JOHN HENRY NEWMAN
AND THE DEVELOPMENT
OF DOCTRINE

JOHN HENRY NEWMAN

AND THE DEVELOPMENT OF DOCTRINE

Encountering Change, Looking for Continuity

...

STEPHEN MORGAN

Foreword by Ian Ker

The Catholic University of America Press
Washington, D.C.

Copyright © 2021
The Catholic University of America Press
All rights reserved

Library of Congress Cataloging-in-Publication Data
Names: Morgan, Stephen, 1965– author.
Title: John Henry Newman and the development of doctrine : encountering change, looking for continuity / Stephen Morgan ; foreword by Ian Ker.
Description: Washington, D.C. : The Catholic University of America Press, [2021] | Includes bibliographical references and index. | Summary: "In focusing on the gestation of "An Essay on the Development of Christian Doctrine" (1845), John Henry Newman's last work as an Anglican and presaging his transition to Catholicism, this book examines how Newman accounted for doctrinal continuity in the face of evidence of change in the history of the church"— Provided by publisher.
Identifiers: LCCN 2021037846 | ISBN 9780813234434 (cloth)
Subjects: LCSH: Newman, John Henry, 1801–1890. Essay on the development of Christian doctrine. | Dogma, Development of. | Catholic Church—Doctrines.
Classification: LCC BT21.3.N493 M67 2021 | DDC 230/.201—dc23
LC record available at https://lccn.loc.gov/2021037846
ISBN 9780813239323

FOR CAROLINE

CONTENTS

Foreword by Ian Ker / ix

Acknowledgments / xiii

List of Abbreviations / xv

. . .

Introduction / 1

Chapter 1 Becoming Aware of the Difficulty: Encountering Change While Looking for Continuity— the Period to 1833 / 19

Chapter 2 Antiquity, the *Via Media*, and a Catholicism of the Word—1833 to 1838 / 75

Chapter 3 From a Catholicism of the Word to a Catholicism of the Church—1839 to 1842 / 133

Chapter 4 From a Catholicism of the Church to the Church of Catholicism—1842 to 1845 / 201

Conclusion / 263

. . .

Bibliography / 279

Index / 309

FOREWORD

Ian Ker

On October 13, 2019, on a hot, gloriously sunny autumn day, Pope Francis declared John Henry Newman to be a Saint, alongside Giuseppina Vannini, Mariam Thresia Chiramel Mankidiyan, Dulce Lopes Pontes, and Marguerite Bays. It was an extraordinarily joyful occasion for the entire church, but for the English-speaking world, it was an event that attracted more people than the Eternal City has seen since Paul VI— now a Saint himself—raised the Forty English and Welsh Martyrs to the altars nearly fifty years ago. My own part in the journey to that day—in my writings and how they led to the two individuals whose miraculous cures opened the way to Newman's canonization—has formed a significant part of my priestly life. Since the publication of *John Henry Newman: A Biography*, in 1988, I have been convinced that Newman could speak to the church of today in a way that few others could. His *Grammar of Assent* and *Idea of a University* stand as works of Philosophy and Educational Theory, respectively, that have scarcely been bettered in the century and a half since they appeared. Yet it is his *Essay on the Development of Christian Doctrine* that has a particular relevance to the church in the twenty-first century.

The *Essay on the Development of Christian Doctrine* was written at a crucial point in Newman's life. It is, in many ways, the written evidence of the intellectual aspect of the existential struggle that had come to preoccupy him and that found its catharsis in his reception into the Catholic Church, by Blessed Dominic Barberi, on October 9,

---

Rev. Ian Ker taught theology at Oxford University, where he is a senior research fellow for the Blackfriars. He has published more than 20 books on Newman including *John Henry Newman: A Biography* and (as co-editor) the *Cambridge Companion to John Henry Newman*.

FOREWORD

1845, three days after the *Essay* was complete. Various analyses of the theology of the *Essay* have been produced, and it has been in print almost continuously since its first publication. What has been lacking in recent years has been a consideration of the genesis of the *Essay* and the influence that genesis had on the theological structure that Newman adopted in it. In *John Henry Newman and the Development of Doctrine*, Stephen Morgan has filled that gap with a book that displays very high-quality scholarship, thorough (and, doubtless, painstaking) archival work, a comprehensive and close reading of the secondary literature, and a sophisticated understanding of the theological issues. The book provides a compelling analysis of the attempts by John Henry Newman to account for the historical reality of doctrinal change within Christianity in the light of his lasting conviction that the idea of Christianity is fixed by reference to the dogmatic content of the deposit of faith.

Arguing that Newman proposed a series of hypotheses to account for the apparent contradiction between change and continuity, Morgan demonstrates that this series begins much earlier than is generally recognized and that the final hypothesis he was to propose, contained in the *Essay*, provided a methodology of lasting theological value. The introduction establishes the centrality of the problem of change and continuity to Newman's theological work as an Anglican, its part in his conversion to Roman Catholicism, and its contemporary relevance to Roman Catholic theology. It also surveys the major secondary literature relating to the question, with particular reference to those works published within the last fifty years. In the first chapter, covering the period to the publication of his first major work, *The Arians of the Fourth Century*, in 1833, Newman's earliest awareness of the problem and first attempts to solve it are considered. The growing confidence of Newman's Tractarian period and his development of the notion of the *via media* form the second chapter and the collapse of that confidence, the subject matter of the third. The fourth chapter is concerned with the emergence of the theory of development and the writing and content of the *Essay*. The conclusion considers the legacy of the *Essay* as a tool in Newman's theology and in the work of later theologians, finally suggesting that it may offer a useful methodological contribution to the contemporary Roman Catholic debate about continuity and change in the teaching of the church.

This book also makes two further contributions that are significant to the genre of Newman Studies: one historiographical and one theological. Newman's reliability as source of his own opinions and conduct has been the subject of criticism since Charles Kingsley's initial attack. In the last half-century or so, several authors—among them Owen Chadwick, Stephen Thomas, James Pereiro, and Frank Turner—have called into question Newman's own account of the history of his religious opinions in the *Apologia pro vita sua*. Morgan has shown that, while not without faults (even Homer nods), Newman's account can be demonstrated by reference to contemporaneous evidence to be substantially accurate at almost all significant moments. Morgan's further theological contribution is that he shows how the process of theology is conditioned by its subject matter, what Newman called the Idea of Christianity. By tracing the evolution of Newman's thought, Morgan illustrates how theology must always ground itself in a close engagement with the deposit of faith, taken as facts and not opinion.

ACKNOWLEDGMENTS

It is impossible to bring a work like this to publication without the assistance of enormous numbers of people. It is similarly impossible to list them all without running the risk of overlooking one or two: the risk, however, does not excuse me from the attempt.

First among those I want to thank is my wife, Caroline. It is a cliché to refer to wives as long-suffering, but here it is entirely accurate. Without her steadfast and loving support over thirty years, I would simply not have had the opportunity, confidence, or determination to have set foot on the road. In return for her constant belief in and affectionate, patient forebearance, *parturiet mons, nascetur ridiculus mus*. My children—Peter, Sophia, and Hugo—also deserve my thanks for allowing their Daddy to lock himself away with his books when he should, perhaps, have been more engaged with them. I am also deeply grateful for Hugo's help in putting bibliography and footnotes in the proper form and to Dr. Francis Young for compiling the index.

Next, grateful acknowledgment is due my most constant friend Ed Morgan, whose idea it was that I embark on the task of writing about Newman and development, and to Fr. David O'Sullivan, who offered unstinting hospitality, superb food, pretty decent wine, and great conversation while I was undertaking research for the volume.

Thanks are also due to those whose encouragement to apply myself to the study of theology has at last brought forth some fruit: Frs. Michael House, Dermot Fenlon, Alexander George, Cyril Law, John Redford, and Bernard Green—the last two now in the merciful hands of God. To my Bishops, Crispian Hollis and Philip Egan, both of Portsmouth, and to Stephen Lee Bun-sang of Macao, for creating the space for this small part of my diaconal service, I am also deeply grateful. These acknowledgments would be incomplete if they omitted the debt I owe to the University of Saint Joseph, Macao: my students, colleagues—especially the university librarian, Francisco Peixoto—and my predecessor as rector, Fr. Peter Stilwell, during whose term I was able to complete this manuscript.

My doctoral supervisor, Mark Chapman, deserves more credit than a simple acknowledgment can convey—for teaching me how to write with some precision, some conciseness, and a modicum of fluency. In every respect, he was a model *Doktorvater* and my pattern now in supervising my own students. Others in Oxford (then and now) deserve my gratitude too: among them Sarah Foot, Charlotte Methuen, Werner Jeanrond, and, above all others, Fr. Ian Ker. It was his unparalleled biography that first whetted my appetite for John Henry Newman. His scholarly assistance and his warm friendship have been indispensable throughout.

Fr. James Bradley's encouragement to approach CUA Press cannot go unacknowledged, and the support of the team there—Trevor Lipscombe, John Martino, et al.—together with the extraordinarily helpful suggestions of my two readers, has turned a rather rough manuscript into this volume. For that, they deserve immense credit: the blame for any shortcomings are entirely my own.

Heavenly assistance has been sorely needed in this project and has been sought and obtained through the Venerable, then Blessèd, and now Saint John Henry Newman. The intercession of Mary, under her titles Our Lady of Victory, Our Lady of Walsingham, and, most often, *Mair Aberteifi* (Our Lady of Cardigan, of the Taper), has sustained me throughout. Finally, I should add my acknowledgment to God, the Most Holy and Undivided Trinity, in Whom firmly I believe and truly.

Macao SAR China

ABBREVIATIONS

JHN   John Henry Newman

Works by John Henry Newman

Add.   *Addresses to Cardinal Newman and His Replies*

Apo.   *Apologia Pro Vita Sua* (1st Edition)

Ari.   *The Arians of the Fourth Century: Their Doctrine, Temper and Conduct chiefly as Exhibited in the Councils of the Church between A.D.325 & A.D.381*

AW   *John Henry Newman: Autobiographical Writings*

Dev.   *An Essay on the Development of Christian Doctrine* (1845 edition)

Dev. (1878) *An Essay on the Development of Christian Doctrine* (1878 edition)

Ess. 1–2   *Essays Critical and Historical*, 2 volumes (Uniform Edition)

HS 1–3   *Historical Sketches*, 3 volumes (Uniform Edition)

Idea   *The Idea of a University, Defined and Illustrated*

Jfc.   *Lectures on Justification*

LD 1–32   *The Letters and Diaries of John Henry Newman*, 31 volumes

PS 1–8   *Parochial and Plain Sermons*, 8 volumes (Uniform Edition)

SD   *Sermons Bearing on Subjects of the Day* (Uniform Edition)

ABBREVIATIONS

TP 1–2	*The Theological Papers of John Henry Newman*, 2 volumes (Uniform Edition)
Tracts 1–5	*Tracts for the Times*, 1840, 5 volume edition
TTE	*Tracts Theological and Ecclesiastical* (Uniform Edition)
USS	*Fifteen Sermons Preached before the University of Oxford* (Uniform Edition)
VM 1–2	*The Via Media*, 2 volumes (Uniform Edition)

Other Works and Abbreviations

AAS	*Acta Apostolicae Sedis*
ATR	*Anglican Theological Review*
BOA	Birmingham Oratory Archives
CSEL	Corpus Scriptorum Ecclesiasticorum Latinorum
ITQ	*Irish Theological Quarterly*
JEH	*Journal of Ecclesiastical History*
JRH	*Journal of Religious History*
JTS	*Journal of Theological Studies*
ODNB Online	*Oxford Dictionary of National Biography Online*
PG	Patrologiae Cursus Completus, Series Graeca
PL	Patrologiae Cursus Completus, Series Latina
TS	*Theological Studies*

JOHN HENRY NEWMAN

AND THE DEVELOPMENT
OF DOCTRINE

INTRODUCTION

Six weeks after being received into the Roman Catholic Church on October 9, 1845, John Henry Newman published *An Essay on the Development of Christian Doctrine*.[1] In this work, he outlined a theological approach for assessing whether any development in Christian doctrine constituted an authentic development or a corruption of an antecedent doctrine. This work was the last of Newman's Anglican writings, and arguably the first of his Roman Catholic works. It represents the synthesis of a number of ideas with which he had engaged, in a struggle of increasing intensity, for most of the preceding thirty years. In March 1844, John Henry Newman began a new notebook, one in which he was to begin to organize his thoughts regarding the development of doctrine to deal with the intellectual difficulty, the paradox, that history presents in any consideration of Christian doctrine.[2] It was not, however, a theory simply produced in the year and a half between the beginning of the notebook and the publication in November 1845 of the *Essay* but rather one that had grown out of the *cursus* of Newman's entire religious life to date. The theory that was to be fully expressed in the *Essay* both provided the workable hypothesis for which he had long searched and offered an intellectually and historically cogent justification for its concrete expression in the Roman Catholic Church to which Newman had already made his submission.

Newman called the *Essay* "an hypothesis to account for a diffi-

---

1. John Henry Newman, *An Essay on the Development of Christian Doctrine* (London: James Toovey, 1845), hereafter *Dev.* in citations and the *Essay* in text.
2. John Henry Newman, "Copybook on Development," n.d., B.2.8, Birmingham Oratory Archives, hereafter BOA. See also his "Papers and Fragments on the Development of Christian Doctrine," Various dates, B.2.8, BOA and his "Preparatory Notes for the 3rd Edition of Development," n.d., D.7.6, BOA.

culty,"³ and the difficulty to which he referred provides the basis of the enquiry in this book: how does the Anglican Newman account for doctrinal continuity in the light of the evidence of change in the history of the church? This question is not simply one of historical interest or of concern primarily for those engaged in the various aspects of that subgenre of nineteenth-century theology that has come to be called Newman Studies. It is also an issue that goes to the heart of much of the discourse in Roman Catholic theology at the beginning of the twenty-first century. To understand and appreciate both the significance of and potential to contribute to that discourse that Newman's theology of development as set out in the *Essay* represents, it is necessary to first comprehend the process through which he arrived at that theology. This book, therefore, seeks to pinpoint Newman's earliest awareness of the difficulty. It describes and analyzes the successive attempts he made to provide a coherent hypothesis to account for that difficulty. It charts how and why he lost confidence in each of those hypotheses and how, at length, he came to what he called his *"Theory of Developments,"*⁴ the hypothesis that formed the subject matter of the *Essay*. It shows that this definitive hypothesis was characterised by a determination that it should avoid the failings of his earlier attempts at providing an account and argues that this understanding of the hypothesis contributes significantly to the current debate concerning conciliar hermeneutics in the Roman Catholic Church.

The Current Significance of Development of Doctrine in Roman Catholic Thought

The pontificate of Pope Francis has been one in which it might not be inaccurate to say that the only constant has been change. It has been a lived example of John Henry Newman's *dictum*, that "to live is to change"—although we will see in the course of this book that this is an expression all too often taken out of context and used to

---

3. Newman, *Dev.*, 27.
4. Newman, *Dev.*, 27.

INTRODUCTION

actually reverse the point that Newman was seeking to make. Nevertheless, whether it was eschewing the traditional papal red shoes or changing, first *de facto* and then *de jure*, the foot-washing rite of the *Mandatum* on Holy Thursday, it has been clear from the moment he stepped out onto the *loggia* of St. Peter's on March 13, 2013, that this was to be a papacy of change to which Catholics, indeed, the whole world, would need to accustom themselves.

The organization and sartorial changes wrought by Pope Francis and his collaborators are not necessarily matters of concern, at least not on the level of theology, except insofar as they disclose a disposition to what has been handed on. Those changes thus far have been concerned with externals that have themselves undergone enormous transformation, even within living memory, and might be seen as simply prudential decisions concerning nonessential manifestations of the papal office. There have, however, been changes that must concern the theologian and that present a greater challenge. For example, the issues arising out of changes in sacramental discipline indicated in the Post-Synodal Apostolic Exhortation *Amoris laetitia*,[5] which appear to signify alterations in the understanding of the sacraments themselves and the theology of grace, unsettled a number of theologians, the author among them. The May 2018 amendment of paragraph 2267 of the *Catechism of the Catholic Church* to rule out use of the death penalty, seemingly in all circumstances, was justified by the Holy See specifically as a "development of doctrine."[6] This change in what had previously been thought to be the settled doctrine—albeit one with a developing understanding of the prudential judgements to be made in specific circumstances—while largely uncontroversial in the European context, gave rise to a measure of *admiratio* in other parts of the world, not least in the United States.

---

5. Pope Francis, Post-Synodal Apostolic Exhortation *Amoris laetitia* (March 19, 2016), http://w2.vatican.va/content/francesco/en/apost_exhortations/documents/papa-francesco_esortazione-ap_20160319_amoris-laetitia.html.

6. Congregation of the Doctrine of the Faith, "Letter to the Bishops Regarding the New Revision of Number 2267 of the Catechism of the Catholic Church on the Death Penalty," August 1, 2018, paras. 7 and 8, http://press.vatican.va/content/salastampa/en/bollettino/pubblico/2018/08/02/180802b.html.

INTRODUCTION

The development of doctrine is, therefore, not simply a matter of arcane interest to theologians but a live one in ecclesial life. While the pontificate of Pope Francis has brought this into particularly sharp focus, it has been a significant theological question for more than half a century. Writing in the magazine *America* immediately before the beginning of the fourth period of the Second Vatican Council in January 1965, the American Jesuit theologian John Courtney Murray referred to the development of doctrine as "the issue underlying all issues at the Council."[7] Murray was writing in response to the decision of Pope Paul VI, announced on the last working day of the third period of the council, November 20, 1964, by the secretary general of the council, Eugène Cardinal Tisserant, to defer the council's vote on the *schema* on religious liberty.[8] In drafting this *schema*, Murray had collaborated with his fellow *peritus*, Pietro Pavan, then professor of social economics at the Pontifical Athenaeum of the Lateran, later rector of the Lateran University and a cardinal. Their draft *schema* went substantially further than existing Catholic doctrine on religious liberty, and in the *America* article, Murray was setting out his case for this particular development of doctrine.

The manifestation of disquiet that attended Paul VI's decision to defer consideration of the Murray/Pavan *schema* was a foretaste of the lasting theological controversy that was to surround the eventually approved Declaration on Religious Liberty, *Dignitatis humanae*.[9] This conciliar doctrine was to be among the root causes of the 1988 schism with Archbishop Marcel Lefebvre and his followers, and the debate regarding the limits of this doctrine and the extent of the de-

---

7. John Courtney Murray, "The Matter of Religious Freedom," *America*, January 9, 1965, 40–43.

8. For an account of these events, see Luis Tagle, "The 'Black Week' of Vatican II (November 14–21 1964)," in *History of Vatican II: Church as Communion, Third Period and Intersession, September 1964–September 1965*, ed. Giuseppe Alberigo and Joseph Andrew Komonchak, vol. 4 (Leuven: Peeters, 2003), 393–406. This account is itself not uncontroversial. It has received trenchant adverse criticism, including accusations of "severe and partisan bias." See Agostino Marchetto, *The Second Vatican Ecumenical Council: A Counterpoint for the History of the Council*, ed. Kenneth D. Whitehead (Scranton, Pa.: University of Scranton Press, 2010), 219.

9. Pope Paul VI, *Declaratio de Libertate Religiosa*, *AAS*, no. 58 (1966): 929–41.

velopment it entailed continues to the present.[10] The Second Vatican Council was to see other developments, including a demonstrable "increase and expansion in Christian Creed and Ritual"[11] of varying degrees of controversy, and the postconciliar period has been one in which the rate of change has, if anything, accelerated.

The question of the extent to which the conciliar changes can be reconciled with previous Catholic doctrine and the postconciliar changes can be justified by appeal to conciliar authority has become an acute one. Speaking to the members of the Roman Curia in December 2005, Pope Benedict XVI made the issue central to an analysis of the appropriate theological hermeneutic that should be adopted in considering the council itself, its teaching, and postconciliar developments.[12] His proposed "hermeneutic of reform in continuity with the one subject Church" was offered as a *tertium quid* between two radically opposed expressions of what he termed the "hermeneutic of discontinuity and rupture." On the one hand, this rupture has been used to deny the legitimacy of the teachings of the council, postconciliar magisterium, and, at its most extreme, the institutional identity of the postconciliar Roman Catholic Church with the preconciliar body. On the other hand, this same claim that the council marked a decisive rupture with the immediately foregoing period has been used, so Pope Benedict seemed to suggest, to justify radically novel interpretations of the teachings of the council, even going well beyond the conciliar teachings in fidelity to a *soi-disant* "Spirit of Vatican II."

Seeking to propose that a hermeneutic of reform in continuity was essential to a proper understanding of the council and the interpretation of both conciliar and postconciliar doctrinal developments, Pope Benedict confirmed the continuing centrality of the

---

10. Thomas Pink, *What Is the Catholic Doctrine of Religious Liberty*, June 15, 2012, https://www.academia.edu/639061/What_is_the_Catholic_doctrine_of_religious_liberty.

11. Newman, *Dev.*, 27.

12. "Da una parte esiste un'interpretazione che vorrei chiamare 'ermeneutica della discontinuità e della rottura'; essa non di rado si è potuta avvalere della simpatia dei mass-media, e anche di una parte della teologia moderna. Dall'altra parte c'è l' 'ermeneutica della riforma,' del rinnovamento nella continuità dell'unico soggetto-Chiesa," Benedict XVI Pope, *Ad Romanam Curia Ob Omina Natalicia*, *Acta Apostolicae Sedis*, no. 98 (December 22, 2005): 40–53.

issue of development that Murray had identified forty years earlier. The problem of this centrality, however, remains as it was when Murray wrote, that is, the theology of development in Roman Catholicism is still a relatively embryonic field. One possible explanation for this undeveloped state is the phenomenon of magisterial positivism, which achieved one expression in the traditional Ultramontane form, which reached its zenith between the two Vatican Councils, and another in the conciliar positivism of the period since the second. This positivism has been so dominant in popular and scholarly Roman Catholic theological discourse that it has been possible to conduct that discourse without being aware of the need for addressing the question of development except by reference to positivism. A less than thoroughgoing commitment to return *ad fontes*, except where even the vaguest claim to a conciliar mandate is lacking, has arguably marked a period when the "event" of the Second Vatican Council and its "spirit" have often seemed to be justification enough for theological and liturgical novelty.[13] In each of the forms it has taken, this positivism manifests itself in a self-referential sat-

---

13. This appeal to the "event" of the council is expressed well in John O'Malley et al., *Vatican II: Did Anything Happen* (London: Continuum, 2007). Cf. Massimo Faggioli, *Vatican II: The Battle for Meaning* (Mahwah, N.J.: Paulist Press, 2012) and James Sweeney, "How Should We Remember Vatican II," *New Blackfriars* 90, no. 1026 (2009): 251–60. Sweeney's article appeared in the March 2009 edition of *New Blackfriars* containing the proceedings of the 2008 Catholic Theological Association of Great Britain's conference, which had the theme "the challenge of providing the means for the Church to fulfil its mission today as the vantage point for a rereading of both the documents of Vatican II and the ecclesial event that was the Council." It is expressive of a theological position built on an extraordinarily univocal historiographical consensus, derived in no small measure from the approach adopted by those who have collaborated with Giuseppe Alberigo and Joseph Komonchak in their undoubtedly impressive five-volume *History of Vatican II* (Leuven: Peeters, 1995–2005), cited in n. 23 above. This history has been so influential that Gerard Mannion was surely not exaggerating in his review of the work when he called it "a work of the Church" ("History of Vatican II—Edited by Guiseppe Alberigo and Joseph A. Komonchak," *International Journal of Systematic Theology* 12 (2010): 478–84.) A critique of this position is beginning to emerge in works such as Brunero Gherardini, *Concilio Ecumenico Vaticano II: Un Discorso Da Fare* (Turin: Lindau, 2009); *Concilio Ecumenico Vaticano II: Il Discorso Mancato* (Turin: Lindau, 2011); Agostino Marchetto's work cited in n. 23 above; Roberto De Mattei, *Il Concilio Vaticano II. Una Storia Mai Scritta* (Turin: Lindau, 2010); and in a volume of essays that appeared in English edited by Matthew Lamb and Matthew Levering, *Vatican II: Renewal within Tradition* (Oxford: Oxford University Press, 2008).

INTRODUCTION

isfaction with or justification for any particular change by claiming for it the authority of its chosen source of magisterial authority. The fact that none of these several forms of positivism have seemed to provide the necessary impetus for a widespread engagement with the task of working out a proper account of development is regrettable. Such an account would need to be one that takes seriously the claims both of continuity and change. This failure is as much an indictment of the state of Catholic theology as are the attendant clumsy attempts to shore up arguably heterodox positions by proof-texting sacred scripture, the Fathers, St. Thomas, or even Newman himself, and doing so by quoting these authorities not only out of context but also plainly contrary to the meaning of their authors. That is not, however, an exclusively postconciliar phenomenon. Pius XII did the same in *Mediator dei*, article 46, by reversing the sense of Prosper of Aquitaine's dictum *lex orandi lex credendi*—a task facilitated by overlooking the very plain priority of the *lex credendi* in the original form *legem credendi lex statuat supplicandi*.[14] Pope Benedict XVI's insistence on the need for a hermeneutic of reform in continuity, together with the particular challenges posed by the doctrinal changes (apparent or real) of his successor, suggests that seeking to answer the question identified by Murray can no longer be deferred.

That Christian doctrine was static and immutable would have seemed self-evident to those schooled in a theology heavily reliant on the categories of Aristotelian thought, at least in the expression St. Thomas Aquinas and others gave to it. As late as the seventeenth century, the Roman Catholic bishop, historian, and theologian Jacques-Bénigne Bossuet (1627–1704) could claim that "variation in religion is always a sign of error; that the Christian religion came from its Lord complete and perfect; that the true church had main-

---

14. Pope Pius XII, *Mediator dei*, November 20, 1947, http://w2.vatican.va/content/pius-xii/en/encyclicals/documents/hf_p-xii_enc_20111947_mediator-dei.html. For a discussion of what Pius did and indications of its possible consequences, see Christopher Smith, "Liturgical Formation and Catholic Identity," in *Liturgy in the Twenty-First Century: Contemporary Issues and Perspectives*, ed. Alcuin Reid (London and New York: Bloomsbury T & T Clark, 2016), 260–86.

tained immutably, *must* have maintained immutably, the deposit of truth which had been given to it."¹⁵

It was a view that would have seemed entirely unexceptional fifty years earlier when his compatriot, the French Jesuit Denis Pétau (1583–1652), considered the history of Dogma in his *Opus de doctrina temporum*.¹⁶ Yet the very engagement spawned by Bossuet's own work, especially his 1688 work, *Histoire des variations des Églises protestantes*,¹⁷ and the correspondence it engendered with Gottfried Leibnitz (1646–1716), meant that Roman Catholic theology could not remain indefinitely insulated against the currents of European thought that came to be called the Enlightenment. Although Ernst Breisach traces the remote origins of this awareness of doctrinal development in Roman Catholic theology to the high-medieval period, it had certainly become an unavoidable question by the beginning of the nineteenth century, when an awareness of the history of doctrine and the attendant notion of development were beginning to become more widespread.¹⁸

An example of this was the work of Johann Adam Möhler (1796–1838) and Johann Sebastian Drey (1777–1853) at the Roman Catholic faculty of the University of Tübingen. Their work was, on occasion, controversial enough to result in delation to Rome yet important enough to have placed the question at the center of theological discourse. Nearly two centuries later, Karl Rahner (1904–1984) could write, as if it were a quite matter-of-fact observation, that, "as Catholics, we believe in the development of dogma, that as the awareness of our faith becomes more and more developed, we achieve a deeper

---

15. Owen Chadwick, *From Bousset to Newman*, 2nd ed. (Cambridge: Cambridge University Press, 1987), 5–6. Chadwick claims this to be axiomatic, yet nowhere cites the axiom in Bossuet's work. It is, however, an entirely fair representation of the position that Bossuet takes in his *Exposition de Le Foi Catholique* (Paris, 1671).

16. D. Patavius, *Opus de Doctrina Temporum: Auctius in Hac Nova Editione Notis & Emendationibus Quamplurimus, Quas Manu Sua Codici Adscripserat Dionysius Petavius* (Paris: Lutet, 1627).

17. Jacques-Bénigne Bossuet, *Histoire Des Variation Des Églises Protestantes* (Paris: Charpentier, 1844).

18. E. Breisach, *Historiography: Ancient, Medieval and Modern* (Chicago: University of Chicago Press, 2007), 139–41.

INTRODUCTION

understanding of the dogma itself."[19] Rahner treated of the subject of development of doctrine in several other essay-length pieces,[20] and there is an undoubted awareness of development and attempts to engage with it in the theology of other twentieth-century Roman Catholic theologians, such as Yves Congar (1904–1995),[21] Henri de Lubac (1896–1991),[22] and Bernard Lonergan (1904–1984).[23] Although distinct in their methods, approaches, and conclusions, it is true that these three do belong to a distinct strain in twentieth-century Catholic theology, but even in the previously dominant world of neo-scholastic theology, the question of doctrinal development was not entirely overlooked. The Spanish Dominican Francisco Marín-Sola published his *La evolución homogénea del dogma católico* in 1924 and in it considered the question of development in

---

19. Karl Rahner, "The Position of Christology in the Church between Exegesis and Dogmatics," in *Theological Investigations*, vol. 11 (London: Darton, Longman and Todd, 1974), 209.

20. See, for example, "The Historicity of Theology: The Teaching Office of the Church in the Present-Day Crisis of Authority," *Theological Investigations*, vol. 12 (London: Darton, Longman and Todd, 1974), 3–30; "Basic Observations on the Subject of Changeable and Unchangeable Factors in the Church," *Theological Investigations*, vol. 14 (London: Darton, Longman and Todd, 1976), 3–23; "Yesterday's History of Dogma and Theology for Tomorrow," *Theological Investigations*, vol. 18 (London: Darton, Longman and Todd, 1983), 3–34; and "On the Situation of Faith," *Theological Investigations*, vol. 20 (London: Darton, Longman and Todd, 1981), 13–32. Patrick Burke provides an analysis of Rahner's changing theology of development in the chapter "The Development of Dogma" in *Reinterpreting Rahner: A Critical Study of His Major Themes* (New York: Fordham University Press, 2002), 188–225.

21. See, for example, Yves Congar, *Tradition and Traditions*, trans. Michael Naseby and Thomas Rainborough (London: Burns and Oates, 1966); *A History of Theology* (New York: Doubleday, 1968); *The Meaning of Tradition* (San Francisco: Ignatius Press, 2004).

22. See, for example, Henri de Lubac, "The Problem of the Development of Dogma," in *Theology in History* (San Francisco: Ignatius Press, 1996); *The Mystery of the Supernatural*, trans. R. Sheed (New York: Herder and Herder, 1998); and Henri de Lubac, *A Brief Catechesis on Nature and Grace*, trans. R. Arnandez (San Francisco: Ignatius Press, 1984).

23. Lonergan's contribution is considered at length and compared with that of Newman's in an unpublished dissertation, Philip Anthony Egan, "Newman, Lonergan and Doctrinal Development" (PhD diss., Birmingham University, 2004).

Andrew Mezaros's extensive survey of Congar's work and its relation to and dependence upon Newman is particularly useful; see Andrew Meszaros, *The Prophetic Church: History and Doctrinal Development in John Henry Newman and Yves Congar*, 1st ed. (Oxford: Oxford University Press, 2016). Aidan Nichols looks at the idea of development in both Congar and de Lubac in his *From Newman to Congar: The Idea of Doctrinal Development from the Victorians to the Second Vatican Council* (Edinburgh: T & T Clark, 1990).

a manner not without its similarities to Newman's own treatment, particularly in his insistence upon the use of the illative process, by which conclusions can be drawn out of premises.[24] Nevertheless, Newman's *Essay* remains the *locus classicus* for any consideration of the question for theologians who want to consider the insights not only of neoscholastic theology but the call of the Second Vatican Council *ad fontes*. What is more, the singular status of Newman's work is such that any attempt at working out a practical expression of the hermeneutic of reform in continuity to which Pope Benedict called the church needs to take its arguments and their origins very seriously, indeed.

Writing It "Historically"

The first entry in Newman's 1844 notebook, that for March 7, began with the imprecation: *"Write it historically."*[25] No less than in any other area touched on by historical considerations, theology, particularly an account of the theological history of a particular individual or concept, is attended by controversial historiographical considerations. Newman's historiographical self-injunction is not without its difficulties, both in interpreting what he meant and assessing how faithfully he followed his own call.

The extreme reaction of the Oxford historian Simon Skinner[26] to

---

24. Francisco Marin-Sola, OP, *La Evolución Homogénea Del Dogma Católico*, Biblioteca de Tomistas Españoles 1 (Madrid: Valencia La Ciencia Tomista Real Convento de Predicadores, 1923). For a commentary on the similarity between Marin-Sola's ideas and those of Newman, see the unpublished doctoral thesis of Paul G. Crowley, "Dogmatic Development after Newman: The Search for a Hermeneutical Principle in Newman, Marin-Sola, Rahner and Gadamer" (University of Michigan, 1984). See also Joshua R. Brotherton, "Development(s) in the Theology of Revelation: From Francisco Marin-Sola to Joseph Ratzinger: Development(s) in the Theology of Revelation," *New Blackfriars* 97, no. 1072 (November 2016): 661–76.

25. Newman, "Copybook on Development."

26. Simon Skinner, "History versus Hagiography: The Reception of Turner's Newman," *Journal of Ecclesiastical History* 61, no. 4 (2010): 764–81. This article was a "review of the reviews" and was a sustained polemic arguing that Roman Catholic scholars are incapable of the necessary scholarly detachment when writing in the field of history concerning their coreligionists.

INTRODUCTION

Ian Ker's admittedly stinging review[27] of Frank Turner's *John Henry Newman: The Challenge to Evangelical Religion*[28] suggests that any attempt by a Roman Catholic scholar to give an account of Newman's life, or even to contribute to the general academic discourse, risks particularly trenchant adverse criticism from certain quarters. It is difficult to read Skinner's argument without coming to the conclusion that he would want to silence the voice of Roman Catholic scholarship. While conceding nothing to Skinner's overblown allegations of disreputable hagiographic intent on the part of Roman Catholic authors, of Ker, in particular—allegations that Duffy has more than adequately dealt with[29]—nor to a wider historiographical consensus in favor of a methodological agnosticism, this work is written by a Roman Catholic scholar who accepts that Newman is a controversial figure, hardly less so today than in his own lifetime, and one with whom the author shares a confessional attachment. The book has been written, therefore, with a constant consciousness of the author's biases and religious sympathy with the position to which Newman came at the end of the period under consideration. The issues that arise concerning his position in the Roman Catholic Church typically give less occasion for neuralgic and pungent reaction than does his time as an Anglican, particularly the period leading up to his conversion to Rome. That is not to say that he has not been a controversial figure within the Roman Communion, both during his life and since. In the last thirty years or so, attitudes toward Newman have often been proxies for other theological controversies. Since this work is principally concerned with the period up to his conversion to Roman Catholicism, however, a measure of caution is not only necessary but desirable. Nevertheless, the call for a "religious

---

27. Ian Turnbull Ker, "Slow Road to Rome," *Times Literary Supplement*, December 6, 2002, 32.

28. Frank Miller Turner, *John Henry Newman: The Challenge to Evangelical Religion* (New Haven, Conn.: Yale University Press, 2002).

29. Eamon Duffy, "The Reception of Turner's Newman: A Reply to Simon Skinner," *Journal of Ecclesiastical History* 63, no. 3 (2012): 534–48. The editor accorded Skinner the last word in this exchange with a rebuttal of Duffy published in the same issue as Duffy's reply. See Skinner, "A Response to Eamon Duffy," 549–67.

turn" in ecclesiastical history, made most insistently by Sarah Foot in her presidential speech at the Summer Conference of the Ecclesiastical History Society in 2011 and repeated in the second part of her Inaugural Lecture as Regius Professor of Ecclesiastical History at the University of Oxford that same year, requires serious consideration.[30] Foot's argument is that unless the claims that religious belief and practice make on individuals and societies are taken as authentic, sincere, and serious, then any account of the past is necessarily distorted and incomplete. To seek to understand Newman's personal religious history and his theological contribution without this religious turn would necessitate such a distortion and be so incomplete as to entirely lack value.

To give proper weight to these historiographical considerations, this book is written on the basis of treating Newman at any particular point in time as an individual with an open future. We must take seriously both his own freedom and the claims of the present moment on Newman at any specific point rather than overstate the influence of any particular efficient or final cause, let alone to read back, anachronistically, into his present the claims of events that lay in his future. This is not to say there is not great value and significant insight to be gained by reading Newman under a particular biographical event, teleological aspect, or metanarrative theme. Ian Ker's definitive 1988 biography, *John Henry Newman: A Biography*, owes much of its completeness and thorough organization of the material to a structure that presents Newman's work and life as leading up to and flowing away from the religiously and chronologically central event of his conversion to Roman Catholicism.[31] Newman's earlier conversion to an explicitly evangelical religion provides the interpretative key in Sheridan Gilley's *Newman and His Age*.[32] Similarly, Owen Chadwick's reworking of his 1956 Birkbeck Lectures in Cambridge,

---

30. Sarah Foot, "Has Ecclesiastical History Lost the Plot?" *The Church on Its Past, Studies in Church History* 49 (2012): 1–25; Foot, "Thinking with Christians: Doing Ecclesiastical History in a Secular Age," accessed February 23, 2020, http://podcasts.ox.ac.uk/thinking-christians-doing-ecclesiastical-history-secular-age-audio.

31. Ian Turnbull Ker, *John Henry Newman: A Biography*, 1st ed. (Oxford: Oxford University Press, 1988).

32. Sheridan Gilley, *Newman and His Age* (London: Darton, Longman and Todd, 1990).

INTRODUCTION

in his previously cited book, *From Bossuet to Newman*,[33] relies on a number of hermeneutical presuppositions, not the least of which is a profound scepticism of the value of Newman's own account of events, grounded in what he sees as Newman's profound polemical intent.[34]

Stephen Thomas's attempt, in *Newman and Heresy: The Anglican Years*, to understand the place of heresy in forming Newman's theological opinions offers subtle insights that might otherwise be missed, even if he, like Chadwick, doubts Newman's sincerity because of the apologetic and polemic character of much of his published work.[35] John Coulson's account of the influence of Samuel Taylor Coleridge on Newman's adoption of sacramental language as a response to rationalism is another work in which an account is given that privileges certain aspects, such as that sacramental language offers particular perspectives which might otherwise remain obscure.[36] In two works, *Newman the Theologian* and *Unfolding Revelation*, Jan Hendrik Walgrave seeks to arrange Newman's thoughts according to fundamental theological priorities related to the psychological effect of development on the individual subject, specifically on Newman.[37] Nicholas Lash's *Newman and Development* offers a convincing synthetic analysis of the theology of the *Essay* itself and of the influence of concrete events related to doctrinal history on the process of development.[38]

Less successful are those attempts that seek to overstate the place or influence of a particular individual or cause. Pereiro's *"Ethos"* and

---

33. Owen Chadwick, *From Bousset to Newman*, 1st ed. (Cambridge: Cambridge University Press, 1957). The second edition, cited in n. 15, is the edition from which future citations are taken.

34. See, for example, his comments about the alterations made to the *Essay* for its republication in the Longman's Uniform Edition of 1878 in Chadwick, *From Bousset to Newman*, 123, 188–89.

35. Stephen Thomas, *Newman and Heresy: The Anglican Years* (Cambridge: Cambridge University Press, 1991).

36. John Coulson, *Newman and the Common Tradition: A Study in the Language of Church and Society* (Oxford: Clarendon Press, 1960).

37. Jan Hendrick Walgrave, *Newman the Theologian: The Nature of Belief and Doctrine as Exemplified in His Life and Works*, trans. A.V. Littledale (London: Geoffrey Chapman, 1960); *Unfolding Revelation: The Nature of Doctrinal Development* (London: Hutchinson, 1972).

38. Nicholas Lash, *Newman on Development: The Search for an Explanation in History* (London: Sheed and Ward, 1975).

INTRODUCTION

the Oxford Movement is one such attempt to make the contribution of S. F. Wood central to the whole question of the development of doctrine by largely minimizing and making derivative, if not completely eclipsing, Newman's contribution.[39] He shares Thomas's and Chadwick's profound scepticism regarding the reliability, even validity, of Newman's own account of his history, accusing him of having "interpreted the past by the final issue of his intellectual course and read development where he had not seen it before."[40] Pereiro is joined in this attempt to deny Newman the accolade of originality, perhaps surprisingly, by several other academics who happen also to be Roman Catholics. One such critic is Professor V. A. McClelland, whose quite understandable devotion to the memory of Henry Manning appears to require of him that he arrive at a distinctly mixed assessment of Newman.[41] Another is Peter Nockles, whose undoubtedly significant *The Oxford Movement in Context* suggests that Newman arrived at his theology of development and, hence, Rome as a result of a reading of the Fathers that was "peculiarly personal [and] imaginative."[42] Elsewhere, he speaks of this reading as leading Newman on a "peculiar religious odyssey."[43] In neither case is "peculiar" a neutral expression. In fact, Nockles proceeds on the basis that Newman's own account of events and manner of arguing is both "disingenuous" and marked by "self-conscious cynicism."[44]

Whatever Frank Turner's lengthy 2002 book *John Henry Newman: The Challenge to Evangelical Religion* brought to the field of Newman studies is thoroughly obscured by the author's clear intimations of dishonesty on Newman's part and by an attempt to impose a metanarrative of almost exclusively antievangelical motive on Newman's

---

39. James Pereiro, *"Ethos" and the Oxford Movement: At the Heart of Tractarianism* (Oxford: Oxford University Press, 2008).

40. Pereiro, *"Ethos,"* 166.

41. It is the overriding motif of a collection of essays he edited, *By Whose Authority? Newman, Manning, and the Magisterium* (Bath: Downside Abbey, 1996).

42. Peter Nockles, *The Oxford Movement in Context: Anglican High Churchmanship 1760–1857* (Cambridge: Cambridge University Press, 1994), 145.

43. Peter Nockles, "Oxford, Tract 90 and the Bishops," in *John Henry Newman: Reason, Rhetoric and Romanticism*, ed. David Nicholls and Fergus Kerr (Bristol: Bristol Press, 1991), 29.

44. Nockles, "Oxford, Tract 90 and the Bishops," 37, 47.

INTRODUCTION

Anglican years that the evidence simply will not support. Turner appears to have been influenced by the attempts at remote and inexpert psychoanalysis that suggest that Newman either suffered from a "delicate self-absorption"[45] and "feline sarcasm"[46] or a neurosis born of suppressed homosexual desire.[47] Furthermore, Turner appears to have lacked a clear understanding of the taxonomy of nineteenth-century Anglican churchmanship, confusing and conflating, at various times, evangelicalism, latitudinarianism, liberalism, and low-church Protestantism. This limitation makes the task of following and sustaining his main thesis particularly difficult.

The body of secondary literature relating to Newman in general and the issue of development, in particular, is both enormous and wide-ranging, which means that it is possible to engage only with such of the secondary literature that is either of greatest significance

---

45. Which was Lytton Strachey's take in his *Eminent Victorians: Cardinal Manning, Florence Nightingale, Dr. Arnold, General Gordon* (London: Chatto, 1918), 69.

46. Diarmaid MacCulloch, *Christianity: The First Three Thousand Years* (London: Penguin, 2009), 841. Elsewhere, MacCulloch referred to the "agonised, perennially self-scrutinising journey of this Victorian cleric from initial religious certainty via another religious certainty to a very different final religious certainty" in a review of John Cornwell's *The Unquiet Grave: The Reluctant Saint* (London: Continuum, 2012) entitled "A Different Cloth—Newman's Unquiet Grave: The Reluctant Saint by John Cornwell," *Literary Review*, June 2010, http://www.literaryreview.co.uk/macculloch_06_10.html.

47. This view is heavily suggested by Geoffrey Faber in his *Oxford Apostles: A Character Study of the Oxford Movement* (London: Faber & Faber, 1933), although the word "homosexual" is notable for its absence. It forms part of the picture of Newman presented by Ellis Hanson in *Decadence and Catholicism* (Cambridge, Mass.: Harvard University Press, 1988). It also emerged as a consistent theme in the broadcast and print media coverage of the run-up to the papal visit to Britain in 2010, during which Pope Benedict XVI was to beatify Newman.

In the review cited in n. 60, MacCulloch goes so far as to write: "Newmanolators cannot abide the idea that he could have been gay. As conservative Roman Catholics, they can't just accept that homosexuality is one unremarkable and morally neutral variant in human behaviour; and so Newman's enthusiastic biographer, Father Ian Ker, has insisted emphatically on Newman's heterosexuality. Reading Cornwell's account of Newman's emotional life—his passionate friendships with other single men (St. John was just the most long-lasting), his tortured opinions about his own sinfulness, his obvious revelling in the homosocial world of early Victorian Oxford—it is difficult to avoid applying to him that useful variant of Ockham's Razor: 'Looks like a duck, quacks like a duck—can it be a duck?'"

So pervasive was this discourse at the time that in the new edition of his definitive biography, issued to coincide with the beatification, Ker felt compelled to add an "afterword," which argued that the biographical and textual evidence demonstrated that the suggestion of homosexuality could not be sustained. See Ker, *Newman: A Biography*, 746–50.

INTRODUCTION

to the wider current discourse in Newman studies or has a claim to consideration by reference to the questions here under consideration. In any event, if the claim that Newman be considered a man with an open future at any particular point in the history of his religious opinions is to be sustained, then it is proper that the primary literature and archival evidence has the first place in this account. Indeed, such is this claim to the priority of the primary evidence that, unless other explicit reasons are given, the works of Newman referred to will be those as originally published. This requires a departure from the common practice of citing Newman's works from the Uniform Edition of his works that Newman reworked for Longman in the late 1870s.[48] In this work, reference will almost always be to the first edition of any particular title. References to the *Essay* are, unless otherwise noted, to the first edition published by James Toovey in 1845. Newman made a number of minor corrections to this text for a second edition in 1846 and substantially reworked the *Essay* for the third edition in the Uniform Edition in 1877. Although Newman was to claim that this third edition had "no substantial alterations," he acknowledged that he had "nearly turned it inside out, as far as arrangement goes."[49] The extent and effect of, and the reasons for, the changes between the first and third editions are outside the scope of this work, except to note that those changes exist and Newman's assertion that they are not substantial might not be taken at face value.[50] Where reference is made to texts of Newman's sermons, it is either made to the first published edition (as with the

---

48. Where, exceptionally, citations are from the Uniform Edition, the abbreviations used are from Joseph Rickaby, *An Index to the Works of John Henry Cardinal Newman* (London: Longmans Green and Co., 1914).

49. JHN to Mrs. William Froude, December 23, 1877, in *The Letters and Diaries of John Henry Newman*, ed. Charles Steven Dessain, Edward E. Kelly, Ian Turnbull Ker et al., vol. 28 (Oxford: Clarendon Press, 1973–1977 [vols. 23–32]), 288–89, hereafter *LD*.

50. Lash certainly believed the alterations did not lack significance in *Newman on Development*, 4. Aidan Nichols, in his *From Newman to Congar*, 45–47, shares this view, as did Chadwick in his *From Bousset to Newman*, 185–91. A full, critical comparison of the two editions exists in the form of an unpublished doctoral dissertation by Gerard McCarren for the Catholic University Press of America in 1998, *Tests or Notes? A Critical Evaluation of the Criteria for Genuine Doctrinal Development in John Henry Newman's Essay on the Development of Christian Doctrine* (Washington, D.C.: The Catholic University Press of America, 1998).

INTRODUCTION

University Sermons) or to the copies to be found in the Birmingham Oratory Archives. Newman's own correspondence and diary entries are cited from the thirty-two-volume series, *The Letters and Diaries of John Henry Newman*, edited by Charles Stephen Dessain and others.

Structure of the Book

The main body of this book is contained in four chronologically arranged chapters, which are divided by reference to the establishment of each of the successive hypotheses. The first of these main chapters, "Becoming Aware of the Difficulty: Encountering Change while Looking for Continuity—the Period to 1833," traces Newman's earliest encounters with issues of change and continuity. The chapter provides an account of how Newman came to believe in the fixed and essentially dogmatic nature of Christianity during his teenage years and then describes his growing awareness, during his studies for Anglican Orders, of the problem that historically observable doctrinal change poses for a religion with a fixed deposit of faith. It charts and explains the emergence of Newman's first hypothesis, the *disciplina arcani*, in the publication of his first major work, *The Arians of the Fourth Century*.

Chapter 2, "Antiquity, the *Via Media*, and a Catholicism of the Word—1833 to 1838," analyses the reasons for Newman's emerging awareness of the limitations of the *disciplina arcani* and his growing dependence on the role of antiquity in securing the connection of later doctrinal expression to Apostolical faith. It notes Newman's first use of the term "development" in the context of the question of change and continuity at a date rather earlier than has hitherto been recognized. The chapter argues that the correspondence with the Abbé Jager played a significant role in working out in Newman's mind the place of tradition and its differing expressions. It shows that the importance of the idea of the Church of England as a *via media* between what he came to see as Roman corruption and Protestant infidelity had a crucial part in producing Newman's next hypothesis. As his confidence in the Tractarian movement grew, Newman sought to establish both the Apostolic and Catholic notes of the Church of England in the written witness of the Fathers.

The third chapter, "From a Catholicism of the Word to a Catholicism of the Church—1839 to 1842," demonstrates how Newman's confidence in the *via media* was deliberately and successfully undermined by Nicholas Wiseman. It shows how, in his unpublished material on Apollinarianism and his attempt to recover from Wiseman's attack, Newman came to recognize the central and indispensable importance of the church as the living organ of the authentication of doctrinal change and his attempt to claim for the Church of England a place within that Catholicism of the Church.

The fourth chapter, "From a Catholicism of the Church to the Church of Catholicism—1842 to 1845," argues that Newman came to understand that the theory of a Catholicism grounded in an authoritative teaching church could not be reconciled with the historical and lived reality of the Anglican Church. The chapter demonstrates that this realization coincided with the loss of Newman's anti-Catholic sentiments, and it describes the emergence of Newman's theory of the development of doctrine, first in his final University Sermon and then in *An Essay on the Development of Christian Doctrine*, and his identification of the church of his theory with the Roman Catholic Church.

The conclusion summarizes the findings of the previous chapters and points forward to the importance of those findings for the evaluation of the reception and legacy of the theory of development outlined in the *Essay*. It contends that the genesis of the theory provides a useful theological hermeneutic for understanding what Newman was attempting in the *Essay*. This, in turn, assists in assessing the limitations of the methodology it outlines and the care with which that methodology should be applied, as exemplified both for Newman himself in his life and work as a Roman Catholic and how it has been treated by other Roman Catholic theologians. Finally, it proposes areas of further work that might usefully be illuminated by the account offered here.

CHAPTER 1

BECOMING AWARE OF THE DIFFICULTY

...

ENCOUNTERING CHANGE WHILE LOOKING FOR CONTINUITY— THE PERIOD TO 1833

This chapter examines the early period of Newman's growing awareness of doctrinal development with the intention of establishing when and how he became explicitly aware of it and how he set about incorporating it into his theology. It argues that the implications of an explicitly dogmatic religious conviction combined with an increasingly firm attachment to notions of tradition and of the necessity of the divinely constituted reality of the church, of which he first became aware during his early years at Oriel, were worked out in his reading of the Fathers from the late 1820s onwards in such a way as to make him recognize not only the fact of doctrinal development but also the necessity of a theory to account for it, one that could accommodate both continuity and change.

The chapter begins by looking at the evidence in Newman's own writing, in his letters, diaries, and sermons, in the period prior to his beginning work on what came to be published as *The Arians of the Fourth Century*, a period when he appears to exhibit little explicit awareness of post-Apostolic doctrinal change but became conscious of several factors that were later to play a significant part in his thinking. It will then assess the effect of the process of writing and the subject matter and methodology of *The Arians* that began to awaken in him a conscious sense of doctrinal development, noting, in particular, how to deal with the difficulties this presented to the previously assumed fixed character of the content of dogmatic truth.

Before *The Arians of the Fourth Century*

When Newman recalled the history of his own religious opinions in writing his *Apologia Pro Vita Sua*, he was at pains to describe the character of the "great change of thought" that had taken place in him during the autumn of 1816.[1] He sketched a childhood religious practice grounded firmly in the reading of the Bible, of perfect knowledge of the catechism but devoid of conviction, until that "great change of thought" that overcame him at the age of fifteen, his conversion to Evangelicalism. The particular character of that conversion, at least as he recalled it forty-eight years later, was one where he "fell under the influences of a definite creed, and received into my intellect impressions of dogma, which, through God's mercy, have never been effaced or obscured."[2] That is to say, Newman's was a conversion to an explicitly dogmatic conception of the Christian faith whose creeds, as he was later to express it, "were facts, not opinions,"[3] and the fundamental underlying "fact" of this revelation was the person of Jesus Christ.[4]

---

1. John Henry Newman, *Apologia Pro Vita Sua: Being a Reply to a Pamphlet Entitled "What Then Does Dr. Newman Mean?"* 1st ed. (London: Longmans, Green and Co., 1864), 58, hereafter *Apo.* in the citations and *Apologia* in the text.

2. Newman, *Apo.*, 58.

3. John Henry Newman, *The Arians of the Fourth Century: Their Doctrine, Temper and Conduct chiefly as Exhibited in the Councils of the Church between A.D.325 & A.D.381*, 1st ed. (London: J. G. and F. Rivington, 1833), 148, hereafter *Ari.* in the citations and *The Arians* in the text.

4. Ian Turnbull Ker, *Healing the Wound of Humanity* (London: Darton, Longman and Todd, 1993), 43–50. See also Terrence Merrigan, *Clear Heads and Holy Hearts: The Religious and Theological Ideal of John Henry Newman*, Louvain Theological and Pastoral Monographs 7 (Louvain: Peeters, 1991), 90–102. Here Merrigan notes that Newman's notion of the

THE DIFFICULTY: THE PERIOD TO 1833

Although it had immediate, profound, affective, and existential consequences, the conversion Newman remembered was one that was primarily about, first, the apprehension of the reality of the existence of God and himself, the "two, and two only luminously self-evident beings,"[5] and, second, the claims of religious truths expressed in propositional form. Nevertheless, there does not appear to be any evidence in his journals or correspondence from this period that with this conversion came a consciousness that the particular doctrines he found impressed on his intellect had a developmental history. His much later claim, in 1844, that he had "always" held "a development of doctrine at least in some great points of theology"[6] clearly was not intended to refer back to this period. Neither is it possible to find supporting evidence from this period for his recollection in the *Apologia* of his having adopted as his own Thomas Scott's maxim, which he encountered in his reading in 1816, that "Growth is the only sign of life."[7] Indeed, although he later referenced Scott's expression in paraphrase in the *Essay*,[8] it would appear that he understood it at the time primarily in a moral rather than a doctrinal sense.[9] It is also worth noting that it was at this same time he first encountered the writings of the Fathers, when he read Joseph Milner's *History of the Church of Christ*.[10] This marked the beginning

---

character of revelation, is that of the revelation of "Christ Himself ... the ground, source of coherence, and the continuing dynamic of Christian life and reflection, in and through which He is now known and apprehended" (Merrigan, 98). Cf. Paul Misner, "Newman's Concept of Revelation and the Development of Doctrine," *The Heythrop Journal* 11, no. 1 (1970): 32–47. Misner contends that Newman's concept of revelation was fundamentally verbal and propositional.

5. Newman, *Apo.*, 59.

6. JHN to Mrs. William Froude, December 23, 1877, in *The Letters and Diaries of John Henry Newman*, ed. Charles Steven Dessain, Edward E. Kelly, Ian Turnbull Ker et al., vol. 28 (Oxford: Clarendon Press, 1973–1977 [vols. 23–32]), 288–89, hereafter *LD*.

He gives as examples of such "great points" the doctrines of the Trinity and Incarnation, which he notes "are intellectual developments of the inspired declarations of Scripture." It would appear that the term "always" was not intended to be construed exactly but rather to convey the sense that this was, in 1844, a long-held view.

7. Newman, *Apo.*, 61.

8. Newman, *Essay*, 73.

9. In support of this contention, it is noted that, in the *Apologia*, he pairs the aphorism with another explicitly moral injunction: "Holiness before peace," 61.

10. Joseph Milner, *History of the Church of Christ*, 5 vols. (London, 1794).

of a fascination with patristics, but, again, there is no evidence in his journals or letters to indicate that his reading of Milner suggested to him any sense of doctrinal development. What Milner did do was to make Newman "enamoured of the long extracts from St. Augustine, St. Ambrose, and the other Fathers" that the five volumes contained.[11] It was to be over ten years before Newman's interest was converted into any kind of systematic reading of the Fathers,[12] but this early encounter had little causal significance to both Newman's first need to propose a theory of development[13] and to his later Catholic conversion.

In *From Bossuet to Newman*, Owen Chadwick argues that Newman's own recollection of such matters was fundamentally unreliable, whether these recollections were written nearly thirty years later in the *Essay* and in his correspondence around the time of his conversion to Roman Catholicism, or nearly fifty years later in the *Apologia*. It is Chadwick's contention that from both psychological necessity and apologetic intent Newman adopted a "passionate devotion to 'consistency,'" and that an "element of self-justification entered into most of what he published between 1840 and 1878."[14] Chadwick suggests this caused Newman to misrepresent the history of his religious opinions and argues that he did this to justify his Roman Catholic conversion as having "relentlessly issued from those trains of thought which he had pursued while he was an Anglican."[15] Chadwick contends that the real reason for the progress through Evangelicalism, incipient liberalism, and Tractarianism to Roman Catholicism was a gradual realization, in both his opinions and ecclesial loyalties, of the principles of development that he had learned, albeit second-hand and in translation, from the work of Johann Adam Möhler (1796–1838), and of which he became consciously aware only toward the end of his life as an Anglican.[16]

11. Newman, *Apo.*, 62.
12. JHN to Harriett Newman, May 1, 1826, in *LD* 2, 284.
13. JHN to Mrs. William Froude, July 14, 1844, in *LD* 10, 297–98.
14. Chadwick, *From Bossuet to Newman*, 123.
15. Chadwick, *From Bossuet to Newman*, 88.
16. Chadwick, *From Bossuet to Newman*, 111–38.

It is true that Chadwick states that Newman was not "influenced by Möhler," noting that: "He was not reading Möhler, nor Wiseman, nor Perrone, nor even Petau. He was reading Justin Martyr, Athanasius, Tertullian, Ambrose, Lactantius, Cyril."[17] It can only be direct first-hand influence that Chadwick is denying, however, since it is certainly Möhler's hand to which he refers when he notes that: "the theory of development . . . coming not from Newman's mind but from across the seas—was in the atmosphere that surrounded Newman at Littlemore."[18] In adopting this position, Chadwick advances a rationale for Newman's changing position that neither accepts Newman's own apologetic of "consistency" nor echoes the suspicions and criticisms of disingenuousness and deception that were continually levelled at Newman since his secession to Rome and were widely hinted at before that event. Chadwick's argument is not unproblematic, however, in so far as it seeks to pin the responsibility for Newman's awareness of doctrinal development upon indirect, atmospheric influence.

James Pereiro, considering the period of the 1840s, when W. G. Ward had certainly exposed Newman explicitly to Möhler's thought, makes use of similar language when he concludes that: "Newman, while not directly influenced by Möhler, would not have escaped the atmosphere around him."[19] The suggestion of an atmospheric cause, whether made by Chadwick or Pereiro, fails to take account of a series of other, more direct influences that are contemporaneously documented in Newman's correspondence, journals and sermons. In the terms framed by Chadwick, the argument has often seemed to be about whether Newman was, from the very beginning of his own religious history, driven by thinking dependent in some way on Möhler's thinking, or whether he was inconsistent in or disin-

---

17. Chadwick, *From Bossuet to Newman*, 118–19. Chadwick here relies on John Henry Newman, "Papers and Fragments on the Development of Christian Doctrine" Various dates, 1, B.2.8, Birmingham Oratory Archives, hereafter BOA.

18. Chadwick, *From Bossuet to Newman*, 119. In the introduction to the second edition, Chadwick moves his ground to suggest that Newman had come to 'see" the fact of development "quite independently" of "a group of South German Catholics," yet he does not revise the argument in the text. See Chadwick, *From Bossuet to Newman*, xv.

19. Pereiro, "*Ethos*," 162.

genuous about the development of his religious opinions in his later accounts. The evidence from Newman's own hand at the time seems to support his later recollections and reveals that although it is not possible to date any explicit, conscious awareness of doctrinal development back to his Evangelical conversion, it certainly significantly ante-dates an explicit encounter with Möhler.[20] In any event, the work of C. Michael Shea and Kenneth Parker in recent years has demonstrated that Chadwick's conclusion is no longer supportable.[21]

What it is possible to demonstrate, however, is that as soon as Newman began any formal, systematic doctrinal study, he did encounter the reality of the development of the propositional forms in which Christian doctrine was expressed. On November 1, 1823, Newman wrote to his mother telling her that he had started to attend a series of private lectures,[22] an initiative of the newly appointed Regius Professor of Divinity, Charles Lloyd[23] that were given to an invited group of four Oriel fellows and four Christ Church students.[24] Newman recorded in his memoir, composed in 1874, revised in 1876, and published posthumously under the title *Autobiographical Writings*,[25] that he started attending these lectures in 1823 and continued to do so until his acceptance of the curacy of St. Clement's in 1824 (on May 16).[26] His journals, however, suggest that he attended these lectures until early 1826, and even then, his nonattendance

---

20. The first time Newman explicitly quoted Möhler, in his 1859 article for the *Rambler*, "On Consulting the Faithful in Matters of Doctrine," he did so from *Symbolik*, but in French with an attribution to Perrone, suggesting that it is possible that even at so late a date, he did not have first-hand knowledge of the work. See John Henry Newman, "On Consulting the Faithful in Matters of Doctrine," *The Rambler*, July 3, 1859, 211.

21. See, for example, Kenneth L Parker and C. Michael Shea, "Johann Adam Möhler's Influence on John Henry Newman's Theory of Doctrinal Development," *Ephemerides Theologicae Lovanienses* 89, no. 1 (2013): 73–95.

22. JHN to Mrs. Newman, November 1, 1823, in *LD* 2, 167.

23. Charles Lloyd, (1784–1829), Regius Professor of Divinity, Oxford (1822–1827), Bishop of Oxford (1827–1829), in which last office he was, it should be noted, Newman's ordinary. See also *ODNB Online*.

24. The fellows of Christ Church, Oxford, are known as "students." The college has singular terminology that differs markedly from that in use in other Oxford colleges.

25. *Autobiographical Writings*, ed. Henry Tristram (London: Sheed and Ward, 1957), 72, hereafter *AW*.

26. Diary entry for Sunday, May 16, 1824, in *LD* 2, 174.

appears to have been initially conceived by him as being a temporary thing.[27] It has been argued that the lectures represent the only formal training in theological and historical method that Newman received and that Lloyd's intent, which was primarily apologetic and controversialist, had a defining influence on Newman's own approach.[28] Lloyd's lectures were, Newman recalled, concerned with "exegetical criticism, historical research, and controversy"[29] and considered in some detail the gradual development of the language used to express doctrinal truth.[30] The effect on his students of the detail and thoroughness of his research was profound. Henry Liddon recorded that the opening lecture, a detailed, even exhaustive exegesis of the first four verses of the Letter to the Hebrews, had the effect of amazing the attendees, among whom were Newman and Pusey.[31] It is not without significance for the present purposes that the underlying theme of the Letter to the Hebrews, that of the relationship between the Jewish and Christian Covenants, had been conventionally used as a scriptural example of the notion of progress in religious truth, certainly since the publication of Joseph Butler's *Analogy*,[32] which Newman was to begin reading in June 1825.[33]

Lloyd's lectures adopted a deliberately historical method and relied heavily on patristic sources. It seems very likely that Newman's own resolve to engage in the previously noted systematic study of the Fathers in May 1826 was not unconnected with the lectures at which he had only recently suspended his attendance. Thomas Bokenkotter has noted that Lloyd's treatment of ecclesiastical history in the

---

27. JHN notes, in his diary entry for Tuesday, January 31, 1826, that "Lloyd's lectures began" and on Thursday, February 9, 1826, writes that he "withdrew for term from Lloyd's lectures," *LD* 2, 275.

28. Thomas Bokenkotter, *Cardinal Newman as an Historian* (Louvain: Publications Universitaires, 1959), 14–19.

29. Newman, *AW*, 71.

30. Edmund S. Ffoulkes, *A History of the Church of St. Mary the Virgin, Oxford: The University Church: From Doomsday to the Installation of The Duke of Wellington, Chancellor of the University* (London: Longmans, Green and Co., 1892), 381–83.

31. Henry Parry Liddon, *Life of Edward Bouverie Pusey*, vol. 1 (London: Longmans Green and Co., 1893), 62–64.

32. Joseph Butler, *The Analogy of Religion, Natural and Revealed, the Constitution and Course of Nature*, 2nd ed. (London: James, John and Paul Knapton, 1736).

33. Diary entry: "began Butler's *Analogy*," Saturday June 25,1825, in *LD* 2, 238.

lectures he gave while Newman was still regularly attending concentrated heavily on the rise and development of papal power:[34] a question that continued to engage Newman at least until the publication of the *Essay* and which, arguably, dogged his footsteps throughout his life.[35] In any event, it was a subject that demanded the recognition of doctrinal development as a demonstrable reality, whether one viewed such development as in conformity with the Christian faith or as a manifestation of the Antichrist predicted in sacred scripture, Newman's position at the time (and by his own account until 1843).[36] Lloyd's own position was much less hostile to Rome than Newman's,[37] and it seems probable, although his journals give no clue as to his reading at the time, that Newman would have encountered a more balanced view of the papacy in the standard works on ecclesiastical history to which Lloyd was directing his students. Lloyd certainly intended his students to read in this connection de Maistre's *Du Pape*,[38] a work which explicitly identifies the development of the doctrine of the papacy as he, an early nineteenth-century ultramontane, conceived it: as having grown from a "germ" in the Apostolic age.[39] Newman does note that when he was preparing *The Arians*, some six or seven years later, he "was not ignorant of

---

34. Bokenkotter relies, here, on the abstract of Lloyd's lectures given in Ffoulkes, *A History of the Church of St. Mary the Virgin*, 381–83.

35. Bokenkotter, *Cardinal Newman as an Historian*, 19.

36. Newman, *Apo.*, 63.

37. In an 1825 article, originally written anonymously, but which he later admitted to having written, Lloyd explicitly disavowed strong language with regard to the Roman Catholic Church and stated that he was "unwilling to fix upon the Romish Church the charge of positive idolatory" and disclaiming even "the most remote intention of bringing any insinuation against Roman Catholics." He was also an enthusiastic proponent of Catholic Emancipation, in favour of which he both organized opinion and spoke out. As Bishop of Oxford, he opposed both the Archbishop of Canterbury and the Archbishop of Armagh when he spoke powerfully and effectively in the second reading of the 1829 Catholic Relief Bill in the House of Lords. For his pains, he was attacked both in Parliament and in the press; these attacks, it was claimed, played no small part in his death less than two months later. See "Obituary - Bishop Lloyd," *Gentleman's Magazine and Historical Chronical*, no. 99 (1829): 560–63. See also W. J. Baker, *Beyond Port and Prejudice: Charles Lloyd of Oxford 1784–1829* (Orono: University of Maine at Orono Press, 1981).

38. Edward Churton, *Memoir of Joshua Watson*, vol. 1 (Oxford: Parker, 1861), 285.

39. Joseph de Maistre, "Du Pape (Originally Published Paris 1819)," in *Ouevres Complètes de J' DeMaistre* (Paris: Vitte, 1928), 34–35. The word used by de Maistre is *"germe."*

the works of Mosheim and other learned Germans,"[40] and remarks in the *Essay* that he was at this time aware of the work of "several distinguished writers of the continent, such as De Maistre and Möhler."[41] Accordingly, Newman must have been conscious of the notions of historical progress and doctrinal development with which many of these works were imbued, although Chadwick is almost certainly correct in his judgment that he did not share their widespread identification between development and progress.[42]

In the autumn of 1825, Newman preached a series of sermons, initially at St. Clement's in Oxford, that would appear to have been heavily influenced not only by the lectures given by Lloyd but also his reading of Joseph Butler, which continued at least until October 12 of that year.[43] Butler's influence on Newman's later work, especially on the *Essay*, has been examined in detail by Klaus Dick, who argues that Newman's real theoretical advance was to extend Butler's use of analogy in theology to the field of history.[44] These 1825 sermons seem to support Newman's own recollection in the *Apologia* that it was Butler's *Analogy* that impressed upon him "the historical character of Revelation,"[45] and that it was, as Thomas Sheridan has observed, an obvious feature of Butler's work that influenced Newman greatly.[46]

The series of sermons began on September 11 and ran until December 11, and set out explicitly "the continuity which exists in the overall plan of salvation whereby God led man generally from natural religion, through the religion of the Old Testament, to that of the New."[47] These sermons contain the first explicit example of Newman

40. John Henry Newman, *Tracts Theology and Ecclesiastical*, Uniform ed. (London: Longmans, Green and Co., 1908), 141–42, hereafter *TTE*.

41. Newman, *Dev.*, 27.

42. Chadwick, *From Bossuet to Newman*, 97.

43. Diary entry: "read Davison on Primitive sacrifice, and part of Butlers Analogy," Wednesday October 12, 1825, in *LD 2*, 262.

44. He also suggests that the structure of the *Essay* is fundamentally identical to Butler's conception of development. Klaus Dick, "Das Analogieprinzip Bei J.H. Newman Und Seine Quelle in J. Butlers Analogy," *Newman Studien* 5 (1962): 9–228.

45. Newman, *Apo.*, 67.

46. Thomas Sheridan, *Newman on Justification: A Theological Biography* (New York: Alba House, 1967), 111.

47. Sheridan, *Newman on Justification*, 111.

expressing any notion of doctrinal development. In the sermon's introduction, used only in the first of the four occasions that he preached the first sermon of the series, Newman laid out his purposes clearly in terms that are redolent with the language of Butler's *Analogy*:

> The *history* of the Christian revelation as connected with and arising out of Judaism, is a subject little attended to by many religious persons.... Whereas we should ... turn our attention to its *history*—i.e. under what circumstances it was made known to the world, by means of what instruments at what successive periods and at what places.[48]

When he preached the sermon a second time at Southampton on October 9, 1825,[49] Newman expanded the introduction slightly in order that the force of his argument was strengthened:

> Doubtless it is more important to understand *what* religion is, than to know *how* it came into the world—to eat the living fruit than to know the particulars of its culture and growth. Yet unless we attend to the *history* of the gospel, as well as its *character and object*, we run the risk of forgetting that there was a time when the true light had not risen, and even at the present day it shines but on a small part of the world.[50]

Newman's notes on the manuscript record that he preached this sermon on four occasions: St. Clement's, Oxford, on September 11, 1825; Peartree Chapel, Southampton, on October 9, 1825;[51] St. Mary the Virgin, Oxford, on June 11, 1826; and Well Walk Chapel, Hampstead, on September 9, 1827.[52] Although Newman frequently used sermons more than once, his use of this one on four occasions over a two-year period might reasonably be taken as an indication of the importance he attached to its message. None of the others in the se-

---

48. Sermon 104, in *John Henry Newman: Sermons, 1824–1843*, vol. 2, ed. Vincent Ferrer Blehl (Oxford: Oxford University Press, 1991), 342–52.

49. The dates that he preached his sermons are recorded on the manuscript notes. His diary entries also often record the number, text or theme of his sermons but, as he noted in his diary for Thursday, June 15, 1826, "My Private Journal only runs from June 13. 1824 to June 13. 1826. while I was Curate at St. Clement's. Now it ceases till 1828, when I took possession of St. Mary's." *LD* 2, 292, where at n. 3 it is noted that "neither date is strictly accurate."

50. *John Henry Newman: Sermons, 1824–1843*, vol. 2, 343.

51. If the date is right (see n. 49), this was twenty years to the day before his submission to the Catholic Church.

52. *John Henry Newman: Sermons, 1824–1843*, vol. 2, 342.

THE DIFFICULTY: THE PERIOD TO 1833

ries seems to have been preached more than once. They were, perhaps, seen by Newman as no more than an expansion of the theme he had outlined in the introduction to the first:[53] a detailed treatment of Christian doctrine considered within an historical context. Even though its conclusions are modest—"We have shown then that the *wisdom of God* is displayed in the gradual introduction of the gospel"[54]—the evidence of this series of sermons suggests that Newman was clearly aware by 1825 of some development in the field of religious doctrine, albeit still only on the level of the various successive biblical covenants and the divine pedagogy of gradual revelation in sacred scripture. There is nothing new in this, and the idea of doctrinal development after the death of the last Apostle, when no new revelation would be expected, is not in Newman's contemplation at this point. Nevertheless, the similarity of expression with the one he was to use in the *Essay*—especially the use of the terms "accounting for" a "difficulty"[55]—is at least worth noting in passing.

These sermons indicate that Lloyd's lectures and the related reading, especially of Butler, had influenced Newman's theology and inculcated in him a sense that religious truth had about it a character that was decidedly not static. It would take the argument too far, however, to suggest that Newman saw that development in dynamic terms. At this stage, he did not appear to consider the possibility of development of the doctrinal truth of Christianity beyond the fulfilment in the Gospel and the Apostolic witness of what he understood to be the prophetic promises of the Old Testament. Indeed, this evidence clearly supports the accuracy of the remark about his views as he recalled them in the 1844 letter to Mrs. Froude already cited, that: "I used to think either that this development was made in the Apostles' lifetime and given by them traditionally to the Church, or at least that it was made by the Church in the *first* ages."[56]

Having been elected to a fellowship at Oriel in 1822, Newman

---

53. In fact, the second, third, fifth, and sixth exist only in outline note form. See A.17.1, BOA.
54. Newman, B.3.4, BOA.
55. *John Henry Newman: Sermons, 1824–1843*, vol. 2, 345.
56. See n. 13.

29

came under the influence of its then—senior fellow and soon to be provost, Edward Hawkins.[57] Although they were later to have irreconcilable differences, Newman credited Hawkins with having been his guide and critic in his pastoral ministry at St. Clement's. It was he who gave Newman the curacy in what was then a chapel of ease to St. Mary the Virgin, where Hawkins was vicar. Newman recorded with gratitude Hawkins's influence on the style and content of his early sermons.[58] Of greater significance for the present purposes, however, was his being "the means to great additions to [Newman's] belief,"[59] foremost among which was the notion of tradition.

Following his evangelical conversion, Newman quickly adopted the habit of using sacred scripture as a means of proving the doctrines of the church.[60] It would appear from his own writings that he took to this approach on his own initiative, even to the extent of proof-texting the articles of the Athanasian Creed.[61] He was to find a resonant echo of this methodology in a sermon that he heard Hawkins preach in 1818, a copy of which Hawkins gave him and urged him to study.[62] The sermon, entitled *Unauthoritative Tradition*,[63] was preached as a university sermon at the University Church on May 31, 1818, and there seems no reason to doubt Newman's recollection of having heard it then, even though there is no mention of it made in his journal. Newman recalled that study of the sermon "made a most serious impression upon me."[64] The accuracy of this memory and the evidence of the sermon's influence over his views are supported by its content.

---

57. Edward Hawkins (1789–1882), tutor of St. John's College, Oxford (1812–1813), fellow of Oriel College, Oxford (1813–1882), vicar of the University Church of St. Mary the Virgin, Oxford (1823–1828), and provost of Oriel College, Oxford (1828-1882), *in ODNB Online*.
58. Newman, *Apo.*, 65.
59. Newman, *Apo.*, 66.
60. Newman, *Apo.*, 60.
61. Newman, *Apo.*, 60.
62. Newman, *Apo.*, 60.
63. Published as Edward Hawkins, *A Dissertation upon the Use and Importance of Unauthoritative Tradition, as an Introduction to the Christian Doctrines; Including the Substance of a Sermon upon 2 Thess. Ii, 15* (London: J. Parker and F. C. and J. Rivington, 1819), hereafter *Unauthoritative Tradition*.
64. Newman, *Apo.*, 60.

Hawkins's original sermon notes do not appear to have survived,[65] but the published version of the sermon runs to eighty-eight octavo pages. Newman recalls that it seemed at the time to be a long sermon, and it may be supposed that if the original was of the same length as that which was published, it would have taken nearly an hour to preach. Newman's patience in listening, and his later close study, would have revealed to him why the sermon became "celebrated."[66] It is not necessary to rely upon Newman's account for evidence of its celebrity. Another of Newman's contemporaries as a fellow of Oriel, Thomas Arnold, recalled sourly at the height of the Tractarian success in May 1836 that Hawkins's sermon had "contributed to their mischief."[67]

The sermon was not original in its treatment of the subject—Newman suggests that it did not go "one step" beyond the standard High Church Anglican position[68]—nor was Hawkins unique in his treatment of the matter;[69] nevertheless, *Unauthoritative Tradition* was a systematic treatment of a question that had become unavoidable in the face of powerful currents in the historical and biblical scholarship of the time. The work of German scholars such as Hermann Samuel Reimarus (1694–1768), Johann Gottfried Eichhorn (1752–1827), and Friedrich Schleiermacher (1768–1834) meant that the relationship between the various parts of sacred scripture and the growing awareness of the interrelationship between the historical data of the early Christian centuries and the contents of the Bible needed to be addressed. For Anglicans, the normative status of Article VI of the Thirty-Nine Articles[70] meant that it was important

---

65. Hawkins's papers and correspondence are in Oriel College Archives, PRO 2/41/1–9, but contain no notes of this sermon.

66. Newman, *Apo.*, 66.

67. Thomas Arnold to Richard Whately, May 4, 1836, in Arthur Penrhyn Stanley, ed., *Life and Correspondence of Thomas Arnold, D.D., Late Head Master of Rugby School and Regius Professor of Modern History in the University of Oxford*, vol. 2 (London: Fellowes, 1844).

68. Newman, *Apo.*, 66.

69. George Glover, *Remarks on the Bishop of Peterborough's "Comparative View of the Churches of England and Rome"* (London, 1821), 108. Glover was relying here on the necessity and importance of oral tradition.

70. Article VI, entitled "*Of the Sufficiency of the Holy Scriptures for Salvation*" reads "Holy Scripture containeth all things necessary to salvation: so that whatsoever is not read therein,

to establish a clear Protestant course between the Scylla of an apparently increasingly untenable *sola scriptura* and the Charybdis of thoroughgoing Latitudinarianism. Hawkins's sermon was addressed to this very issue and sought to establish such a course.

At the beginning of *Unauthoritative Tradition*, Hawkins claims that it was written specifically to answer the question: "Why are so many of the Christian doctrines so *indirectly taught* in the Scriptures?"[71] He wondered why it seemed that these doctrines were "rather implied than taught; why we have to learn them in great measure from incidental notices of them in books written upon particular occasions, controversies, or heresies."[72] There is here a striking similarity with Newman's own developed view of how doctrinal development actually took place as he was to set it out nearly thirty years later in the *Essay*. If Chadwick is correct when he contends that the thought of Möhler played a "decisive role in the debate in the Anglican Church over development before Newman's conversion,"[73] however, then this similarity is not much more than coincidence, an unsurprising one at that. It has been argued, however, that Chadwick's attachment to the thesis that Möhler was the ultimate, albeit indirect, source for Newman's theory of development "leads him to undervalue evidence for other sources."[74] What is clear is that the language used by Hawkins is so similar to that used by Newman that it seems more probable that there is some dependence of the later work on the former, particularly in the light of Newman's consistent recollection. Chadwick's attribution to Newman of a lasting, disqualifying

---

nor may be proved thereby, is not to be required of any man, that it should be believed as an article of the Faith, or be thought requisite or necessary to salvation. In the name of the Holy Scripture we do understand those canonical Books of the Old and New Testament, of whose authority was never any doubt in the Church." See Gerald Lewis Bray, ed., "The Thirty-Nine Articles, 1571," in *Documents of the English Reformation* (Cambridge: James Clarke and Co., 2004), 287–88.

71. Hawkins, *Unauthoritative Tradition*, 1.

72. Hawkins, *Unauthoritative Tradition*, 1.

73. Lawrence Joseph Henry, "Newman and Development: The Genesis of John Henry Newman's Theory of Development and the Reception of His Essay on the Development of Christian Doctrine" (PhD diss., University of Texas, 1973), 6. Henry relies here on the argument advanced by Chadwick in *From Bousset to Newman*, 114–18.

74. Henry, "Newman and Development," 7.

apologetic concern for consistency might well argue against placing too much reliance on the evidence in the *Apologia*,[75] and might even suggest that Newman's claimed dependence on Hawkins for this notion in Tract 85,[76] written at the height of Newman's involvement in the Oxford Movement in 1837, is unreliable evidence. Newman began *The Arians* possibly as early as October 21, 1831,[77] however, and returned to it "after many weeks intermission" shortly before the Christmas of that year.[78] It was completed by July 31, 1832,[79] nearly a year before the beginning of the Oxford Movement and the emergence of suggestions among some of Newman's critics of inconsistency on his part, to which he undoubtedly later felt obliged to give answer. His assertion in *The Arians* of a dependence on Hawkins's *Unauthoritative Tradition* must, therefore, remain free of Chadwick's charge.[80] Peter Nockles notes that Newman's recollections are supported by the arguments of Louis Bouyer and Gunter Beimer.[81] The absence of any evidence in Newman's letters and diaries from either 1818, when he first heard the sermon, or from the 1820s, when he fell under Hawkins's influence at Oriel, taken with Chadwick's demonstrable assertion of a wider contemporary awareness of this particular issue, however, makes a definitive conclusion impossible without further corroborative evidence. That corroboration is found, however, when Hawkins's sermon is compared with the sermons which Newman himself preached in his first years of ordained

75. Particularly the claim, already adverted to above, that "There is one other principle I gained from Dr. Hawkins ... the doctrine of Tradition." Newman, *Apo.*, 65.

76. John Henry Newman, "Tract 85: Lectures in the Scripture Proofs of the Doctrines of the Church" (J. G. F. and J. Rivington and J. H. Parker, 1836), 4–5, in *Tracts 4*. Cf. Hawkins, *Unauthoritative Tradition*, 64.

77. Diary entry: "resumed my task at the Councils (*This was the History of the Arians*), tho' with many interruptions for a while," Friday, October 21, 1831, in *LD* 2, 368.

78. Monday, December 19, 1831, in *LD* 2, 377.

79. Tuesday, July 31, 1832, in *LD* 3, 74.

80. At n. 2, Newman writes, "Vide Dr. Hawkins original and most conclusive work on Unauthoritative Tradition, which contains in it the key to a number of difficulties which are apt to perplex the theological student." *Ari.*, 55.

81. Peter Nockles, *The Oxford Movement in Context: Anglican High Churchmanship 1760–1857* (Cambridge: Cambridge University Press, 1994), 110, first cited in the introduction, n. 42; Louis Bouyer, *Newman: His Life and Spirituality* (London: Burns and Oates, 1958), 63; and Günter Biemer, *Newman on Tradition* (New York: Herder and Herder, 1967), 33–42.

ministry. It is, therefore, necessary to look in some detail at what Hawkins wrote.

Hawkins began *Unauthoritative Tradition* by noting that his own experience of learning Christian doctrines, which he supposed to be common, was that it was tradition and not scripture that had been his first introduction to the various teachings of Christianity. He observed that he had "first collected" doctrine not usually "immediately from the Scriptures," even though those doctrines rested "entirely upon Scriptural authority,"[82] but rather that the tradition of the church was "intended to be the ordinary introduction to them."[83] Claiming to stand in conformity with the position of such High and Dry Churchmen as Daniel Waterland and Jones of Nayland,[84] and praying in aid of his argument Butler's *Analogy*,[85] Hawkins went on to argue that the normative case is "that the Church should carry down the *system*, but the Scriptures should furnish all the *proofs* of the Christian doctrines; that tradition should supply the Christian with the *arrangement*, but the Bible with all the *substance* of divine truth."[86] Although Hawkins cites Waterland and Jones of Nayland in suggesting that he had "collected" doctrine, he could quite as well have gone back to Hooker as authority for his approach. Hawkins's claim to be operating according to the accepted approach of the Standard Anglican Divines[87] is, in reality, one of standing in the tradition, albeit understood as unauthoritative, of collecting the sense of scripture "using a reason informed by the doctrinal truths of Christian tradition" that derives directly from Hooker.[88]

Hawkins was at pains to exclude what he believed to be the characteristic error of "the Romanists," which is the granting of an "in-

---

82. Hawkins, *Unauthoritative Tradition*, 2.
83. Hawkins, *Unauthoritative Tradition*, v.
84. Hawkins, *Unauthoritative Tradition*, 3.
85. Hawkins, *Unauthoritative Tradition*, 13.
86. Hawkins, *Unauthoritative Tradition*, 18.
87. A term used here to include at least Hooker, Andrewes, Taylor, Hall, Laud, and Ussher. See J. Booty, "Standard Divines," in *The Study of Anglicanism*, ed. Stephen Sykes, John Booty, and Jonathan Knight (London: SPCK, 1998), 176–87; see also Michael Ramsey, *Anglican Spirit* (New York: Church Publishing, 2004), 13–15.
88. See Mark D. Chapman, "The Theology of Richard Hooker," in *Anglican Theology* (London: Continuum, 2012), 124.

dependent authority for the traditions conveyed to us by the Church" on the grounds of observable fallibility and a liability to corruption that is intrinsic to its nature.[89] Neither did he allow these traditions a role that is primarily about the "confirmation or interpretation" of doctrines that are revealed in scripture.[90] To do this would privilege them to an extent that would hint at an authoritative status and overturn the plain meaning, to him at least, of that "fundamental Article of the Protestant Faith," Article VI.[91]

It is clearly not part of Hawkins's intent to aim at the unique and privileged place of scripture in Protestant Christianity, but rather to posit the place of tradition in a role auxiliary to it: "It (i.e., Scripture) would appear to be in the want of such a guide that the very difficulty complained of consists.... Now exactly such an aid and guide may surely be found in *tradition*, the traditions conveyed from age to age by the Church in general."[92] This clear conception of the relationship between scripture and tradition is the characteristic theme: indeed, the entire sermon is, in fact, an extended argument for believing that "the Church should *teach*, and the Scriptures *prove*, the doctrines of Christianity."[93] Even a doctrine as central to Christian faith as the divinity of Jesus, Hawkins suggested, rests not on the fragmentary and tentative hints of it provided by scripture but because it is and always has been taught by the church, and that "any uninterrupted tradition brings with it a reasonable *presumption* in its behalf."[94] Drawing his thoughts together, at the end of an exhausting if not exhaustive examination of the working out of this principle across a wide spectrum of doctrine throughout the centuries, he concluded: "Let no one expect more from the Scriptures than they were designed to afford, or spurn that assistance (i.e. tradition) which they themselves imply."[95]

89. Hawkins, *Unauthoritative Tradition*, 20.
90. Hawkins, *Unauthoritative Tradition*, v.
91. Hawkins, *Unauthoritative Tradition*, 28. See also Hawkins, 1 x, where Hawkins also cites *Homily* i from *The Book of Homilies* as authority for this position.
92. Hawkins, *Unauthoritative Tradition*, 17.
93. Hawkins, *Unauthoritative Tradition*, 22.
94. Hawkins, *Unauthoritative Tradition*, 21.
95. Hawkins, *Unauthoritative Tradition*, 86.

THE DIFFICULTY: THE PERIOD TO 1833

The language of Newman's 1825 sermons, in addition to revealing the influence of Newman's reading of Butler, also bears a striking similarity to that employed by Hawkins. It is, however, in the theological method, that is, in the use to which sacred scripture is put, that these sermons most resemble Hawkins's argument. In these sermons, and in others preached on various occasions during this period, Newman consistently argued from the doctrine taught by the church to the scriptural evidence, rather than the other way around. As a then member of the Oxford Association of the Bible Society, which he had supported since June 1823[96] and to which he had been a full subscriber since May 1824,[97] it might have seemed more usual to have followed the pattern of his earlier sermons and to have engaged, in the classical evangelical manner, in a detailed biblical exegesis.[98] What he did, however, was to set out what he took to be the teaching of the church and then use scripture to provide the evidential support for the ecclesial doctrine. In this series of sermons, Newman did not seek to stretch scripture to prove a point, nor did he engage in an exercise in proof-texting. In this way, the argumentation reflected Hawkins's insistence on the distinction between doctrinal *arrangement* and *substance* and foreshadowed the distinctive method that Newman adopted in his use of patristic sources.

This use of tradition, even if only in a strictly *unauthoritative* way, sat awkwardly with the evangelical principles to which Newman had heretofore been committed and to which he had only recently publicly recommitted himself in his subscription to the Bible Society. Indeed, this adoption of Hawkins's approach "struck at the root of the principle on which the Bible Society was set up,"[99] although Newman did not feel compelled to remove his name from the subscription list to that body until 1830.[100] Whatever his motives for remaining

---

96. Newman, *AW*, 192.
97. Diary entry for Saturday, May 15, 1824, in *LD 1*, 174.
98. See, for example, Sermon 12, preached first at St. Clement's on August 15, 1824, or Sermon 40, preached at St. Clement's on December 5, 1824, both in B.3.4, BOA.
99. Newman, *Apo.*, 66.
100. Diary entry: "withdrawing my name from the Bible Society," Thursday June 8, 1830, in *LD 2*, 228.

a member of the Bible Society for so long, Newman's own recollection in his *Autobiographical Writings* that, through his adoption of Hawkins's position, he "had taken the first step towards giving up the evangelical form of Christianity,"[101] is supported by his letter of November 26, 1826, to Samuel Rickards. In it, he suggests that his correspondent's expertise in the teachings of the Anglican Divines of the sixteenth and seventeenth centuries might be applied to the purpose of acting as "a band of witnesses for the truth" by treating them "*as a whole*, a corpus theologicum et ecclesiasticum, *the* English Church."[102] It is an argument for tradition that went certainly as far as Hawkins. Furthermore, it is clear even at this early date that Newman saw the unavoidable connection between tradition and the development of doctrine. Writing of the scope of theological questions to which this tradition could be applied, he writes that: "This is, indeed, a large head of inquiry, for it includes questions of ... the gradual development of doctrines."[103]

It would be too much to suggest that at this date Newman had a notion of the development of doctrine beyond that implied in Lloyd's lectures: that is, of a gradual development of the language used to express doctrinal truth.[104] Nevertheless, when taken with the homiletic evidence, it suggests a conscious acceptance of unauthoritative tradition sufficiently early in Newman's life to suggest that Newman himself recalled correctly, in 1864, when he wrote that "there is one other principle which I gained from Dr. Hawkins, more directly bearing upon Catholicism, than any other I have mentioned; and that is the doctrine of Tradition."[105]

Alongside this notion of tradition, and intrinsically implied by it, Newman was at this time becoming ever more explicitly aware of the necessity of the church as a vehicle for tradition. Hawkins's influence was also not insignificant here, for on August 19, 1824, he had given Newman a copy of John Bird Sumner's *Apostolical Preaching considered*

---

101. Newman, *AW*, 78.
102. JHN to Samuel Rickards, November 26, 1826, in *LD 1*, 310.
103. JHN to Samuel Rickards, November 26, 1826, in *LD 1*, 310.
104. Ffoulkes, *A History of the Church of St. Mary the Virgin*, 381–83.
105. Newman, *Apo.*, 66.

in an Examination of St. Paul's Epistles.[106] Newman recorded in his journal that he finished reading the book exactly one week later.[107] Like Hawkins's sermon, Sumner's book explicitly confronted the problem that the scriptural evidence for many doctrines is largely implicit and indirect. In its constant resort to the fact of "Apostolical preaching" as the source for and justification of doctrine, that is, to preaching in accordance with teaching of the Church of Apostolic times, Sumner's argument presented Newman with an historical challenge. Sumner had used "germ," a direct translation of de Maistre's "germe," to describe the presence in scripture, albeit in a hidden and implicit way, of later doctrines such as the Trinity, and there is evidence of its wider use with reference to Christian doctrine.[108] The challenge, then, was, Sumner contended, to understand how such a germ could be brought to ever fuller expression. For Sumner, the answer was clear: it was through Apostolic preaching in the church. As Stern has shown, Sumner accepted the notion of the church as a self-evident fact and, in this, Newman was inclined to follow Sumner, even where, as Sheridan demonstrates, he found it uncongenial and inconvenient so to do.[109] Sumner's ecclesiology may have evoked echoes of Newman's nearly contemporaneous reading of Butler, but it was William James, who, despite Newman's later recollection of being "impatient of the doctrine" when introduced to it by James, first caused Newman to take an interest in Apostolical Succession.[110] The ideas to which James had introduced Newman were to be explored in detail, however, through the work of another of the Oriel grandees who exercised so profound an influence on Newman at this time: Richard Whately.[111]

106. Diary entry: "Hawkins gave me Sumner's Apostolical Preaching." Thursday, August 19, 1824, in *LD 1*, 185. See John Bird Summer, *Apostolical Preaching Considered in an Examination of St. Paul's Epistles* (London: John Hatchard, 1815), 185.

107. Diary entry: "and finished Sumner's apostolical preaching." Thursday, August 26, 1824, in *LD 1*, 186.

108. See, for example, Kathleen Coburn, ed., *The Notebooks of Samuel Taylor Coleridge*, vol. 1 (London: Routledge, 1957), 264.

109. Jean Stern, *Bible et Tradition Chez Newman: Aux Origines de La Théorie du Développement* (Lyon: Éditions Aubier-Montaigne, 1967), 62–65. See also Sheridan, *Newman on Justification*, 82–85.

110. Newman, *Apo.*, 67.

111. Richard Whately (1787–1863), fellow of Oriel (1810–1821), principal of St. Alban Hall (1825–1831), Archbishop of Dublin (1831–1863), in *ODNB Online*.

Newman had first come into close contact with Whately after his election to the Oriel fellowship. Whately had entered Oriel in 1805 as an undergraduate, and by the time Newman was elected a fellow in April 1822, had himself been a fellow for eleven years and had just given that year's Bampton Lectures. Although his marriage necessitated giving up his fellowship in August 1823, he returned to Oxford two years later as principal of St. Alban's Hall and asked Newman to assist him as vice-principal. Newman readily admitted that he was in Whately's debt, not just for the "gentle and encouraging" way in which he handled him when, as a new fellow he was still "awkward and timid," but because he recalled that he had "emphatically, opened my mind, and taught me to think and to use my reason."[112] It was not specifically his influence in this area that is of the most interest for the present purposes, however, but rather for the ecclesiological ideas to which Whately introduced Newman:

> What he did for me in point of religious opinion, was first to teach me the existence of the Church, as a substantive body or corporation; next to fix in me those anti-Erastian views of Church polity, which were one of the most prominent features of the Tractarian movement.[113]

This recollection Newman repeated in his *Autobiographical Writings*:

> He found that one momentous truth of Revelation, he had learned from Dr. Whately, and that was the idea of the Christian Church, as a divine appointment, and as a substantive visible body, independent of the State, and endowed with rights, prerogatives, and powers of its own.[114]

Whately's opinions in this regard are clearly expressed in his anonymous 1826 publication, *Letters on the Church by an Episcopalian*.[115] Sheridan argues that this work "gives us a good clue to the subjects treated in his conversations with Newman" on the subject of the church, and Newman's journals make clear that he and Whately had opportunities for many such conversations throughout 1825 and

---

112. Newman, *Apo.*, 68.
113. Newman, *Apo.*, 69.
114. Newman, *AW*, 12.
115. Richard Whately, *Letters on the Church by an Episcopalian* (London: Longman, Rees, Orme, Brown and Green, 1826).

1826.¹¹⁶ There seems, therefore, to be no reason to call into question Newman's accounts of Whately's effect upon his views.

At St. George's Chapel, Brighton, on Christmas morning 1826, Newman preached a sermon on Daniel 7:13–14, entitled "Sermon for Christmas Day—On the Mediatorial Kingdom of Christ."¹¹⁷ He preached it again, with a slightly altered conclusion, a month later on January 28, 1827, before his own congregation at St. Clement's, Oxford. In what was, in fact, as much a consideration of Trinitarian doctrine and of the relationship of the person of Jesus Christ to God the Father than anything else, the sermon is testimony to the dogmatic character of Newman's faith. But more than that, the sermon provides evidence of Newman having, as early as the end of 1826, an inescapable awareness of the historical nature and condition of Christian Revelation together with an embryonic notion of tradition as the place in which that revelation was expressed in doctrinal form and of the necessity of the church within Christianity as the vehicle that carries forward that tradition.

The argument Newman was attempting to make in the sermon draws on all these notions to present what is, in the event, a not entirely satisfactory doctrinal synthesis of Trinitarian and Christological orthodoxy, which points forward to what was to become an abiding interest over the next six years: the Arian controversy. The Trinitarian theology of the sermon certainly flirted with the subordination of the Son to the Father, and in a memorandum, written on May 13, 1827, Newman notes that he "must be more or less wrong, for B[lanco] White, Whately and Hawkins all think me so."¹¹⁸ Hawkins more explicitly accused him of "Arianizing."¹¹⁹ The obvious and direct influence of these men on Newman made him feel their criticism all the more keenly. It is this criticism that appears to have led to his taking comfort in arguing that he had not attempted a systematic account of the Trinity but had given merely "*a partial view* of the

---

116. Sheridan, *Newman on Justification*, 116, n. 11.
117. Newman, Sermon 158, in B.3.4, BOA.
118. JHN, "Memorandum: Sermon "On the Mediatorial Kingdom of Christ," May 13, 1827, in *LD* 2, 15.
119. Newman, *Apo.*, 71.

doctrine ... the truth (supposing so) but not the whole truth" and to further admitting "I ... cordially dislike all discussions concerning the *nature* of God."[120] What is certain is that in his attempt at so doing, Newman was to point forward to what was to become an abiding interest over the next few years: the Arian controversy. It is not, however, the doctrinal content of the sermon that is of most interest here but rather the purpose that determined the manner in which Newman was arguing. In terms that once again closely prefigure the language he was to use twenty years later in the *Essay*, Newman noted that in this sermon, he was advancing a position that "was given *to account for a difficulty*" and that "for *particular purposes*, according to particular occasions, it may be useful to represent Catholic doctrine in this or that form."[121] He went even further in suggesting that some form of contingency attended the outward expression of the doctrine precisely as it had been expressed in former times:

> For some years certain texts have perplexed me—I have tried different solutions—(one to understand "the Son" always of our Lord's human nature)—at least I have acquiesced in that question—and was emboldened to declare [it to] the satisfaction (if possible) of others similarly perplexed, from considering it to have been the church's doctrine from the beginning—tho' (as I now admit) not the *whole* doctrine.[122]

Quite apart from the fascinating insight this passage gives into the Christological struggle Newman was engaged in and into at least one of his attempts to resolve the "Arianizing" for which he had been criticised, the expression, "tho' (as I now admit) not the *whole* doctrine," indicates an explicit awareness of the partial nature of the church's attempts at the dogmatic expression of her doctrines.

Newman was clearly uncomfortable with the need to define closely and in dogmatic form the core content of the Christian faith and yet saw that not to do so was an inadequate response to beliefs that were to come to be rejected as incompatible with that faith.

---

120. Memorandum of May 13, 1827, in *LD* 2, 15–16. The italics here are Newman's. Cf. Newman, *Dev.*, 27.
121. Newman, *LD* 2, 16.
122. Newman, *LD* 2, 16.

Though not yet proposing a solution, Newman was now aware of the problem, and although by no means the fully developed theology of 1845, nor yet anything like it, this memorandum is undoubtedly evidence that by May 13, 1827, Newman was beginning to grapple with questions that would lead him, in time, to need to propose an hypothesis of continuity in the development of doctrine to account for the difficulty of change.

Writing *The Arians*

A recurrent challenge in tracing the history of Newman's opinions on any subject is that of providing an account of the intermissions, sometimes of long duration, during which there is little or no evidence of him engaging with the particular subject matter. Newman was not, however, an academic engaged primarily in research for whom the pursuit of his various projects might be seen as his principal preoccupation. In the three or four years leading up to the commissioning of the work that eventually became *Arians*, Newman's letters, diaries, and autobiographical writings reveal a man thoroughly occupied with the teaching and wider tutorial duties at St. Alban's Hall and Oriel, together with the pastoral work that went with his incumbency of the University Church. Even in the long vacations of 1828, 1829, and 1830, his diaries provide evidence that his long-planned systematic reading of the Fathers had to be squeezed in between rounds of parish visiting and other pastoral duties, and his familial obligations to his mother, sisters, and other relatives. Nevertheless, a number of pieces of work that Newman undertook during this apparent intermission formed a propaedeutic period for the project that became *The Arians*, the subject matter of which provided him with both difficulty and hypothesis—and the manner in which the church attempted to deal with the emergence of heresy through terminological change and the use of the *disciplina arcani*.

Newman had conceived his desire to engage in this patristic reading as a way in which "to trace the sources from which the corruptions of the Church, principally the Romish, have been derived,"[123] and it emerged at a time when his view of the Fathers was hardly complimentary. Indeed, he recorded in the *Apologia* that his attitude was one of "a certain disdain for antiquity" which 'showed itself in some flippant language against the Fathers in the Encyclopedia Metropolitana."[124] Newman's articles in the *Encyclopedia Metropolitana* had begun in the spring of 1824, at the instigation of Whately, with an article on Cicero.[125] This first article was well received, and Whately had little trouble persuading the editor, Edward Smedley, to commission Newman to write another article that would require him to engage seriously with patristic writing. The subject was the first-century neo-Pythagorean philosopher Apollonius of Tyanæus,[126] principally renowned as a miracle worker, and Newman's article led him to consider both the likelihood of the reliability of the particular accounts of Apollonius's miracles and, more widely, the whole concept of the miraculous in general. The latter half of the article is, in fact, an almost separate essay in which Newman seeks to draw a distinction between the miracles of sacred scripture and those occurring in pagan religions and the later life of the church.[127] Written between June 1825 and the following spring, the language he used in the article regarding the reliability of patristic witness to the events recalled is dismissive, although his real target—the pagan miracles—is always subject to more explicit disdain.

In the article, Newman sought to set up the conditions under which a claim to the miraculous can be sustained, conditions designed to reflect well on the miracles of sacred scripture, and, by contrast, to enable other classes of miracles to be discounted. In language that pointed forward twenty years to the *Essay*, he entitled one section: "On the antecedent Credibility of a Miracle considered as a Divine Interposition,"[128] and, on grounds of antecedent probability,

---

123. JHN to Jemima Newman, May 1, 1826, in *LD* 2, 285.

124. Newman, *Apo.*, 72.

125. Newman, "Marcus Tullius Cicero," in *Encyclopedia Metropolitana* (London: Mawman, 1824), 279–94.

126. Newman, "Apollonius of Tyanaeus," in *Encyclopedia Metropolitana* (London: Mawman, 1826), 619–44.

127. Newman, "Apollonius," 624–44.

128. Newman, "Apollonius," 628.

concluded that "the claims to supernatural power in the primitive Church are in general questionable."[129] He then went on to examine the character of the witnesses to miracles, since, he argued, "the credibility of Testimony arises from the belief we entertain of the character and competency of the witnesses."[130] In his comparison between the miracles of scripture, on the one hand, and those of pagan religions and the primitive and later church, on the other, he wrote:

> *A previous character for falsehood* is almost fatal to the credibility of a witness of an extraordinary narrative, *e.g.*, the notorious insincerity and frauds of the Church of Rome in other things, are in themselves enough to throw a strong suspicion on its Testimony to its own Miracles. The primitive Church is in some degree open to a charge of a similar nature.[131]

And again, later: "Men are always ready to believe what flatters their own opinions.... This consideration invalidates at once the testimony commonly offered for Pagan and Popish Miracles, and in no small degree that for the Miracles of the primitive Church."[132]

This language may convey a certain disdain by association, but it can hardly be called flippant. These quotations represent the strongest terms Newman used in the entire article, and yet it is clear that it was Rome and not the Fathers that he wished to discredit. While the embarrassed recollection of the *Apologia* is, perhaps, a little overemphasised, the entire tone of the article and its heavy reliance, as the footnotes attest, on Hume and Bentham[133] nevertheless support Newman's contention that this was a period in his life when he "was beginning to prefer intellectual excellence to moral" and "was drifting in the direction of liberalism."[134]

In early 1827, as part of an ongoing dispute with his brother Francis, Newman had researched, written, and distributed both to his

---

129. Newman, "Apollonius," 631.
130. Newman, "Apollonius," 639.
131. Newman, "Apollonius," 640.
132. Newman, "Apollonius," 642.
133. Although he also relies on Butler's *Analogy*, at least in outlining the place of miracles within the witness of sacred scripture.
134. Newman, *Apo.*, 72.

THE DIFFICULTY: THE PERIOD TO 1833

brother and his sisters a paper on infant baptism.[135] The paper runs to sixty-six quarto pages, and since it professed to treat the history of the practice, one might have expected he would draw on the patristic study in which he had been engaged. In fact, the paper makes almost no use of patristic material, but Newman's opportunity to embark on a properly systematic reading of the Fathers was served by the arrival of a set of works of the Fathers, delivered from Pusey, then in Germany, that awaited him on his return to Oxford at the beginning of Michaelmas term, 1827.[136] It is not at all clear why Newman asked Pusey to acquire these volumes, but his academic duties, along with an increase in his pastoral duties,[137] prevented Newman from reading them until the Long Vacation of 1828, but by June 23, he had begun to read the Apostolic Fathers.[138]

He had shared his reading plan with Charles Lloyd, the new Bishop of Oxford, formerly his teacher and now his ordinary. Newman recorded Lloyd's encouragement, and in his journal entry for February 21, 1827, he gave a tantalizing glimpse of his own self-awareness, particularly regarding the development of his own theological opinions: "Lloyd is the new Bishop of Oxford. He is very kind and takes great interest in my plan of reading the Fathers; but he says that our theological systems do not agree. They agree more than when I was in class with him, but I do not tell him so."[139]

The following summer was given over to this reading, as was that of 1830, at least after the dispute over the Oriel tutorship had concluded and he had discharged his filial duties by visiting his mother, aunt, and sisters in Brighton.[140] It is clear that he had made suffi-

---

135. See Newman, *LD* 2, 5, n. 1.
136. Diary entry: "*went to Oxford by this time the Fathers, which Pusey had bought me in Germany had arrived*," not later than Saturday October 13, 1827, in *LD* 2, 30. Oxford University organizes its teaching in three terms. The first term of the academic year runs from late September until early December. The feast of St. Michael falls on September 29 and gives the term its name, "Michaelmas."
137. He was instituted vicar of St. Mary the Virgin, the University Church, on Friday, March 14, 1828. Newman, *LD* 2, 62.
138. His diary reads: "MONDAY 23 JUNE 1828 began the Patres Apostolici with Barnabas," in *LD* 2, 76.
139. Newman, *AW*, 210.
140. Thursday, July 1, 1830, in *LD* 2, 246.

cient progress in this chronologically systematic reading such that when he received an invitation from Hugh James Rose in March 1831 to write an article on the history of the church councils of the fourth and fifth centuries,[141] he was "well disposed towards it," a disposition qualified only by a concern as to whether he had sufficient time to complete the work.[142] The writing of this book, which eventually became *The Arians*, represents the next principal episode in Newman's engagement with the question of development and the first attempt at proposing a hypothesis to account for the difficulty that he perceived it created.[143]

From the very first, Newman had agreed with Rose's proposal that any *History of the Councils* would only work if it was conceived of as an introduction to a theological consideration of the "articles in which the great doctrines of Christianity are treated."[144] Rose's conception for the Theological Library was that under the hand of a number of authors, "handy little volumes, uniform, and with appropriate embellishments" would be published and that they would promote serious theological study among Anglican clergy.[145] Newman's articles in the *Encyclopaedia Metropolitana* had recommended him to Rose and his coeditor Lyall, although, as Pattison argues, it seems likely that they labored under the misapprehension that Newman was a "moderate" Anglican, like themselves,[146] rather than the "hot headed man"[147] he conceived himself to be. That Lyall and Rose should be so misinformed as to Newman's actual views is, perhaps, surprising in view of the correspondence in March 1831 between Rose and Newman. As previously mentioned, Rose had written to Newman

---

141. Hugh James Rose to JHN, March 9, 1831, in *LD* 2, 321.
142. JHN to Hugh James Rose, March 28, 1831, in *LD* 2, 321–22.
143. The article was never published as such but only in an expanded form as *The Arians* and is hereafter referred to under that title.
144. Hugh James Rose to JHN, March 9, 1831, in *LD* 2, 321.
145. Thomas Mozley, *Reminiscences Chiefly of Oriel College and the Oxford Movement*, vol. 1 (London: Longmans Green and Co., 1882), 247.
146. Robert Pattison, *The Great Dissent: John Henry Newman and Liberal Heresy* (Oxford: Oxford University Press, 1991), 100.
147. JHN to Harriett Newman, October 16, 1831, in *LD* 2, 367.

seeking his views on a number of "controversial Articles,"[148] and it had been his purpose, as he later explained, only to ascertain the extent to which Newman would take a position in accordance with "the principles of the Church of England."[149] Newman's response was to state baldly that he was "not aware that [he] differ[ed] in any material point from our standard writers," while hinting heavily that things were not quite as straightforward as all that: "I should be unwilling to allow any alteration without the concurrence of my own judgement—and, if the change required were great, should cheerfully acquiesce in my M.S. being declined, rather than consent to suppress or modify any part of it which I deemed of importance."[150] If Rose and Lyall had expected a conventional history, then it was clear that such was not what Newman intended to produce.

In his initial response to Rose's invitation, Newman had set out a detailed plan of the work,[151] with which Rose expressed his contentment,[152] and after a brief correspondence concerning the practical and business arrangements surrounding the project,[153] Newman was able to begin the work in earnest at the beginning of the 1831 Long Vacation.[154] Thirty years later, in the controversy surrounding the writing of the *Apologia*, Newman recalled the effect this work had in fashioning in him an attachment to the principle of antiquity as a guarantor of doctrinal authenticity. He expressed himself in characteristically poetic language: "It was launching myself on an ocean with currents innumerable; and I was drifted back first to the ante-Nicene history, and then to the Church of Alexandria.... The course of reading which I pursued in the composition of my work was directly adapted to develope [sic] it in my mind."[155]

---

148. Hugh James Rose to JHN, March 9, 1831, in *LD 2*, 321.
149. Hugh James Rose to JHN, March 30, 1831, in *LD 2*, 323.
150. JHN to Hugh James Rose, March 28, 1831, in *LD 2*, 322.
151. JHN to Hugh James Rose, March 28, 1831, in *LD 2*, 321–22.
152. Hugh James Rose to JHN, March 30, 1831, in *LD 2*, 323–24.
153. JHN to Hugh James Rose, April 5, 1831, in *LD 2*, 324; Francis Rivington to JHN, April 21, 1831, referred to in n. 1 of *LD 2*, 324, and in the diary entry for Friday, April 22, 1831, in *LD 2*, 327.
154. Wednesday, June 22, 1831, in *LD 2*, 338.
155. Newman, *Apo.*, 87–88.

Rowan Williams, rather more prosaically, has suggested that the mechanics of his work on this project had a direct effect on Newman's conception of doctrine and mark a distinct step forward from the position that he had held only four years earlier:

> His sense of the legitimacy and the necessity of doctrinal definition seems to have developed actually *in* the process of endeavouring to write Church history; and the various comments in *The Arians of the Fourth Century* directed against those who are lukewarm about dogmatic definition ... are the direct fruit of the experience of writing the book, and in some degree, addressed to the Newman of 1827.[156]

Rose's original invitation had not specified which councils were to come within its purview: he merely suggested to Newman that "as a preliminary to a work on those Articles ... a *History of the Councils*, in which so many of them (one may say *all*) were discussed would be very valuable."[157] Newman sought clarification concerning this point in his response of March 28, 1831,[158] and, in his reply, Rose proposed that since the *History of the Councils* was to be an introduction to one of the articles of the Christian faith, then "The Councils consequently to be dwelt on are those in which the great points of faith were discussed or heresies censured."[159]

The first works that Newman read as he began work on *The Arians* were the secondary accounts rendered by Gibbon and Maimbourg, together with the quasicanonical *Defensio* of Bishop Bull, on which the final work was so heavily to rely.[160] Recognizing the ultimately dogmatic purpose of this introductory work, he broadened his reading to include works by the Anglican Divines Daniel Wa-

---

156. Rowan Williams, "Newman's Arians and the Question of Method in Doctrinal History," in *Newman after a Hundred Years*, ed. Ian Turnbull Ker and Alan G. Hill (Oxford: Clarendon Press, 1990), 263.

157. Hugh James Rose to JHN, March 9, 1831, in *LD 2*, 321.

158. JHN to Hugh James Rose, March 28, 1831, in *LD 2*, 321–22.

159. Hugh James Rose, March 30, 1831, in *LD 2*, 323.

160. G. Bull, *Defensio Fidei Nicaenae, Ex Scriptis, Quae Exstant, Catholicorum Doctorum Qui Intra Tria Prima Ecclesiae Christianae Saecula Floruerunt. In qua Obiter Quoque Constantinopolitana Confessio, de Spiritu Sancto, Antiquiorum Testimoniis Adstritur* (Oxford, 1685). Newman cites Bull's *Defensio* twelve times in the text of *The Arians* and a further thirty-two times in the notes to the text.

terland, Samuel Clarke, and Samuel Horsley.[161] It is not clear why he began with this scheme of reading rather than with a review of the patristic writing with which he was by that time familiar, but the overview these works provided him with served to develop his conception of the project and the work of that summer, interrupted briefly by a holiday in Devon, and significantly altered Newman's original notion of the size and scope of the project.[162] He advised Rose in August 1831 that the work would need to be at least three volumes if it were to cover the range Rose had suggested and that they would be better arranged thematically than chronologically.[163] Rose's response to this expanding project was to attempt to rein in Newman. Rose's response has not survived, but its existence is attested to in a diary note of its receipt on September 8, 1831,[164] and by Newman's September 12, 1831, response, in which he acknowledged "the service which your letter has been to me in disengaging me from the entanglements in which I had become involved by the extent and abundance of my subject."[165] Nevertheless, Newman still retained a broad vision of the extent of his commission, recognizing that it could conceivably include within its conspectus a consideration of the Council of Trent—albeit that this would require a separate work.[166] Rose does not appear to have responded to this later letter, which Newman seemingly took as a green-light to go ahead with the project according to his own instincts.

Throughout the rest of 1831 and into 1832, Newman worked on the project alongside his other duties, which had expanded still further with his appointment as rural dean on September 1, 1831.[167] He had come to perceive a particular moral purpose in his work on *The Arians*, a dimension that was never far from his controversialist and apologetic writing for the rest of his life. It was certainly strong enough for him to turn down Whately's second invitation to become

---

161. Wednesday, June 22, 1831, in *LD* 2, 338.
162. Ker, *Newman: A Biography*, 43.
163. JHN to Hugh James Rose, August 24, 1831, in *LD* 2, 352–53.
164. Thursday, September 8, 1831, in *LD* 2, 358.
165. JHN to Hugh James Rose, September 12, 1831, in *LD* 2, 358–59.
166. JHN to Hugh James Rose, September 12, 1831, in *LD* 2, 359.
167. Thursday, September 1, 1831, in *LD* 2, 357.

once more the vice-principal of St. Alban's Hall (an office he had given up on becoming a tutor at Oriel in 1826), and demonstrated again, when writing to his sister Harriett, in October 1831, to explain his own appreciation of the task at hand in terms that are heavily suggestive of an acute sense of moral purpose. Upon "Whately's promotion" to Archbishop of Dublin, Newman had expected his friend to invite him 'some time or other to join him at Dublin'[168]—although he later ruefully noted, "He never did. He knew me better than I knew myself."[169] His rationale for refusing any such offer that might come is expressed in terms that indicate his awareness of the importance of the work in which he was engaged, its wider context, and the part that he, and perhaps only he, had to play. His words have an almost prophetic quality:

> I think my mind is quite made up that it is my duty to remain where I am; so remain I shall.... My reasons for remaining are these:—first, I am actually engaged to Mr. Rose, for a succession of works, the composition of which is quite incompatible with the duties of a post about an Archbishop—next, this engagement will be in itself a channel of extensive usefulness, which I should be abandoning just as I had begun it—thirdly the study of theology is very much neglected at Oxford, and I may be doing a peculiar service to the place (by "peculiar" I mean what others will *not* do) by cultivating it—fourthly, if times are troublous, Oxford will want hot headed men, and such I mean to be, and I am in my place.[170]

He again expressed the moral character of the work to Simeon Lloyd Pope, when he wrote that he was engaged "on an extremely important subject" that was not merely of academic or historical significance but that was "resisting the innovations of the day, and attempting to defend the work of men indefinitely above me (the Primitive Fathers) which is now assailed."[171] Wilfrid Ward observed the purpose

---

168. JHN to Harriett Newman, October 16, 1831, in *LD* 2, 367.
169. Newman, *LD* 2, 367, n. 3.
170. JHN to Harriett Newman, October 16, 1831, in *LD* 2, 367.
171. JHN to Simeon Lloyd Pope, April 9, 1832, in *LD* 3, 43. Quite apart from the evidence that this letter provides for Newman having abandoned what he had perhaps overclaimed was his earlier dismissive and flippant attitude toward the Fathers, it provides a clear and early refutation of Frank Turner's hypothesis in *The Challenge* that it was the fight against evangelicalism that was the motivating purpose of Newman's writing rather than

in undertaking the commission: "For Newman himself it was not an exercise of historical research for its own sake, but an essential link in the rational justification of existing Orthodox Christianity for educated men and thinkers—the central object of all his work."[172]

To achieve this object, Newman had to devise a rhetorical strategy that would simultaneously fix the same character to the errors of the third and fourth centuries and to those of the nineteenth. Jay Hammond describes this strategy in detail in his "Interplay of Hermeneutics and Heresy in the Process of Newman's Conversion 1830–1845," in which he outlines a complex twin dialectic. He argues that Newman's theology operated around the twin poles of belief and faith on the one hand, and development and church on the other. Hammond contends that it is the dialectic between conscience and dogma that defines the belief/faith pole, with that between probability and imagination shaping the development/church pole.[173] Much of the evidence he considers belongs to the period immediately after the writing of *The Arians*. Nonetheless, throughout the period from 1830 to 1845, Hammond maintains that Newman's "own theological preoccupations against liberalism were the primary impetus for his historical study. He looked into the past to help him discern the theo-political events of the present ... to construct a rhetorical strategy against his adversaries."[174]

Newman's sense of urgent moral purpose was strengthened by the methodological challenge he faced in the process of researching and writing *History of the Councils*. In the previously quoted letter to Rose of August 1831, he framed the methodological question before him in terms that would have a profound impact upon not just

---

against religious liberalism—which is clearly what Newman meant by "the innovations of the day."

172. Wilfrid Philip Ward, *Last Lectures of Wilfred Ward Being the Lowell Lectures, 1914 and Three Lectures Delivered at the Royal Institution, 1915* (London: Longmans, Green and Co., 1918), 40.

173. Jay Hammond, "Interplay of Hermeneutics and Heresy in the Process of Newman's Conversion from 1830–1845," in *Authority, Dogma, and History: The Role of Oxford Movement Converts on the Papal Infallibility Debates*, ed. Kenneth Parker and Michael J. G. Pahls (Palo Alto, Calif.: Academica Press, 2009), 45–76.

174. Hammond, "Interplay of Hermeneutics and Heresy," 46.

The Arians but upon his repeated attempts at proposing an adequate account of doctrinal continuity in the face of historical evidence of significant development and change. His reading had led him to a definite plan:

> For the last six weeks I have given some time to the examination of my materials—and am of the opinion that I shall best answer the object of making an useful work by giving a *connected* history of the Councils—i.e. not taking them as isolated, but introducing so much of Church History as will illustrate and account for them. Do not suppose that I mean to evade the strict discussion of the subjects settled in the Councils—this is the main object of the whole work—but since only the conclusions come to, not the arguments and controversy are given in the Acts ... to analyze these would be doing nothing. What light would be thrown on the Nicene Confession *merely* by explaining it article by article? to understand it, it must be prefaced by a sketch of the rise of the Arian heresy.[175]

Newman felt that he needed to write a work that took proper account of the events and arguments that provided the immediate historical backdrop to the councils of the early church and, more significantly in the context of the matter under consideration here, within which the dogmatic statements of the Christian faith arose. The task he had set himself in responding to the invitation to write this *History of the Councils*, the task he attempted to fulfill in writing *The Arians*, was neither one of systematic theology nor history but rather one of what Newman considered to be a truly ecclesiastical history. His reading had provided no real model for this, as he confided to Samuel Rickards: "The standard Divines are magnificent fellows, but then they are Antiquarians or Doctrinists, not Ecclesiastical Historians—Bull, Waterland, Petavius, Baronius and the rest—of the historians I have met with I have a very low opinion—Mossheim, Gibbon, Milner, etc—Cave and Tillement are highly respectable, but biographers."[176] He had a sense that he was, therefore, on his own and that he had to write a "*connected* history" such that it was both good history and good theology: respecting the norms of each discipline. Newman

---

175. JHN to Hugh James Rose, August 24, 1831, in *LD* 2, 352.
176. JHN to Samuel Rickards, October 30, 1831, in *LD* 2, 371.

THE DIFFICULTY: THE PERIOD TO 1833

understood that this meant that what he wrote would have to account for the process that led up to the Nicene symbol and the symbol itself in such a way that gave proper weight to historically verifiable events, while also reflecting on the definitive nature of the revelation of God in the person, acts, and teaching of Jesus Christ. His correspondence gives some hint of his awareness of the ever-expanding scope of work that this methodology necessitated. The August 1831 letter to Rose recorded his unease: "I have a difficulty in combining history and doctrinal discussion, which besides the irregularity which it might occasion in the work by causing frequent digressions, may render it heavy, *load the text with notes at the foot* of the page, and after all prevent the complete investigation and elucidation of various points of doctrine."[177]

Newman went through several iterations of a structure for the work that he believed would enable him to resolve the difficulty of giving an account that was properly both historical and theological: each successive plan expanding the size and number of volumes necessary to adequately answer Rose's initial concept. Rose's intervention in September 1831[178] settled the fundamental structural concerns and, in Newman's words in his reply, had disengaged him "from the entanglements in which I had become involved by the extent and abundance of my subject."[179]

By early 1832, the publishers were chasing him to produce the work, and his letters and diaries for the first half of that year record his determination to finalize it.[180] In a diary entry on Thursday, June 7, 1832,[181] he recorded that it was completed, but as the editors of the third volume of *Letters and Diaries* observe, "presumably the writing

---

177. JHN to Hugh James Rose, August 24, 1831, in *LD 3*, 353. The seriousness with which Newman expressed this difficulty, if one takes him at his word, is evidence against Stephen Thomas's description of the work as a "narrative," in which Newman does not engage in the historian's proper task of "the impartial sifting of evidence"—however such impartiality might be defined, let alone attempted—but "rather ... incorporates the historian's interest in causality and origins into a story in which argument and narrative are carefully woven to make the greatest popular appeal" (Thomas, *Newman and Heresy*, 35).

178. Thursday, September 8, 1831, in *LD 2*, 358.

179. JHN to Hugh James Rose, September 12, 1831, in *LD 2*, 358–59.

180. JHN to Richard Hurrell Froude, January 8, 1832, in *LD 3*, 3–4.

181. Thursday, June 7, 1832, in *LD 3*, 54.

out still remained to be done."[182] At the beginning of July, Newman had sent Rose, by way of Rivington and Turrill, the first third of the manuscript.[183] He had intended to deliver the second third directly to Rose when he went to Cambridge on July 16, but his intentions were frustrated by Rose's absence from Cambridge due to illness.[184] In any event, the work was finally completed on July 31, 1832,[185] as Newman's diary records with relief, and from Brighton just over a week later, he and Rose were in correspondence regarding the latter's editorial observations.[186] This correspondence continued throughout August and September,[187] and by October, Newman had become anxious. Rose had passed the manuscript to his coeditor William Rowe Lyall, the Archdeacon of Maidstone, and Newman was certainly aware of this when he wrote to Froude in September.[188] On October 23, Newman received a letter from Rose[189] that also included a letter from Lyall to Rose,[190] which Newman recorded in his diary as "*plucking my 'Arians*,'" that is, rejecting it as unacceptable.[191]

Newman's reaction to Lyall's editorial criticism and to Rose's implicit decision not to publish the work as part of the Theological Library was dignified and indicated that he could see the force of the editorial stance. Lyall's letter recorded that he had admired the scholarship and style of the work: "It is full of learning, and the tone and spirit in which it is written are excellent—the style also I like particularly: it is thoroughly *English*, and in many places strikingly

---

182. Newman, *LD* 3, n. 1.
183. JHN to Hugh James Rose, July 5, 1832, in *LD 3*, 65.
184. JHN to Mrs. Newman, July 16, 1832, in *LD 3*, 66–67.
185. Tuesday, July 31, 1833, in *LD 3*, 74.
186. JHN to Hugh James Rose, August 8, 1832, in *LD 3*, 77.
187. JHN to Hugh James Rose, August 16, 1832, in *LD 3*, 78–79; diary entry for Thursday, August 24, 1832, in *LD 3*, 80; JHN to Jemima Newman, August 27, 1832 in *LD 3*, 82; JHN to Richard Hurrell Froude, September 13, 1832, in *LD 3*, 94; and diary entry for Thursday, September 27, 1832, in *LD 3*, 97.
188. JHN to Richard Hurrell Froude, September 13, 1832, in *LD 3*, 94.
189. Hugh James Rose to JHN, October 21, 1832, in *LD 3*, 104.
190. William Rowe Lyall to Hugh James Rose, October 19, 1832, in *LD 3*, 104–5.
191. Tuesday, October 23, 1832, in *LD 3*, 103. The expression "*plucking*" refers to the ancient voting practice in the Oxford University convocation, whereby a vote against a proposition was indicated by a member grasping the gown of a proctor as he passed through the assembly to take the vote. See entry for "plucking" at *Oxford English Dictionary Online*.

good."[192] He also recognized, however, that it was a poor fit for the Theological Library, not least because it was manifestly not the commissioned *History of the Councils* but rather "a History of *Arianism*."[193]

Newman's reply to Rose, written on the day of the receipt of Rose's letter, recognized that this assessment was a fair one and accepted that he had "completed a history of Arianism," but he sought Rose's support in getting the manuscript published as a stand-alone work.[194] Newman's response to the theological criticisms made by Lyall, on the other hand, indicated that on that point, he parted company with his editor. Lyall had suggested that Newman's argument, which had made much of the *disciplina arcani* and tradition, was "directly adverse to that which Protestant writers of our church have contended for."[195] It will be necessary for us to consider this observation and those made in Lyall's later letters in greater detail when the text of the published work is considered.[196] In his response to Rose, however, Newman conceded only to having committed minor solecisms:

Believe me to be quite sensible of the absurdity of committing the paradoxes and mistakes in minor points to which you allude—and, though I ever wish to have the command of my own views and to preserve that individuality of opinion, (so to call it) on which I conceive the prospect of permanent usefulness to depend, yet it is my anxious desire to avoid every position which may give a handle to opponents or to perplex the honest reader who agrees with me in the main.[197]

Rose promised full support to Newman in attempting to get the manuscript published,[198] and on November 5, Lyall contacted Rivington, the intended publishers, to secure their agreement.[199] Rivington wrote to Newman that same day to confirm that they would, indeed, publish the work in an edition of 750 copies and hoped so to

---

192. William Rowe Lyall to Hugh James Rose, October 19, 1832, in *LD 3*, 104–5.
193. William Rowe Lyall to Hugh James Rose, October 19, 1832, in *LD 3*, 105.
194. JHN to Hugh James Rose, October 23, 1832, in *LD 3*, 103–4.
195. William Rowe Lyall to Hugh James Rose, October 19, 1832, in *LD 3*, 105.
196. That is, those of November 3 and 9, 1832, respectively, in *LD 3*, 112, 133.
197. JHN to Hugh James Rose, October 23, 1832, in *LD 3*, 103.
198. Hugh James Rose to JHN, October 29, 1832, in *LD 3*, 104, n. 1.
199. William Rowe Lyall to Rivington, November 6, 1832, in *LD 3*, 112, n. 3.

THE DIFFICULTY: THE PERIOD TO 1833

do as soon after Easter 1833 as suited Newman.[200] As it was, Newman had agreed to accompany Froude and his father to the Mediterranean over the winter of 1832 to 1833,[201] a journey that was to take Newman away from Oxford on December 3 1832,[202] not returning until July 9, 1833,[203] and so the work did not appear until November 5, 1833.[204]

Five days after Newman's return to Oxford, on July 14, 1833, Keble preached the Assize Sermon in St. Mary the Virgin, under the title "National Apostasy." Newman had been away for much of the period covering the events that had led to Keble's remarks, but he was keenly aware of the issues. The Catholic Relief Act of 1829[205] had caused trouble enough—Newman's part in the campaign against the MP for Oxford University, Robert Peel, who as Home Secretary had guided the bill through the House of Commons,[206] may have been, in part, at the root of the difficulties he had had with Hawkins over the Oriel tutorship, each of them having canvassed "energetically" on opposite sides[207]—but the Church Temporalities (Ireland) Act of 1833[208] had been more than he and many of those of like mind were prepared silently to bear. Keble's sermon attempted to lay bare the full Erastian nature of the act and to identify the existential threat it posed to the very conception of the Church of England that he, Newman, and others held as being of its essence. There were other events that summer that may have been the initial catalyst for the Oxford Movement, the meeting at Rose's Hadleigh Rectory being chief among them,[209]

---

200. William Rowe Lyall to JHN, November 6, 1832, in *LD 3*, 112, n. 3.
201. Richard Hurrell Froude to JHN, September 9, 1832, in *LD 3*, 92–93; JHN to Richard Hurrell Froude, September 13, 1832, in *LD 3*, 93–94.
202. Monday, December 3, 1832, in *LD 3*, 121.
203. Tuesday, July 9, 1833, in *LD 4*, 3.
204. Tuesday, November 5, 1833, in *LD 4*, 85.
205. "An Act for the Relief of His Majesty's Roman Catholic Subjects," (1829) 10 Geo. 4, 7.
206. Peel felt compelled to resign and stand for reelection to his parliamentary seat, as he was representing the graduates of Oxford University (many of whom were Anglican clergymen) and had previously stood on a platform of opposition to Catholic Emancipation. Peel lost the subsequent by-election in February 1829.
207. Ker, *Newman: A Biography*, 32.
208. "An Act to Alter and Amend the Laws Relating to the Temporalities of the Church in Ireland," (1833) 3 & 4 Will. 4, 37.
209. Peter Nockles calls the Hadleigh Rectory meeting the movement's "famous inaugural conference" (Nockles, *The Oxford Movement in Context*, 124).

but because Newman was present and the lecture was given from his pulpit, he thereafter held that Keble's sermon was the starting gun for the movement.[210]

It is ironic that the sermon attracted little contemporary notice, and its immediate effect appears to have been slight.[211] Newman's energies were diverted into the movement—although it had not, by this time, attained this or any other name—such that, between his return to Oxford and the eventual publication of the book in November 1833, he made but one further mention of the book in his correspondence to H. A. Woodgate, and that was but a remark in passing.[212] These months were a period of intense activity during which, among other things, Newman planned and organized the first of the *Tracts for the Times*, writing at least six and possibly seven of the first ten, and he was heavily engaged in the organization of the nascent movement. Most of the concerns regarding the text of *The Arians* had been settled prior to his departure for the Mediterranean the previous December. Nevertheless, bearing in mind the extraordinary lengths to which he had gone in producing *The Arians*, the immediate pre- and postpublication silence in his letters and diaries is surprising, even allowing for the fact that the frenetic activity around the first months of what would come to be called the Oxford Movement had left little time for other concerns.

The Text of *The Arians*

The work that had originally been conceived as a volume in Rose and Lyall's Theological Library, with the title *A History of the Councils*, was finally published under the title of *The Arians of the Fourth Century, Their Doctrine, Temper, and Conduct, Chiefly as Exhibited in the Councils*

---

210. "I have ever considered and kept the day, as the start of the religious movement of 1833." Newman, *Apo.*, 100.

211. Mark D. Chapman, "John Keble, National Apostasy, and the Myths of 14 July," in *John Keble in Context*, ed. K. Blair (London: Anthem Press, 2004), 47.

212. JHN to H. A. Woodgate, August 7, 1833, in *LD 4*, 28. Keble twice refers to the sermon in letters to Newman, but Newman's replies do not mention it. See John Keble to JHN, August <or July> 1833 and November 5, respectively, in *LD 4*, 19, 86; <...> denote Newman's interpolation.

THE DIFFICULTY: THE PERIOD TO 1833

of the Church, between A.D. 325, and A.D. 381 on November 5, 1833. Extending to 436 pages of slightly larger than Octavo, comprising eleven pages of preface and 425 pages of text, it bore a dedication to John Keble and an advertisement that made reference to its genesis as part of Rivington's Theological Library, noting that, "as it seemed, on its completion, little fitted for the objects with which that publication has been undertaken, it makes its appearance in an independent form."[213] It was arranged in six chapters, which, when preparing the work for publication as part of the complete edition published by Longmans in 1878, Newman conveniently grouped into a first part dealing with doctrinal matters, containing the first two chapters of the original work, and a second part dealing with historical matters, containing the remaining chapters of the first edition.

Newman later claimed that, "What principally attracted me in the ante-Nicene period was the great Church of Alexandria, the historical centre of teaching in those times,"[214] and this attraction certainly appears to have influenced the text of *The Arians*. In the first chapter, he immediately sets up an opposition between the Church of Alexandria, which he portrays positively, and that of the Church of Antioch, to which he ascribes almost entirely negative characteristics. As soon as Newman had introduced his readers to the Church at Antioch, he confronts them with the stark statement that "This ancient and celebrated Church, however, is painfully conspicuous in the middle of the century" [i.e., the third century], "as affording so open a manifestation of the spirit of Antichrist, as to fulfil almost literally the prophecy of the Apostle in 2 Thess. Ii."[215] He could hardly be clearer about his position than when he wrote, "Antioch is the metropolis of the heretical, as Alexandria of the orthodox party."[216] In the following thirty or so pages, Newman never lost an opportunity to point up the adverse characteristics of the Church of Antioch,

---

213. Newman, *Ari.*, advertisement.
214. Newman, *Apo.*, 88.
215. Newman, *Ari.*, 3–4.
216. Newman, *Ari.*, 10.

linking it directly to the development of the heresy of Arianism, by way of Judaism, Sophism, and the Antiochene church's own "disputatious character."[217] The language applied to Antioch never fails to be loaded with adverse inferences, with terms such as "artifice" and "sceptical,"[218] "pugnacious," and "satirical"[219] being typical examples. The vocabulary used about the Church of Alexandria is, in contrast, almost entirely positive. Even the fact that Arius himself was a Presbyter of the Church of Alexandria is excused by reference to the fact that he was "educated at Antioch," and that, "so far from being favourably heard at Alexandria, he was on the first promulgation of his heresy, expelled from the church in that city."[220] The Church of Alexandria is described as "supplied in especial abundance, both of the materials and instruments prompting to the exercise of Christian zeal,"[221] and its catechetical practices, especially with reference to the use of the principle of reserve, are held up by Newman as the exemplar of the best practice of the early church.[222] His purpose in setting up this duality would appear to be apologetic: not with reference to the heresies of the early church but, by analogy, to the ecclesiastical controversies of his own day. Stephen Thomas argues that: "In *The Arians of the Fourth Century*, for the first time, there appears, clearly enunciated, the analogy between heresy and the forces of Newman's own time which he regarded as enemies of church and Christianity. It is, indeed, the political aspect of heresy which he takes for his peroration, pointing to the present significance of the past."[223]

Newman himself conceived the task in apocalyptic terms, which certainly suggests that he was quite as "hot headed" as he had previously suggested to his sister as he intended to be.[224] He commented:

---

217. Newman, *Ari.*, 28.
218. Newman, *Ari.*, 29.
219. Newman, *Ari.*, 30.
220. Newman, *Ari.*, 43.
221. Newman, *Ari.*, 45.
222. Newman, *Ari.*, 46–54.
223. Thomas, *Newman and Heresy*, 38.
224. JHN to Harriett Newman, October 16, 1831, in *LD* 2, 367.

Meanwhile, we may take comfort in reflecting, that, though the present tyranny has more of insult, it has hitherto less of scandal, than attended the ascendancy of Arianism; we may rejoice in the piety, prudence, and varied graces of our Spiritual Rulers; and may rest in the confidence, that, should the hand of Satan press us sore, our Athanasius and Basil will be given us in their desired season, to break the bonds of the Oppressor, and let captives go free.[225]

This use of the principle of historical parallel was certainly novel, although it was to become a defining characteristic of Newman's controversial style both before, during, and after his conversion to Roman Catholicism—indeed, it will be shown in chapter 3 that it was instrumental in that conversion. Williams, who has noted that one of the major challenges for Newman in writing *The Arians* was the lack of a model in other writers for a work of this kind,[226] suggests that, despite the doctrinally and ecclesiologically conservative agenda in *The Arians*, this use of historical parallel is "a disturbingly radical view of the history of theology."[227] The purposes to which Newman was to put the use of this principle varied with the occasion and specific controversial issues, but in *The Arians*, it seems clear that, as Avery Dulles observed, it is used to provide "an allegory of the Oxford of Newman's day: the Alexandrians represent the Oxonian Platonists, whom Newman supports; his attacks on Antioch are disguised censures of the rationalists of contemporary Oxford."[228] Taking a similar view, Jan-Hendrik Walgrave has suggested that "Newman's study of the fathers and of the great heresies and schisms of early Church history gradually presented to his view the ancient church as it really was and positions taken up by both sides in the controversies of the patristic era. He found these ideas, principles and standpoints analogous to those of the disputants of his own day."[229]

---

225. Newman, *Ari.*, 422.
226. Williams, "Newman's Arians," 265.
227. Rowan Williams, ed., introduction to *The Arians of the Fourth Century, Their Doctrine, Temper, and Conduct, Chiefly as Exhibited in the Councils of the Church, between A.D. 325 and A.D. 381*, by John Henry Newman, Millennium (Leominster: Gracewing, 2001), XXI.
228. Avery Dulles, *Newman* (London: Continuum, 2002), 3.
229. Jan Hendrick Walgrave, *Newman the Theologian: The Nature of Belief and Doctrine*

THE DIFFICULTY: THE PERIOD TO 1833

Having introduced the main theological schools by reference to the *dramatis personae* of the churches at Antioch and Alexandria, Newman then went on to describe the practice of the *disciplina arcani* as exhibited in the catechetical practice of the Alexandrian Church.[230] This practice, that of keeping in reserve the specific doctrinal truths of Christianity prior to the baptism of the neophyte, is justified by Newman by his reference to the practice of the early church, not so much as a practice but as a principle. Newman defined this *disciplina arcani* as that "self-restraint and abstinence practised, at least partially, by the primitive church in the publication of the most sacred doctrines of our religion,"[231] and he identified the practice as arising from the proper use of sacred scripture as the "vindication" of the church's teaching.[232] He made reference at this point in the text to the work of Hawkins, referred to in detail above, which he describes as being "the key to a number of difficulties which are apt to perplex the theological student."[233] Newman contrasted the proper principle of "the Church to teach the truth and then appeal to Scripture in vindication of its own teaching,"[234] with the approach of heretics, here specifically referring to the Arians, as neglecting "the information provided for them" by the teaching of the church, and then attempting "themselves a work to which *they* are unable," that is, "the eliciting ... a systematic doctrine from the scattered notices of the truth which Scripture contains."[235]

At the heart of the practice of the *disciplina arcani* for Newman was the distinction between exoteric and esoteric teaching in the practice of Christian antiquity. Newman argued that, for the ante-Nicene church, the exoteric practice was one of reserve adopted for apologetic reasons, with the esoteric being revealed in the in-

---

as Exemplified in His Life and Works, trans. A.V. Littledale (London: Geoffrey Chapman, 1960), 38.

230. Newman, *Ari.*, 55–71.
231. Newman, *Ari.*, 55.
232. Newman, *Ari.*, 56.
233. Newman, *Ari.*, 55, n. 2.
234. Newman, *Ari.*, 56.
235. Newman, *Ari.*, 56.

struction of those already admitted to the community of the church of those "truths reserved for the baptised Christian," which "were not put forward as the arbitrary determinations of individuals, as the word of man, but rather as an *apostolical legacy*, preserved and dispensed by the Church."[236] The private interpretation of scripture was insufficient, and indeed likely to lead into error,[237] for, as he had learned from Hawkins, it is for "the Church to teach the truth, and then appeal to Scripture in vindication of the truth."[238] More specifically, and on the authority of Irenaeus, Newman argued that:

> we derive the doctrine of our salvation through none but those who have transmitted to us the gospel, *first preaching it*, then (through God's mercy) delivering it to us in the Scriptures, as a basis and pillar of our faith. Nor dare we affirm, that their statements were made previously to their attaining perfect knowledge, as some presume to say, boasting that they amend the apostles.[239]

Newman, as a good Churchman, was committed to preserving the notion of the sufficiency of scripture and therefore felt it necessary to quote with approbation the words of Irenaeus, "it must not be supposed, that this appeal to tradition in the slightest degree disparages the sovereign authority and sufficiency of Holy Scripture, as a record of the truth."[240] Yet in a passage that goes rather beyond the view expressed by Hawkins, and beyond a strictly *unauthoritative* tradition, Newman asserted that "In the passage from Irenaeus above cited, apostolical tradition is brought forward, not to supersede Scripture, but in conjunction with Scripture, to refute the self-authorised arbitrary doctrines of the heretics."[241] The dogmatic content of this tradition, kept secret by the *disciplina arcani*, was, Newman argued, finally revealed and brought to light, when:

---

236. Newman, *Ari.*, 59.
237. Newman, *Ari.*, 59.
238. Newman, *Ari.*, 59. See also Hawkins, *Unauthoritive Tradition*, 18.
239. Newman, *Ari.*, 59–60.
240. Newman, *Ari.*, 61.
241. Newman, *Ari.*, 61.

It was authoritatively divulged and perpetuated in the form of symbols according as the successive innovations of heretics called for its publication. In the creeds of the early Councils, it may be considered as having come to light, and so ended; so that whatever has not been thus authenticated, whether such was prophetical information . . . or comment on the past dispensations . . . is from the circumstances of the case, lost to the church.[242]

Here, then, was a potential hypothesis to account for the difficulty of the apparent change from the teaching of the ante-Nicene church to the developed doctrinal language of the Council of Nicaea itself. It was a hypothesis that attempted to account not just for the apparent change but for the reasons behind such a change. The consequence of the operation of the principle of reserve under the *disciplina arcani*, Newman suggested, was that the vocabulary of theological discourse in the period prior to the "coming to light," that is, in the ante-Nicene period, would appear inconsistent, ambiguous, and incomplete, at least "from the standpoint of developed orthodoxy."[243] Nowhere was this inconsistency, ambiguity, and incompleteness more to be found than in the language used in the primitive church to express its Trinitarian beliefs.

For Newman, the reconciliation of Trinitarian language used in the ante-Nicene and post-Nicene church was but a particular example of a general problem, and in the light of his avowed use of the principle of historical parallelism, it was a question that had implications that went wider than concerns about terminological consistency in the teachings of the primitive church. The apparent differences between the Church of England in his own age and the primitive church required of him a resolution: he needed to be able to show that the church of third-century Alexandria and nineteenth-century England were one and the same. His problem was the appearance of radical dissimilarity and discontinuity between the two. In his reading for *The Arians*, especially in his encounter with the work of Bishop Bull, Newman was drawn to the rule of faith of the fifth-century Gallic monk, St. Vincent of Lerins. This rule of faith,

---

242. Newman, *Ari.*, 61–62.
243. Williams, "Newman's Arians," 269.

the so-called Vincentian Canon, was that the Catholic faith was that "quod semper, quod ubique, quod ab omnibus creditum est."[244] Newman's understanding of the force and application of the Vincentian Canon was to be tested, as will be discussed in subsequent chapters, in his 1834 and 1835 correspondence with the Abbé Jager and fully developed in his *Lectures on the Prophetical Office of the Church*.[245] It continued to serve him until 1839, as will be seen, when it came into conflict in his thinking with another maxim drawn from the Latin Fathers, this time St. Augustine, which led to Newman's having to radically reinterpret the meaning of St. Vincent's dictum.

All that was, however, in the future at the time of the publication of *The Arians*; in 1833, the direct import of this axiomatic rule of faith for Newman was to underline the belief that the faith of the primitive church had to be the faith of the church in every age. Newman saw that the Church of England in the nineteenth century could impose nothing more to be believed as necessary for salvation upon its adherents than that which the early church had prescribed; the corollary was that the Church of England in the nineteenth century had to prescribe as being necessary for salvation the whole of that faith which bound the early church: the dogmatic nature of the Christian faith demanded continuity. With this general question in mind, then, the particular problem for Newman with regard to the evidence he had accumulated in *The Arians* was how to explain the apparently radical discontinuity, at least between the terminology used by the ante-Nicene Fathers and the language adopted at Nicaea and in the subsequent councils.

Newman's thinking regarding the pedagogical purpose of the use of the principle of reserve under the *disciplina arcani*, taken together with the operation of the notion of economy, went some way toward resolving the difficulty. The principle of economy, or as Newman defined it, the "accommodation to the feelings and prejudices

---

244. Vincent of Lérins, "Commonitorium," in Corpus Christianorum: Series Latina, vol. 64 (Turnhout: Brepols, 1953), 149.

245. John Henry Newman, *Lectures on the Prophetical Office of the Church Viewed Relatively to Romanism and Popular Protestantism* (London: J. G. and F. Rivington, 1837).

of the hearer, leading him to the reception of a novel or unacceptable doctrine,"[246] provided him with sufficient room to accommodate the theological imprecision of the ante-Nicene language to the later expression of orthodoxy. Nevertheless, a strict application of the principle of economy would also suggest that the person making use of it had "knowledge possessed but not fully communicated" of the doctrine as it later came to be fully expressed, in this case by the Council of Nicaea.[247] The language used by the ante-Nicene father, St. Cyril of Alexandria, regarding the substance of God, for example, is specifically rejected by the council, and the use of the language adopted by the council had been specifically rejected by Cyril.[248] The clear import of this, for Newman, was that far from possessing the full Nicene faith, kept in reserve for the purposes of economy, under the rule of the *disciplina arcani*, what was under consideration was a discontinuity in the explicit doctrinal content of belief.

Newman could see further examples of this apparent discontinuity in the various terms used to describe the relationship of the Son to the Father—and, indeed, the very use of the term "son" at all. The rationalization that Newman offers draws its methodology from the very apologetic and controversial nature of his own work. He proposed that it was not for pedagogical reasons that the principle of economy was used to express doctrines fully conceptually understood but that the systematization of doctrine itself arises because of apologetic or controversial reasons. As Newman himself wrote: "False doctrine forces us to analyse our own positions in order to exclude it."[249] That is to say, the formal expression in dogmatic form of the Christian faith came about, and, indeed, continued to come about, specifically to counter the emergence of heresy. Williams describes Newman's understanding of the process thus: "each formulation, even the hallowed word 'son' for the Second Person, and each figure of Scripture is in itself inadequate and calls for some coun-

---

246. Newman, *Ari.*, 79.
247. Williams, "Newman's Arians," 271.
248. Newman, *Ari.*, 201–18.
249. Newman, *Ari.*, 180.

terbalancing concept or image. Until crises arise, systematization is unnecessary."[250]

Newman, at this point, understood the process as being one in which, to counter error, the terms used to describe the mysteries of faith have to be refined to create a technical theological language that comes to replace or supersede the broader, less specific vocabulary of an earlier age. He contended that the process worked as follows: "There are two characteristics of opinions subjected to this intellectual scrutiny; first, they are *variously* expressed during the process; secondly, they are expressed *technically*, at the end of it."[251]

The operation of this process allowed Newman to close his survey of the Catholic theology of the ante-Nicene period with an examination of the language used by five ante-Nicenes: Athenagoras, Tatian, Theophilus, Hippolytus, and Novatian. His very use of the expression "Catholic doctrine" is itself notable, since the usual term at the time was to speak of "Orthodox doctrine."[252] He concedes that a superficial reading of their works, by reference to the vocabulary of post-Nicene orthodoxy, might make their language suspect of the heresy that was Arian doctrine but that, far from being heretical, "the orthodoxy of the five writers in question, is ascertained by a careful examination of the passages from which the accusation has been brought against them."[253] The very process of the refinement of terms and the adoption of technical vocabulary meant that it was anachronistic to attempt to judge the use of terms in an earlier age by the standards of a later. It allowed Newman the conclusion that although the ante-Nicene divines might not have recognised the full expression of Trinitarian orthodoxy in the symbol of Nicaea as, at once, identical with their own beliefs, their expressions of Trinitarian faith and the expressions of Trinitarian faith of the Council of Nicaea were at least compatible with one another.

250. Williams, "Newman's Arians," 269.
251. Newman, *Ari.*, 197.
252. Newman uses the term "Catholic doctrine" four times in his survey of ante-Nicene theology and even closes the section of the chapter with the statement, "And thus closes our survey of Catholic Ante-Nicene theology." Newman, *Ari.*, 218. See also *Ari.*, 197, 207, 212, and 217.
253. Newman, *Ari.*, 216.

THE DIFFICULTY: THE PERIOD TO 1833

As has been already noted, Archdeacon Lyall had very serious misgivings about the implications of the account that Newman had given. His views, expressed to Rose in the letter that Rose sent on to Newman, are candid and worth reproducing here at length:

The present system of Orthodox Christianity is grounded upon Scripture under the sanction and continued authority which is furnished by *Tradition*, of which the Councils are the authentic organs—The question is, what is the proper province and the true value of *human authority* in the matter of Divine Revelation? Now, in no way could this question I think be so well handled, as in a general history of the principal councils accompanied with critical remarks upon their proceedings, showing when they had *outstepped* their proper office, and when their authority was *binding*—Of course the *constitution* of the councils, the *manner* in which they conducted their deliberation etc would have formed part of such a work, and the different views taken of the matter by the Churches of England and of Rome, would have afforded ample subjects of illustration—I am here only briefly stating what my own conception would have been of the History of the Councils—if Mr Newman's work shall be published in the *Theological Library*, there are several parts that will require consideration—particularly in those places where he speaks of the *disciplina arcani*—I do not pretend to make my opinion the rule—but Mr Newman's notions about tradition appear to me directly adverse to that which Protestant writers of our own church have contended for—according to them a 'secret tradition" is no tradition at all—quod semper, quod ubique, quod ab omnibus, is the very definition of authentic tradition. Mr Newman's views seem to me more favourable to the Romanist writers, than I should like to put forward in the *Theological Library*—There are also several other passages and expressions which made by [sic][254] hyperorthodox nerves *wince*—a little—and which we must talk about hereafter if Mr Newman's book is published with *our names* appended.[255]

Although he attempted to defend himself in a letter to Newman two weeks later, claiming that he had "only hazarded an opinion; I did not deliver judgement,"[256] Lyall appears to have recognized that this is not traditional Anglican theology. In particular, he had recognized that Newman's use of the Fathers differed in many respects

---

254. The text says "by," but the sense demands "my."
255. William Rowe Lyall to Hugh James Rose, October 19, 1832, in *LD 3*, 105.
256. Archdeacon Lyall to JHN, November 3, 1832, in *LD 3*, 112.

from the way in which they had traditionally been used by Anglican Divines.

Anglican scholars of the sixteenth and seventeenth centuries were rightly revered for their work on the Fathers, yet the use to which patristic writings had been put in the Church of England, like the theological place of tradition itself, had long been ambiguous. As Jean-Louis Quantin demonstrates, the shifting the ground of the disputes about doctrine during the forging of a distinctly Anglican theology in these centuries, had led to an attempt by churchmen to the claim that the consensus of the Fathers was the sure mark of orthodoxy, that such a consensus could be established and that it was a consensus that, conveniently, supported the Anglican view.[257]

Newman's approach to patristic sources—and the extent to which it was distinctive—will be analysed in greater detail when his contribution to the *Tracts* is considered in the next chapter, but for the present purposes, it is sufficient to note that Lyall had foreseen that Newman's approach, that of taking the Fathers on their own terms, was perilous. In his suggestion that Newman's view was "favourable to the Romanist," he was looking beyond the text of *The Arians* to a notion of tradition: not to the unauthoritative tradition of Hawkins's sermon, of the "Protestant writers of our own church," of Anglicanism, but to the authoritative tradition as proclaimed by Rome. He had seen what Newman had not: that Newman's reading of the Fathers would need to find a solution to lack of a univocal patristic doctrinal witness that would need more than the Vincentian Canon could supply.

Despite the clarity of the November 3rd letter, Lyall was concerned that he had not properly explained his reservations to Newman, and, on November 9, 1832, he again wrote to Newman to further acquit himself of having charged him with unorthodox positions. It, too, bears quoting at length:

If I used the word orthodox, it must have been in that improper sense in which a Protestant, or Church of England divine is used to say ... I dif-

---

257. Jean-Louis Quantin, *The Church of England and Christian Antiquity: The Construction of a Confessional Identity in the 17th Century* (Oxford: Oxford University Press, 2009), 5–6.

fer almost as widely from the generally received estimate which Protestant writers have made of the value of Patristical testimony, and of tradition in general, as I do from the views entertained by Romanists—it seems to me, that my own views do not very widely differ from yours on those points— But then my duty as editor is not to sanction my own views, but only those of Protestant churches—to which I think your views of tradition somewhat opposed—indeed I have not been accustomed to consider any tradition has a value, under the conditions implied in your discussion of the *disciplina arcani*... if it were true that the ante-Nicene fathers had not spoken strongly and openly and frequently about these doctrines, it would be difficult not to believe that they had not interpreted Scripture as we do-a supposition that would be almost fatal to the doctrines as it seems to me.[258]

Lyall had other objections to Newman's work, for example, to his having ascribed value to "the dispensation of Paganism,"[259] even if on the eminently sound patristic authority of St. Clement of Alexandria, but his principal problem with the text was that it implied a change in doctrine against which even the Vincentian Canon itself was not proof. He had identified a trend which he thought sufficiently dangerous for him to want to dissociate himself from the work. To quote Rowan Williams again, what Lyall had seen was this:

Once grant that not everything is openly professed by ante-Nicene writers, even if the substance of what is believed is the same as that of the Nicene faith, and the appeal to a unanimous voice of the "undivided Church" is significantly weakened.... Lyall, in short, has correctly seen the spectre of the *Essay on Development* behind Newman's tortuous and sometimes confused pages on the *disciplina arcani*.[260]

This argument, whilst persuasive and in many ways seeming to be the obvious conclusion to be drawn from Lyall's remarks, is not without its critics. Pereiro, for example, holds that such analyses of the Newman of *The Arians* are fundamentally anachronistic. He

---

258. Archdeacon Lyall to JHN, November 9, 1832, in *LD 3*, 113.
259. Newman, *Ari.*, 89. Here Newman is quoting St. Clement of Alexandria. He had first used this expression in the second University Sermon, preached on April 13, 1830. See *Fifteen Sermons Preached before the University of Oxford between AD 1826 and 1843* (London: Longmans, Green and Co., 1909), 21, hereafter *USS*.
260. Williams, "Newman's Arians," 273.

argues that Newman's awareness of development at this early date should be understood strictly according to the rule that true doctrine is fixed and does not develop, whereas heresy is precisely what does arise when the moral flaws of individuals lead them to attempt to go beyond the deposit of faith. He argues that the work on *The Arians* and his studies of other early Christian heresies had led Newman to a view that "heresy was the mature and natural fruit of an *ethos* characterized by intellectual pride, worldliness, or other moral deficiencies; within heresy, different ethical characters generated different types of error."[261] Defining development as "the progressive and necessary unfolding of a principle, a concept, or an idea into its proper corollaries," Pereiro further argues that it was not until much later that Newman countenanced even the possibility of "doctrinal development in orthodoxy."[262] The role of the *disciplina arcani* in this synthesis is that of place-holder: Newman had not yet come to the point where he could accept that the church had a binding authority to pronounce on tradition or the meaning of scripture. The *disciplina arcani* may be used, at least in the absence of any other available alternative, as a hypothesis that appears to account for change without having to accept development understood in the terms outlined by Pereiro.

Although recognizing that the method Newman employed in *The Arians* to give an account of the development of heresy "resembled his later theory of development,"[263] Pereiro suggests that the close personal engagement of Newman with Blanco White's personal religious trajectory—from Roman Catholicism to Unitarianism by way of the intellectual Anglicanism of the Oriel Common Room—reinforced the view that it was always heresy that resulted from development, not orthodoxy. White's religious history had, indeed, made a profound impression on Newman and proved to him just "how persuasive liberal heresy can be."[264] Newman shared with Keble a profound

---

261. Pereiro, "*Ethos*," 130.
262. Pereiro, "*Ethos*," 132.
263. Pereiro, "*Ethos*," 131.
264. Hammond, "Hermeneutics and Heresy," 61.

dislike of what they both called "paper logic," not least because they both believed it to lead to overly systematized theology. The Newman of the 1830s, Pereiro contends, rejected this approach because he saw it as grounded in the moral deficiency of pride—exhibited for him in the contemporary example of Blanco White—whereby what was involved was "an effort on the part of the human mind to impose its law on revealed truths."[265] It was as accurate an assessment of fourth-century error as it was of nineteenth, and the parallel, dangerous as it was, was lost no more on Newman than it had been on Archdeacon Lyall.[266]

Pereiro's argument is both cogent and coherent but fails to take account of the evidence adduced above for the explicit awareness of doctrinal development, orthodox and otherwise, in Newman's writing in the 1820s. He is, however, surely correct to point to the force of Newman's conviction that the moral dimension of an individual has a direct influence on how that person will approach the truths of revelation. The evidence would seem to support an ambiguity toward doctrinal development in Newman's work at the time of writing *The Arians* rather than a clear rejection of orthodox development. In *The Arians*, Newman had noted how in scripture, "no prophet ends his subject: his brethren after him renew, enlarge, transfigure or reconstruct it."[267] This process, he suggested, takes place because of the action of the human mind, albeit divinely inspired, engaging in the natural contemplation of religious truth. Williams sees that this represented a wider awareness of development by Newman, wider certainly than Pereiro will allow, suggesting that, if by development is meant "adumbrating greater truths under the image of lesser, implying the consequence or the basis of doctrines in their correlatives,"[268] then it is nothing more or less than "the operation of a general principle of our nature."[269] This view supports Newman's own recollection in the *Apologia* of his position, where he, almost

265. Pereiro, "*Ethos*," 133.
266. Newman, *Ari.*, 103–4.
267. Newman, *Ari.*, 64.
268. Newman, *Ari.*, 62.
269. Newman, *Ari.*, 63.

wistfully, recalled his preference in the late 1820s for ante-Nicene positions over what he then thought to be the "unnecessarily scientific" ones of the period after that council.[270] As Williams puts it, for Newman at the time of writing *The Arians*, "the advance of dogma is something almost tragic, a poignant ideological puberty," wherein, through "the novel and risky business of refining terms, excluding or qualifying what was once acceptable, even baptizing, by clarification, what was once suspect (as with the "ομοούσιον" itself) we move towards the 'technical' language, superseding the innocent variety of earlier days."[271] Newman's complete manifesto for this position is to be found early in *The Arians*:

If I avow my belief, that freedom from symbols and articles, is abstractedly the highest state of Christian communion, and the peculiar privilege of the primitive Church, it is not from any tenderness towards that proud impatience of control in which many exult, as in a virtue: but first, because technicality and formalism are, in their degree, inevitable results of public confessions of faith; and next, because when confessions do not exist, the mysteries of divine truth, instead of being exposed to the gaze of the profane and uninstructed, are kept hidden in the bosom of the Church far more faithfully than is otherwise possible.[272]

Tragically, poignant or not, it is, nonetheless, still the advance of dogma: it is still development. It might only be "a *Verfallstheorie* of dogmatic language, the notion of formulation itself being a kind of betrayal of some richer truth; but it is a necessary fall, a *felix culpa*, given that the Church lives in a history of change, contingency, and human sinfulness, and that the Gospel must be preached in a variety of contexts."[273]

The flaw in Pereiro's argument stems from a confusion between Newman's rhetorical strategy, accurately outlined by Hammond, and the purpose to which that strategy was deployed. It is true that Newman had not, by the date of the completion of the manuscript of *The Arians* in July 1832, arrived at a fully worked out notion of the devel-

---

270. Newman, *Apo.*, 71.
271. Williams, "Newman's Arians," 270.
272. Newman, *Ari.*, 41.
273. Williams, "Newman's Arians," 270.

opment of doctrine, but he could no longer hold that only heterodoxy could develop. He was certainly not describing a process of development that could only take a heterodox turn when he wrote about the doctrine of the Trinity that "there will, of course, be differences of opinion in deciding how much of the ecclesiastical doctrine as above described, was derived from direct Apostolical tradition, and how much was the result of intuitive spiritual perception in scripturally-informed and deeply religious minds."[274]

Those who are "scripturally-informed and deeply religious" were manifestly not, in Newman's conception, the heretics; they were not those who are marked by the *ethos* identified by Pereiro as characterized by intellectual pride, worldliness, or other moral deficiencies. They were, instead, those engaged in a process that might, at this point, only be concerned with the development of the language used to express that faith *quod semper, quod ubique, quod ab omnibus creditum est*, rather than to the development of doctrine understood as the development of the conceptual understanding of the data of revelation and contained in doctrinal formulae. Nevertheless, Williams is surely correct when he writes that, for Newman at this time, "a crack has been opened in the confident assertion that doctrine does not change, even if only in the recognition that its idiom changes."[275] It is—its limited scope admitted—the beginning of an understanding of a genuine process of development: that is, of development as a process that, as already has been seen, he defines as "the progressive and necessary unfolding of a principle, a concept, or an idea into its proper corollaries."[276]

When *The Arians* went to press, on the eve of the beginning of what became the Oxford Movement, Newman was certainly explicitly conscious of change in doctrinal expression. He saw that this presented a difficulty in his search for continuity, in that "definite creed" that he had received into his intellect as "impressions of dogma," and which, he recalled, "through God's mercy, have never

---

274. Newman, *Ari.*, 195.
275. Williams, "Newman's Arians," 270.
276. Pereiro, "*Ethos*," 132.

been effaced or obscured."[277] He thought, however, that he had a hypothesis that would account for this difficulty in terminological development protected by the *disciplina arcani* and the rule of faith of the Vincentian Canon. Events would prove that the hypothesis could provide but a limited answer.

277. Newman, *Apo.*, 58.

CHAPTER 2

ANTIQUITY, THE *VIA MEDIA*, AND A CATHOLICISM OF THE WORD— 1833 TO 1838

The events that led to the Oxford Movement are a matter of record but also hotly contested. Distant causes, for example, that it was part of the conservative reaction to the French Revolution of 1789 and the collapse of the Holy Alliance just prior to the European revolutions of 1830,[1] and proximate causes, such as the Peel election in Oxford following Catholic Emancipation[2] and the Church Temporalities (Ireland) Act,[3] can all claim some part in its genesis. So too can the individuals involved, the principal ones, at least, having

---

1. Palmer of Worcester, writing only ten years after the beginning of the Oxford Movement, located the impetus for action precisely in "the first sound of the tocsin of revolution at Paris in 1830." See William Patrick Palmer, *A Narrative of Events Connected with the Publication of the Tracts* (Oxford: John Henry Parker, 1843), 97. See also Nigel Aston, *Christianity and Revolutionary Europe, c. 1750–1830* (Cambridge: Cambridge University Press, 2002), 297–332. Cf. Jonathan C. D. Clark, *English Society 1688–1832: Ideology, Social Structures and Political Practice During the Ancien Regime* (Cambridge: Cambridge University Press, 1985), 418, where he concisely describes the state of flux thus: "Hereditary rule, primogeniture and religion were society's organising principles.... What had changed was that, relatively suddenly, a particular description of a social nexus had been unseated from its intellectual and constitutional hegemony." See also Clark, 527–47.
2. "An Act for the Relief of His Majesty's Roman Catholic Subjects," (1829) 10 Geo. 4, 7.
3. "An Act to Alter and Amend the Laws Relating to the Temporalities of the Church in Ireland," (1833) 3 & 4 Will. 4, 37.

been blessed with what are, by any standards, a combination of extraordinary intellectual, personal, and spiritual gifts that made them a prime example of Hall's epithet, "*stupor mundi Clerus Britannicus*."[4] The extent to which this event or that person influenced what came to be called the Oxford Movement is an area of debate that is colored as much by churchmanship, historiographical assumptions, and ecclesiastico-political positions as it is by any other consideration. As Peter Nockles has argued, "for a period, it was simply the need for all conservative forces in Church and State to unite in the face of what seemed then like a common enemy, that helps explain the wide appeal of the Movement at Oxford."[5] This highly contested area falls outside the scope of this work, but what falls firmly within it is the influence that the beginnings of the Oxford Movement had on Newman's search for a lasting hypothesis to account for continuity of doctrine in the face of apparent change, the need for which he was aware by 1832.

The first hypothesis that Newman had proposed—that of terminological development protected by the twin sentinels of the *disciplina arcani* and the Vincentian Canon—had come under serious attack even before *The Arians* was published. The Vincentian Canon was uncontroversial enough, but the notion of the *disciplina arcani* and the use to which Newman had put it in *The Arians* was not. The criticisms that were made of his approach undermined his confidence in the first hypothesis and heavily influenced his search for a replacement. This chapter will, therefore, look first at the critical assault on the *disciplina arcani* and the undermining of Newman's first proposed solution to his "difficulty" before moving on to a consideration of the effect that his involvement in the early period of the Oxford Movement had on his development of a replacement hypothesis.

That the Oxford Movement had a profound impact on Newman's theological trajectory cannot be denied, nor can the reciprocal effect

---

4. Joseph Hall, "Bishop Hall's Latin Theology, with Translations," *The Works of Bishop Hall*, vol. 9 (Oxford: Talboys, 1839), 16.

5. Peter Nockles, "Oxford, Tract 90 and the Bishops," in *John Henry Newman: Reason, Rhetoric and Romanticism*, ed. David Nicholls and Fergus Kerr (Bristol: Bristol Press, 1991), 31.

of Newman's theological trajectory on the growth and course of the movement: he was an integral part of its early years, and it of him. Over the course of this chapter, this complex interaction will be considered in connection with the published product of Newman's engagement with the Oxford Movement, primarily in the *Tracts for the Times*, the correspondence with the Abbé Jager, and the *Lectures on the Prophetical Office of the Church*. What will emerge from this analysis is the outline of a hypothesis that Newman believed could provide him with precisely the adequate guarantee of continuity in the face of change that he sought. It was to be found in what has been called a "Catholicism of the Word,"[6] located within the Church of England, taking its Vincentian stronghold in antiquity and understood as the *via media* between Protestant error and Roman corruption.

The Assault on the *disciplina arcani*

In the previous chapter, we examined Archdeacon Lyall's criticisms and suggestion that Newman's use of the idea of the *disciplina arcani* was going well beyond a position conformable with "that which Protestant writers of our church have contended for."[7] Newman's first hypothesis could account for apparent change in the church's doctrine only if it was possible to argue that the terminological developments, of which the Nicene language was the most significant example, were the public statements of what had previously been believed always, everywhere, and by everyone but that had been shielded from public view, from the written record, by the *disciplina arcani*. Despite its "strikingly intense rhetoric of initiation, revealed-but-concealed mystery, the holy community guarding its integrity against a hostile

---

6. This expression is taken from Mark D. Chapman, "A Catholicism of the Word and a Catholicism of Devotion: Pusey, Newman and the First Eirenicon," *Journal for the History of Modern Theology* 14, no. 2 (2007): 167–90. He uses it to describe the largely text-based and text-bound religion, initially shared by Newman and Pusey, which the former abandoned in the late 1830s but to which the latter remained attached. The idea is further explored in his "Temporal and Spatial Catholicism: Tensions in Historicism in the Oxford Movement," in *The Shaping of Tradition: Context and Normativity*, ed. Colby Dickinson (Leuven: Peeters, 2014), 17–26.

7. William Rowe Lyall to Hugh James Rose, October 19, 1832, in *LD 3*, 105.

world,"[8] Newman's use of this idea could command little support even among those within the Church of England whose views were, in other matters, closest to his own. While calling *The Arians* "the book of a scholar," a cause for "rejoicing," and a "volume ... earnestly and warmly recommended," James Rose could not but take exception to Newman's position when he reviewed the work for the *British Magazine*:

> the only considerable point on which he [i.e., the reviewer—Rose] differs from Mr. N. [i.e., Newman] is, on Disciplina Arcani. He cannot bring himself to think that it was so early, or so widely extensive as Mr. N. does; nor can he think that the authorities to which Mr. N. refers bear him out. They all appear to refer to the 3rd or 4th centuries, and not to the practice of the primitive church.[9]

Newman was grateful for the review—"your praise of me has quite overcome me"[10]—but he was also conscious of the reviewer's criticism. In a passage that hints at the two-fold system of doctrine he would develop in the coming years, here "Catholic Verities" and "Theological Verities" standing duty for what would later become the "Apostolical or Episcopal Tradition" and the "Prophetical Tradition," Newman reaffirmed his position:

> I find you still discontented with my Disciplina Arcani. I had altered it a good deal since you saw it in MS. Indeed re-written it. The whole of that chapter (which I doubt not will get me into trouble) was written at least four times.—I have no reluctance to confess I have made a mistake in what is not one of the "Catholic Verities"—Do you not think the Roman Catholic distinction between them and the "Theological Doctrines" a most useful one? Thus one can symbolize with the Evangelicals. There is no reason one should be ashamed at changing any Theological Doctrine for one's certainty of them is indefinitely below that which we have of the Catholic Verities— Yet I do not see why I should change. Why is poor Clement not a witness of

---

8. Williams, introduction to *The Arians*, xxxiv.

9. James Rose, "Notices and Reviews: The Arians of the Fourth Century, Their Doctrine, Temper, and Conduct," *British Magazine*, 5 (1834): 67–68. Rose was the editor, together with Samuel Roffey Maitland, and Newman's letter to him of January 1, 1834, in *LD 4*, 156, presupposes that Rose was the author of the review.

10. JHN to Hugh James Rose, January 1, 1834, in *LD 4*, 156.

a Disciplina Arcani? in spite of Mosheims [sic.] attempt to give a different direction to his words?[11]

He did not have to wait long for the detailed and (perhaps most significantly having regard to his own sensibilities) episcopally provided answer to his question in the response of Bishop Kaye of Lincoln.

John Kaye had been appointed Bishop of Bristol in 1820. He held the see in plurality with his mastership of Christ's College, Cambridge (to which he had been appointed in 1814 when only thirty) and the Regius Chair of Divinity in the same university, to which he had been elected unopposed in 1816. He was translated (the church's term used when a bishop is transferred from one diocese to another) to Lincoln in 1827, giving up the professorship and, eventually, the mastership. Kaye's patristic scholarship has been credited with "fostering the general revival in patristic studies which helped incubate Tractarianism,"[12] although, as will be shown later in this chapter, that there was a revival implies that patristic scholarship was previously moribund, a contention that is far from obvious. Fittingly for an appointment made on the advice of the Tory prime minister, Lord Liverpool, once a bishop, he quickly aligned himself with the largely Tory High-Church Hackney Phalanx.[13]

In 1826, Kaye had already expressed his view of the *disciplina arcani* in a consideration of Tertullian's suspicions. He outlined a position that stood firmly within the Anglican and specifically high church consensus:

Having already delivered our opinion respecting the mischievous consequences which have arisen to the Church from the countenance lent by the writings of Clemens Alexandrinus to the notion of the Disciplina Arcani—

---

11. JHN to Hugh James Rose, January 1, 1834, in *LD 4*, 159.

12. John Kaye, Bishop of Lincoln (1783–1853), in *ODNB Online*.

13. The term "Hackney Phalanx" was first used by Dr. Williams Hales, the rector of Killesandra, Ireland, "to describe the motley group of London High Churchmen who entertained him on visits to the capital." See Edward Churton, ed., *Memoir of Joshua Watson*, 2 vols. (Oxford: John Henry and James Parker, 1861), 97. The term came to describe pre-Tractarian High Churchmen who were "in the years immediately prior to 1828 ... in the political ascendancy and in effective control of ecclesiastical patronage" (Nockles, "Oxford, Tract 90 and the Bishops," 64).

we shall now only express our regret that Protestant divines, in their eagerness to establish a favourite point, should sometimes have been induced to resort to it.[14]

Bishop Kaye saw this appeal to a secret tradition as an appeal to no tradition at all, as had Lyall. Therefore, when Rose sent him the text of *The Arians* before publication, Kaye returned in detail to a critique of *disciplina arcani* and to the particular use Newman had sought to put it.[15]

Part of Kaye's criticism was that Newman had misread Clement and hence misrepresented him. In fact, Newman's approach to translation may have contributed to this difficulty. Writing to Rose on January 3, 1834, about an accompanying manuscript of the fifth volume of *Church of the Fathers*, Newman had admitted to "translations" that were "not over exactly literal—i.e., word for word critically," to which he defensively added: "The meaning is always his [i.e., in this case, Basil's], as near as I could give it."[16] In the context of the genre of *Church of the Fathers*, this mattered little. These works were intended to offer to the less scholarly reader a selection of translations of patristic writings to create and support the ethos that Newman and his fellow Tractarians thought an absolutely necessary substrate for a proper appreciation and reception of their controversial writings.[17] Translation by strict construction was less important in these works than an approach that might now be called "dynamic equivalence," where the sense of the text is of more concern than terminological or idiomatic fidelity. This freedom with the text, which Kaye had suggested was responsible for Newman's misdirection about the *disciplina arcani* in Clement, was perhaps a manifestation of a tendency that Rowan Williams identifies in his introduction

---

14. John Kaye, *The Ecclesiastical History of the Second and Third Centuries, Illustrated from the Writings of Tertullian* (Cambridge: J. Deighton and Son, 1826), 251.

15. William Rowe Lyall to Hugh James Rose, October 19, 1832, in *LD 3*, 104–5.

16. JHN to Hugh James Rose, January 3, 1834, in *LD 4*, 162.

17. For a consideration of the genre and its effect, see G. B. Tennyson, *Victorian Devotional Poetry: The Tractarian Mode* (Cambridge, Mass.: Harvard University Press, 1981). The most popular work of this kind, published well before the movement began, was John Keble, *The Christian Year* (London: C. and J. Rivington, 1827), which by 1834 had seen twelve editions and was to remain in print for the remainder of the nineteenth century.

to the Birmingham Oratory Millenium edition of *The Arians*: "Newman's own perspectives and proposals are often flawed by a colossally over-schematic treatment and carelessness in detail."[18]

Newman's response to Kaye was to make initial notes that he then worked up into a memorandum, clearly intended to form part of a reply.[19] The memorandum has a "degree of defensive awkwardness,"[20] which suggests that Kaye's criticisms had rattled Newman:

> If I have any where implied that the Disciplina was a strict *rule* I am sorry—I meant it rather as a principle and feeling, to be observed, as *far as possible* in *all* ages. This I have implied in my remarks on the Evangelists—and I have expressly said so, but cut it out at a friend's demurring. My notion is that it was *no* strict rule. Had any heathen asked the Apostles, "*What* do you believe about a Trinity?" they would have told—only they did not put it forward—They used their *discretion*. This *first* secrecy was at an end by AD 180 (say)—i.e. the Christian doctrine had gone into the stock of public knowledge as far as the grand outlines were conceived.... I grant that the 4th Cent. Fathers systematized about the Arcanum far beyond the Primitive Church.[21]

In his book *Newman and the Alexandrian Fathers*, Benjamin King remarks that there is no evidence of Newman sending Kaye the memorandum and suggests that, even had he done so, it would not have "satisfied" his critic.[22] Indeed, these notes appear only to have satisfied Newman himself by the use of a device he attempted to construct: suggesting that Kaye's criticisms were not of his doctrine but merely of his history. Henry Wilberforce had also heard of the attack and wrote to Newman of the criticism in a letter that does not appear to have survived.[23] In his response to Wilberforce, Newman attempt-

---

18. Williams, introduction to *The Arians of the Fourth Century*, xxxvi.
19. JHN, a "Memorandum," January 11, 1834, in *LD 4*, 169, n. 1
20. Williams, "Newman's Arians and the Question of Method in Doctrinal History," 274.
21. JHN, a "Memorandum," January 11, 1834, in *LD 4*, 169, n. 1.
22. Benjamin John King, *Newman and the Alexandrian Fathers: Shaping Doctrine in Nineteenth-Century England* (Oxford: Oxford University Press, 2009), 133.
23. The letter is not found in any of the collection of letters from Henry Wilberforce cited in the *ODNB Online*. JHN's diary for January 20, 1834, records, "while at Derby I had letters from H.W." (*LD 4*, 178). That the letter referred to Kaye's criticism can be inferred from JHN's response to Henry Wilberforce, January 17, 1834, in *LD 4*, 177.

ed to justify himself by resort to the distinction between the history and the theology:

> As to the Disciplina [arcani], Rose objects to my *history* not my doctrine. He says I begin it too soon. So does the Bishop of Lincoln in some notes Rose has sent me from him—indeed he thinks (of course—for, writing for the Theological Library I could not give my authorities) I have made a "confusion"—have not read the books etc etc—Now I have grounds, whether good or bad—and do not mean to knock under. I have begun by being too candid to the Provost and James—what a goose I was!—and they have so taken it, that I will cut candour in future all my life—I have studied the Bishop's ground before I published, and will give my views, should the book come to a second edition.[24]

In letter to John Frederic Christie on January 14, 1834, Newman had already resorted to this defense when he referred to Kaye's remarks as having

> been flooring part of my book—viz. the *historical* part of the Disciplina. I have got my grounds, though I have not published them—so I suppose if the book comes to a second edition, it will be much larger. So many subjects are touched on in it, it was impossible to give my reasons in a work *intended for* the Theological Library—so I expect to be thought ignorant on points, which I have examined and (rightly or wrongly) decided on.[25]

Newman was, knowingly or not, thoroughly misrepresenting the Bishop of Lincoln's position, for Kaye objected both to the history and to the theology. In his *Some Account of the Writings and Opinions of Clement of Alexandria*, Kaye expanded on the criticisms he had offered in his notes to Rose.[26] He argued that Newman had incorrectly projected back the uncontested fourth-century evidence of the *disciplina arcani* into the ante-Nicene period, and that Newman had conflated this post-Nicene understanding of the *disciplina arcani* with Clement of Alexandria's "Esoteric system."[27] Kaye had little enough

---

24. JHN to Henry Wilberforce, January 17, 1834, in *LD* 4, 177.
25. JHN to John Frederic [sic.] Christie, January 14, 1834, in *LD* 4, 174–75.
26. John Kaye, *Some Account of the Writings and Opinions of Clement of Alexandria* (London: J. G. and F. Rivington, 1835).
27. Kaye, *Some Account of the Writings and Opinions of Clement of Alexandria*, 368.

time for Clement's notion, dismissing it as being "destitute of solid foundation,"[28] but even such a flawed notion could not, he argued, be identified with the later methodology, as Newman had done in *The Arians*. Furthermore, he contended that Newman's argument risked the "Romish" error of requiring the present-day believer to believe "as necessary to salvation" doctrines about which there was a "total silence" in "the first ages of Christianity."[29] Finally, he was not even prepared to accept the accuracy of Newman's account of Clement. Newman's coupling of the *disciplina arcani* with the principle of economy, the former as the ethos underpinning the operation of the latter, rested on Clement, and Kaye explicitly rejected the connection: "The authority of Clement has been quoted in support of a mode of interpretation κατ' οἰκονομίαν, but in my opinion, erroneously."[30]

Newman was always particularly sensitive to episcopal criticism, as will be seen in the next chapter when the responses to a number of the *Tracts for the Times*, especially Tract 90, will be considered. It is no surprise, therefore, that his various defenses of the *disciplina arcani* were careful to attempt to answer Kaye's criticisms. In a letter to Thomas Falconer at the beginning of the controversy, Newman unsurprisingly uses the same language that he had used in his note of January 10 and 11, claiming that the *disciplina arcani* existed "rather as a feeling and principle than as a rule in the early Church" and "the existence in cent. 4 [as] evidence of the existence of the *principle* in the first."[31] He was similarly confident of his grounds when he wrote to Keble in February 1834 that "I have been looking at Faber's Apostolicity of Trinitarianism—and he so entirely agrees with me about the Disciplina Arcani that I am quite easy as to my Lord of Lincoln's strictures."[32]

The claim that Faber, a "moderate Evangelical"[33] and therefore

---

28. Kaye, *Some Account of the Writings and Opinions of Clement of Alexandria*, 368.
29. Kaye, *Some Account of the Writings and Opinions of Clement of Alexandria*, 367.
30. Kaye, *Some Account of the Writings and Opinions of Clement of Alexandria*, 397.
31. JHN to Thomas Falconer, about January 26, 1834, in *LD 4*, 180. This letter is marked, in Newman's hand, as "Not sent."
32. JHN to John Keble, February 9, 1834, in *LD 4*, 190.
33. King, *Newman and the Alexandrian Fathers*, 132. Faber's "brand of Anglicanism was

free of any suggestion of "Romish" tendencies, "entirely agrees with me" was perhaps to overstate the case, ever so slightly.[34] Faber certainly held that there were those in the ante-Nicene Church to whom the fullness of the church's doctrine had been taught and others "who were as yet instructed only in the shadow of the Word,"[35] but he nowhere claimed quite as much for the *disciplina arcani* as did Newman in *The Arians*. In suggesting that those "in the shadow of the Word" were gradually "made acquainted with the true Word in the opened heaven,"[36] Faber was not going nearly as far as Newman, for whom the move toward a technical, nonscriptural language is identified as an inevitable, almost necessary corollary of the gradual unveiling of teachings previously protected from view by the *disciplina arcani*.[37] Faber, although distinctly not of the same party within the Church of England as Lyall, Rose, or Kaye, was still keen to maintain "the classical Anglican apologetic" of an appeal to the belief of the undivided church, which Rowan Williams argues Newman "is undermining" in *The Arians*.[38]

The unsent letter to Falconer contained a sentence that is remarkable for the completeness of the conception of development that it contains, given the date of its composition. When speaking of the relationship between the *disciplina arcani* and the principle of reserve, Newman wrote:

---

strongly evangelical, and he stressed the protestant doctrines of the necessity of conversion, justification by faith, and the sole authority of scripture as the rule of faith." See *ODNB Online*.

34. Although Newman may have been more justified in claiming Faber's full support than at first glance. Faber had written that, "Our present business, however, is: partly, with *the amount of their antiquity*; and, partly, with *the nature of the grand secret which they professed to communicate*. I. In regard to the *antiquity of the Christian mysteries*, Origen and Clement of Alexandria seem inclined to carry it up even to the time of Christ and his Apostles." See George Stanley Faber, *The Apostolicity of Trinitarianism*, 2 vols. (London: J. G. and F. Rivington, 1832), 1:210. He then proceeds to discuss the "secret" for the next several pages.

35. Faber, *The Apostolicity of Trinitarianism*, 1:43.

36. Faber, *The Apostolicity of Trinitarianism*, 1:43.

37. Newman, *Ari.*, 197. Faber's view—that "the *technical phraseology* of the Mysteries implies the *existence* of the Mysteries themselves: for the Mysteries, no doubt, gave birth to the phraseology" (Faber, *The Apostolicity of Trinitarianism*, 1:213)—makes a similar point to Newman but lacks the latter's obvious sense of regret alluded to in the previous chapter.

38. Williams, "Newman's Arians," 297.

CATHOLICISM OF THE WORD, 1833–1838

This is the case with the greater part of the theological and ecclesiastical system, which is implicitly contained in the writings and acts of the Apostles but was developed at various times according to circumstances. I should in a certain sense say this was true of the doctrine of the Trinity—and of the Incarnation as opposed to Nestorianism.... Our Creeds, our Liturgies, our canons are for the most part developed and determined by a definite period after the time of the Apostles.[39]

This clear statement by Newman of the observable fact of the development of doctrine lacked a description of the method by which the development takes place, although the remarks about the Incarnation and Nestorianism hinted at the relationship between development and the need to combat heresy, which Newman would later make much of. Neither did it contain any suggestion of when the "definite period" would come to an end. Nevertheless, the language adopted by Newman is strikingly similar to that adopted in his final University Sermon in the *Essay on Development* and even in the *Apologia*. This is not the theory of development in its final form, but it is very early evidence that, as Selby has argued, "a direct link may be traced between the theory of development and the principle of reserve,"[40] and it seems to confirm Newman's claims in letters to his sister Jemima and to Mrs. William Froude that he had held to some notion of doctrinal development since 1831 or so.[41]

In his extensive and painstaking examination of the papers of S. F. Wood, Pereiro dismisses Selby's assertion and argues that Newman's rejection of Wood's ideas about development are *prima facie* evidence that "the evidence against Newman having held a theory of development before 1840 is compelling."[42] In taking this position,

---

39. JHN to Thomas Falconer, January 26, 1834, in *LD 4*, 180.
40. Robin Selby, *The Principle of Reserve in the Writings of John Henry Cardinal Newman* (Oxford: Oxford University Press, 1975), 72.
41. JHN to Mrs. John Mozley, January 23, 1843, in *LD 9*, 213–14. Mrs. John Mozley was Newman's sister Jemima, who had married John Mozley, on April 28, 1836; see the note, in Newman's hand, to the letter from his mother of April 12, 1836, the last before Mrs. Newman's death on May 17, 1836, in *LD 5*, 276, and his diary entry for April 28, 1836, in *LD 5*, 290. Newman's elder sister, Harriett, married John Mozley's brother Thomas later the same year; see Tuesday, September 27, 1836, in *LD 5*, 363. See also JHN to Mrs. William Froude, July 14, 1844, in *LD 10*, n.d., 297.
42. Pereiro, "*Ethos*" 166.

he agrees with Chadwick, who—in the light of the unsent letter to Falconer—incorrectly refers to the final University Sermon as Newman's "first utterance upon the subject" of development.[43] Pereiro further claims support from Newman's own stance in the correspondence with the Abbé Jager and in his *Lectures on the Prophetical Office* to contend that "it is therefore unlikely that he [Newman] would have professed in 1834 what he would so emphatically deny some months later."[44] These rejections and denials of particular presentations of development by Newman, to which this chapter will later return, do not, however, constitute rejection of the idea *tout court*. One resolution of this apparent difficulty may be provided by Chadwick, who observed that for Newman, who "believed in religious progress as little as he believed in secular progress, and that was not at all,"[45] the use of the term "development" did not imply the adoption of the sense in which the word was used by "contemporary evolutionary philosophy."[46] Even at this very early stage, Newman was using the term to express what he could not fail to observe: that "the Church of antiquity herself bore the marks of inner growth in the history of her own thought and life."[47] The vocabulary and obvious sense of the letter to Falconer is irrefutable evidence that Newman held to some kind of a theory of development in January 1834, even if only to a theory in which developments in creeds, liturgies, and canon, that is, development of "the theological and ecclesiastical system, which is implicitly contained in the writings and acts of the Apostles,"[48] were seen as "another way of expressing the object of faith," which "itself remained identical and invariable."[49]

Newman continued to appeal to both his chronology for and con-

---

43. Chadwick, *From Bousset to Newman*, 89.
44. Pereiro, "Ethos," 165.
45. Chadwick, *From Bousset to Newman*, 98.
46. Chadwick, *From Bousset to Newman*, 102.
47. Chadwick, *From Bousset to Newman*, 97.
48. JHN to Thomas Falconer, January 27, 1834, in *LD* 4, 180. It is the same point that Newman was to make, later the same year, in Tract 41, as will be demonstrated in the next section of this chapter.
49. Louis Allen, *John Henry Newman and the Abbé Jager: A Controversy on Scripture and Tradition (1834–1836)* (London: Oxford University Press, 1975), 13.

cept of the *disciplina arcani* when in March 1834 he wrote to Edward Burton.[50] Burton was seeking Newman's views on the ante-Nicene use of the term ὁμοούσιον, particularly on some arguments put to Burton by Faber on the disavowal of the term at the Council of Antioch in the third century. Newman's argument was that the term was "not *condemned*, but merely *abandoned*," that is, that the principle of economy meant that, in the absence of a compelling reason to insist upon the use of ὁμοούσιον in its formulae, the Fathers avoided it for apologetic reasons.[51] Newman spelled out this contention in the letter to Burton: "The effect of objections is surely to make men guarded. Especially Heads of the Church in Council assembled, deposing the Metropolitan himself of the place where they meet, and him a shrewd disputant, are not likely to lay themselves open to criticism by volunteering a difficulty. There was no *call* on them to use it."[52]

Newman was using the same language nearly two years later when he wrote to Rose that he "never meant it was a *Church* rule, but a self-imposed rule for individuals," still claiming, increasingly implausibly, that "the Bishop of Lincoln grants that Clement holds it."[53] Yet by the middle of the following year, 1836, Newman's attachment to the *disciplina arcani*, or at least to his earlier claim of patristic authority for its early uses, was less sure. The patristic witness to the sufficiency of scripture, without a tradition protected by the *disciplina arcani* was now "an irrefragable argument."[54] He had not, however, abandoned his earlier belief that the *disciplina arcani* was a part of the system of belief in the early church, arguing as late as September 1838, in words quoted from Hawkins,[55] that "the more fundamental the doctrine ... the more likely would it be rather implied than directly taught in the writings of the Apostles."[56]

50. JHN to Edward Burton, March 1, 1834, in *LD 4*, 194–97.
51. JHN to Edward Burton, March 1, 1834, in *LD 4*, 195.
52. JHN to Edward Burton, March 1, 1834, in *LD 4*, 196.
53. JHN to Hugh James Rose, December 15, 1835, in *LD 5*, 178.
54. John Henry Newman, "Tract 71: On the Mode of Conducting the Controversy with Rome" (J. G. F. and J. Rivington and J. H. Parker, January 1, 1836), 139, in *Tracts 3*.
55. Edward Hawkins, *A Dissertation upon the Use and Importance of Unauthoritative Tradition*, 64.
56. John Henry Newman, "Tract 85: Lectures in the Scripture Proofs of the Doctrines

Newman had initially suggested to Christie that he should offer a comprehensive answer to the critics of his use of the *disciplina arcani* in the first edition of *The Arians* in a "much larger" second edition.[57] In a letter to Richard Hurrell Froude dated June 14, 1834, and dealing with so many different issues that the letter is of exceptional length,[58] Newman refers to the Bishop of Lincoln's criticism and his plan to "publish a series of dissertations in a second volume, for example, "on the 'disciplina arcani'"[59] in order to answer Kaye's charges.

Work on other projects intervened, and by August 1834, it was clear to him that he would not soon be able to return to the question,[60] although he still entertained the notion of revision as late as December 1836.[61] Even three decades later, when the idea of a second edition of *The Arians* was mooted, Newman, by this time freed from apologetic necessity and in changed confessional circumstances, was able to recognize that *The Arians* was "a very imperfect work."[62] Still later, he corrected an admirer: "But, please do not call my Volume on the Arians 'great' it is not even little ... hitting no mark at all."[63] Nonetheless, he did not take the opportunity to add his "series of dissertations" that preparing the text for the 1871 edition afforded him, and the text remained substantially unaltered, Newman explaining to another correspondent who had cited *The Arians* approvingly:

When at a comparatively late date I was led to re-publish it, I should have liked to mend it, but I found that if I attempted it would come to pieces, and I should have to write it over again. In saying this, I have no intention of withdrawing from the substance of what you quote from me; on the con-

---

of the Church" (J. G. F. and J. Rivington and J. H. Parker, 1836), 4–5, in *Tracts 5*. Tract 85 appeared on September 21, 1838.

57. JHN to John Frederic Christie, January 14, 1834, in *LD 4*, 174.
58. JHN to Richard Hurrell Froude, June 14, 1834, in *LD 4*, 268–79.
59. JHN to Richard Hurrell Froude, June 14, 1834, in *LD 4*, 275.
60. JHN to John William Bowden, August 10, 1834, in *LD 4*, 320.
61. JHN to Henry Wilberforce, December 29, 1836, in *LD 5*, 399.
62. JHN to Malcolm MacColl, February 1, 1867, in *LD 23*, 46.
63. JHN to Robert Charles Jenkins, February 27, 1877, in *LD 28*, 172.

trary, I hold it as strongly as I did fifty years ago when it was written; but feel the many imperfections of the wording.[64]

As Williams remarks, in the way Newman deployed the *disciplina arcani*, "he is on the verge of admitting that doctrine—not merely doctrinal idiom—changes" even if he remained "still sufficiently part of the tradition of Bull to believe that the ante-Nicene faith needed only a minimal definition of form and vocabulary to require no further refinement."[65] Kaye's criticisms had undermined Newman's assertions in *The Arians* and the language with which Newman attempted to defend them in his correspondence lacked the confidence of the earlier work. Yet he was anxious to hang on to the *disciplina arcani*, if only to attempt to provide an Anglican apologetic that connected the beliefs of the ante-Nicene Church with post-Nicene orthodoxy. His critics, however, Kaye chief among them, had shown how this exposed Newman to the risk of a need for an authoritative tradition. This was a position that Newman could not yet permit himself to admit, even if, as Jay Hammond points out, he had been perfectly content as early as 1832 with the view that "the creeds which made the *disciplina arcani* public 'were facts, not opinions' that guided the interpretation of scripture" and "ensured orthodox dogma."[66]

Tracts for the Times

On July 14, 1833, at Newman's invitation, John Keble preached the sermon in St. Mary the Virgin at the opening of the Oxford Assizes. Newman remarked in the *Apologia* that he "ever considered and kept the day, as the start of the religious movement of 1833,"[67] yet, as has been seen in the previous chapter, there is little contemporaneous evidence in his letters and diaries to corroborate the recollection

---

64. JHN to W. S. Lilly, June 27, 1882, in *LD 30*, 105.
65. Williams, "Newman's Arians," 276.
66. David Hammond, "Imagination and Hermeneutical Theology: Newman's Contribution to Theological Method," *The Downside Review*, 106 (1988): 58. The embedded quote is from *Ari.*, 134.
67. Newman, *Apo.*, 100.

or to suggest that the importance Newman claims to have accorded the occasion was widely shared at the time. The diary entry for July 14 does nothing more than record the bald facts: "6 Trinity Assize Sunday did duty morning and afternoon at St. Mary's Keble preached in morning Assize Sermon for me in evening."[68] Even his letter to Keble on August 5, 1833, makes not even a passing reference to the event despite being almost entirely concerned with the same subject matter.[69] Although Newman does make several oblique references to the sermon in his letters over the following weeks and months,[70] his appreciation of the significance of the event as the starting pistol of the Oxford Movement began to crystallize only toward the end of the year, when he was to describe the "Assize Sermon ... and the Advertisement prefixed to it" as "the first intimation of what was to follow on our part."[71]

Newman had returned from the Mediterranean and found himself pitched into precisely the sort of controversy for which his temperament and skills seemed best suited: it was precisely the work for a "hot headed man," to which, as was shown in the previous chapter, he had previously looked forward with such eager anticipation.[72]

Although he was not present at the meeting at Hugh James Rose's rectory at Hadleigh in Suffolk, where Palmer of Worcester and Hurrell Froude represented the Oxford voice of those outraged at the Church Temporalities (Ireland) Bill, Newman very quickly found himself—or more precisely ensured that he found himself—heavily engaged in organizing activities to protest against both the presuppositions and consequences of that legislation.[73] Writing to Bowden, Newman acknowledged the necessity of meetings and committees, petitions to Parliament, and addresses to archbishops, but he believed that his own talents would be better directed through his pen "to rouse the clergy, to inculcate the Apostolical Succession and to

---

68. Diary entry for Sunday, July 14, 1833, in *LD 4*, 5.
69. JHN to John Keble, August 5, 1833, in *LD 4*, 20–22.
70. For example, JHN to Charles Portales Golightly, July 30, 1833, in *LD 4*, 13–14, and JHN to John Frederic Christie, August 6, 1833, in *LD 4*, 25–27.
71. "FRAGMENTARY DIARY," December 6, 1833, in *LD 4*, 10.
72. JHN to Harriett Newman, October 16, 1831, in *LD 2*, 367.
73. JHN to Charles Portales Golightly, July 30, 1833, in *LD 4*, 13–14.

defend the Liturgy" through the publishing of tracts.[74] By the end of 1833, twenty tracts had been published, eleven of which Newman had himself written and a further thirty were to be published in 1834, eight of them by Newman.[75] He fully recognized their sententious character and their tendency to incite controversy, even among those of his party: that was precisely, for Newman, their purpose. Writing in July 1834 to Arthur Perceval, author of Tracts 23, 35, and 36, he observed:

> As to the first Tracts, everyone has his own taste. You object to some things, another to others—If we altered to please everyone the effect would be spoiled. They were not intended as symbols é Cathedrâ—but as the expressions of *individual* minds—and individuals feeling strongly, while on the one <other> hand they are incidentally faulty in mode of language, are still peculiarly *effective*.[76]

The purpose of the tracts was quite clear: they represented a conscious attempt to present the Apostolical case in polemical form. In the advertisement that was attached to the publication of a volume of the first forty-six, published by Rivington in 1834, Newman wrote that the tracts had been written to deal with concerns that could be briefly described thus:

---

74. JHN to John William Bowden, August 31, 1833, in *LD 4*, 33. By the time Newman came to write *Apologia*, he was less convinced of the value of the structural apparatus of movements, observing, by way of an explanation for the eventual distancing of Rose from the Oxford Movement, due to, among other things, his attachment to such apparatus, that "Living movements do not come of committees" (*Apo.*, 107).

75. Because of their controversial nature, there was little or no indication of the authorship on the face of the first tracts. The first tract to bear the initials of its author (Pusey) was Tract 18, published on December 21, 1833, although only two days earlier, in a letter to Frederic Rogers, in *LD 4*, 146, Newman remarked: "I have a most admirable tract from Pusey, but his name must not yet be mentioned." The first complete list of authors of the tracts appeared in Henry Parry Liddon, *Life of Edward Bouverie Pusey*. He identified Newman as the author of twenty-nine of the tracts (1, 2, 3, 6, 7, 8, 10, 11, 19, 20, 21, 31, 33, 34, 38, 41, 45, 47, 71, 73, 74, 75, 76, 79, 82, 83, 85, 88, and 90) and as having revised and completed Palmer of Worcester's Tract 15, as well as having written the various advertisements to the bound volumes. Liddon's scheme of attribution is uncontroversial and is confirmed by the work of Vincent Blehl in *John Henry Newman: A Bibliographical Catalogue of His Writings* (Charlottesville: University Press of Virginia, 1978), 115–21, C52–83.

76. JHN to Arthur Perceval, July 20, 1834, in *LD 4*, 308; <...> denotes Newman's interpolation. He recalled this letter in an account of the tracts in *Apo.*, 110–11.

The Apostolic succession, the Holy Catholic Church, were principles of action in the minds of our predecessors of the 17th century; but, in proportion as the maintenance of the Church has been secured by law, her ministers have been under the temptation of leaning on an arm of flesh instead of her own divinely provided discipline.... A lamentable increase of sectarianism has followed; being occasioned (in addition to other more obvious causes) first, by the cold aspect which the new Church doctrines have presented to the religious sensibilities of the mind, next to their meagreness in suggesting motives to restrain it from seeking out a more influential discipline.[77]

In the five and a half months between Keble's sermon and the end of the year, almost every letter of substance that Newman wrote touched upon the issues in controversy, and those same issues were also the subject of a series of six letters he wrote to the editor of *Record*, five of which were published, under the signature "A.CHURCHMAN."[78] Newman's diaries and correspondence for 1833 and 1834 provide ample evidence of an almost frenetic activity in support of the nascent Oxford Movement, and the effort was not wasted. Nockles remarked on the wide appeal of the tracts and noted how "Tractarian élan harnessed to the restatement of old truths enshrined in the Church's formularies seemed an irresistible combination."[79] Even if Newman believed himself to have got into "all sorts of scrapes with my Tracts—abused in every quarter,"[80] he could see that his efforts in "the right cause"[81] were "going on most prosperously."[82] Later reflecting on this period in the *Apologia* in terms which accord closely with the tone of his correspondence at the time and which provide a useful corrective when looking closely at the texts of Newman's contributions to the tracts, he was to write:

---

77. JHN, advertisement, *Tracts 1*, iii.
78. The letters were dated October 21, 1833, in *LD 4*, 63–65, and October 31, 1833, in *LD 4*, 76–78. The date given is that of publication, per *LD 4*, 76, n.1; November 7, 1833, in *LD 4*, 87–88; November 11, 1833, in *LD 4*, 94–96; and November 14, 1833, in *LD 4*, 101–3. The sixth was not published: the editor gave his reasons in a note to Newman, dated December 4, 1833, in which he remarked that "the Tracts countenanced by the New Society at Oxford" were "the fruit of something nearly akin to Infatuation." See *LD 4*, 136, n. 2.
79. Nockles, *The Oxford Movement in Context*, 274.
80. JHN to Hugh James Rose, November 23, 1833, in *LD 4*, 120.
81. JHN to Hugh James Rose, December 15, 1833, in *LD 4*, 142.
82. JHN to Richard Hurrell Froude, December 15, 1833, in *LD 4*, 140.

Nor was it only that I had confidence in our cause, both in itself, and in its controversial force, but besides, I despised every rival system of doctrine and its arguments.... I thought... that the Apostolical form of doctrine was essential and imperative, and its grounds of evidence impregnable. Owing to this confidence ... [m]y behaviour had a mixture in it both of fierceness and of sport; and on this account, I dare say, it gave offence to many.[83]

Establishing the "Apostolical form of doctrine" as "essential and imperative" to the identity of the Church of England dominated Newman's own contributions to the tracts in 1833 and 1834. If the encroachments of political power were to be resisted in a country where an Erastian conception of the relationship between the church and state had held sway for such a long time, Newman understood that it was first necessary to carve out for the church—especially for her clergy—an ecclesiology that looked back beyond the crown and Parliament for the source of the church's authority. He sought to establish for the Church of England not an independence from the nation of England and its constitutional and political arrangements, indeed, Newman explicitly disavowed any such aim while countenancing its possibility, but rather to remind his readers that the Church of England had a wider context and a source of authority distinct from that which it drew from the state.[84]

In the "advertisement" that prefaced the first bound edition of the *Tracts*, Newman refers to the Church of England as the "English branch" of "the Church of Christ."[85] This language stood firmly in the tradition of the High Churchmen and drew upon the understanding of the Caroline Divines of the seventeenth century, but Newman deployed it here, however, not to assert the Church of England's claims to catholicity—a conventional purpose[86]—but to introduce its claims to apostolicity. If he could but convince his readers "to maintain the doctrine of the Apostolical Succession,"[87] then it would be possible to resist the "sheer Tyranny," as he characterized

83. Newman, *Apo.*, 113–14.
84. JHN to Charles Portales Golightly, August 11, 1833, in *LD 4*, 28.
85. Newman, advertisement, *Tracts 1*, v.
86. Nockles, *The Oxford Movement in Context*, 153–54.
87. JHN to R. F. Wilson, September 8, 1833, in *LD 4*, 44.

them, of the assaults of the state on the prerogatives of the Church of England.[88] Newman's accounts of his first introduction to the notion of Apostolical Succession varied. In a letter to Keble in November 1844, he credits Froude with having been the agent in 1829,[89] yet in the *Apologia*, as was seen in the previous chapter, the credit is more plausibly given to the Oriel fellow William James in 1823.[90] The origins of his first acquaintance with the doctrine may be uncertain, but the centrality it was to assume in his contributions to the tracts is not in doubt. Each of the eleven tracts Newman wrote in 1833[91] dealt either directly or substantially with this issue, as well as the seven he wrote from 1834.[92] The very first tract, *Thoughts on the Ministerial Commission*, is a reminder to the clergy that the bishops are not merely officers of the Crown but "the SUCCESSORS OF THE APOSTLES" and asks "on *what* are we to rest our authority, when the State deserts us?"[93] He supplied his own answer, which revealed the theological premises undergirding the tracts: it is a statement of intent, a manifesto for the tracts, for the movement, and for Newman's involvement in it:

I fear we have neglected the real ground on which our authority is built, - OUR APOSTOLICAL DESCENT.

We have been born, not of blood, nor of the will of the flesh, nor of the will of man, but of GOD. The LORD JESUS CHRIST gave His SPIRIT to His Apostles; they in turn laid their hands on those who should succeed them; and these again on others; and so the sacred gift has been handed down to our present Bishops, who have appointed us as their assistants, and in some sense representatives.[94]

This concern to establish the distinctive origins and authority of the church and the attendant claim to those origins and that au-

88. JHN to H. A. Woodgate, August 7, 1833, in *LD 4*, 27.
89. JHN to John Keble, November 21, 1844, in *LD 10*, 425.
90. Newman, *Apo.*, 67. William James (1787–1861) had been one of Newman's examiners for the Oriel Fellowship in 1822 and had recommended his election. See *LD 10*, 425, n. 3.
91. That is, tracts 1, 2, 3, 6, 7, 8, 10, 11, 15, 19 and 20, in *Tracts 1*.
92. That is, tracts 21, 31, 33, 34, 38, 41 and 45, in *Tracts 1*.
93. John Henry Newman, "Tract 1: Thoughts on the Ministerial Commission Respectfully Addressed to the Clergy" (Messrs. Rivington's, September 9, 1833), 1, in *Tracts 1*.
94. Newman, Tract 1, 2, in *Tracts 1*.

thority for the Church of England, caused Newman to have to address two matters that would have a significant effect in developing his notion of the *via media*: how to treat those doctrines that are not clearly delineated in sacred scripture, and what to say of the position of what he then called the Roman Communion. If he was to claim for the Church of England this "real ground" in an unassailable "apostolical descent," then it was essential that he offer a cogent account of its attachment to doctrines that it professed and yet which could hardly come up to the standard of proof demanded by the sixth of the thirty-nine articles: that any doctrine "not read therein [i.e., in sacred scripture], nor may be proved thereby, is not to be required of any man, that it should be believed as an article of the Faith, or be thought requisite or necessary to salvation." He also needed to provide a method that in answering this first question would not open him up to accusations that he was either claiming for the Church of England or allowing to the Church of Rome the capacity that he believed the latter to assert: that of having the power to add to the deposit of faith.

The Thirty-Nine Articles of Religion had been adopted by the Convocation of the Church of England in 1563 and finalized in 1571.[95] Assent and subscription to them had since been a condition of matriculation at both universities[96] and for advancement to Holy Orders in the Established Church. Since 1662, they had been published as part of the *Book of Common Prayer* and, as part of that book, were considered to be part of the defining formularies of the Anglican Church. Their purpose was to establish the doctrine of the Church of England with particular reference to settling the theological controversies of the sixteenth century and to determine its position on the questions of dispute between it and both the Roman Catholic Church

---

95. Bray, *Documents of the English Reformation*, 284. For an account of the theological genesis of the articles, see chapter 3, "Settling Anglican Theology: Elizabeth I, John Jewel and the Thirty-Nine Articles," in Chapman, *Anglican Theology*, 43–71.

96. Oxford maintained the precept until 1856, whereas, from 1772 on, Cambridge imposed a religious test only on the taking of a degree, and that test was merely a simple declaration of *bona fide* membership of the Church of England rather than the formal subscription to the articles that was previously required. See Denys Arthur Winstanley, *Unreformed Cambridge* (Cambridge: Cambridge University Press, 1935), 313.

and the Anabaptists. The extent to which there was a received reading of the articles that could be described as acceptable to Anglicans, together with the attempt Newman later made to present a synthesis of them that challenged this received reading, will be considered in the next chapter in the context of the writing of and the reaction to Tract 90. However, it is necessary here to consider the use Newman made of the articles, particularly the sixth, in writing the early tracts and in seeking to develop a coherent hypothesis to account for doctrinal change.

The sixth article was entitled "Of the sufficiency of the Holy Scripture for Salvation," which addresses the question of where the sources of Christian revelation are to be found. It begins:

> Holy Scripture containeth all things necessary to salvation: so that whatsoever is not read therein, nor may be proved thereby, is not to be required of any man, that it should be believed as an article of the faith, or be thought requisite or necessary to salvation.[97]

Like many of the other articles, the sixth charts a careful course; it is not so much about scripture as about how doctrine should be formed.[98] The concern of the sixth article is to lay out correct principles for the use of scripture in establishing Christian doctrine without conceding anything resembling what was to become the position of the Tridentine *duplex fons*.[99] It proclaims the sufficiency but not

---

97. "06. Of the Sufficiency of the Holy Scripture," in Bray, *Documents of the English Reformation*, 287.

98. For a full discussion of the purpose and use to which the sixth article was put, see Oliver O'Donovan, *On The Thirty Nine Articles: A Conversation with Tudor Chrisitanity* (London: SCM Press Ltd., 2011), 45–51. Cf. "Quo vadis, Petre?" in H. Oberman, *The Dawn of the Reformation: Essays in Late Medieval and Early Reformation Thought* (Edinburgh: T & T Clark, 1992), 280–97.

99. The Tridentine teaching was itself a *via media* between the Lutheran *sola scriptura* and a position argued at the Council of Trent by, among others, Giovanni Maria Cardinal del Monte (later Pope Julius III), who proposed that divine revelation was to be found "partim in libris scriptis, partim in sine scripto traditionibus." Trent instead decreed that "perspiciensque, hanc veritatem et disciplinam contineri in libris scriptis et sine scripto traditionibus, quae ab ipsius Christo ore ab Apostolis acceptae, aut ab ipsis Apostolis Spiritu Sancto dictante quasi per manus traditae." "*Decretum primum: recipiuntur libri sacri et traditionis apostolorum.*" See Concilium Tridentinum, Sessio IV, April 8, 1546, in Heinrich Denzinger, *Enchiridion Symbolorum, Definitionum et Declarationum de Rebus Fidei et Morum*, ed. Peter Hünermann, Robert Fastiggi, and Anne Eglund Nash, 43rd ed. (San Francisco: Ignatius Press, 2012), 369–70,

the exclusivity of scripture and does not deny that there is profit to be had from teaching external to the canon.[100] The article later goes on to delimit the canon in a manner that sides decisively with the Protestant rather than the Roman Catholic side, but the subtlety of the text regarding sufficiency leaves a place for tradition, albeit understood as outside the strict deposit of faith. Relying to a greater or lesser degree on these nuances had been a staple of Anglican Divines from Hooker on.[101] For Hooker, "collecting" the sense of scripture involved the careful use of "techniques that allow the reader to grasp what is necessary to salvation. . . . Scripture is not always plain but has to be "collected together."[102] Newman understood this to mean reading it in the light of the Apostles Creed, not because the latter determined what the former meant but that the creed represented

---

para.1501. The conciliar definition rejects the notion of two separate, complete, sufficient (to use the sixteenth-century terminology) sources: it is *duplex fons* properly construed as the "twin founts" (sacred scripture and holy tradition) of the single source (divine revelation). See M. Schmaus, *Dogma 1: God in Revelation* (London: Sheed and Ward, 1968), 218. Cf. J. R. Geiselmann, *The Meaning of Tradition* (London: Burns and Oates, 1966), 82.

100. Indeed, the original text of the article as it appeared, as Article 5 in the Forty-Two Articles of 1553, explicitly supported just such a notion. It read: "Holy Scripture containeth all things necessary to salvation: so that whatsoever is neither read therein, nor may be proved thereby, although it be sometime received of the faithful, as godly and profitable for an order and comeliness: yet no man ought to be constrained to believe it as an article of the faith, or repute it requisite to the necessity of salvation" (Bray, *Documents of the English Reformation*, 287).

101. For Hooker's position on this question, see Richard Hooker, "Of the Laws of Ecclesiastical Polity: Book 1, Chapter Xiv," in *The Works of That Learned and Judicious Divine, Mr. Richard Hooker: With and Account of His Life and Death*, ed. John Keble (Oxford: Clarendon Press, 1876), 267–72. The conventional view has been that Hooker was a proponent of a *via media avant la lettre*, Newman and Keble being among the most persuasive advocates of position. More recently, this has been critically reexamined by, for example, Diarmaid MacCulloch, who in "Richard Hooker's Reputation," in *The English Historical Review* 117 (2002): 773–812, notes: "nowhere in any of his writings does Hooker use either the word Anglicanism or the phrase *via media*. That may suggest that the legacy of Hooker is not as straightforward as it has sometimes been portrayed; indeed, it may mean that Anglicanism and the *via media* are more interesting and fluid concepts that the complacent version of Anglican historiography has sometimes made them." See Diarmaid MacCulloch, "Richard Hooker's Reputation," *The English Historical Review* 117, no. 473 (2002): 773. For a distinct take from the perspective of an Anglican Evangelical, see Nigel Atkinson, *Richard Hooker and the Authority of Scripture, Tradition and Reason* (London: Paternoster Press, 1997).

102. Chapman, *Anglican Theology*, 114, 117. Chapman remarks that "While this could perhaps be regarded as consonant with the *sola scriptura* of the Reformation, it undoubtedly pushes the idea to its limits" (117).

the distillate of the church's response to the scripture. In the mid-1830s, Newman was certainly not going beyond Hooker. In addressing in the tracts the question of how to provide an account of those doctrines that were considered to be a settled and binding part of the Anglican system—not least in the face of the attacks of *sola scriptura* Evangelicals—and yet for which little scriptural support could be garnered, Newman took a conventional line in asserting scriptural sufficiency:

> You wish to have my opinion on the doctrine of "the Holy Catholic Church," as contained in Scripture, and taught in the Creed.... It seems that true doctrine and warm feelings are not enough. How am I to know what *is* enough? you ask. I reply, *by searching Scripture*.... Let us join issue then on this plain ground, whether or not the doctrine of "the Church," and the duty of obeying it, be laid down *in Scripture*.[103]

It was a view of the doctrinal value of sacred scripture that would have seemed entirely uncontroversial to the standard Anglican Divines.

In the eighth tract, "The Gospel a Law of Liberty," published on October 31, 1833,[104] Newman conceded that sufficiency was but one aspect of the question and sought to address the paucity of scriptural support for "the ecclesiastical system under which we find ourselves." He argued that far from being a matter of surprise, it was a direct consequence of the very relationship between Christ and his church:

> When a man gives orders to those whom he thinks will mistake him, or are perverse, he speaks pointedly and explicitly; but when he gives directions to friends, he will trust much to their knowledge of his feelings and wishes, he leaves much to their discretion, and tells them not so much what he would have done in detail, as what are the objects he would have accomplished.... Accordingly, there is no part perhaps of the ecclesiastical system, which is not faintly traced in Scripture, and no part which is much more than faintly traced.[105]

---

103. "Tract 11: The Visible Church (In Letters to a Friend)" (Messrs. Rivington's, November 11, 1833), Letter 1, 1–2, in *Tracts 1*.

104. "Tract 8: The Gospel a Law of Liberty" (Messrs. Rivington's, October 31, 1833), in *Tracts 1*.

105. Tract 8, 1.

He returned to the same point in December 1833 in the nineteenth tract to be published, the tenth Newman himself had written, in which the matter of the proofs for Apostolical Succession are directly under consideration. Newman conceded that while,

> MEN are sometimes disappointed with the proofs offered in behalf of some important doctrines of our religion; such especially as the necessity of Episcopal Ordination, in order to constitute a Minister of CHRIST. They consider these proofs to be not so strong as they expected, or as they think desirable.[106]

Yet he asserted that:

> such persons should be asked, whether these arguments they speak of are in their estimation weak as a guide to their own practice, or weak in controversy with hardheaded and subtle disputants. Surely, as Bishop Butler has convincingly shown, the faintest probabilities are strong enough to determine our *conduct* in a matter of duty ... [w]e should reply (and most reasonably too), that, *considering the undeniable fact* that ordination has ever been thought necessary in the Church for the Ministerial Commission, our interpretation is the most probable one, and therefore the safest to act upon[107]

This tutioristic appeal to probability was to form a significant part of his defense of those Anglican teachings or those doctrines of the wider church held by Anglicans that could rely on little obvious, explicit scriptural support. It was an early deployment of an apologetic and epistemological tool to which he was to have frequent resort for the rest of his life: that of antecedent probability. He was to go further in Tract 34 when considering the various rites and customs of the church that could make little or no claim to a pedigree *sola scriptura*. Indeed, he quoted St. John Chrysostom at the head of the tract in a way that would appear to leave behind the ground he had shared with Hawkins: "He who is duly strengthened in faith, does not go so far as to require argument and reason for what is enjoined, but is satisfied

---

106. "Tract 19: On Arguing Concerning the Apostolical Succession. On Reluctance to Confess the Apostolical Succession" (Messrs. Rivington's, December 23, 1833), 1, in *Tracts 1*.
107. Tract 19, 2, in *Tracts 1*.

with the *tradition* alone."[108] Taking as his point of departure St. Paul's words in 1 Corinthians 9: 2–16 concerning obedience to "customs" of the church—in that case the cutting short of the hair of men and the head covering of women in church—Newman argued in Tract 34 that St. Paul's authority itself attached to various Anglican practices, such as the baptism of infants, for which scriptural evidence was wanting. Hooker had used the same reasoning to justify the use of "rites and customs serving for the seemliness of church-regiment" and cited as his authority the position taken by Whitaker in his controversy with Bellarmine.[109] Newman's position here, then, once again stands in a classical Anglican tradition, but whereas both Whitaker and Hooker were concerned to establish with certainty the fact of these "rites and customs being known to be Apostolical,"[110] Newman was prepared to be satisfied with probability:

> These instances, then, not to notice others of a like or a different kind, are surely sufficient to reconcile us to the complete ritual system which breaks upon us in the writings of the Fathers. If any parts of it indeed are contrary to Scripture, that is of course a decisive reason at once for believing them to be additions and corruptions of the original ceremonial; but till this is shown, we are bound to venerate what is certainly primitive, and probably is apostolic.
>
> It will be remarked, moreover, that many of the religious observances of the early Church are expressly built upon words of Scripture, and intended to be a visible memorial of them, after the manner of St. Paul's directions about the respective habits of men and women, which was just now noticed.[111]

Newman readily granted that this question of scriptural sufficiency was not a new one to the church nor even a controversy dating

---

108. "Tract 34: Rites and Customs of the Church" (Messrs. Rivington's, May 1, 1834), 1, in *Tracts 1*.

109. William Whitaker, *Disputatio de Sacra Scriptura, Contra Huius Temporis Papistas, Inprimis Robertum Bellarminum Iesuitam ... Pontificium in Collegio Romano, & Thomam Stapletonum Regium in Schola Duacena Controversiarum Professorem: Sex Quoestionibus Proposita et Tractata* (Cambridge: Ex officina Thomae Thomasii, florentissimae Cantabrigiensis Academiae Typographi, 1588), chap. 6, quaest. 6., cited in Hooker, "Laws," para. 1, bk. 1, ch. xiv.

110. Hooker, "Laws," para. 1, bk. 1, ch. xv.

111. Tract 34, 4, in *Tracts 1*.

only to the Reformation. Later, in Tract 34, he cited both Tertullian[112] and St. Basil[113] in support of "a tradition of observances independent of Scripture" dating to Apostolic times and founded originally on a *disciplina arcani* by which "Apostles and Fathers who modeled [sic] the Churches, were accustomed to lodge their sacred doctrine in mystic forms, as being secretly and silently conveyed."[114] Newman had outlined a presumption in favor of the binding nature of primitive tradition, unless a particular observance was actually contrary to the warrant of scripture, in the sentence from Tract 34 already quoted, and relied upon the following passage from St. Basil:

> Of those articles of doctrine and preaching, which are in the custody of the Church, some come to us in Scripture itself, some are conveyed to us by a continuous tradition in mystical depositories. Both have equal claims on our devotion, and are received by all, at least by all who are in any respect Churchmen. For, should we attempt to supersede the usages which are not enjoined in Scripture as if unimportant, we should do most serious injury to Evangelical truth: nay, reduce it to a bare name.[115]

This same tradition of religious practice, Newman suggested, operated under a dual dispensation of implicit scriptural sanction and explicit traditional prescription, whereby "rites and ordinances, far from being unmeaning, are in their nature capable of impressing our memories and imaginations with the great revealed verities; [they are] far from being superstitious, are expressly sanctioned in Scripture as to their principle, and delivered to the Church in their form by tradition."[116]

Admittedly, Tract 34 was concerned primarily with such "rites and ordinances," but the link made between the impressions created by the rites and the "revealed verities," taken together with the citation from St. Basil with its reference to 'sacred doctrine" is sufficient evidence that Newman saw the principle as having a wider doctrinal application not limited merely to liturgical or devotional custom.

112. Tract 34, 5, in *Tracts 1*.
113. Tract 34, 6.
114. St. Basil, "On the Holy Spirit," para. 66, as quoted in Tract 34, 7, in *Tracts 1*.
115. St. Basil, "On the Holy Spirit," para. 66, as quoted in Tract 34, 6–7, in *Tracts 1*.
116. Tract 34, 7.

This was certainly to go beyond Hooker, who had been careful to distinguish between "rites and customs" and "supernatural necessary truth."[117] Newman was reluctant to make that distinction and in Tract 45 asks: "*who* made us judges of essentials and non-essentials? *how* do we determine them?"[118]

While continuing to hold to the notion of scriptural sufficiency, in terms that he believed to be entirely conformable to Article VI, Newman provided with this argument in Tract 34 a rationale within which even a doctrine as central to Christianity as the Trinity—"necessary doctrine, doctrine the very highest and most sacred"—for which he willingly conceded there was "though *most conclusive*" but "indirect and circuitous" scriptural proof, could be accommodated.[119]

In Tract 45, published first on St. Luke's Day, October 18, 1834, he went further and asked: "Where is this solemn and comfortable mystery formally stated in Scripture, as we find it in the creeds?"[120] The absence of the standard of proof demanded by Article VI had been quoted to him as a reason to doubt the received teaching on Episcopacy—which he describes as "but a case of *discipline*"[121] rather than "a case of *doctrine*"[122]—by those who, Newman implied, would never seek to doubt the doctrine of the Trinity, the scriptural evidence for which was equally scanty. He was later to state with rhetorical force and clarity in Tract 71, under the title *On Controversy with the Romanists*, what "this majestic evidence" was and in what this certainty of doctrine that the approach gave him consisted. "It was," he wrote:

a very great mercy that the Church Catholic all over the world, as descended from the Apostles, does at this day speak one and the same doctrine about the Trinity and Incarnation, as it has always spoken it, excepting in one

---

117. Hooker, "Laws," para. 4, bk. 1, ch. xiv.
118. "Tract 45: The Grounds of Our Faith" (Messrs. Rivington's, October 18, 1834), 4, in *Tracts 1*.
119. Tract 45, 6.
120. Tract 45, 6.
121. Tract 45, 5.
122. Tract 45, 6.

single point, which rather *probat regulam* than interferes with it, viz. as to the procession of the HOLY GHOST from the SON. With this solitary exception, we have the certainty of possessing the entire truth as regards the high theological doctrines, by an argument which supersedes the necessity of arguing from Scripture against those who oppose them.[123]

Newman's argument explicitly depended on the witness of antiquity to Apostolical origins and on a consensus of the witnesses who asserted its catholicity. It was an argument grounded in a theological method of historical parallelism that was to characterize both Newman's and the other Tractarians' work. It was also "exactly the sort of history that he [Newman] liked best—a presentation of the past that gave a clear moral for the present."[124] The moral for the present is put by Newman into the mouth of the imaginary "Laicus" in Tract 41, when he says:

I think I quite understand the ground you take. You consider that, as time goes on, fresh and fresh articles of faith are necessary to secure the Church's purity, according to the rise of successive heresies and errors. These articles were all hidden, as it were, in the Church's bosom from the first, and brought out into form according to the occasion. Such was the Nicene explanation against Arius; the English articles against Popery: and such are those now called for in this Age of schism, to meet the new heresy, which denies the holy Catholic Church.[125]

His interlocutor "Clericus" concurs, and looking back on this tract five decades later when preparing the Uniform Edition for Longmans within *The Via Media of the Anglican Church*, volume 2,[126] Newman noted that, "here, as above, the principle of doctrinal development is accepted as true and necessary for the Christian

---

123. Tract 71, 132, in *Tracts 3*.
124. King, *Newman and the Alexandrian Fathers*, 31. For a treatment of Newman's historical method, see Jay Hammond, "Interplay of Hermeneutics and Heresy in the Process of Newman's Conversion from 1830–1845." Cf. Thomas, *Newman and Heresy*; Thomas Fergusson, "The Enthralling Power: History and Heresy in John Henry Newman," *Anglican Theological Review* 85, no. 4 (2003): 641–62.
125. "Tract 41: Via Media No. II" (Messrs. Rivington's, August 24, 1834), 5, in *Tracts 1*.
126. John Henry Newman, *The Via Media of the Anglican Church*, Uniform ed., vol. 2, (London: Longmans, Green and Co., 1885), hereafter *VM 2*.

Church."[127] Pereiro's comment that "the picture does not seem as simple as Newman painted it many years after the events" carries the implied accusation that the 1885 gloss is anachronistic eisegesis, yet the sense of the text of the tract is straightforward enough to acquit Newman of the charge.[128] The device of the dialogue between Clericus and Laicus is direct enough, and it is clear that Clericus was intended to stand for Newman himself. The words of Laicus, "I think I quite understand the ground you take," confirm that the process described is the opinion not of Laicus but of Clericus. This expression of a notion of the development of doctrine by Newman in 1834, before his exchange of correspondence with S. F. Wood, does not fit with Pereiro's thesis that it was Wood who introduced and eventually convinced Newman of the reality of development. Nonetheless, it is difficult to read the passage any other way than that it admits of a notion of development. The objection that Newman subsequently condemned the Roman Catholic idea of development, as he understood it, in his correspondence with the Abbé Jager is no objection at all. As will be seen, it is clear from the correspondence with Jager that Newman appeared to believe that the Roman Catholic concept of development consisted in a Magisterial positivism constrained by little more than papal ambition, and it was this he was anxious to reject. Arguing that by opposing the Roman Catholic position as he conceived it, Newman opposed the idea of development altogether, however, is simply not sustainable when the evidence of the tracts and the unsent letter to Falconer are considered.[129] Pereiro makes no reference in "*Ethos*" to this letter, and his criticism is one with which Thomas concurs, suggesting that the later Newman overlooks the confusion in his earlier work between "essential 'articles of faith' ... and local, disciplinary 'articles of religion.'"[130]

The difficulty of distinguishing between these two was to form a considerable part of the rhetoric of the dispute with the Abbé Jager and was a problem not unique to Newman among Anglican Divines,

127. Newman, *VM* 2, 40.
128. Pereiro, "*Ethos*," 165.
129. JHN to Thomas Falconer, January 27, 1834, in *LD* 4, 180.
130. Thomas, *Newman and Heresy*, 185.

Daniel Waterland having engaged with the matter a hundred years earlier.[131] Chadwick, Pereiro, and Thomas are, however, committed *a priori* to the thesis that Newman did not come to recognize the idea of development of doctrine (as opposed to the development of heresy) until a period later than that currently under consideration: for Chadwick, Newman "crossed the Rubicon" only between 1841 and 1843.[132] Pereiro argues, "It is beyond dispute that a theory of development had already taken shape in Newman's mind by 1840,"[133] and Thomas claims that it belongs in the period immediately prior to his conversion to Roman Catholicism.[134] The evidence examined in the previous chapter and this and the succeeding chapter, however, suggests that they cannot be right. Indeed, the passage here in Tract 41 outlines an approach that, while admittedly is not the principle of doctrinal development in the final completeness of its 1845 form, is, nonetheless, a clear expression of Newman's awareness of development. Furthermore, it is a significant move forward from mere textual development, and although the notion of the *disciplina arcani* is not entirely dispensed with, his hypothesis now seems to depend more on apostolicity and the catholic consent of antiquity than on the operation of the principle of reserve in the manner Newman had suggested the previous year in the unsent letter to Falconer.[135] The question remained, however: was this any bulwark against the claims of Roman Catholicism?

If it were possible that the "very highest and most sacred doctrines," for example, that of the Trinity, doctrines certainly falling within the definition of "necessary to salvation," could be dependent for their content not on the plain words of scripture but rather were rather derived, at least in their form, from nonscriptural tradition, then it seemed to many that the door had been left open for the claims of the Roman Catholic Church to exercise the teaching office of that nonscriptural tradition. Conscious from the first that

---

131. Biemer, *Newman on Tradition*, 9–10.
132. Chadwick, *From Bousset to Newman*, 120.
133. Pereiro, "*Ethos*," 171.
134. Thomas, *Newman and Heresy*, 236–47.
135. JHN to Thomas Falconer, January 27, 1834, in *LD 4*, 180.

he would be accused of opening that door to "the solicitations of Romanism,"[136] Newman was anxious to spell out his differences with Roman Catholic claims, or at least what he and most of his readers believed them to be. He did so from the very beginning, when in the advertisement to the first volume of the tracts he proclaimed their purpose, and by extension, the Oxford Movement, as having "the object of contributing something towards the practical revival of doctrines" in order to, among other things, "repress the extension of Popery."[137]

Having asserted in Tract 11 the doctrine of the visible church and conceded that schism is wrong, even sinful, he set out in some detail in the remainder of the tract the doctrine of the visible church as one and as divinely willed, citing scriptural authority for this position. He wrote:

Moreover Scripture directly insists upon the doctrine of the Visible Church, as being of importance. E.g. St. Paul says;—"There is *one body*, and one SPIRIT, even as ye are called in one hope of your calling; one LORD, one faith, one baptism, one GOD and FATHER of all." Ephes. iv. 5, 6. Thus, as far as the Apostle's words go, it is as false and unchristian, (I do not mean in degree of guilt, but in its intrinsic sinfulness), to make more bodies than one, as to have many Lords, many Gods, many Creeds.[138]

By the end of Tract 11, the obviousness of the apparent flaws is stark.

If the purpose of Newman's early tracts was to firmly establish Anglican claims to Apostolical Succession, then it was necessary to deal with the criticism that this made the Church of England in some way dependent upon Rome. Newman could see that the criticism had two limbs: first, that Apostolical Succession could only have come to the Church of England from her Roman Catholic antecedents, as her current position as separated from the communion of Rome suggested, or at the very least that she was in schism, and second, that Rome's claims to the capacities attendant upon Apostolical Succession, to popery, which surely included what he called an infalli-

---

136. JHN to H.A. Woodgate, August 7, 1833, in *LD 4*, 27.
137. JHN, advertisement, *Tracts 1*.
138. Tract 11, 3, in *Tract 1*.

ble teaching authority, were at odds with the Anglican position. In his next contribution to the series, Tract 15, Newman confronts the problem head on:

WHEN Churchmen in England maintain the Apostolical Commission of their Ministers, they are sometimes met with the objection, that they cannot prove it without tracing their orders back to the Church of Rome; a position, indeed, which in a certain sense is true. And hence it is argued, that they are reduced to the dilemma, either of acknowledging they had no right to separate from the Pope, or, on the other hand, of giving up the Ministerial Succession altogether, and resting the claims of their pastors on some other ground; in other words, that they are inconsistent in reprobating Popery,

It is intended, in the pages that follow, to reply to this supposed difficulty.[139]

The "flat denial of the alleged" fact that the Church of England initiated the schism with Rome is the cornerstone of the argument that follows.[140] It is an argument that draws heavily upon a hermeneutic of continuity that would become a staple of Tractarian historiography. Newman contended that the Church of England was one and the same body that had subsisted in England before the Reformation:

The English Church did not revolt from those who in that day had authority by succession from the Apostles. On the contrary, it is certain that the Bishops and Clergy in England and Ireland remained the same as before the separation, and that it was these, with the aid of the civil power, who delivered the Church of those kingdoms from the yoke of Papal tyranny and usurpation, while at the same time they gradually removed from the minds of the people various superstitious opinions and practices which had grown

---

139. "Tract 15: On the Apostolical Succession in the English Church" (Messrs. Rivington's, December 13, 1833), 1, in *Tracts 1*. William Palmer (named for his Oxford College Palmer of Worcester, to distinguish him from another Oxford Tractarian, similarly eponymously named Palmer of Magdalen) produced the initial draft of this tract, which Newman revised and completed, the former having decided to give up contributing to the tracts following a disagreement with Newman concerning the form of an advertisement for "An Association of Friends of the Church." See William Palmer to JHN, November 29, 1833, in *LD 4*, 128–30.

140. Tract 15, 3.

up during the middle ages, and which, though never formally received by the judgment of the whole Church, were yet very prevalent.[141]

The argument appears to be that it is Rome that is in schism from the Apostolical Church "by virtue of her "tyranny and usurpation," and that it was the papal attempt "to gain *power* over the whole Church" and "to *lord it* over GOD's heritage" that put Rome, not England, in the wrong.[142] Furthermore, the "various religious and ecclesiastical usages"[143] forced upon the Church in England and Ireland by this papal aggression made it a religious duty for the English church to take the action they did:

our Bishops, at the time of the Reformation, did but vindicate their ancient rights; were but acting as grateful, and therefore jealous champions of the honour of the old Fathers, and the sanctity of their institutions.... And, if England and Ireland had a plea for asserting their freedom under any circumstances, much more so, when the corruptions imposed on them by Rome even made it a duty to do so.[144]

Rome had neither the legitimate interest of patriarchal authority over England nor kept to Apostolical doctrine, Newman argued.[145] Therefore, even with its orders derived from the same source as those claimed by Rome, the Church of England had, in Newman's conception, the duty of submission neither to Rome nor to the corruptions in practice and "false doctrine and error which Romanists now maintain" and that "adulterated the sincerity of the Christian verity, and brought the Church into miserable bondage."[146] Lest his readers be left in any doubt of the extent of Newman's differences with it, at least since the time of Trent, he describes the Ro-

141. Tract 15, 4.
142. Tract 15, 6.
143. Tract 15, 6.
144. Tract 15, 9.
145. Tract 15, 6. A somewhat improbable claim abandoned by the following summer, when in Tract 38, Newman puts into the mouth of his cipher Clericus a distinction between Geneva and Rome: "I like foreign interference, as little from Geneva, as from Rome. Geneva at least never converted a part of England from heathenism, nor could lay claim to patriarchal authority over it." See "Tract 38: Via Media No. I" (Messrs. Rivington's, July 25, 1834), 27, in *Tracts 1*.
146. Tract 15, 10.

man Communion as "heretical," as having "apostatized" and having bound "itself in covenant to the cause of Antichrist."[147] By the end of 1833, in Tract 20, while still protesting "the very enmity I feel against the Papistical corruptions of the Gospel,"[148] Newman was able to express this ecclesiology clearly: the Church of England was to be understood "as a true branch of the Church universal, yet withal preserved it free from doctrinal error. It is Catholic and Apostolic, yet not Papistical."[149]

The emergence of this ecclesiology of the Church of England as the *via media* between Protestant error and Roman Catholic excess in the thought of Newman marked a decisive step in his attempt to develop a replacement hypothesis to account for the difficulty of change and continuity. The clear commitment to a doctrine of the visible church as a prerequisite for the invisible[150] represented a further move away from Newman's Calvinist youth. He set out his first complete attempt at expressing the meaning of this *via media* in Tracts 38 and 41, which, together with Tract 71, were to be incorporated into the second volume of a two-volume collection under the title *The Via Media of the Anglican Church* in 1836.[151] The *via media* of these tracts was no *via negativa*: it was not conceived of as not this, nor that; not Protestant nor Catholic. It was instead presented by Newman in entirely positive terms: it was the Protestant and the Catholic who were to be understood in the negative sense because they were not Anglican. In proposing this synthesis, Newman was adopting the position he believed taken by Hooker and the Caroline

---

147. Tract 15, 10.
148. "Tract 20: The Visible Church, Letter III" (Messrs. Rivington's, December 24, 1833), 1, in *Tracts* 1.
149. Tract 20, 3.
150. Tract 11, 2–3.
151. John Henry Newman, *The Via Media of the Anglican Church: Illustrated in Lectures, Letters and Tracts Written between 1830 and 1836*, 2 vols. (London: J. F. and G. Rivington, 1836). The critical edition of *the Via Media of the Anglican Church*, edited by H. D. Weidner, reveals the extent of the alterations Newman made to the text of the various lectures, letters, and tracts between the first edition in 1836 and the second in 1837. See John Henry Newman, *The "Via Media" of the Anglican Church*, ed. H. D. Weidner (Oxford: Clarendon Press, 1990). The work was further revised in 1841 and again for the Uniform Edition for Longmans in 1885 appearing as *VM* 1 and 2.

Divines. Newman writes of the Church of England's position as a positive choice: "The glory of the English Church is, that it has taken the VIA MEDIA, as it has been called. It lies *between* the (so called) Reformers and the Romanists."[152] It was "not a matter of compromise but a positive position, witnessing to the mystery and the universality of God and God's kingdom working through the fallible, earthly *ecclesia Anglicana*."[153] England alone had kept to the deposit of faith, Newman argued, whereas the continental Protestants and domestic nonconformist Dissenters had mistakenly fallen into the error that was the natural product of *sola scriptura*. Rome's error, Newman observed, had been to seek to add to the faith: the "presumption" of "adding to the means of salvation set forth in Scripture ... the Church of Rome has added other ways of gaining heaven."[154] Newman maintained that the *via media*, to which the Church of England had remained faithful, had protected it from the dangers attendant upon other systems of theology. Whereas the decrees of Trent had driven Rome away from the right path, the Thirty-Nine Articles—which he maintained was "not a body of divinity"[155]—had ensured the Church of England remained true:

Our Articles are one portion of that accumulation. Age after age, fresh battles have been fought with heresy, fresh monuments of truth set up. As I will not consent to be deprived of the records of the Reformation, so neither will I part with those of former times. I look upon our Articles as in one sense an addition to the Creeds; and at the same time the Romanists added their Tridentine articles. Theirs I consider unsound; ours as true.[156]

The vocabulary of "fresh battles" and "fresh monuments of truth set up" placed alongside the language of "accumulation" and not parting with the records "of former times" hints strongly at the positive and practical nature of the *via media* and places it within the context of Newman's search for a coherent explanation for continuity

---

152. "Tract 38: Via Media No. I," 28, in *Tracts 1*.
153. John Booty, "Standard Divines," *The Study of Anglicanism*, ed. John Booty, Stephen Sykes, and Jonathan Knight (London: SPCK, 1998), 176.
154. Tract 41, 37, in *Tracts 1*.
155. Tract 41, 32.
156. Tract 41, 31–32.

in the face of change: for a stronghold in antiquity protected from the twin errors of self-will and the corrupting influence of ecclesiastical power. As he expressed it in Tract 45,

> EVERY system of theology has its dangers, its tendencies towards evil. Systems short of the truth have this tendency inherent in themselves, and in process of time discover it, and work out the anticipated evil, which is but the legitimate though latent consequence of their principles. Thus, we may consider the present state of Geneva the fair result on the long run of the system of self-will which was established there in the sixteenth century. But even the one true system of religion has its dangers on all sides, from the weakness of its recipients, who pervert it. Thus the Holy Catholic doctrines, in which the Church was set up, were corrupted into Popery, not legitimately, or necessarily, but by various external causes acting on human corruption, in the lapse of many ages.[157]

Such was Newman's position at the end of 1834, on the eve of a controversy that was to hone his notion of the *via media* and ground it thoroughly within the tradition of the Anglican Divines of the sixteenth and seventeenth centuries. Before looking at this controversy in the correspondence with the Abbé Jager and the *Lectures on the Prophetical Office of the Church*, which were its direct product, it is first necessary to consider the use Newman had made of patristic sources in the tracts of 1833 and 1834 and on the purposes that underlay his publication of other patristic material during that period.

Newman's Early Tractarian Use of the Fathers

In his 2009 *The Church of England and Christian Antiquity*, Jean-Louis Quantin sought to examine in detail, take on, and then deconstruct the widely accepted "*idées reçues*"[158] of Tractarian historiography that there had been a constant practice within the Church of England stretching back to Cranmer, Jewel, and Hooker whereby the Fathers of Christian antiquity had been the constant subject of particular study and were appealed to in support of this doctrine or that. Writ-

---

157. Tract 45, 1.
158. Quantin, *The Church of England and Christian Antiquity*, 1.

ing in 2001, Arthur Middleton—in a work Quantin dismisses as one of *"haute vulgarisation,"*[159]—claimed that "the *appeal to the Fathers* has been a seminal feature of the Anglican theological tradition since the sixteenth century" and is chiefly responsible for the "peculiar character" of Anglicanism.[160] In making this claim, Middleton was doing no more than echo the opinion of the seventeenth-century Maurist, Dom Denys de Sainthe-Marthe, that "those of the English people that are called Episcopalians, and who compose the greatest part of the State ... profess to hold the Fathers in much greater respect than other Protestants do."[161]

Quantin's thesis is, however, that no matter how widely held this view is, the reality is less obvious and more complex. Furthermore, Quantin argues that Sabine Baring-Gould's suggestion that Anglicans derived "their definite orthodoxy ... from Catholic tradition and the study of the Fathers" was little more than a conventional platitude hallowed by frequent repetition.[162] He suggests, rather, that the evidence simply does not support Newman's claim that:

> our Divines at and since the Reformation have betaken themselves to the extant documents of the early Church, in order to determine thereby what the system of Primitive Christianity was; and so to elicit from Scripture more completely and accurately that revealed truth, which though revealed there is not on its surface, but needs to be *deduced* and *developed* from it.[163]

What Quantin seeks to demonstrate is that the reality is neither as static nor as univocal as Newman here suggested. Whether Newman's position constituted quite the "audacious feat of legerdemain" in re-presenting "the English Reformation and, all its tomes, as a sort of patristic revival,"[164] as Stephen Thomas suggests, however,

---

159. Quantin, *The Church of England and Christian Antiquity*, 7.
160. Arthur Pierce Middleton, *Fathers and Anglicans: The Limits of Orthodoxy* (Leominster: Gracewing, 2001), 6–7.
161. D. de Sainte-Marthe, *Histoire de S.Gregoire Le Grand, Pape et Docteur de l"Eglise* (Rouen, 1697), 282, cited in Quantin, *The Church of England and Christian Antiquity*, 1.
162. Sabine Baring-Gould, *The Church Revival: Thoughts Thereon and Reminiscences* (London: Methuen, 1914), 75.
163. John Henry Newman, "Preface to the Catechetical Lectures of St. Cyril of Jerusalem, in R. R. Church, Library of the Fathers," vol. 2 (Oxford: J. G. and F. Rivington, 1839), x.
164. Thomas, *Newman and Heresy*, 200.

is quite another thing. It was certainly not "legerdemain" to suggest that Hooker and the other standard Anglican Divines of the sixteenth and seventeenth centuries had regularly sought to marshal proof-texts from the Fathers to provide evidence for the antiquity of particular teachings that formed part of the Anglican system. On the contrary, as Peter Nockles has observed, it was a staple of the theological method of the Old High Churchmen that the opinions of Christian antiquity were to be treated as "a corroborative testimony to the truth of the Church of England's formularies and the teaching of her standard divines."[165] What Quantin and Nockles agreed on was that the Tractarian myth of the rediscovery of the Fathers, that they had rescued Anglicanism by going back to the authentic theological methods of their sixteenth- and seventeenth-century forebears, was simply not supportable: "The Fathers were not 'rediscovered': they had never been forgotten."[166]

Quantin argues that the manner in which the Anglican Divines of the sixteenth and seventeenth centuries had deployed patristic authority—which had been taken up by the Old High Churchmen[167]—"was an art of manipulating authorities, as part of what might be called a technology of truth."[168] The Fathers stood as witnesses, and nothing more, to "what is agreeable to the teaching of the Old or New Testament" and evidence of "what the Catholic fathers and ancient bishops have collected from this self-same doctrine."[169] While such an approach might have satisfied those who were content to accept as *fait accompli* the appeal to the Fathers that had been made by the Anglican Divines, it was not an approach that could provide Newman with sufficient material to construct what he believed to be the necessary bulwark against an Erastian attack on the Apostolical authority—and therefore the divine origin—of

165. Nockles, *The Oxford Movement in Context*, 114.
166. Quantin, *The Church of England and Christian Antiquity*, 15; Nockles, *The Oxford Movement in Context*, 109.
167. Quantin, *The Church of England and Christian Antiquity*, 15.
168. Quantin, *The Church of England and Christian Antiquity*, 18.
169. "Canon 6: Concerning Preachers, from the Canons of 1571," in *Documents Illustrative of English Church History*, ed. Henry Gee and William Hardy (London and New York: Macmillan, 1896), 496.

the Church of England. It was, he believed, precisely the limitation imposed by the self-denying ordinance against going beyond conventional High Church patristic proof-texting that had opened the Church of England up to the predations he had witnessed. This, at least, would appear to be the import of his aside about "Conservatism" in his March 1834 letter to Henry Wilberforce[170] and his letter to Hugh James Rose later in the same month.[171]

Other authors of the tracts and other members of the movement might have been content to follow conventional practice with regard to the use of the Fathers, but it did not serve to create the imaginative impression of antiquity that Newman intended to deploy through the use of historical parallelism in order to serve his apologetic purpose. That Newman was able to adopt such a methodology was in part due to the unconventional route by which he first became familiar with the Fathers, his early reading, according to Nockles, of Joseph Milner's *History of the Church of Christ*, to which reference has been made in the previous chapter, rather than by the more conventional Anglican starting point in the study of the Caroline Divines.[172] Gareth Bennett concurred about the methodology but located the source somewhat later in Newman's reading: what he believed to be the distorting influence of George Bull, whose work, and particularly the *Defensio*, Newman took up in preparation for the writing of *The Arians*.[173] Newman's own recollection, in the *Apologia*, was of the decisive influence of Bull in leading him "to consider that Antiquity was the true exponent of the doctrines of Christianity and the basis of the Church of England," and the heavy reliance in *The Arians* on the authority of Bull gives support to his memory.[174] Whether it was Milner or Bull who was primarily responsible, "the seeds of Newman's divergence of approach to antiquity from that of the Caroline Divines and old High Churchmen" had been sown in the impression on his

---

170. JHN to Henry Wilberforce, March 10, 1834, in *LD 4*, 202.
171. JHN to Hugh James Rose, March 17, 1834, in *LD 4*, 206–7.
172. Nockles, *The Oxford Movement in Context*, 111.
173. Gareth Vaughan Bennett, "Patristic Tradition in Anglican Thought 1660–1900," in *Tradition in Luthertum und Anglikanismus: OEcumenica 1971/71*, ed. Gunther Grassman and Vajta Vilmos (Gütterslo: Mohr, 1972), 82.
174. Newman, *Apo.*, 88.

CATHOLICISM OF THE WORD, 1833-1838

imagination made by the "age of martyrs,"[175] and he would utilize this familiarity with the Fathers, deployed as his natural "hot-headed"[176] skills as a controversialist dictated, to provide a model of a living church—the church of antiquity—that he wished to see reproduced in the nineteenth century.[177]

This model of a living church was to be created, Newman believed, not only in the apologetic form of the tracts but also in literary forms that would create impressions as much on the imagination as the intellect. Newman had conceived of a poetic contribution in order "to bring out certain truths and facts, moral, ecclesiastical, and religious, simply and forcibly" as early as November 1832.[178] Appearing in Rose's *British Magazine* under Newman's suggested title "Lyra Apostolica" in June 1833, Newman eventually wrote forty-six of the 179 poems to appear. The tone he adopted and the use to which he put the Fathers in these poems is well illustrated by the verses he wrote *en route* to Algiers the previous December[179] but which were not to appear in the *British Magazine* until August 1834.[180] Entitled "Athanasius," Newman nonetheless marshaled Cyprian, Chrysostom, and Ambrose in addition to the eponymous hero in verses that suggested that he understood precisely that the Church of England was in time of trial:

> When shall our northern Church her champion see,
> Raised by high heaven's decree,
> To shield the ancient faith at his own harm?
> Like him who stayed the arm
> Of tyrannous power, and learning's sophist tone,
> Keen-visioned Seer, alone.
>
> The many crouched before an idol-priest,
> Lord of the world's rank feast.
> In the sad night, mid the Saints' trial sore,

---

175. Nockles, *The Oxford Movement in Context*, 112.
176. JHN to Harriett Newman, October 16, 1831, in *LD 2*, 367.
177. Nockles, *The Oxford Movement in Context*, 113.
178. JHN to Hugh James Rose, November 26, 1832, in *LD 3*, 120.
179. JHN to Mrs. Newman, December 19, 1832, in *LD 3*, 155–62.
180. Vincent Ferrer Blehl, *John Henry Newman: A Bibliographical Catalogue of His Writings* (Charlottesville: University Press of Virginia, 1978), 84.

> He stood, then bowed before
> The sacred mysteries; he their likest sign,
> Weak vessel yet divine.
>
> Cyprian is ours, since the high souled primate laid
> Beneath the traitorous blade
> His silvered head. And Chrysostom we claim
> In that clear eloquent flame
> And learned zeal in the same woe, which shone
> Bright round a Martyr's-throne.
>
> And Ambrose' pastoral might we celebrate,
> Tho' with unequal fate,
> When in dark times our champion crossed a king.
> - But good in every thing
> Comes as ill's cure. Dim Future! shall we NEED
> A Prophet for truth's creed?[181]

The poetry may not be of the first rank—although it is certainly not doggerel—but the reader could be left in no doubt as to Newman's message, addressed as much to the imagination as to the intellect, nor to his intention of eliciting a sympathetic hearing by "catching people when unguarded."[182] As Ker observes, Newman "had been unable to help comparing unfavourably the divided and threatened Church of England with that fresh vigorous Power of the first centuries."[183]

The tracts and poems or "ballads"[184] of the "Lyra Apostolica" were accompanied by *Records of the Church*,[185] a series of translations of patristic material, "extracts from Eusebius etc.... little stories of the Apostles, Fathers etc., to familiarize the imagination of the reader to an *Apostolical state* of the Church."[186] Newman was not responsible for the translations, those being the work of "several Ch[rist] Ch[urch] men,"[187] but he was responsible for their publica-

---

181. JHN to Mrs. Newman, December 19, 1832, in *LD 3*, 156.
182. JHN to John William Bowden, November 17, 1833, in *LD 4*, 109.
183. Ker, *Newman: A Biography*, 56.
184. JHN to John William Bowden, November 17, 1833, in *LD 4*, 109.
185. "Records of the Church Nos. I-XVIII," November 11, 1833, in *Tracts 1*.
186. JHN to John William Bowden, November 17, 1833, in *LD 4*, 109.
187. JHN to Richard Hurrell Froude, December 15, 1833, in *LD 4*, 141. Newman later

tion, and it is considered probable that he furnished them with their introductions, accompanying notes, and conclusions.[188] Writing to Froude in December 1833, he recorded that "we have 12 Numbers out of Records of the Church":[189] seven of these were translations of Ignatius of Antioch's letters and four others accounts of the martyrdom of Ignatius, of the martyrs of Lyons and Vienne, of James the Apostle, and of Polycarp.

Newman continued with this concentration on the subject of persecution. In August 1833, he sent Rose a series of letters about the fourth century for publication in the *British Magazine*.[190] Three were about the way Ambrose of Milan withstood imperial pressure, and the fourth was about the opposition of Basil of Caesarea to the Emperor Valens' incursions into the church. The parallels could not have been clearer, as King notes:

The tone of impending persecution of the English church was there from the beginning of the first Ambrose article, for political reform "makes it a practical concern for every churchman to prepare himself for a change, and a practical question for the clergy, by what instruments the authority

---

noted, "[NB. Liddell, Thornton, Scott of Balliol?]," *LD 4*, 141, n. 5. At the time of Newman's letter to Froude, Liddell was still at Christ Church before his election the following year to a fellowship at Balliol. He and Scott are best known for their jointly compiled Greek-English Lexicon, first published in 1843. See Henry Liddell and Robert Scott, *A Greek-English Lexicon* (Oxford: Clarendon Press, 1843). Liddell was later dean of Christ Church and vice chancellor of Oxford University. He was also the father of the girl Alice, whom his fellow Christ Church don Charles Dodgson memorialised in his fantasy novels pseudonymously published as Lewis Carroll, *Alice's Adventures in Wonderland* (London: Macmillan and Company, 1865) and *Through the Looking Glass and What Alice Found There* (London: Macmillan and Company, 1871). Robert Scott was another Anglican priest and Oxford don: successively, Master of Balliol College, Oxford, Dean Ireland Professor of the Exegesis of Holy Scripture in the same university, and dean of Rochester Cathedral. The Thornton, to whom Newman refers was Charles Thornton, youngest son of the abolitionist and Clapham Sect member Henry Thornton. For biographical details on Liddell, Scott, and both Thorntons, see *ODNB Online*.

188. King, *Newman and the Alexandrian Fathers*, 31, n. 15.

189. JHN to Richard Hurrell Froude, December 15, 1833, in *LD 4*, 141. For dating and attribution of the records, see Rune Imburg, *In Quest of Authority: The "Tracts for the Times" and the Development of the Tractarian Leaders 1833–1841* (Lund: Lund University Press, 1987), 23, n. 12.

190. JHN to Hugh James Rose, August 16, 1833, in *LD 4*, 30.

of Religion is to be supported, should the protection and patronage of the government be withdrawn."[191]

At the beginning of the Oxford Movement, during the meeting at Rose's rectory, Arthur Perceval had set the nascent movement within the context of a time of persecution, albeit in his case, the historical parallel was with the death of Charles I.[192] With the publication of *Records*, Newman had used the same "sense of persecution" as "the impetus for action,"[193] but he had moved the parallel to Christian antiquity. It was to prove a decisive move, both for the future of the movement and for Newman's own theological trajectory.

The Correspondence with the Abbé Jager

Jean-Nicolas Jager (1790–1868) was a Roman Catholic priest of the Diocese of Nancy, who in the summer of 1834 had met Newman's acquaintance, Benjamin Harrison.[194] Harrison, a Christ Church don, was already the author of three of the tracts.[195] Jager was interested in the position of the Church of England and had read some of the tracts, together with Bishop Milner's *The End of Religious Controversy*,[196]

---

191. King, *Newman and the Alexandrian Fathers*, 32. King is quoting here Newman in *Historical Sketches*, vol. 1 (London: Longmans, Green and Co., 1906), 339.

192. Arthur Phillip Perceval, *Collection of Papers Connected with the Theological Movement of 1833* (London: J. G. and F. Rivington, 1842), 2.

193. King, *Newman and the Alexandrian Fathers*, 30.

194. Harrison had been a pupil of Newman's brother Francis, and, in June 1832, he was recommending him to Samuel Rickards as a tutor for Lord Maidstone. Newman there described him as "a treasure ... a man of the deepest and soundest principles." See JHN to Samuel Rickards, June 5, 1832, in *LD 3*, 53, n. 4. The meeting took place during Harrison's visit to Paris while "arabicizing with De Saci." See JHN to Richard Hurrell Froude, November 12, 1834, in *LD 4*, 360.

195. "Tract 16: Advent" (Messrs. Rivington's, December 17, 1833); "Tract 17: The Ministerial Commission: A Trust from Christ for the Benefit of His People" (Messrs. Rivington's, December 20, 1833); and "Tract 24 The Scripture View of the Apostolical Commission" (Messrs. Rivington's, January 25, 1834), all in *Tracts 1*. Later in 1834, he also wrote "Tract 49: The Kingdom of Heaven" (Messrs. Rivington's, December 25, 1834) in *Tracts 2*.

196. Joseph Milner, *The End of Religious Controversy, in a Friendly Correspondence between a Religious Society of Protestants and a Roman Catholic Divine. Addressed to the Bishop of St. David's, in Answer to His Lordships Protestant Catechism* (London: Thomas Burgess, 1824).

a "classic statement of the Roman-Anglican controversy from the Roman side."[197] He was also familiar with Lepappe de Trevern's *Discussion amicale sur l"établissement et la doctrine de l"Église anglicane et en général sur la Réformation*.[198] Jean François Marie Lepappe de Trevern had been a French emigré clergyman living in exile in England during the period of the imposition, in postrevolutionary France, of the Civil Constitution of the Clergy.[199] Because of his presumed familiarity with England and its national church, the book, which had been written as his licentiate thesis at the Sorbonne, was seen in France as a reliable guide and served as "a handbook of Anglican beliefs for French writers over several decades."[200] Jager had also read Bishop John Jebb of Limerick's *Pastoral Instructions*.[201] This book, first published in 1815, contained a tract initially largely written by Alexander Knox, but which by 1831 Jebb had expanded.[202] Called *A tract for all times, but most eminently for the present: Peculiar Character of the Church of England; as distinguished, both from other branches of the reformation, and from the modern Church of Rome*, it picked up on a theme that had emerged in the correspondence between Knox and Jebb. The former had commented to the latter, in a letter of 1813: "What perverse influence the nickname of Protestant has had upon our Church.... It will perhaps be at length discovered, that there is

197. Louis Allen, *John Henry Newman and the Abbé Jager: A Controversy on Scripture and Tradition (1834–1836)* (London: Oxford University Press, 195), 5.

198. Jean-François-Marie Le Pappe de Trévern, *Discussion Amicale Sur l"établissement et La Doctrine de l"Église Anglicane et En Général Sur La Réformation*, 2 vols. (London, 1817).

199. Dominic Aiden Bellenger, *The French Exiled Clergy in Great Britain after 1789: A Working List* (Bath: Downside Abbey, 1986), 178.

200. Allen, *Newman and Jager*, 5. Allen claims that Le Pappe de Trévern was bishop of Vannes before being translated to Strasbourg. This is incorrect. Before going to Strasbourg as archbishop in 1826, he had been the bishop of the restored Diocese of Aire for three years. Allen's confusion may have arisen because Lepappe de Trevern was a Breton, born in Morlaix. See "Bishop Jean-François-Marie Le Pappe de Trévern [Catholic-Hierarchy]," accessed February 21, 2020, http://www.catholic-hierarchy.org/bishop/blpdt.html.

201. John Jebb, *Sermons, on Subjects Chiefly Practical, with Illustrative Notes and an Appendix, Relating to the Character of the Church of England, as Distinguished Both from Other Branches of the Reformation, and from the Modern Church of Rome*, 1st ed. (London: Cadell & Davies, 1815).

202. Jebb, *Sermons, on Subjects Chiefly Practical*, 3rd ed. (London: Cadell & Davies, 1831).

a *medium* between the two extremes."²⁰³ The letter and both the title and theme expressed a notion that, as Louis Allen noted, "anticipated the Via Media by two decades."²⁰⁴

When Harrison wrote to Newman from Paris on September 1, 1834, suggesting that Newman might "gratify the Abbé's wish" and enter into an "amicable controversy" about the tracts,²⁰⁵ Harrison had already resolved to participate in such an exchange. His involvement was, as Allen remarked, clearly entered into with the intention of "withdrawing from the controversy as soon as possible and persuading Newman to take his place."²⁰⁶

Jager's first challenge was published in Migne's new newspaper, *L'Univers religieux*,²⁰⁷ on August 30, 1834, and Harrison replied three weeks later, on September 18.²⁰⁸ In these initial exchanges, Harrison and Jager limited themselves to identifying a measure of common ground in acknowledging the place of tradition within Christianity, while disagreeing about where it was to be found and how it was to be applied. They both accepted the rule of the Vincentian Canon, but whereas for Jager it was a rule that argued for binding ecclesiastical authority in determining the locus and content of tradition,²⁰⁹ for Harrison it was "an invitation to make a judgment about what Tradition is, on the evidence."²¹⁰ Faithful to the Anglican consensus,

---

203. Alexander Knox to John Jebb, in Charles Forster, ed., *Thirty Years Correspondence between John Jebb and Alexander Knox* (London, 1834), 122.

204. Allen, *Newman and Jager*, 6.

205. JHN to Hugh James Rose, September 4, 1834, in *LD 4*, 326, n. 2.

206. Allen, *Newman and Jager*, 4.

207. Jacques-Paul Migne (1800–1875) was a priest, translator, editor, and publisher of extraordinary industry. He is remembered for his Patrologiae cursus completus, comprised of the Series Graeca (PG) and the Series Latina (PL), which together eventually ran to 386 volumes, published between 1844 and 1858, but his interests were wider than patristic scholarship. For an account of his life and work, see R. H. Bloch, *God's Plagiarist: Being an Account of the Fabulous Industry and Irregular Commerce of the Abbé Migne* (Chicago: University of Chicago Press, 1994).

208. For the chronology of the publication of the exchanges between Harrison and Jager in *L'Univers religieux* and between Newman and Jager, first in *L'Univers religieux* and from March 1835 in its associated weekly, *Le Moniteur religieux*, see Allen, *Newman and Jager*, 4–6. This present work relies on the text of the various contributions to these exchanges as published by Allen in *Newman and Jager*.

209. Allen, *Newman and Jager*, 23.

210. Allen, *Newman and Jager*, 22.

its historic formularies, and standard Divines, Harrison, whose two letters were published under the cover of anonymity,[211] argued that tradition existed only as an unauthoritative, interpretative tool of the sole authoritative source, scripture, and that of what it consisted was chiefly an historical question.[212] Jager's position was consistent with the Tridentine synthesis of the *duplex fons*: he contended for the position of the church's Magisterium in defining the content of divine revelation.[213] Such was the position by the end of October 1834 when Harrison had succeeded in "entangling" Newman in the controversy.[214]

Newman did not see at first that the correspondence would amount to much, and indeed, the manner in which he left off the controversy—simply allowing it to lapse when he failed to send off the second part of his second letter to the Abbé[215]—suggested that he did not understand at any time throughout its duration that it would occupy "a crucial position in his intellectual history."[216] Nevertheless, as he explained in another letter to Jager that he did not send, Newman considered it "a duty" to become embroiled in the exchange and wondered "who was likely to undertake this service if [he] declined it." He wrote: "I consider I ought not to decline the challenge, believing as I do that truth is on my side."[217] In any event, his initial prediction—"I do not expect any thing will come of it"[218]—could not have been less accurate, because, as Allen observed, "the key text of the Via Media, and the main idea behind the *Essay*, are directly derived from this controversy."[219] In fact, it was "the often uncomfortably acute enquiries of the tenacious Abbé"[220] that enabled Newman to express "a distinction, drawn possibly for the first time by [him]

---

211. Allen, *Newman and Jager*, 4.
212. Allen, *Newman and Jager*, 22.
213. Allen, *Newman and Jager*, 26.
214. JHN to Archdeacon Froude, October 25, 1834, in *LD 4*, 347.
215. Allen, *Newman and Jager*, 8.
216. Allen, *Newman and Jager*, 1.
217. JHN to the Abbé Jager, end of October 1834, in *LD 4*, 350.
218. JHN to Archdeacon Froude, October 25, 1834, in *LD 4*, 347.
219. Allen, *Newman and Jager*, 3.
220. Thomas, *Newman and Heresy*, 186.

and later to play a great part in his work, between apostolical tradition transmitted by bishops, and prophetical tradition."[221] Newman had been initially dismissive of Jager, calling him 'so weak that so far [the controversy] is no fun,"[222] and later "the most ignorant of men and the most inconsequent of reasoners."[223] Later still, picking up on Jager's prolixity, he described him as "a chattering French Abbé, who says three words where one would do," yet he recognized the "stimulus for reading" the Fathers that the exchange provided.[224] Newman saw that the correspondence at least served the purpose of his becoming more thoroughly acquainted with the issues, or "to get up the controversy," as he put it, and to show that he was not "a papist."[225] Newman later felt obliged to play down the significance of the exchange and deny its crucial role in developing his theology,[226] preferring instead to locate the influence in the exchanges covering similar ground, five years later, with the Irish Roman Catholic priest, Charles William Russell of Maynooth College.[227] Given the relative proximity to Newman's conversion, his claim that Russell "had, perhaps, more to do with my conversion than any one else,"[228] it is per-

---

221. Allen, *Newman and Jager*, 7.
222. JHN to John William Bowden, February 8, 1835, in *LD 5*, 25.
223. JHN to Richard Hurrell Froude, July 16, 1835, in *LD 5*, 100.
224. JHN to Robert Isaac Wilberforce, August 30, 1835, in *LD 5*, 133.
225. JHN to Richard Hurrell Froude, July 16, 1835, in *LD 5*, 100.
226. JHN to the Abbé Jager, 1845 or 1846, in *LD 11* (London: Thomas Nelson, 1961–1972 [vols. 11–22]), 81–82. Jager had written to Newman "to ask whether I did not owe my conversion to him, or some such question. I was obliged to answer, No." See NB to JHN to Joseph Epiphane Darras, February 20, 1868, in *LD 24*, 37. Darras was writing a biographical note of the recently deceased Jager. The letter to Jager was not nearly as direct as this note implies. See JHN to the Abbé Jager, 1845 or 1846, in *LD 11*, 81–82.
227. Russell (1812–1880) was professor of humanity at Maynooth from 1835, then from 1845, professor of ecclesiastical history, and finally from 1857 until 1879, the president. See *ODNB Online*. Newman and Russell had first corresponded in the spring of 1841, when Russell wrote to Newman "protesting against various misunderstandings of Roman Catholic doctrines, particularly of Transubstantiation in *Tract 90*." See Ker, *Newman: A Biography*, 225. This correspondence continued through the following two years (see *LD 8*, 171–75, 180–83, 186–88, and 288; *LD 9*, 154–56, 162, 164–65, 210, 228, 448, 450–51, and 462.). The character and import of the exchange is dealt with in the third chapter of Ambrose Macaulay, *Dr Russell of Maynooth* (London: Darton, Longman and Todd, 1983), 65–98. The men were fitfully to carry on a correspondence almost until Russell's death. Newman's last letter to him is dated September 19, 1879 (*LD 29*, 177–78).
228. Newman, *Apo.*, 317. Further evidence for the veracity of the claim is found in the

fectly reasonable to see the correspondence between Newman and Russell as the more immediately significant: nevertheless, Jager has some claim to have been the first to introduce the argument to Newman. In writing the *Apologia*, he was prepared to acknowledge some debt to this episode in terms that certainly reflect the textual reliance of the *Prophetical Office* on the Jager letters,[229] into which "great portions" of those letters were "incorporated."[230]

Newman's first letter to Jager was published in *L'Univers religieux* on Christmas Day 1834, accompanied by Jager's reply—which was typeset in larger print than Newman's letter.[231] This publishing sleight of hand was indicative of the control of the process Jager was to exert throughout the correspondence.[232] Newman's first reply was printed on successive days at the end of January 1835 and was answered by Jager in three letters published between January 30 and March 18 of that year.[233] The first part of Newman's second response was published in *Le Moniteur religieux* in two sections, the first in

---

fact that when Newman revised *Loss and Gain* for Longman's Uniform Edition in 1874, it contained an affectionate dedication to Russell. See John Henry Newman, *Loss and Gain: The Story of a Convert*, Uniform ed. (Longmans, Green and Co., 1874).

229. Newman, *Apo.*, 140.

230. Newman, *VM 1*, xi. The correspondence is, as Allen has claimed, undoubtedly "not only in the mainstream of the perennial debate between Gallicans and Anglicans on the nature of the Church, but also part of the detailed picture of the Anglican Church which was continuously presented to French Catholic readers between 1830 and 1850." See Allen, *Newman and Jager*, 3. It certainly gives the lie to Tristram's dismissal of "the astonishing insularity of Tractarian Oxford." See Henry Tristram, "In the Lists with the Abbé Jager," in *John Henry Newman: Centenary Essays* (London: Burns, Oates and Washbourne, 1945), 203. Tristram's view seems even more unsupportable in the light of Pusey's early awareness of German Protestant biblical scholarship or Newman's reading of French and German authors (albeit, for the latter, in translation) in preparation for *Ari.*, noted in the previous chapter.

231. Allen, *Newman and Jager*, 6.

232. Jager wrote to Harrison in early 1836 to announce that he intended to publish the entire correspondence in book form containing his own answer to Newman's second response as the final word in the debate even before he had received the second part of Newman's second response (which was, in the event, never sent). The book appeared later that year as Jean-Nicholas Jager, *Le Protestantisme Aux Prises Avec La Doctine Catholique, Ou Controverses Avec Plusiers Ministres Anglicanes, Membres de l"Université d"Oxford* (Paris: Débécourt, 1836). It seems not inconceivable that Newman's decision to let the correspondence lapse was not unconnected with this precipitate and unilateral action. See Allen, *Newman and Jager*, 8.

233. Allen, *Newman and Jager*, 6.

December 1835 and the second in February 1836, alongside Jager's seventh letter and the *de facto* close of the correspondence.

Newman's argument in the correspondence with Jager sought to draw a distinction, with which the Abbé had been hitherto unfamiliar,[234] between the fundamental articles of faith, "doctrines . . . necessary for Church Communion," and other traditional teachings. The former, which Newman saw as identical with "the articles of the Creed," were to be proved from scripture, even if mediated through tradition, and had about them a fixed content, "ever one and the same, admitting of no addition and imperishable."[235] To the tradition through which this "fundamental creed"[236] was handed on, Newman gave the name "Apostolic Tradition," later "Episcopal Tradition." Of this "fundamental creed," Thomas, who is here as elsewhere, perhaps, overly anxious to point up the shortcomings of Newman's argument,[237] suggests that Newman "does not clarify its relation to the various Creeds which came into existence in the Early Church."[238] Although the correspondence with Jager does not make this relationship clear, Newman is quite clear in a letter of July 1835 in which he summarized the state of the debate for the benefit of Froude: "I will receive as necessary for Church Communion all the articles conveyed by [Apostolical Tradition]. *But I do already*. They are the Apostles Creed."[239] Newman had already confirmed to Jager that those doctrines necessary for church communion were identical to the "doctrines necessary for salvation."[240] In the same letter, Newman ascribed to this Apostolical tradition an authority that seemingly went beyond the received reading of Article VI and the strict limits he had encountered in Hawkins: "But here we come to

---

234. Thomas, *Newman and Heresy*, 186.
235. Allen, *Newman and Jager*, 36.
236. Allen, *Newman and Jager*, 40.
237. Thomas uses terms such as "rather confusing" (which he adopts following Stephen Sykes, *The Identity of Christianity* [London: SPCK, 1984], 100), as well as rather stronger language such as "*structural* incoherence" and "grotesque elaborate precision." See Thomas, *Newman and Heresy*, 186.
238. Thomas, *Newman and Heresy*, 187.
239. JHN to Richard Hurrell Froude, July 20, 1835, in *LD 5*, 103.
240. Allen, *Newman and Jager*, 40.

the other sense of Tradition, viz that strict Traditio from one hand to another, from definite person to definite person, official and exact, which I may call *Apostolical* or *Episcopal*. I will allow that such a Tradition does carry its sanction with it as fully as Scripture does."[241]

In the essay he contributed to the *British Critic* in July 1836, occasioned by the publication of "*The Brothers" Controversy*,[242] Newman was to write in similar terms: "This, then, is what is meant by Catholic tradition ... not by arguing and deducing from Scripture ... but as being a separate apostolic information, parallel with Scripture, verified by, but not subsisting in it."[243] Here he was, of course, writing against Hampden, whose appointment to the Regius Chair of Divinity at Oxford had been made in February and whom Newman considered to be entirely unsuitable to hold the post.[244] It is, however, a clear statement of the theology he had been laying out in his letters to Jager.

Newman had suggested in his first letter a second strain of tra-

---

241. JHN to Richard Hurrell Froude, July 20, 1835, in *LD 5*, 103.

242. Charles Thomas Longley and Richard Davenport, "*The Brothers" Controversy: Being a Genuine Correspondence between a Clergyman of the Church of England and a Layman of Unitarian Opinions: Chiefly on the Questions How Far Belief Is an Act of the Will; on the Use of Reason in the Study of the Bible; and How Far It Is the Duty of Unlearned Christians to Examine or Implicitly Abide by the Religion of Their Education* (London: Fellowes, 1836).

243. John Henry Newman, "'The Brothers' Controversy, Being a Genuine Correspondence between a Clergyman of The Church of England and a Layman of Unitarian Opinions," *British Critic, and Quarterly Theological Review* 20 (1836): 194. The article was rewritten and published in the Uniform Edition as "Apostolical Tradition," *Essays Critical and Historical*, 2 vols. (London: Longmans, Green and Co., 1907), 102–37 (hereafter *Ess. 1* or *Ess. 2*), where this passage, as might be imagined, had been rhetorically strengthened by the then–Roman Catholic Newman to read: "Granting that Scripture does not force on us its full dogmatic meaning, that cannot hinder us looking for that meaning elsewhere. Perhaps Tradition is able to supply both interpretation and dogma ... an Apostolical Tradition, supplementary to and interpretative of Scripture." See *Ess. 1*, 115.

244. In the note to "Apostolical Tradition," as it appeared in Newman, *Ess. 1*, 137, Newman describes the essay as "being a continuation of a series of protests" against Hampden's theology. It had been sent to Rose, for the *British Critic*, on February 12, 1836, hard upon Hampden's election to the Divinity Chair. See JHN to Hugh James Rose, February 12, 1836, in *LD 5*, 233, n. 1. See also Ker, *Newman: A Biography*, 125–26. Newman's relationship with Hampden had been strained from the first, Hampden having beaten Newman to the Chair of Moral Philosophy in March 1834. See JHN to Henry Wilberforce, March 10, 1834, in *LD 4*, 201. The two exchanged hostile and ill-tempered letters in May and June of 1835 following Newman's circulation in the Oriel Common Room of a pamphlet written by Henry Wilberforce and published anonymously. See *LD 5*, 73–74 and 83–85.

dition "in matters of doctrine not fundamental and of discipline," which here he calls "pure Tradition."[245] By July, Newman was calling this *"prophetical Tradition,"* which, in terms that would hardly have surprised Hooker, he told Froude was "the voice of the body of the Church, the received system in the Church, the spirit circulating through it and poured out through the channel of its doctors and writers... the system taught, interpretative, supplementary, applicative, of the Scripture doctrine."[246] In the first part of Newman's second letter, he elaborates the point. The "Prophetic Tradition" permeates "the body of the Church like an atmosphere.... This is that body of teaching which is offered to every individual according to his capacity... although it be not necessary to submit to it without proof."[247]

This tradition is not unproblematic, as Jager was quick to point out in terms that were not dissimilar to Froude's criticism of them.[248] Newman's distinction between articles of faith and articles of religion—the former fundamental, necessary for salvation, provable from scripture, and the ground of communion; the latter "ecclesiastical doctrines which are not fundamental"[249]—immediately begs the question of which doctrines belong in which category. Newman's earlier inclusion of the Nicene ὁμοούσιον in the latter category, suggesting that there was a distinction to be drawn between "general doctrine" of Nicaea and its terminological expression,[250] had drawn from his interlocutor the "blunt demand for him to spell out what the fundamentals are,"[251] and when he repeated the assertion in the second letter, it was clear that Newman's distinction had limitations in the way it could deal with the problem of heresy.

Jager believed that the answer to this problem lay in the authority of the church. He wrote:

---

245. Allen, *Newman and Jager*, 36.
246. JHN to Richard Hurrell Froude, July 20, 1835, in *LD 5*, 102.
247. Allen, *Newman and Jager*, 95.
248. Allen, 107. Cf. Richard Hurrell Froude to JHN, July 17, 1835, in *LD 5*, 101.
249. Thomas, *Newman and Heresy*, 189.
250. Allen, *Newman and Jager*, 86.
251. Thomas, *Newman and Heresy*, 189.

No doubt, there is a difference between apostolic tradition and prophetic exposition. The prophets or the doctors of the Church are obliged to define, to comment, to develop the mysteries of religion, and to put them within the people's reach. But as Vincent says, they must do it "while preserving the same doctrine, the same sense, the same judgment." When you develop a truth, you do not change it, on the contrary, you give it more force, more lustre, greater scope. That is what the Fathers and the Doctors of the Church did. The Church took care to warn those who had the misfortune to stray from the apostolic doctrine in their explanations, she pointed out their errors, and condemned them when necessary. And so apostolic tradition has remained pure and intact until our own day and will remain so until the end of time.[252]

In the light of the use by Newman of an exactly parallel argument in the introduction to the *Essay*, citing the same Vincentian authority to make precisely the same point Jager was making,[253] it comes as "little wonder that Jager thought he had some effect on Newman's idea of development."[254]

In fact, there are other parallels between the correspondence and Newman's later work that reveal just how significant an effect the controversy had on him. The very idea of the prophetical tradition, even if confined within the parameters Newman had applied to it, opened the door to development because, as Allen contended, "The notion of a developing agency is obviously contained in this idea of a prophetical tradition."[255] Indeed, although Newman was to assert that "to develop is not to create,"[256] Allen was surely also correct to argue that:

While proclaiming the stability of Anglican doctrine and at the same time being aware of change, Newman brings forward at various times interpretations of change which gradually expand and are clarified under his hostile gaze until at last he finds that this elaboration of arguments to render change and development explicit is beginning to act as a justification of it.[257]

252. Jager, *Le Protestantisme*, 424.
253. Newman, *Essay*, 7–27.
254. Allen, *Newman and Jager*, 18.
255. Allen, *Newman and Jager*, 16.
256. Allen, *Newman and Jager*, 95.
257. Allen, *Newman and Jager*, 12.

Pereiro suggests that to read this awareness of change within the prophetical tradition as a support for the idea of development is to invert the argument. He contends that Newman's purpose in allowing for change here is to "exclude" the development of doctrine.[258] Again, this would appear to be confusing the notion of the development of doctrine with the specifically Roman Catholic conception of it as Newman then incorrectly perceived it. Indeed, it would appear that Pereiro himself is aware of this confusion, for immediately after asserting that because, as Allen says, for Newman at the time of the Jager correspondence, "the object of faith ... itself remained identical and invariable,"[259] he admits that what was at issue was not whether there were developments in doctrine but whether "they could be imposed by the Church, as truths to be believed by the faithful."[260] Despite his assertion that "the evidence against Newman having held a theory of development before 1840 is compelling,"[261]—an assertion that was considered and called into question in the previous chapter in connection with the link between the principle of reserve and that of development identified by Selby[262]—Pereiro here explicitly admits that Newman did, indeed, hold a theory of development, at least in embryo, earlier than the exchange with Wood, and certainly by the time of the Jager correspondence.

What he is justified in arguing is that the theory of development that Newman demonstrably held at the time was one different from that which he understood the Abbé and Rome to be proposing. Newman's misconceptions of the Roman position have been alluded to earlier. Despite Jager's careful, if prolix, explanation, Newman still seemed to think that the Roman position allowed an untrammeled license to positive action to develop doctrine by Magisterial *fiat*. It was some time until he was to accept that this was not the Roman position, in fact, not until after his engagement with Wiseman that will be considered in next chapter. However, in his later years,

---

258. Pereiro, *"Ethos,"* 167.
259. Allen, *Newman and Jager*, 13.
260. Pereiro, *"Ethos,"* 167.
261. Pereiro, *"Ethos,"* 166.
262. Selby, *The Principle of Reserve*, 72–73.

particularly in the period surrounding and, more particularly, after the first Vatican Council, Newman was to encounter more than enough Roman Catholics who appeared to hold to precisely such a notion.

In view of later developments, perhaps the most surprising parallel that Newman draws in the controversy with Jager is that between the position of the Church of England and that of the Donatists. In the first part of his second letter, he admits that Anglicans stand in the same position with regard to the Roman Communion as the Donatists did to the undivided Catholic Church of the fourth and fifth centuries: that is, judged by the whole Church to be in the wrong. Newman excuses the Church of England from the same fate for reasons of the uncertainty of ecclesial authority rather than doctrinal content: "We are ... in that stage of doubt on the *universality of the teaching*, and *many bishops* share our views."[263] Newman's purpose in engaging with the Abbé had been to defend the Church of England and to expose the Roman system. It is not surprising, then, given the polemical purpose of the correspondence, Newman was not to see the inconsistency of his position. In the next chapter, the effect of his study of various heresies of the fourth and fifth centuries on his view of the case will be examined: suffice for the present to record Allen's comment that "indirectly, then, the conjunction which so startled him in 1839, of Donatists, Anglicans, and St. Augustine, had been present to his mind in 1835; without producing the dramatic effect it had later. In this point, too, though, Jager might well make a claim that his arguments had, however circuitously, produced their effect."[264]

Newman was to refine his problematical terminology in order to deal with the unresolved problem of what was fundamental and what was not when he returned to the matter in a review of the series of lectures Wiseman had given at St. Mary Moorfields in Lent 1836.[265]

---

263. Allen, *Newman and Jager*, 104.
264. Allen, *Newman and Jager*, 20.
265. "Wiseman's Lectures on the Church," *British Critic, and Quarterly Theological Review* 20 (1836): 373–403. Wiseman's lectures were published as Nicholas Wiseman, *Lectures on the Principal Doctrines and Practices of the Catholic Church*, 2 vols. (London, 1836).

Newman had reprised many of the arguments from the Jager correspondence in a series of lectures given in the Adam de Brome Chapel of the University Church throughout 1835, and responding to Wiseman's lectures gave him further opportunity to examine the material. In so doing, he chose to revise his vocabulary and to use words that Thomas has described as being "more immediately communicative": words such as "necessary" or "essential," instead of "Fundamentals." He also chose to avoid the problematical distinction between "essential" and "saving" on which Jager had pressed him so hard.[266]

In the Wiseman review, and even more so in the *Lectures on the Prophetical Office of the Church*, Newman mapped out a *via media* that was both faithful to the tradition of Hooker, Laud, and Stillingfleet and yet contained his own distinctive idea.[267] The *Lectures on the Prophetical Office* represented Newman's definitive presentation of the material from the controversy with Jager. He wrote to Maria Giberne that he had "re-written some parts of it an incredible number of times," but that he seemed "to be making way very remarkably here, in Apostolical views ... may it be supernatural."[268] That the work as first published continued to enjoy Newman's confidence can be reasonably inferred from the fact that the only change he was to make to the work when the third edition appeared in 1877[269] was the addition of a preface in which he sought to clarify "first, how far and with what argumentative force these Lectures, published just forty years since, bear upon the teaching in faith and morals of the Catholic Church, against which they were more or less directed; and next what satisfactory answer can be given in explanation of the main charges in which they issue."[270]

The product of the controversy with the Abbé was in an ecclesiological concept of the *via media* understood as expressing "the wisdom required to decide correctly the virtuous middle course

---

266. Thomas, *Newman and Heresy*, 192.
267. JHN to Richard Hurrell Froude, November 12, 1834, in *LD 4*, 360.
268. JHN to Miss M. R. Giberne, November 27, 1836, in *LD 5*, 385.
269. Newman, *VM 1*, xv–xciv.
270. Newman, *VM 1*, xv.

between alternate vices in the life of the Church."[271] Whereas Rome had defined "points of faith *beyond* Scripture," adding to the "points necessary to be believed in order for salvation," the Church of England, alone in all of Christendom it would seem, had maintained "what is agreeable to Scripture doctrine," and, using Hooker's expression, "what the Catholic Fathers and ancient bishops have collected from this selfsame doctrine."[272] It was this doctrine that Newman argued could be determined by reference to the written testimony of scripture and the writings of the Fathers of the ancient and undivided church. It was no accident that Newman chose here to quote the words of the sixteenth-century canon.[273] It was a conscious statement of Anglican orthodoxy, redolent of Hooker's assertion regarding tradition, that "neither may we in this case lightly esteem what hath been allowed as fit in the judgment of antiquity, and by the long continued practice of the whole Church."[274] Newman was proposing a church—proposing, for as he admitted in the preface to the *Lectures on the Prophetical Office*, "the *Via Media*, viewed as an integral system, has never had existence except on paper"[275]—that took a *via media* between the "infidelity" of Protestantism, whether of the continental variety or of domestic dissent, and Roman "corruption of the gospel": a church "Catholic and Apostolic, yet not Roman."[276] As Nockles has noted, in seeking to establish this "integral system," Newman was attempting "to supplement the existing incoherent [Anglican] system" so that the Church of England could "literally ... represent the church of antiquity in doctrinal fullness" in order "to compete with the Church of Rome."[277] In the hands of Pusey, this would eventually resolve into what Nockles has dubbed a "patristic

---

271. W. Allen, "Newman's Model of the Church," in *A Thankful Heart and a Discerning Mind: Essays in Honour of John Newton*, ed. John A. Newton and Mervyn Davies (London: Lonely Scribe, 2010), 172.
272. Newman, "Wiseman's Lectures on the Church," 379.
273. Gee and Hardy, *Documents Illustrative of English Church History*, 476.
274. Hooker, "Laws," 30.
275. Newman, *VM I*, 16.
276. Newman, "Lectures on the Prophetical Office," in *VM* 1, 20.
277. Nockles, *The Oxford Movement in Context*, 130.

fundamentalism,"²⁷⁸ but that would take place long after Newman had been forced to abandon the position. For the time being, the apostolicity of this *via media* would be found in its fidelity to the scripture doctrines of the written witnesses of Christian antiquity; it would be a Catholicism not guaranteed by Rome but by scripture and the Fathers; it would be a Catholicism of the Word.

278. Nockles, *The Oxford Movement in Context*, 145.

CHAPTER 3

FROM A CATHOLICISM OF THE WORD TO A CATHOLICISM OF THE CHURCH— 1839 TO 1842

Almost as soon as it was proposed, the theory of the *via media* as the guarantor of the Catholicism of the Word began to creak under the strain of Newman's continued scholarly examination and reexamination of the Christological heresies of the fourth and fifth centuries. As an ecclesiological construct, notwithstanding his comments about its essentially untried nature,[1] it served to bolster Newman's position in the Church of England and to provide him with some rational justification for his continued prejudice against the Church of Rome.[2] Nevertheless, its utility to him, even in this latter regard, was to fail as he struggled further to make sense of the early history of Christian doctrine. The structural deficiency in his argument, proposing a *via media* between the "most simplistically dogmatic and the nihilist-relativist" without examining fully the properly ecclesiological consequences was, as Cameron argues, at the heart

---

1. Newman, *VM 1*, 16. See also Newman, *Apo.*, 70–71, 73–74.
2. As late as February 1841, Newman wrote: "while Rome is what she is, union is impossible.... Rome must change first of all in her spirit. I must see more sanctity in her than I do at present. Alas! I see no marks of sanctity—or if any, they are chiefly confined to converts from us" (JHN to J. R. Bloxham, undated, in *LD 8*, 42).

133

of the weakness.³ It was one which arose from Newman's conviction at this point that those two extremes did not exist in the early church: therefore, the ecclesiological dimensions that might need to be fleshed out if the theory were to hold did not suggest themselves to him.⁴ Indeed, Dietz has suggested that the fatal flaws in the *via media* are to be found in the fact that as a "multi-faceted proposition," it begs a whole series of questions that Newman consciously avoided attempting to answer because, she argues, he knew that the answers would lead him Romeward.⁵ Whether or not that is so, the use against him of his own favored rhetorical device of historical parallelism, together with several events in the life of the Church of England in which Newman was to a greater or lesser extent a protagonist, were to reveal that the construct, when tried, lacked the robustness needed to survive. These weaknesses ensured that by 1842, he could see that the claims of this Catholicism of the Word were largely illusory.

Newman had suspected as much even as the theory was first beginning to take shape in his writings. In the text of the *Via Media*, he had written: "what has been said is but a dream, the wanton exercise, rather than the practical conclusion of the intellect."⁶ Newman came to believe that this hypothesis was dependent on a heavily confessional predetermined reading of history and that the untried nature of the theory in real life was a direct result of what he came to believe was its unreality. As Stephen Thomas observes: "The collapse of the 'Via Media' did not happen just because events turned against him, but also because he found his position inadequate to an ever-increasing, erosive, inner criticism: the *experimentum crucis* to which he refers in the *Apologia*."⁷

This chapter first looks at how Newman's continued study of heresy undermined the foundations of his Catholicism of the Word,

---

3. Euan Cameron, *Interpreting Christian History: The Challenge of the Churches' Past* (Oxford: Blackwells, 2005), 6.

4. Newman, *VM 1*, 16.

5. K. Dietz, "John Henry Newman and the Fathers of the Church: The Birth of an Ecclesiology" (S.T.D. thesis, Pontifical University of St. Thomas, Rome, 2007), 92.

6. Newman, *VM 1*, 331.

7. Stephen Thomas, *Newman and Heresy*, 202.

before moving on to a consideration of the effects on him of a series of articles by Nicholas Wiseman in the *Dublin Review*.[8] This chapter contends that the intermediate solution of "possession," which he proposed in response to Wiseman, was little more than a place-holder that was unable to stand the double assault of the response within the Church of England to Newman's Tract 90, especially from the Bishops, and the establishment of the Jerusalem bishopric. It argues that Newman came to see that the dichotomy that he had originally posed between catholicity and apostolicity was false. Furthermore, it shows that, in order to provide a sustainable hypothesis that could offer an account of the evidence of change that did not undermine his commitment to the principle of continuity in the doctrine of Christianity, Newman came to an emerging awareness of the necessity of the church as a living organ of authority. In so doing, Newman laid out, in correspondence with his brother Francis, the outlines of what would become his theory of development: one which was able to offer the possibility of determining whether a change was, to use the terminology Newman was to adopt in *An Essay on the Development of Christian Doctrine*, an authentic development or a corruption.

Researching the Monophysites

The notion of the church, with its four creedal notes, but particularly its catholicity and apostolicity, anchored in the presumed univocal written testament of Christian antiquity, lay at the heart of the 'supreme confidence" that Newman later recalled had characterized his own "controversial *status*" within the Church of England at the beginning of 1839.[9] The presumption of this unanimous testimony, which gave the theory of the *via media* its capacity to dismiss both Roman corruption and Protestant infidelity with equal ease, had be-

---

8. Nicholas Wiseman, "Tracts for the Times: Anglican Claim of Apostolical Succession," *Dublin Review* 4 (1838): 307–35; "Tracts for the Times: Anglican Claim of Apostolical Succession," *Dublin Review* 5 (1838): 285–309; and "Tracts for the Times: Anglican Claim of Apostolical Succession," *Dublin Review* 7 (1839): 139–80.

9. Newman, *Apo.*, 180.

come a given for Newman as he looked forward at the beginning of the Long Vacation of 1839 to returning to the material of early heresies. If anything, it had, indeed, been reinforced by Newman's studies of heresy prior to 1839. Even as far back as his work on the *Arians*, Newman had proceeded on the basis that the voice of orthodoxy was demonstrably univocal, and his 1835 study of Apollinarianism had especially singled out for criticism the "speculations of a self-willed and presumptuous intellect" in the face of that "which Scripture had prescribed, and the Catholic Church witnessed."[10] Newman believed that it was heresy that was pluriform and heresiarchs who were inconsistent, even self-contradictory, in their positions: it was to be expected that contradictions, inconsistencies, and incoherence would be found in the historical record of heresy. No such evidence was to be expected in the historical record of orthodoxy because it was always faithful to its Apostolic root even as it became more explicit, even as "fresh and fresh articles of faith" were necessarily defined "to secure the Church's purity" against "the rise of successive heresies and errors."[11] "Truth alone is consistent with itself," he had written in *Lectures on the Prophetical Office*.[12] When Newman turned to examine the history of the Monophysite heresy, his conviction that such a simplistic distinction could be drawn between the development of heresy and the clarification of orthodoxy was to be fatally undermined.

Newman's correspondence in July 1839 records his evident pleasure in being in residence at Oriel alone for the opportunities it gave him to return, after a gap of four years, to a systematic reading of the Fathers. In his letter to Isaac Williams, he delighted in the prospect it afforded: "I am solus in College and am likely to be—a comfort I have not had for several Long vacations—It is my hope to be able to return to my own subject, the doctrines of the Holy Trinity and the

---

10. John Henry Newman, "Apollinaris" History," 1835, B.2.5, 11, BOA.

11. It was to this remark that Newman added the note in the Uniform Edition "[Here, as above, the principle of doctrinal development is accepted as true and necessary for the Christian Church.]" in *VM* 2, 40.

12. Newman, *VM* 1, 37.

Incarnation, which I have read little or nothing about since 1835."[13]

Less than two weeks later, he wrote in reply to Frederic Rogers that although his correspondent had "no business to ask me whether I have got on with my reading in so short a time," he had done "satisfactorily," despite having "wasted some days in doing nothing":

> I have got up the question of the parentage, etc., of the works given to Dionysius the Areopagite. I have got up the history of the Eutychian controversy, got hold of the opinions of Eutyches, and the turning point of the controversy (no easy matter in Theology), have read through the Acts of the Council of Chalcedon, have got up St. Leo's works, and (though last, not least) have at length, by further reading and hunting about, *proved*, as I think, what I have long believed, that the word *Persona*, or Πρόσωπον, was not a technical word in the controversy of the Incarnation till after 350–360.[14]

This remarkable level of industriousness was, he told Rogers, to be followed by reading through the Monophysite controversy and the Nestorian in order "at once to finish Dionysius." Writing the same day to Robert Wilberforce, he explained that he hoped to "be able to finish an Edition of Dionysius of Alexandria" that he "long had on hand for the University,"[15] and in a further letter to Isaac Williams, Newman recorded that he "had got through more than I had expected."[16] He also promised Williams a paper for the Theological Society, perhaps the untitled eleven-page manuscript on the Monophysite controversy dated 1839.[17] This was one of three works on the subject that Newman produced over that summer. These provide the first written evidence of his growing unease with the *via media* as "an approximation to a required solution"[18] to the problem of reconciling what had by now become to Newman the clear evidence of doctrinal change within the fundamentally static nature of the truths of revelation.

---

13. JHN to Isaac Williams, July 1, 1839, in *LD* 7, 99.
14. JHN to Isaac Williams, July 1, 1839, in *LD* 7, 104–6.
15. JHN to R. I. Wilberforce, July 12, 1839, in *LD* 7, 106–7.
16. JHN to Isaac Williams, July 18, 1839, in *LD* 7, 110–11.
17. "Papers and Fragments on the Development of Christian Doctrine," Various dates, B.2.8, BOA.
18. Newman, *VM* 1, 31.

The three unpublished papers on the Monophysite controversy, which are dated to the summer of 1839, are of differing character and length. The untitled manuscript referred to above is the shortest of the three and, indeed, has the character of a paper intended to be heard rather than simply read: the longest is entitled *The Monophysite Heresy*, dated August 23.[19] At eighty-three manuscript pages, it is the longest of Newman's works to remain unpublished and is a systematic account of the origins and character of both Eutychianism and Monophysitism, as well as more general observations on the nature and character of heresy. The third document is found in a privately printed paper, also containing Newman's 1835 paper *Apollinarianism*.[20] In the manuscript held in the Birmingham Oratory Archives, the fourteen pages on the Monophysite controversy begin with a prefatory note in Newman's own hand that makes clear its connection with *The Monophysite Heresy*: "The following is an abstract of a MS of this date, with Notes and References."[21] Of the three works, it is the longest; *The Monophysite Heresy*, unsurprisingly, provides the fullest account of Newman's thinking concerning this particular controversy but also clear evidence of the effect that his reading had had on his confidence in the theory of the *via media*.

In its opening pages, Newman mapped out the origins of the heresy in the reaction within the Egyptian church to the challenge of Arianism: as an overreaction to the attack on Christ's divinity that the Antiochene heresy posed. Stephen Thomas observes that *The Monophysite Heresy* picked up where Newman "left off when treating of Apollinarianism,"[22] both in terms of the chronology—Newman here began the paper with an explicit dating of its *terminus post quem* in 361[23]—and in terms of "its method and schematizing the heresy."[24] Thomas's point here is to argue that Newman's own recollection in the *Apologia* is fundamentally unreliable, and he argues that,

19. John Henry Newman, "The Monophysite Heresy," August 23, 1839, B.2.9, BOA.
20. John Henry Newman, "Apollinarianism," 1835, B.2.9.a, 17–31, BOA.
21. Newman, "Apollinarianism," 17.
22. Thomas, *Newman and Heresy*, 208.
23. Newman, "The Monophysite Heresy," 1.
24. Thomas, *Newman and Heresy*, 205.

unlike many other passages in the *Apologia*, Newman's version of events here is not supported by contemporaneous evidence: that is, he cites no letters or other works in support of his memory. The language of the *Apologia* is dramatic. Newman wrote that "It was during the course of reading that for the first time a doubt came upon me of the tenableness of Anglicanism."[25] He went on:

> My stronghold was Antiquity; now here, in the middle of the fifth century, I found, as it seemed to me, Christendom of the sixteenth and the nineteenth centuries reflected. I saw my face in that mirror, and I was a Monophysite. The Church of the *Via Media* was in the position of the Oriental communion, Rome was where she is now; and the Protestants were the Eutychians.[26]

Surely, Thomas argues, if Newman's reaction to his Long Vacation reading had, indeed, been so dramatic, then:

> what particularly provokes suspicion is that Newman does not support this splendid piece of self-dramatisation by any corroboration of letters or memoranda of the time—something he always does in the *Apologia*—by drawing upon what was by 1864 a large personal archive.[27]

Benjamin King, in *Newman and the Alexandrian Fathers*, follows Thomas's line, commenting: "Yet the connection that Newman claims to have seen thereafter, between the Donatist-Anglican analogy and Monophysitism, hardly appears in Newman's work at the time."[28] It would appear, however, that King has oversimplified the rather more subtle argument that Thomas advances and overlooks those allusions in *The Monophysite Heresy* that Thomas concedes might support Newman's own record. Commenting that "what Newman does *not* draw upon to substantiate his reminiscences are the

---

25. Newman, *Apo.*, 208.
26. Newman, *Apo.*, 208–9.
27. Thomas, *Newman and Heresy*, 205.
28. Benjamin John King, *Newman and the Alexandrian Fathers*, 162. King remarks, at n. 90 on that page: "The only connection that Thomas can find in late 1839 is the 'might seem' of the first sentence of this quotation from the 1840 article 'The Catholicity of the English Church': 'The Monophysites got possession of whole districts, and might seem, if any men, identified with the local Churches in those districts'—the point being that Anglicanism 'might seem' to be identified with a district, too."

papers on Monophystism which he actually wrote in 1839,"[29] Thomas argues that this is because "they present a very different picture ... from that which he put forward in 1845, 1850 or 1864."[30]

Thomas and King do both offer persuasive evidence that the work on the Monophysites was a continuation of Newman's 1835 work on

---

29. Thomas, *Newman and Heresy*, 205.

30. Thomas, *Newman and Heresy*, 205. It is Thomas's contention that, driven by "the exigencies of later rhetorical strategies" the accounts of the events of the summer of 1839 Newman produced in the *Essay on Development*, *Difficulties of Anglicans* and the *Apologia* are "a later rhetoricisation of past experience" (204). Yet, in his analysis of *The Monophysite Heresy*—an analysis King seems to overlook entirely—Thomas points to exactly the kind of contemporaneous corroboration whose absence he claims and even offers an explanation of its tentative character, recalling that, "the sense that Newman might have been, as early as 1839, beginning unhappily to find points of correspondence between himself and the Monophysites emerges most clearly in the opening pages of *The Monophysite Heresy* (206). Thomas, in fact, does not accept this himself, despite having argued it, opting instead for what he calls the "more probable solution," that Newman did see the parallel between Monophysitism and the church of *via media* but not until later in 1839 when he encountered Wiseman's *Dublin Review* article (218). However, as will be seen in the next section of this chapter, Thomas's treatment of that later episode is deeply problematical. In drawing a conclusion that completely ignores or is unaware of evidence in two letters from Newman in the autumn of 1839, Thomas denies both Newman's own recollection and contradicts what he has claimed here as the "more probable solution."

Thomas's governing theory in *Newman and Heresy* is that the habit of historical parallelism and engagement in the polemic of his day provides the only proper hermeneutic for understanding Newman's treatment of heresy. Indeed, *Newman and Heresy* is a detailed and largely convincing analysis of Newman's intellectual history as an Anglican seen from this perspective. Occasionally, however, it seems as if this theory is read back into events rather than established by reference to them, and here is one such example. In looking at the works on Monophysitism, Thomas appears to be simply not prepared to countenance Newman's own assertion in the *Apologia* that, rather than being engaged in a controversial project in his reading over the Summer of 1839, he "was absorbed in the doctrinal question" (Newman, *Apo.*, 208). If, however, Newman's recollection of his doctrinal preoccupation is correct, then comment on sixteenth- or nineteenth-century parallels would be of at least secondary importance, if not entirely out of place. Thomas's insistence here on seeing a methodology and purpose in Newman's work on the Monophysites that prejudicially predetermined his approach to the historical record is, at best, confused. He has offered an explanation from *The Monophysite Heresy* that is at least as probable as his own chosen "more probable solution" and one which corresponds to Newman's own recollection. That this explanation does not easily cohere with Thomas's overarching theory seems a poor reason to discount it. To dismissively describe the account in the *Apologia* as a 'splendid piece of self-dramatisation" (Thomas, *Newman and Heresy*, 205) is to fail to recognize that, as Ker has argued, "Newman had every reason at the time to keep quiet about this devastating bombshell for fear of unsettling his Tractarian followers." See Ian Turnbull Ker, "Newman, Councils and Vatican II," in *Newman and Faith*, ed. Ian Turnbull Ker and Terrence Milligan (Louvain: Peeters, 2004), 122, n. 12.

Apollinarianism. The letters from Newman to Williams, Rogers, and Wilberforce in July 1839 suggest that that was precisely how Newman himself saw it.[31] The parallels that he had drawn in 1835, in both *Apollinaris' History* and in *Letter XVI*, entitled *Apollinaris* in his *Letters on the Church Fathers*, which appeared in the *British Magazine* in July 1836,[32] were used explicitly to support Newman's Tractarian position. They highlight how Apollinaris, although initially faithful to Athanasius, had, through the exercise of private judgment, gradually slipped into error and heresy. It is clearly a criticism by historical parallel of liberalism in religion, as Thomas observes: "This could almost be Blanco White: the rationalism, though the outcome of an unregenerate *ethos*, is tragically concealed from its exponent by delusion."[33] When writing for publication, lest the parallel was lost on the reader, Newman ended the account by spelling out the implications of the parallel. The story of Apollinaris illustrated for him that the Tractarian insistence on the need for precise definitions of faith was the only bulwark against the infidelity of liberalism. The historical parallels Newman had drawn in 1835 served to bolster his Tractarian position, whereas those he recalled having seen in 1839 undermined it. Such parallels could hardly be said to support Newman's "supreme confidence" in his "controversial *status*" nor to enhance his "great and still growing success, in recommending it to others."[34] A certain reserve in communicating any doubts that his reading had occasioned was only to be expected, as Thomas concedes: "To include the parallel between the Monophysites and the Tractarians in his 1839 writings would have been to turn his guns on his own friends, allies and disciples, and on the position which he still publicly stood for. He was not yet ready to do that."[35]

Scarcely less problematical than his refusal to accept Newman's

---

31. JHN to Isaac Williams, July 1, 1839, in *LD* 7, 99; JHN to Frederic Rogers, July 12, 1839, in *LD* 7, 104–6; JHN to R. I. Wilberforce, July 12, 1839, in *LD* 7, 106–7; and JHN to Isaac Williams, July 18, 1839, in *LD* 7, 110–11.

32. John Henry Newman, "Letters on the Church Fathers: Letters XVI," *British Magazine* 10 (July 1, 1836): 35–41.

33. Thomas, *Newman and Heresy*, 144.

34. Newman, *Apo.*, 180.

35. Thomas, *Newman and Heresy*, 218.

account of the 1839 parallel is Thomas's analysis of text of *The Monophysite Heresy*. He sees clearly that Newman's account of the "topology" of the various heresies "hints at a frightening sense of closeness here: if Syria was the seat of rationalism and humanitarianism, then did its antithesis, 'Egypt'—he cannot quite bring himself to write 'Alexandria'—the home of Clement, Athanasius and Cyril, eventually spawn the most perduring and divisive heresy in the history of the early Church?"[36] He also notes Newman's "certain sympathy with the Monophysite *ethos*,"[37] quoting him as observing that "As the Monophysite heresy is contrary to Arianism in doctrine, so, as might be expected, is it in its ethical character. It was far more subtle, specious and attractive to pious minds."[38] He goes so far as to suggest that here "an ominous, though dim, recognition of the face in the mirror has been registered."[39] Thomas then goes on to identify, in Newman's

> meticulously fair distinction between Eutychianism and Monophysitism ... a quite new sense of the danger of a moderate position—of a "Via Media"—in dogmatic controversies ... Newman, then, was confronted with a moderate position eschewing both Eutychianism proper and Chalcedonian orthodoxy, which maintained itself by the highly self-conscious and theoretical adoption of fine distinctions.[40]

Yet he still notes that although Newman "*may* have seen a parallel between this and his own "Via Media" ... he did not remark on it."[41]

Newman's analysis of the Monophysite heresy was essentially conservative, that is, he understood it as consisting in one of resisting dogmatic innovation. This provides Thomas with his final hint in *The Monophysite Heresy* at the disquiet the reading had engendered in Newman. He notes that between 1833 and 1839, Newman had 'so often expressed"[42] the view that innovation was the mark of heresy,

---

36. Thomas, *Newman and Heresy*, 206.
37. Thomas, *Newman and Heresy*, 206.
38. Newman, "The Monophysite Heresy," 2.
39. Thomas, *Newman and Heresy*, 207.
40. Thomas, *Newman and Heresy*, 207.
41. Thomas, *Newman and Heresy*, 207.
42. Thomas, *Newman and Heresy*, 207.

whereas here he was forced to observe that it was the Monophysites who "claimed but the use of what was already received."[43] The parallel with the Tractarian position that Rome had added to the faith is clear, and this was a matter which Newman had argued throughout his correspondence with the Abbé Jager. Although admitting that it cannot have been lost on Newman, Thomas nevertheless comments: "But, again, although we may imagine that this may have disturbed Newman, he makes little of it."[44] This is to ignore the obvious import of Newman's letter to Rogers on September 22, 1839. Written shortly after he had read the Wiseman article and realizing the force of its argument, as will be shown shortly, Newman observed to his friend that "the whole history of the Monophysites has been a sort of alterative."[45] The term "alterative" has the clear meaning of a medicine acting upon internal processes rather than causing an external reaction.[46] Thomas suggests that this letter is nothing more than further evidence that it was the occasion of Wiseman's article "rather than the scholarly researches of his closet some weeks before,"[47] that first began to undermine Newman's belief in the church of the *via media*.[48] On the contrary, the choice of a particular word with such a specific meaning, with closely associated vocabulary ("stomach-ache," "dose")[49] and the relative proximity in time to the events recalled, supports the contention that the account in the letter to Rogers is the more probable and that Newman's later recollections, although admittedly written with rhetorical purpose, are reliable. It seems at least as likely as any other explanation, particularly in the light of the evidence in the text of *The Monophysite Heresy*, and Newman's near contemporaneous recollection in the letter to Rogers, that it was, indeed, his Monophysite research that was the first intimation to him of the parallel he was soon to see more starkly.

    43. Newman, "The Monophysite Heresy," 58.
    44. Thomas, *Newman and Heresy*, 208.
    45. JHN to Frederic Rogers, September 22, 1839, in *LD 7*, 154.
    46. *Oxford English Dictionary Online*.
    47. Thomas, *Newman and Heresy*, 219.
    48. Although, as will be shown in the next section, Thomas is ultimately not prepared to concede even that.
    49. JHN to Frederic Rogers, September 22, 1839, in *LD 7*, 154.

It is important to record, at this point, that Newman's reading of the fifth-century controversies shared with his earlier work on those of the previous century that sense of a necessary but unwelcome "*Verfallstheorie* of dogmatic language," commented on by Rowan Williams in his essay "Newman's Arians."[50] By the time of *The Monophysite Heresy*, however, this goes beyond merely a change in the language to an acknowledgement that the understanding of the underlying "richer truth" has itself moved, "superseding the innocent variety of earlier days."[51] Newman's theological sympathies, again in parallel to fourth-century controversy, were with the doctrinal formulae of the *status quo ante*: then with Cyprian, now with Cyril. It is not, however, the Christological questions that primarily absorbed Newman in 1839. As Daley observes: "What is interesting in Newman's reading of these fifth and sixth century controversies over Chalcedon is that his attention is focussed almost exclusively on the questions they raised about the teaching authority in the Church."[52] It was a focus that would come to dominate Newman's search for a hypothesis to account for the difficulty of doctrinal development in the years that remained to him as an Anglican.

Wiseman's *Dublin Review* Article

In a three-part article, published in the April and October 1838 and August 1839 editions of the Catholic quarterly periodical the *Dublin Review*, Nicholas Wiseman published a review of the tracts that sought to undermine the basis upon which the principles of the Oxford Movement had been constructed. Wiseman's aim was to demonstrate as illusory the claim of the authors of the tracts, among them Pusey, Keble, and Newman, that the Church of England was a legitimate branch of the universal church, enjoying the rights, powers, and privileges of that church, and in full possession of its

---

50. Williams, "Newman's Arians," 270.
51. Williams, "Newman's Arians," 270.
52. Brian Daley, "Newman and the Alexandrian Tradition," in *Newman and Truth*, ed. Terrence Merrigan and Ian Turnbull Ker (Louvain: Peeters, 2008), 179.

sacramental and doctrinal economy through a share in Apostolic Succession.

On September 19, 1839, Newman was shown the article and the effect on him was profound, something he recorded both in correspondence at the time and in retrospective recollection.[53] That a single piece of controversialist apologetic should have such a dramatic effect on Newman seems extraordinary and demands explanation. His reaction would, in the absence of his Monophysite research, suggest that the claim on Newman of the hypothesis of the *via media* was fragile in the extreme. It is critical to understanding how Newman came to abandon the church of the *via media*, with its claims to apostolicity grounded in the Catholicism of the Word, to establish why he should have reacted so strongly to the article and its claims. Particular attention must be given to the manner in which Wiseman put his case and to Newman's theological preoccupations at the time, both of which made him particularly susceptible to Wiseman's argument.

Furthermore, if the article had such an effect on Newman, its effect on the other leaders of the movement also needs to be considered. In order to be able to attempt to address these issues, it is necessary to look closely at both the form and the substance of Wiseman's article, at Newman's entries in his diaries at this point, his correspondence, and his other works, together with the correspondence of the other Tractarians. This analysis demonstrates that Newman's reaction was determined in no small measure by Wiseman's compelling use of a methodology that closely echoed Newman's own. Considering the particular theological questions that had occupied him in the early part of 1839 and the distinctive nature of the ecclesiology of the *via media*, Newman's reaction to Wiseman's article will be shown to be almost unavoidable and the lack of reaction in the other leaders of the movement scarcely surprising. Although in the later months of 1839 and in 1840, Newman appeared to regain much

---

53. JHN to Frederic Rogers, September 22, 1839, and October 3, 1839, *LD* 7, 154–55, 150–60; JHN to S. F. Wood, September 29, 1839, in *LD* 7, 156–57; JHN to J.W. Bowden, October 20, 1839, and November 4, 1839, in *LD* 7, 166–68, 177; the unsent letter to Robert Williams of November 10, 1839, in *LD* 7, 180; Henry Wilberforce, "F. Newman's Oxford Parochial Sermons," *Dublin Review* (*New Series*) 12 (1869): 327; and Newman, *Apo.*, 116–18.

of his prior confidence in Anglicanism, it will show that the ultimate effect of Wiseman's article was to force Newman to recognize that the Church of England could not provide him with the hypothesis he needed to account for the difficulty of doctrinal development.

Founded in 1836, the *Dublin Review* was a Catholic quarterly with which Nicholas Wiseman was intimately connected. Wiseman had been awarded his DD after public examination before he was quite twenty-two years old, held a Roman professorship at twenty-five, and became rector of the Venerable English College in Rome at twenty-seven.[54] He was to be consecrated a bishop at the unusually early age of thirty-seven and later, in 1850, became the first Archbishop of Westminster and the first cardinal resident in England since the death of Pole nearly three hundred years earlier. On a brief return to England in 1835, Wiseman had been concerned about the small number of English Catholics capable of, or interested in, entering into discussion with non-Catholics. In establishing the *Dublin Review*, which he edited jointly with Michael Quinn and Daniel O'Connell, he hoped to provide a means of addressing Catholic issues and of responding to non-Catholic critics. The *Dublin Review* soon acquired a wide readership, and by the autumn of 1839, it was not in any sense surprising that former Oxford acquaintances of Newman such as Henry Manning, then a rural dean in Sussex, or Robert Williams, a banker, barrister, and Tory MP for Dorchester, would be reading it and drawing Wiseman's articles to his attention.

The article that both Manning and Williams placed before Newman in September 1839[55] was a paradigmatic example of what Wiseman had intended the *Dublin Review* to achieve. It was a serious engagement by a Catholic author (in this case Wiseman himself) with the ideas and discourse of non-Catholics: in this case, the theology of the tracts, particularly with the notion of Apostolical Succession,

---

54. For an account (albeit hardly impartial) of Wiseman's stratospheric trajectory, see Wilfrid Philip Ward, *The Life and Times of Cardinal Wiseman*, 2 vols. (London: Longmans, Green and Co., 1912). See also Richard J Schiefen, *Nicholas Wiseman and the Transformation of English Catholicism* (Shepardstown, W.Va.: Patmos Press, 1984), which strikes a less breathless tone and sees Wiseman's rise as less unstoppably inevitable.

55. By Williams, in person, see September 19, 1839, in *LD* 7, 153, and by Manning, by way of correspondence, H. E. Manning to JHN, September 17, 1839, in *LD* 7, 153–54.

which underpinned, both for Newman and the other Tractarians, the notion of the *via media*.[56] The subject of Apostolical Succession held a central place in the tracts, occurring in the titles of no fewer than five[57] (three by Newman) and central to the treatment of the particular subject matter in twenty-nine others. Taken together with the Branch Theory and the *via media*, this was the ground that Wiseman set out to occupy.

In the article, published in three parts in 1838 and 1839, Wiseman purported to review the tracts.[58] The review was not, however, a simple literary assessment of the tracts but a systematic, concerted, and sustained attack on their theology. It would be a mistake, however, to view this as an attack conceived aggressively. Wiseman wrote: "The times, Heaven knows, are sufficiently bad. It is a work of charity to try to mend them. The collection of Tracts . . . which forms the three volumes before us, was published for this purpose. As a well-intentioned attempt, it deserves our sympathy."[59] Nor should this be seen as a case of Wiseman patronizing the "well-known knot of divines at or from Oxford,"[60] still less damning them with faint praise. He not only knew the quality of his interlocutors but also respected them, within limits: "Will they succeed? We firmly believe they will: nay, strange to say, we hope so. As to patching up, by their prescriptions, the worn-out constitution of the poor old English Church, it is beyond human power."[61]

Wiseman recognized that he would have to take on the arguments of these interlocutors using the self-same methods with which they had first advanced them. While Catholic apologetic since the sixteenth century had most often been expressed in the categories and

56. For background to this revival in Anglican claims to Apostolical Succession, see Nockles, *The Oxford Movement in Context*, 146–83.

57. Tracts 4, 15, 19, 24, and 74, the first four in *Tracts 1*; the last in *Tracts 3*. Keble had written number 4; Newman numbers 15, 19, and 74; and Harrison number 24.

58. Nicholas Wiseman, "Tracts for the Times: Anglican Claim of Apostolical Succession," *Dublin Review* 4: 307–35; "Tracts for the Times: Anglican Claim of Apostolical Succession," *Dublin Review* 5: 285–309; and "Tracts for the Times: Anglican Claim of Apostolical Succession," *Dublin Review* 7: 139–80.

59. Wiseman, *Dublin Review* 4, 307.
60. Wiseman, *Dublin Review* 4, 308.
61. Wiseman, *Dublin Review* 4, 308.

language of the controversies of that century, Wiseman realized that if he were to achieve his purpose, he would have to go further back. In his *Lectures on Justification*, Newman had done the same to present an approach to the classic Catholic/Protestant difference regarding faith and good works. To deal with the present issue, therefore, Wiseman would do the same. "Antiquity and authority are their watchwords,"[62] he noted and so those would be the tools he used to counter them.

In the first two parts, Wiseman concentrated on arguments from authority to attempt to prove that "the Anglican Church could not sustain any claim on her part to a share in apostolical succession."[63] He believed that, in doing so, he had proved beyond a shadow of doubt that the Church of England was, at the very least, in a state of schism from the Catholic Church. In the third part, it was his intention to deliver the *coup de grace* to the ecclesiology of the Tractarians, using the witness of antiquity, demonstrating that the Church of England was not just in a state of schism but, "according to the principles of the ancient Church," that such a state of schism "is a state of sin, of outlawry, and deprivation."[64] The third part begins with a restatement of what Wiseman claimed to have achieved in the earlier parts and a rehearsal of the methodology he had adopted thus far, including those concessions that he had made to Anglicanism, "in order to simplify the controversy."[65] He went on to make a further concession: that for the sake of progress, he was prepared to lay aside any charge of heresy against Anglicans and proceed solely on the basis of the charge of schism. Although he by no means conceded that Anglicans were not heretics and believed that it was practically improbable that a schismatic should remain long a schismatic without falling into heresy,[66] Wiseman recognized that to insist on this position would be to introduce a deeply controversial and emotive

---

62. Wiseman, *Dublin Review* 4, 308.
63. Wiseman, *Dublin Review* 7, 140.
64. Wiseman, *Dublin Review* 7, 141.
65. Wiseman, *Dublin Review* 7, 139.
66. Wiseman, *Dublin Review* 7, 141, where he cites both Augustine and Jerome as patristic authorities for this position.

issue that need not be addressed in fulfilling his present purpose. He wrote that his objective in this third article was to demonstrate that the counsels of antiquity were against even the possibility of the Branch Theory[67] and that his chosen method would be to examine the question "by the light of antiquity and judge it entirely by the rules laid down and determined by the fathers of the primitive Church."[68]

Wiseman took as his example the case of the conflict between St. Augustine and the Donatists. While he was at pains to lay out the ecclesiological terms of the controversy, he gave no detailed account of the underlying historical background or doctrinal differences at issue. At first glance, this might appear to be an oversight or a lack of thoroughness on his part; it is, in truth, the methodological key to the theological core of his argument. Wiseman confined his argument tightly to an attempt to use the voice of antiquity to convict the English church of schism: all other issues, doctrinal, sacramental, or historical, were surplus to his apologetic requirements. That is not to say that he did not use particular parallels to drive home the point: he drew a parallel between the position of Lucilla, whose opposition to Caecilian had done so much to occasion the Donatists' crisis, with that of Anne Boleyn as an agent of the schism,[69] as he does the issue of the confiscation of sacred vessels by the Donatists with the dissolution of the monasteries,[70] and that both justified their actions by reference to supposed corruptions.[71] He even notes that both the Donatists and the Tractarians insisted on being called Catholics[72] and that both held themselves to be a "branch" of the Church Catholic.[73] Wiseman's examination of the Donatist controversy was, he contended, applicable to the case of Anglicanism, even if some of the details of the parallels are somewhat strained or distorted be-

---

67. The idea that the [Roman] Catholic Church, the Orthodox Church, and the Church of England (and its communion) were three legitimate branches of the one Catholic Church.
68. Wiseman, *Dublin Review* 7, 143.
69. Wiseman, *Dublin Review* 7, 144.
70. Wiseman, *Dublin Review* 7, 144–45.
71. Wiseman, *Dublin Review* 7, 149, 150, and 155.
72. Wiseman, *Dublin Review* 7, 146.
73. Wiseman, *Dublin Review* 7, 160.

cause the fundamental parallel is not dogmatic but ecclesiological.[74] This methodology allowed Wiseman to look in detail at the manner in which the Catholic Fathers dealt with the Donatists and then let the parallels speak for themselves with regard to the position of the Anglican Church.

The primary means by which the Catholic Church attempted to deal with the Donatists was in denying the latter's claim to be a part of the Catholic Church. This response was, Wiseman said, "simple and clear"[75] and consisted in demonstrating "the fact of the Donatist Church, however numerous its Bishops and its people, being excluded from communion by other Churches."[76] Wiseman quotes both Optatus and then Augustine in his letters against Parmenianus, Petilianus, and Cresconius "as sufficient to prove that the Churches in communion must be true to the exclusion of all that stand in separation from them."[77] He then noted that, just as the Donatists justified their separation from Catholic communion on the grounds of the alleged corruption of the Catholic Church, so did Anglicans. Citing both the *Book of Homilies* and John Jewel's, *The Apology of the Church of England*, as precise parallels with the Donatist argument, Wiseman quoted St. Augustine as authority. He wrote: "Either the Church was so corrupted before your reformers came, that it had ceased to be the Church of God, or not. If it was, then had Christ's promise failed, which secured perpetuity to his Church; if not, whence did those who separated from it derive their authority?"[78] This argument, it seems, was sufficient for Wiseman, as he observed: "These passages hardly require any comment; any reader of ordinary judgment will see how St. Augustine must, upon his principles, have judged the case of the English Church.... These principles, if applied to the modern controversy, will go a great way towards deciding the respective positions of the Catholic and Anglican Churches."[79] This

---

74. Wiseman, *Dublin Review* 7, 143.
75. Wiseman, *Dublin Review* 7, 148.
76. Wiseman, *Dublin Review* 7, 148.
77. Wiseman, *Dublin Review* 7, 149.
78. Wiseman, *Dublin Review* 7, 153.
79. Wiseman, *Dublin Review* 7, 153.

must hold, he argued, even if the doctrinal differences are not in any sense parallel between the case of the Donatists and the Anglicans, since it is necessary that there is some method by which such differences, whatever they may be, can practically be judged. Antiquity itself, in the person of Augustine, provided just such a method: "Qua propter securus iudicat orbis terrarum, bonos non esse qui se dividunt ab orbe terrarum in quaecumque parte orbis terrarum."[80]

The remaining twenty-five pages of Wiseman's article are given over to working out the consequences of this primary argument and dealing with any possible objections he can foresee. Wiseman continued to resort to the authority of the Fathers to show that "it is easy at once to ascertain who are the Church Catholic, and who are in a state of schism, by simply discovering who are in communion with the See of Rome, and who are not."[81] In support of this contention, Wiseman quoted not only Augustine but Ambrose, Jerome, Aurelian, John of Constantinople, Gregory the Great, and even the Third Council of Carthage, which warned Catholics to be on their guard against Donatist Bishops, "ne quis Donatistorum cum honore suo recipiatur sed in numero laicorum."[82] The overall impression reading the article is of Wiseman seeking to and—in the light of future events—succeeding in delivering an almost interminable series of patristic blows against the ecclesiological arguments of the Tractarians and any possible justification for them. The style is consistent and utterly relentless, indeed, Wiseman admitted as much: "We here close our article, not from want of materials, but from fear of wearying."[83] He had set out to use the voice of antiquity against the arguments of the Tractarians, and he believed that he had successfully done so:

The voice of antiquity is, therefore, clear and loud upon the claims to apostolical succession of any Church involved in schism, that is, which is not in communion with other Churches, and especially with that of Rome. Implicated in a crime which no possible circumstances can justify; exercising

---

80. Wiseman, *Dublin Review* 7, 154, quoting from St. Augustine, *Contra Epistolam Permaniani*, bk. III, ch. IV, para. 24, in PL 43: 101.
81. Wiseman, *Dublin Review* 7, 163.
82. Wiseman, *Dublin Review* 7, 175.
83. Wiseman, *Dublin Review* 7, 180.

their functions, even when validly, still without profit to the souls of men; styled wolves rather than shepherd; admitted into the Church only as laymen—can bishops so characterized have been considered by the ancient Church descendants and representatives of the apostles?[84]

Although he had already seen it, Newman's attention was again drawn to Wiseman's article on September 19, 1839, by Robert Williams. The tone of Williams's correspondence with Newman suggests that, despite his own achievements, he still related to Newman in many ways as a student overly eager to impress a don. On a visit to Oxford, he showed Newman the article. Newman's recollection of the event in the *Apologia* records that, on first reading, he "did not see much in it,"[85] until Williams drew to his particular attention "the palmary words of St. Augustine ... Securus judicat orbis terrarium."[86] He wrote that the effect on him of hearing Williams repeat those words time and again was as the effect on Dick Whittington hearing the bells of London calling him to return or of Augustine hearing the child's voice repeating the phrase "Tolle lege, tolle lege."[87] Newman recorded that Augustine's words "gave a cogency to the Article, which had escaped me at first. They decided ecclesiastical questions on a simpler rule than that of Antiquity ... here then Antiquity was deciding against itself ... the theory of the Via Media was absolutely pulverized."[88]

The kind of "corroborative evidence from the period in question" that Thomas finds lacking in the account of the parallel with Monophysitism[89] is, however, available with regard to the account of the effect on Newman of the Wiseman article. For example, Newman's letter to Frederic Rogers on September 22, 1839, in which he wrote of the effect of reading the article, Newman admitted: "I have had the first real hit from Romanism which has happened to me.... I seriously think this is a most uncomfortable article on every account ...

84. Wiseman, *Dublin Review* 7, 175.
85. Newman, *Apo.*, 211.
86. Newman, *Apo.*, 211.
87. Newman, *Apo.*, 212.
88. Newman, *Apo.*, 212.
89. Thomas, *Newman and Heresy*, 219.

there is an uncomfortable vista opened which was closed before."[90] This language is strikingly similar to that recalled by Henry Wilberforce in an article for the *Dublin Review* in 1869, where he records Newman as having confided to him an "astounding confidence" in October 1839 that "for the first time since I began the study of theology, a vista has been opened up before me, to the end of which I do not see."[91]

Wilberforce also recalled Newman as being resolved of the importance of a reply to Wiseman: "It is quite necessary that I should give a satisfactory answer to it, or I shall have the young men around me ... going over to Rome."[92] The necessity of a response he had certainly alluded to in the letter to Rogers, and he made similar remarks in a letter to S. F. Wood on September 29, 1839, where he refers to his desire to persuade Keble to answer the article and to hear Pusey's views on the matter.[93] In November, Newman wrote to Bowden in clear terms: "You should read the late article in the Dublin—it is the best thing that Dr Wiseman has put out. It is paralleling the English Church and the Donatists; and certainly the parallel is very curious—the only question is whether Augustine's notions are Catholic on this point—*he* certainly does seem to make for Dr. W."[94]

Later in the same month, writing this time to Robert Williams—a letter written but not sent—Newman used similar language to that he had used earlier to Wood, and which Henry Wilberforce recalled.[95] Here he suggests that he has yet to have the "view" that might lead to Rome, whereas he had earlier suggested to Wood and, assuming that his (Wilberforce's) recollection is accurate, to Wilberforce that he had already seen the "vista," even if he was not sure to where it would lead. Nevertheless, allowing for his intent in urging caution on Williams, the imagery Newman chose is sufficiently consistent

---

90. JHN to Frederic Rogers, September 22, 1839, in *LD* 7, 154–55.
91. Wilberforce, "Oxford Parochial Sermons," 327.
92. Wilberforce, "Oxford Parochial Sermons," 327.
93. JHN to S. F. Wood, September 29, 1839, in *LD* 7, 156–57. For a consideration of the wider Tractarian engagement with the competing claims of catholicity and antiquity in the development of doctrine, see Pereiro, "*Ethos*," 130–85.
94. JHN to J. W. Bowden, November 4, 1839, in *LD* 7, 177.
95. JHN to Robert Williams, November 10, 1839, in *LD* 7, 180.

to provide corroboration for Wilberforce's recollection. His later recollection in *Apologia* is of an almost evanescent experience: what Newman had seen was, as he was later to say, a ghost.[96]

It is not only the use of language that prefigures Newman's later work, nor that it was written but not sent, that is remarkable about the letter to Williams: the nervousness it conveys is also striking. In it, Newman can offer Williams no better an argument against Wiseman than the risk of private judgment leading one into making a move that might later be wrong. Such prudential caution, such care in the exercise of private judgment, is characteristic of Newman—in many respects, the *Apologia* is an extended account of that caution—but here, particularly if Frank Turner's argument is correct that Newman's preoccupation at the time was the behavior of the younger members of the Oxford Movement (an argument that can hardly account for Newman not having sent the letter to Williams),[97] it seems inadequate. Newman appears to have recognized the unsatisfactory nature of the letter. Sending it to Wood, he wrote: "I have stupidly written the inclosed [sic] on half a sheet, and have so miserably written it that you will be plagued by reading it."[98] If Turner's thesis is to be maintained, and the effect of the Wiseman article had not been nearly as dramatic as claimed, the weakness of the unsent letter to Williams, written when Newman was composing his response for the *British Critic*, an article certainly complete by November 29, 1839,[99] is inexplicable.[100]

Newman had not claimed that his research into the Monophysites had changed his entire view of the *via media*. In writing the letter to Rogers on September 22, 1839, that has already been cited,

---

96. Newman, *Apo.*, 213.
97. Turner, *The Challenge*, 337.
98. JHN to S. F. Wood, November 10, 1839, in *LD* 7, 181.
99. JHN to Mrs. John Mozley, November 29, 1839, in *LD* 7, 187.
100. Thomas offers a different account than Turner. In looking to discount Newman's account of the effect of the Monophysite research and suggesting that it was only after receiving the "hit" from Wiseman that Newman came to see "an analogy between the 'Via Media' and Monophysitism" (Thomas, *Newman and Heresy*, 218), Thomas accords the Wiseman article a greater significance than does Turner. Nevertheless, he, too, seems determined to overlook the language Newman used. Newman had not claimed that his research into the Monophysites had changed his entire view of the *via media*.

Newman made the explicit claim that the Monophysite research had been "a sort of alterative" to which Wiseman's article was the "dose" and one which had given him a "stomach-ache."[101] As shown when looking earlier, in considering Thomas's critique,[102] this was the use of a very precise expression, which, given the use of related vocabulary ("stomach-ache" and "dose"), admits of only tight construction. Newman was not suggesting that the Monophysite parallel had been a major crisis but that it had unsettled him such that the force of the Wiseman article was able to do real damage.[103] In the absence of other evidence that calls into question the reliability of each and every recollection of an individual, even a recollection of an experience less than six weeks old, this is exactly the sort of evidence that accords with the "common sense ... view that individuals have private access to their own experiences" the recollection of which is, indeed, "uncriticisable."[104] It was, indeed, precisely the interior unsettling of his position caused by the "alterative" of the Monophysite episode that made possible the exterior reaction to the "dose" of the Wiseman article.

Newman's own account of the effect of the Wiseman article on him in the *Apologia*, albeit an account of theological controversy later recollected in tranquility, would appear, on the basis of the contemporaneous evidence, to be substantially accurate. Early the following year, Newman wrote again to Bowden. Using imagery that, as will be seen, would reoccur in the *Essay*, Newman leaves no doubt as to the magnitude of the effect upon him of Wiseman's article:

101. JHN to Frederic Rogers, September 22, 1839, in *LD* 7, 154.
102. See n. 30.
103. Thomas Fergusson, "The Enthralling Power: History and Heresy in John Henry Newman," *Anglican Theological Review* 85, no. 4 (2003): 654–59.
104. Thomas, *Newman and Heresy*, 218. Yet still Thomas is unwilling to concede the veracity of Newman's own account, arguing against such a "common sense" view. He suggests, instead, that what is going on in the "remarkable piece of introspection" that forms the body of Newman's November 24, 1843, letter to his brother-in-law, James Mozley (*LD* 10, 29), is the existence of "two rhetorics, two patterns of argument proceeding coterminously: the one, centred on Monophysitism, is submerged, an erosive inner inquest, Newman's own rhetoric turned upon himself; the other is both a public argument to justify the continuing viability of Tractarianism, *and* an attempt, only partially successful, to quieten the working of the inner counter-pattern of argument, which he only embraced unreservedly after 1843" (219).

As to Dr Wiseman's article I do not think you have hit the point of it. It made a very great impression here—and, to say what of course I would only say to such as yourself, it made me for a while very uncomfortable in my own mind. He maintains first that the present *look* of Christendom is such, that St. Austin or St. Basil coming among us would say at once, "*That* is the Catholic Church—and *those* are heretics" meaning Rome and us respectively.[105]

The previous month, Newman had similarly written to Pusey to express the discomfort Wiseman had caused him: "since I read Dr. W's article I have desponded much—for, I said to myself, if even I feel myself pressed hard, what will others who have either not thought so much on the subject or have fewer retarding motives?"[106]

The evidence from Newman's letters, diaries, and literary output suggests that one significant reason why the effect on him was comparatively so intense may have been that he had been occupied with purely theological questions for well over a year prior to his exposure to the article, whereas the other Tractarian leaders had quite other preoccupations. Pusey had spent the four years up until 1839 with children of fragile health and an increasingly incapacitated wife, who died in May of that year. His own correspondence at the time is unsurprisingly filled with touching sorrow, although he does find time late in the year to advert to the Wiseman article.[107] Seeking evidence in support of the Anglican position against Wiseman, Pusey enquired of Manning: "Do you know any other (other than Hammond on Schism) good clear book, shewing that the absence of inter-communion does not involve schism?"[108] Several weeks later, he asked Manning to research evidence regarding the relative sizes of Eastern Orthodox churches with the purpose of further attacking Wiseman's premise.[109] These are the only extant letters of Pusey on the controversy, and they are all to Manning, who had clearly been struck by the Wiseman article when it was first published. By the time

---

105. JHN to J. W. Bowden, February 21, 1840, in *LD* 7, 241.
106. JHN to E. B. Pusey, January 15, 1840, in *LD* 7, 214.
107. Pusey to Manning, December 11, 1839, in Henry Liddon, ed., "Correspondence of Dr Pusey, Liddon Bound Volumes," vol. 109, 39, Dr. Pusey's Library Archives, Pusey House.
108. Pusey to Manning, December 26, 1839, in *LD* 7, 40.
109. Pusey to Manning, February 4, 1840, in *LD* 7, 41.

he received the letters from Pusey, Manning had already written to Newman expressing his concern that he was "half glad to find it, and three-fourths afraid of it."[110] By coincidence, Newman received Manning's letter on the very same day that Williams had shown him the article. Keble's correspondence at the time is filled with the parochial concerns of the vicar of Hursley and with the ill-starred scheme for the Church of the Holy Saviour, Leeds. In none of his correspondence does he make any reference either to the Wiseman article or the effect that it was having on Newman or anyone else. Similar practical considerations fill the letters at this time of the other Oxford men such as the Wilberforces and Gladstone: Newman's life at the time contained none of these distractions. Newman had become editor of the *British Critic* in February 1838 (Skinner describes the publication having been "commandeered" in a kind of Tractarian *putsch*)[111] and set about turning it into the organ of Tractarian opinion that some already assumed it was.[112] The tracts continued, Newman gave a further series of lectures in the Adam de Brome Chapel at the University Church,[113] and he was, as has been seen, engaged in a reading of the Fathers that fully occupied his time. It seems reasonable to conclude that, in the absence of the distractions of pastoral or familial duties and, therefore, fully "absorbed in the doctrinal question,"[114] the effect of Wiseman's article was much greater upon Newman than it could have been on the other Tractarians.

Another significant reason for Newman's reaction, and a further reason to distinguish him from Pusey and Keble, was his own theological history. Whereas the other two were profoundly grounded (Keble from childhood) in High Church ecclesiology, Newman had had to work his own way to it. Pusey and Keble were the direct inheritors of the ecclesiological tradition of Hooker, carried down to them through the Caroline Divines and the Non-jurors of the sev-

---

110. H. E. Manning to JHN, September 17, 1839, in *LD* 7, 153.

111. Simon Skinner, *Tractarians and the "Condition of England": The Social and Political Thought of the Oxford Movement* (Oxford: Clarendon Press, 2004), 31.

112. Ker, *Newman: A Biography*, 158.

113. Later published as John Henry Newman, "Tract 85: Lectures on the Scripture Proofs of the Doctrines of the Church" (J. G. F. and J. Rivington, 1838), in *Tracts 5*.

114. Newman, *Apo.*, 208.

enteenth century and by those such as Jones of Nayland who had kept the flame of High Church tradition alive following the suppression of Convocation and the dry season of eighteenth-century Latitudinarianism. The operative ecclesiological model was that of the seventeenth-century unity of king, church, and state,[115] justified for Pusey on the basis of divine act witnessed by history and for Keble on the authority of sacred scripture. The Church of England they might dearly wish to have reformed in a very particular way, but it was their church, and they saw it as a given.

Newman was from a different stable. Despite his remark that he did "not expect anything so blessed again, Charles is the King, Laud the Prelate, Oxford the sacred city, of this principle,"[116] this was not an ecclesiology with which he had grown up. The convert to Anglican Calvinism who, through the Gathers, pastoral ministry among the humble parishioners of St. Clement's, and the company of the other Tractarians had become a sacramental catholic,[117] had every reason to adopt this ecclesiology. He did adopt it, but largely as a theoretical system in abstract rather than as one first experienced as a concrete lived reality. Because his ecclesiology was, at this point, primarily an intellectual construct, he was concerned to ensure a "harmony of parts" within his theoretical model.[118] This meant that he faced a problem. The fact that Branch Theory resulted in "Popery in Rome and Zwingli-Lutheranism in England ... was a difficulty for Newman, although not for Palmer or the old High Churchmen,"[119] nor even for Keble and Pusey, for whom it was a lived, experienced, and largely comfortable reality. Newman's theological development had led him to attempt to work out his ecclesiology from first principles, and this attempt contained within it the seeds of its own downfall. His reading of the Fathers and his Mediterranean journey of 1832 and 1833 had brought about a realization that "there was something greater than the Established Church, and that was the Church Cath-

115. Skinner, *Tractarians*, 87–133.
116. Skinner, *Tractarians*, 121.
117. Ker, *Newman: A Biography*, 21–23.
118. Nockles, *The Oxford Movement in Context*, 174.
119. Nockles, *The Oxford Movement in Context*, 174.

olic and Apostolic."[120] If there was indeed this "something greater," it was a work of necessity for Newman to establish what it was and how the Church of England was related to it. That task had given him the church of the *Via Media* and, while the theory of the *via media* held, all was well and good, but the combined efforts of Eutyches and Wiseman had left it looking decidedly fragile. It was the development of his understanding of patristic ecclesiology, confirmed by his reading of Wiseman, that compelled him "to acknowledge that his theory of the *via media* had failed ... such was the realization that shattered Newman's Anglo-Catholic allegiance."[121]

It was to be another six years before he finally submitted to the logic of what he had first confronted in the Long Vacation of 1839. Nevertheless, from the moment Williams's insistent repetition of Augustine's words had made such a firm impression upon him, Newman was set on a very specific course. It was one that Newman's own theological history, personal circumstances, and controversialist methodology had predisposed him to take and, "the stomachache, the leak, the vista, the shadow of a hand, the ghost, the rising spirit, the opening heaven, like the Monophysite in the mirror and the incantatory power of the words themselves, convey Newman's subtle movement."[122] The evidence in the documentary record is such that the very particular effect that the article had on Newman should provoke little surprise, notwithstanding the skepticism of Kingsley, Thomas, and Turner. Nicholas Wiseman had written such an article, in such a manner and at such a time, that Newman was almost bound to have reacted in the way he did.

Newman did not long languish in the uncertainty that Wiseman's article had provoked. He was later to describe his state of mind as one of excitement and recalled that: "After a while, I got calm, and at length the vivid impression faded away."[123] Indeed, the language of

---

120. Newman, *Apo.*, 95.
121. Avery Dulles, "Newman: The Anatomy of a Conversation," in *Newman and Conversion*, ed. Ian Turnbull Ker (Edinburgh: T & T Clark, 1997), 29.
122. Sheridan Gilley, *Newman and His Age* (London: Darton, Longman and Todd, 1990), 190.
123. Newman, *Apo.*, 213.

the *Apologia* concerning this period is among the most vivid in that entire work. He wrote:

I had seen the shadow of a hand upon the wall. It was clear that I had a good deal to learn on the question of the Churches, and that perhaps some new light was coming upon me. He who has seen a ghost, cannot be as if he had never seen it. The heavens had opened and closed again. The thought for the moment had been, "The Church of Rome will be found right after all"; and then it had vanished. My old convictions remained as before.[124]

The imagery is, as has been shown, consistent with that used in contemporaneous comment and correspondence,[125] but the passage contains within it an apparent difficulty. How, if the impressions had been so very vivid, did they so readily vanish?

The answer to this apparent evanescence may be found in the allusions Wilberforce recalled and which are encountered in the correspondence with Rogers and Wood. Wiseman's article had caused Newman to be concerned at the possibility that its arguments would cause "young men around [him] . . . going over to Rome."[126] Newman's reference in the *Apologia* to the sermon "Divine Calls" provides further evidence of his state of mind at the time, within which such impressions could be both experienced so powerfully and yet fade from view. Newman's conception of faith as an act of the will, assisted by divine grace, is succinctly but powerfully captured in the passage of the sermon that he quotes in the *Apologia*:

O that we could take that simple view of things, as to feel that the one thing which lies before us is to please God! What gain is it to please the world, to please the great, nay even to please those whom we love, compared with this? What gain is it to be applauded, admired, courted, followed,—compared with this one aim, of "not being disobedient to a heavenly vision"? What can this world offer comparable with that insight into spiritual things, that keen faith, that heavenly peace, that high sanctity, that everlasting righteousness, that hope of glory, which they have, who in sincerity love and follow our Lord Jesus Christ? Let us beg and pray Him day by day to reveal Himself to our souls more fully, to quicken our senses, to give us sight

---

124. Newman, *Apo.*, 213.
125. See n. 53.
126. Wilberforce, "Oxford Parochial Sermons," 327.

and hearing, taste and touch of the world to come; so to work within us, that we may sincerely say, "Thou shalt guide me with Thy counsel, and after that receive me with glory. Whom have I in heaven but Thee? and there is none upon earth that I desire in comparison of Thee. My flesh and my heart faileth, but God is the strength of my heart, and my portion for ever."[127]

The "old convictions" to which Newman referred provide a further clue. They were, he recalled in the *Apologia*, "the principle of dogma, the sacramental system and anti-Romanism."[128] As recently as 1838, Newman had written, in Tract 83 of Rome as the Anti-Christ,[129] and it is far from clear that the distinction between the city of Rome and the Church of Rome that he made in the *Apologia* is as clear in either that tract or, as he claimed, in *Home Thoughts from Abroad*.[130] The language of the comment to Wilberforce and the correspondence with Rogers and Wood is clear enough, and Newman's residual anti-Romanism is corroborated in these two nearly contemporaneous works. The fact that he was able to return to the field of controversy so quickly, with his attempted refutation of Wiseman's article in his own "Catholicity of the English Church" in the January 1840 issue of the *British Critic*,[131] should not be taken as evidence of the unreliability or mendacity of the account in the *Apologia*, as Newman's critics, Thomas and Turner among them, have suggested. It is more likely to have been the reaction of one for whom what he claimed to have seen simply did not accord with what he thought possible. It may also be further evidence of the Tractarian habit of continually practicing the principle of reserve. If Rome was Anti-Christ, then the momentary thought that "The Church of Rome will be found right after all"[132] was a notion of antecedent improb-

---

127. JHN, Sermon 542, "Divine Calls," preached October 27, 1839, in St. Mary the Virgin, Oxford, in *Parochial and Plain Sermons*, vol. 8 (London: Longmans, Green and Co., 1907), 2, and quoted in Newman, *Apo.*, 213–14.

128. Newman, *Apo.*, 216.

129. "Tract 83: Advent Sermons on Anti-Christ" (J. G. F. and J. Rivington, 1838), 71, in *Tracts 4*.

130. Newman, *Apo.*, 217.

131. John Henry Newman, "Catholicity of the English Church," *The British Critic and Quarterly Theological Review* 27 (1840): 40–88.

132. Newman, *Apo.*, 213.

ability, deeply uncongenial, and any intellectual attraction that the notion held for Newman needed to be kept reserved. Moreover, if Newman's fear that "nothing but a quasi miracle" could prevent the Tractarians from surviving "the trial with no proselytes whatever to Rome,"[133] then a convincing answer to Wiseman needed to be provided.

This Newman attempted to do in his *British Critic* article the following January, but the argument there advanced was not the same as that which had characterized his Catholicism of the Word in the *Via Media*, nor was it carried forward with anything approaching the rhetorical bravura that had marked his controversial writings until only a few months earlier. It was a more measured, even tentative, piece than he had been accustomed to publishing and one which implicitly revealed Newman's growing understanding of the need for a Catholicism of the Church.

The Theory of Possession

Having secured control of the *British Critic* in 1838, Newman had a ready forum for his controversial writing: it was to this forum he turned when his excitement had calmed and he was ready to answer Wiseman. Published in January 1840 under the title "Catholicity of the English Church,"[134] it was, as he wrote to Bowden, an attempt "to stop up the leak in our boat which [Wiseman] has made."[135] When talking to Henry Wilberforce the previous October, Newman had said that despite the force of Wiseman's article, he "felt confident that when he returned to his rooms and was able fully and calmly to consider the matter, he should see his way completely out of the difficulty."[136] He had now had the opportunity for that full and calm consideration, and "Catholicity of the English Church" was his response; it was a response that he recognized from the first, however, lacked his customary rhetorical swagger. As has been noted previ-

---

133. JHN to W. Dodsworth, November 19, 1839, in *LD 7*, 186.
134. Newman, "Catholicity of the English Church," 40–88.
135. JHN to J. W. Bowden, January 5, 1840, in *LD 7*, 202.
136. Wilberforce, "Oxford Parochial Sermons," 327.

ously, Newman recalled himself as having begun the Long Vacation of 1839 secure in the 'supreme confidence" of his own "controversial status,"[137] but here, less than six months later, he was decidedly less self-assured. He wrote to his sister that he had "written an article for the B.C. in reply to one of Dr Wiseman's in the Dublin, which had fidgeted me a good deal. It is the only formidable thing I have seen on the Roman side—but cannot deny it is good and strong, and calculated to do harm, considerable harm. I have done what I can by way of an answer. But it is a large subject."[138]

In the guise of an approving review of a work on Apostolic Succession by his fellow Tractarian, Arthur Perceval,[139] Newman began the article by contending that Perceval had made his case: "We do trust and believe that the question of English Orders is now settled once for all ... at all events the controversy is at an end for the present."[140] Approving Perceval's work was not, however, Newman's purpose: the opportunity of the review was, in reality, simply a device to allow him to make an attempt at stopping up the leak. He proceeded to frame the issue between Rome and the English Church as being, he claimed, not about the validity of Anglican Orders—which "for argument's sake," along with the charge of heresy, Wiseman had not disputed in the Donatist article[141]—but about schism:

The objection which we have in mind, concisely stated, is this: on the one hand, that unity is the tenure of divine favour; that communion with our brethren is the means of communion with our Lord and Saviour; that the Church is not only Apostolic, but Catholic; that schism cuts off the fountains of grace; and that estrangement from the Christian world is schism; and, on the other, that in matter of fact our Church is emphatically in a state of estrangement, having intercourse with no other Christian body in any part of the world, excepting her own dependencies and offshoots.[142]

---

137. Newman, *Apo.*, 180.
138. JHN to Mrs. John Mozley, November 29, 1839, in *LD* 7, 187–88.
139. Arthur Phillip Perceval, *An Apology for the Doctrine of Apostolical Succession: With an Appendix on the English Orders* (London: J. G. F. and J. Rivington, 1839).
140. Perceval, *An Apology*, 2.
141. Wiseman, *Dublin Review* 7: 139.
142. Newman, "Catholicity of the English Church," 42.

The importance of the question for Newman can be in no doubt, and his selection of military metaphors served to heighten the sense of both the importance and the urgency of the task:

> But though we have gained this point, it does not follow that we have driven the enemy from the field and put an end to the war. There is another important and difficult post which the Roman party have not yet surrendered, and from which we must dislodge them.[143]

It was not, he well understood, an easy task and one about which he had "no pretences and ... no hopes of doing justice to it."[144] Nevertheless, it was work he could not avoid if he was to save the "boat" of both the Tractarian cause and his own stronghold of antiquity within it—his Catholicism of the Word. The way he went about tackling the task reveals that he had moved beyond the conception of the church as the passive vehicle of tradition that he had derived from Milner, Hawkins, Sumner, and Whately, the church of his dispute with the Abbé Jager, and had now come to understand the centrality of the church in establishing, protecting, and verifying the very stronghold itself.

In the aftermath of Wiseman's article, Manning had written to Newman suggesting that part of the plausibility of the article was down to Wiseman "treating the Roman Jurisdiction in England as anything but an usurpation."[145] It was this sense of being in possession that was to underpin Newman's "vigorous re-assertion of Tractarian principles" in his *British Critic* response.[146] The Roman Church might well be a part of the true church, but so was the Church of England, and it was the latter that was present and in possession of England: it was the Catholic Church in England. In order to make this case, Newman had to be able to argue that it was possible to be not only Apostolic but also to be Catholic and yet not be in communion with the pope: that is what he set out to do.

Early in the article, Newman, using the Socratic technique he had

---

143. Newman, "Catholicity of the English Church," 41.
144. Newman, "Catholicity of the English Church," 42.
145. H. E. Manning to JHN, October 23, 1839, in *LD* 7, 173.
146. Thomas, *Newman and Heresy*, 221.

deployed in a number of the tracts,[147] constructed an imaginary dialogue between an Anglo-Catholic and a Roman Catholic: "by setting down the arguments on the one side and the other in the form of a dialogue, which shall be conducted favorably to the Church of Rome, so as to bring matters to an issue."[148] When revising the work for the Uniform Edition, Newman shortened the dialogue and sharpened it somewhat, ending with an exchange that expresses the issue with a clarity that is explicitly absent, although implicitly present, in the original:

> *Angl.*—We go by Antiquity; that is, by the Apostles. Ancient consent is our standard of faith.
> *Rom.*—We go by Catholicity. Universal consent is our standard of faith.
> *Angl.*—You are cut off from the old Fathers.
> *Rom.*—And you are cut off from the present living Church.[149]

The dialogue, in a lengthier form in the original than in the revised, lays out the grounds upon which this issue is to be decided. The Roman Catholic begins by asserting that oneness and Catholicity are notes of the church, and the Anglo-Catholic concedes that this is so and that schism is a sin; the Anglo-Catholic claims purity and primitiveness (i.e., apostolicity) for the Church of England and alleges corruption against Rome: "We are pure because we are primitive. You are corrupt because you are novel."[150] The Roman then asks a question that goes to the heart of Wiseman's article and Augustine's "palmary words,"[151] a question to which Newman simply had to provide an answer if he was to stop the leak in the boat: "Who is to judge antiquity?"[152] Other questions remain in the rest of the longer, original version of the dialogue: if the textual additions to the creed were permissible, why not later expansions? The Roman Catholic,

---

147. See, for example, that between Clericus and Laicus, in "Tract 38: Via Media No. I" (Messrs. Rivington's, July 25, 1834); "Tract 41: Via Media No. II" (Messrs. Rivington's, August 24, 1834), in *Tracts 1*.
148. Newman, "Catholicity of the English Church," 42–43.
149. Newman, "Catholicity of the English Church," in *Ess.* 2, 6.
150. Newman, "Catholicity of the English Church," 43.
151. Newman, *Apo.*, 211.
152. Newman, "Catholicity of the English Church," 44.

in language close to that which Newman would later deploy in his own arguments, suggests that what the Anglo-Catholic calls corruptions—e.g., prayer to the saints and the doctrine of Purgatory—are no different from the various additions to the creed in that they "but interpret and fulfil" the Apostolic faith: "We realize what you only profess."[153] Finally, Newman put into the mouth of his Roman Catholic the underlying ecclesiological issue that he sought to deal with in the remainder of the article:

> This is your theory; we have an opposite theory, which is as good as yours. You say the many went wrong because they were corrupt; we say they could not but go right, because they were promised infallibility. But now observe the contrast between your system and ours, how simple is ours, how perplexed yours. You move on two foundations, we on one; you hold by the primitive Creed *and* the Church; you count it a duty to keep to the Creed and to keep to the Church, making no due provision for the case of a discordance between them, yet maintaining that very case to have happened. We have but one rule, to follow the Church; for in following the body, we are sure to be adhering to the faith. The society which we are to *join* is the teacher of what we are to *believe*. Accordingly in our view heresy and schism are never disjoined. You, on the contrary, almost assert that we are heretics, and almost grant that you are schismatics; yet maintaining withal we are both one Church, and both have one faith.[154]

It was as succinct a statement of the issue to be determined as could be made, allowing for the simplification of caricature made necessary by the literary form of the Socratic dialogue.

It was not Newman's primary purpose in this article to disprove the Roman case but rather to make the Anglo-Catholic one. Nevertheless, before he did the latter, he sought simply and wittily to do the former, and in doing so, he reveals his explicit awareness of the problems posed by the historical reality of doctrinal development given the fixed nature of the Apostolic faith.

Rehearsing the history of the Deutero-Nicene Council, when "for the first [time], a general council, or what is called so, made an ar-

---

153. Newman, "Catholicity of the English Church," 45.
154. Newman, "Catholicity of the English Church," 46.

ticle of faith, in addition to, not in development of, the Creed,"[155] Newman noted the circumstances of that council, which called into question its doctrine: deficiencies which speak to the fundamental grounds of several of the arguments he had previously used to attempt to reconcile change and continuity. These included the fact that this council "was the first... which rested the proof of its decree on grounds short of scripture"; that Deutero-Nicaea "violated the doctrine of adherence to the practice or received opinion of antiquity"; and, a key deficiency in the light of Newman's argument later in the article, the council was "the first which was held in a divided state of the Church."[156] These were, in Newman's account, clear deficiencies: Hooker, *sola scriptura*, and Article VI were abrogated by the first deficiency; St. Vincent of Lérins, antiquity, and the Catholicism of the Word were contradicted by the second; and Newman's theory of the *via media* was vindicated by the third deficiency of the council. Because of these deficiencies, Deutero-Nicaea had resulted in the doctrine that was, Newman argued, simply not reliable: "Now what has it issued in? in [sic] an assemblage of doctrines which, as was observed above, whether right or wrong, have scarcely more connection with the doctrines whether of the primitive Creed or the primitive Church than the doctrines of the Gospel have with those of the law."[157] This, for Newman, was the natural result of the deficiencies, the source of the corruption. It found expression, he argued, in a fundamental rejection of the Christocentric principle in the Christian doctrine of antiquity in the Roman doctrines of Purgatory and in worship of "St. Mary and the Saints," indeed, in "a radical change of inward temper and principle,"[158] one might even say ethos.

His criticism of the Roman position gave Newman the opportunity to indulge in savagely witty polemic. It is an example of Newman's capacity for the very effective use of sarcasm: "Does the Church, according to the Romanists, know more now than the Apos-

155. Newman, "Catholicity of the English Church," 47.
156. Newman, "Catholicity of the English Church," 47.
157. Newman, "Catholicity of the English Church," 48.
158. Newman, "Catholicity of the English Church," 48.

tles knew?"¹⁵⁹ He enquired as to the Marian faith of St. Paul, whether he believed "that the merits of St. John the Baptist should be imputed to him" and whether "he did or did not hold that St. Peter could give indulgences to shorten the prospective sufferings of the Corinthians in purgatory."¹⁶⁰ He offered an excuse for these imaginings in conceding that even as St. Paul "certainly does bring out his thoughts only in answer to express questions asked, and according to the occasion," rather than as a systematic treatise, and St. John "has written a Gospel as later, so also more dogmatic than his fellow Evangelists, in consequence of the rise of heresy," so might they have held doctrines beyond those expressed by them in their extant writings, nonetheless there had to be a limit to what was believable, even by Roman Catholics. He ended this passage with the most acerbic of his parallels, with a remark that implied precisely the same disingenuousness in the Roman Catholic, of which he was himself was later to be accused:

> But still there are limits to these concessions; we cannot imagine an Apostle saying and doing what Romanists say and do; can they imagine it themselves? Do they themselves, for instance, think that St. Paul was in the habit of saying what Bellarmine and others say,—"Laus Deo et *Virginque Matri*?" Would they not pronounce a professed epistle of St. Paul's which contained these words spurious on his [sic] one ground?¹⁶¹

Earlier in the article, Newman had suggested that the only way the Roman Catholic argument could be at all sustained was "to make light of the judgement of antiquity, or to maintain that revelation is progressive";¹⁶² now, without any apparent sense of irony, he suggests that "this difficulty has led some Roman writers to the theory of a *disciplina arcani*."¹⁶³

However witty Newman's attack on the Roman Catholic position, the Anglican (or, more properly, the Anglo-Catholic) case still needed to be made. Newman understood that pointing out the weak-

---

159. Newman, "Catholicity of the English Church," 50.
160. Newman, "Catholicity of the English Church," 51.
161. Newman, "Catholicity of the English Church," 51.
162. Newman, "Catholicity of the English Church," 48–49.
163. Newman, "Catholicity of the English Church," 52.

nesses in the Roman Catholic position was one thing, but making the Anglo-Catholic case was quite another, and it was only the latter that would begin to undo the damage Wiseman's article had done.

When Newman had argued with the Abbé Jager, seeking to construct the hypothesis of the *via media* to provide adequate protection for antiquity and advance his Catholicism of the Word, the difficulty of the English church's separation had not seemed so great a difficulty. Now, in the aftermath of Wiseman's article and the light of Augustine's *securus iudicat orbis terrarum*, Newman acknowledged that it was the central question to be addressed. He recognized that "the English difficulty, was that the Church being "one body," how can we, estranged as we are from every part of it except our own dependencies, unrecognized and without intercommunion, maintain our right to be considered part of that body?"[164]

The remainder of Newman's piece was an attempt to provide a convincing answer to that question. He knew he would have to demonstrate that intercommunion was, even if desirable, unnecessary, that its absence did not necessarily imply schism, and that the life of grace within a particular church could be maintained even if schism were conceded. He needed to reassert the claims to apostolicity for the Church of England that had been part of the narrative and apologetic of the Oxford Movement from its inception, but in a way that met Wiseman's objections. Unsurprisingly, perhaps, he found his ammunition in the works of the Anglican Divines and in the Fathers, but before that, he had to prepare the ground of battle.

Having stated the standard Tractarian position that Apostolic descent, rather than unity, was what constituted the "essential completeness" of the church, Newman provided a justification for the particular claims and nature of the Church of England in terms that are surprisingly Erastian.[165] Allowing for the fact that he was, indeed, an occasional writer, shaping his arguments to the matter in controversy, his assertion that "each branch [of the Church] is bound to conform to the country," such that "they are in consequence, as

---

164. Newman, "Catholicity of the English Church," 53.
165. Newman, "Catholicity of the English Church," 54.

Churches, under the supremacy of the state or monarch whom they obey in temporal" is unexceptional.[166] The immediately following claim that the monarch might, therefore, use the church "as one of the functions of his Government, as his ministers of public instruction," is, however, worthy of note, remarkable even. The extent of Newman's deployment of an Erastian position is immediately made clear: "Ordination is a bishop's prerogative; but everything else save ordination comes from the king. The whole jurisdiction is his; his are all the spiritual courts; his the right of excommunication; his the control of revenues; his the organization of dioceses; his the appointment of bishops."[167]

While seemingly incompatible with his 1833 reaction to the Irish Church (Temporalities) Act, conceding so much to the Erastian position was necessary if Newman was to deploy Cranmer, Stillingfleet, Barrow, Dodwell, and Hickes to argue that each communion, indeed each diocese, is essentially a complete church and "mutual intercourse ... but an *accident* of the Church, not of its essence."[168] When he came to the patristic material, he was anxious to claim St. Ignatius of Antioch and St. Cyprian for this position, citing, for example, the latter's "Episcopatus unus est, cujus a singulis in solidum pars tenetur."[169] Newman held that the "Anglican theory of ecclesiastical unity" was the same as the patristic theory, and, he believed, the testimony of the Fathers supported his contention "that each Church is naturally independent of every other; each bishop a complete channel of grace, and ultimate centre of unity; and all unions of see with see but matters of ecclesiastical arrangement."[170] He did not go as far as to suggest that this authority extended to allowing the particular church to "lay down on her own authority Articles of Faith," and the distinction he had so laboriously set out in the correspondence "Catholicity of the English Church" with the Abbé Jager between Articles of Faith and Articles of Religion should not be overlooked here.

166. Newman, "Catholicity of the English Church," 54.
167. Newman, "Catholicity of the English Church," 54.
168. Newman, "Catholicity of the English Church," 55.
169. Newman, "Catholicity of the English Church," 61.
170. Newman, "Catholicity of the English Church," 62–63.

Nonetheless, Newman came close at this point in the *British Critic* article to deploying an argument that gave to the particular church wide doctrinal authority. It was a position that Pusey had explicitly contradicted in correspondence with him only days before Newman had read Wiseman's article.[171] Pusey had written a critical review of Christopher Benson's *Discourses upon Tradition and Episcopacy*[172] for the *British Critic*, which Newman had published in October 1839.[173] In the review, Pusey had noted that Benson was critical of the Tractarians for seeming to hold that particular churches had the power to determine "things necessary to salvation." Pusey argued that this was a "mistake" on Benson's part, deriving from the latter's lack "of a notion of the Catholic Church," precisely the place in which that power was located.[174] That the disunity between the churches meant that the Catholic Church could not exercise this power was not to deny to it the faculty itself.

In adopting this conception of the rights and capacities of the particular church, Newman was prepared to acknowledge that the patristic witness was not univocal. He noted that St. Augustine's view was different, one "more nearly approaching to the Roman."[175] He could not, however, accept his argument regarding another of St. Cyprian's arguments from *De Unitate*: "Tear the ray from the sun's substance, unity will not admit this division of light; break a branch from the tree, it will not bud when broken; cut off the channel from the spring, the channel will dry up."[176] Newman would follow Dodwell and adopt the position that these analogies do not apply, as St. Augustine claimed, to the whole body of the church, the *orbis terrarum*, but to each individual diocese, to the "episcopal and diocesan unit."[177] What is more, Newman went on to argue that even if one were to accept St. Augustine's position, even those within the Roman

---

171. E. B. Pusey to JHN, September 12, 1839, in *LD* 7, 147.
172. Edward Bouverie Pusey, "Notice of 'Discourses upon Tradition and Episcopacy' by Christian Benson," *Quarterly Theological Review* 26 (1839): 508.
173. Pusey, "Discourcess upon Tradition," 508.
174. E. B. Pusey to JHN, September 12, 1839, in *LD* 7, 147.
175. Newman, "Catholicity of the English Church," 63.
176. Newman, "Catholicity of the English Church," 64.
177. Newman, "Catholicity of the English Church," 64.

Communion could see and argue that this meant "that *Catholicity* and not the *Pope*, is the essence of the Church."[178] If the Gallicans could hold to this view and not be cast off from the Roman Communion, then perhaps the issue in England, Newman suggested, was not a quarrel with "*Catholicity*" but a "special quarrel which we have with Rome."[179]

The doctrinal consequences of his argument were immediately apparent to Newman, and here he claimed St. Augustine in support of his position. If the latter's argument that the part must yield to the whole, "Et concilia posteriora prioribus apud posteros praeponuntur, et universum partibus semper jure optimo praeponitur,"[180] then as surely as the Church of England "yields to a general council," so, surely, must Rome be prepared to submit Trent to "a Council yet to come."[181] Quite apart from the logical inconsistency between his claim here for the authority of General Councils over the Church of England with his assertions earlier in the article about state or monarchical prerogatives, not to mention Article 21 of the Thirty-Nine Articles, what Newman here, and in the remainder of the article, failed adequately to grasp was the contention underlying Wiseman's—indeed, the whole Roman—position, that there was a substantial identity between the Roman Communion and the Catholic Church. Even if St. Augustine's argument is understood in the terms of conciliarism, for Wiseman and Rome, Trent *was* a General Council of the church and there simply was no question of its supersession by "a council yet to come."

Although he had not fully grasped—or, more likely, felt it unnecessary and inconvenient for his present purposes to engage with it fully—the implications of the underlying claim were not lost on Newman. He well understood that it underpinned the Roman defense against the Anglican charge of novelty. He expressed it in terms that, because it foreshadows the very imagery that he was to use in the *Essay*, are worth quoting in full:

178. Newman, "Catholicity of the English Church," 65.
179. Newman, "Catholicity of the English Church," 65.
180. Newman, "Catholicity of the English Church," 69.
181. Newman, "Catholicity of the English Church," 69.

When we object to the Romanists that their Church has changed in the course of years, they not unfrequently acknowledge it, and are philosophical on the subject. They say that all systems have their development; that nothing begins as it ends; that nothing can come into the world *totis numeris*, that the seed becomes a tree, and the child a man. And they urge, moreover, that the full grown fulfilment, to superficial observers, necessarily seems different to what it was in its rudiments, just as a friend, not seen for many years, is strange to us at first sight, till, by degrees, we catch the old looks, or the well-remembered tones, or the smile or the remark, which assure us that, with whatever changes of age or circumstance, he is the same.[182]

Newman conceded that this was a powerful argument and one which, he presciently wrote, "does seem to reconcile one to much that otherwise it is difficult to comprehend in the history of religion."[183] Its flaw, however, was that it lacked a mechanism that Newman could accept that would enable one to distinguish when a development "departed from antiquity and forfeited its trust."[184] Absent a living organ to determine between developments and corruption, then, Newman argued, the Roman contention made Dionysius "the forerunner of Arius" and called into question the status of his beloved St. Cyprian because of his erroneous baptismal doctrine.[185] In the patristic period, Newman argued, a number of these developments led to the temporary suspension of intercommunion between the churches. The mechanisms for the resolution of these suspensions were unclear and took differing forms at different times: sometimes it was the judgment of the pope, at others of councils against the pope, and at others the decision of the Fathers against either or both pope and councils. Newman uses the words of St. Augustine to support his argument: "this does nothing to prejudice the Catholic Church diffused over the whole world."[186] This being so, Newman argued:

---

182. Newman, "Catholicity of the English Church," 69–70.
183. Newman, "Catholicity of the English Church," 70.
184. Newman, "Catholicity of the English Church," 70.
185. Newman, "Catholicity of the English Church," 70.
186. Newman, "Catholicity of the English Church," 71.

Directly it is granted that active intercourse is not *absolutely necessary* as a note of the Church... then, in spite of our being separated from Greece and Rome, shut up in ourselves and our dependencies, and looked on coldly or forgotten by the rest of Christendom, there is sufficient ground for still believing that the English Church is at this time the Catholic Church in England.[187]

The remainder of the article proceeds from the point of this assertion that the Church of England is the Catholic Church in possession of England and its dependencies. Newman had already demonstrated, both in the article and elsewhere, that, to his own satisfaction, both the descent and the doctrine of the Church of England were such as to satisfy the creedal note of apostolicity and, in the foregoing pages, he had seemed to suggest that the note of unity was desirable but not essential. His theory of possession sought to define catholicity in a manner that served his own argument. Wiseman's parallel of the Church of England with the Donatists failed, Newman claimed, because "the Donatists had not possession; their only tenure of existence was hatred and opposition to the rest of Christendom,"[188] and Roman claims to catholicity were compromised by separation and absence from Greece and Russia.[189] Whatever creedal catholicity meant, then, it was not, for Newman at this point, what Rome claimed.

In the final pages of the article, Newman staked out the Church of England's claim to the note of sanctity in support of his theory of possession. Newman argued that Rome could not resist the Church of England's claim to be part of the Catholic Church—albeit one Rome might assert was in schism—"if the Anglican communion had but that one note of the church upon it—sanctity."[190] Newman's examination of the Church of England's claim to sanctity is, however, little more than an assertion and condemnation of Roman devotional corruption. It was an argument that he had deployed against the Abbé Jager three years earlier, and he was to return to the same point in the letter to Bloxam in early 1841, noted above:

187. Newman, "Catholicity of the English Church," 72.
188. Newman, "Catholicity of the English Church," 73.
189. Newman, "Catholicity of the English Church," 74.
190. Newman, "Catholicity of the English Church," 86.

Rome must first change in her spirit. I must see more sanctity in her than I do at present. Alas! I see no marks of sanctity—or if any, they are chiefly confined to converts from us ... I do verily think that, with all our sins, there is more sanctity in the Church of England and Ireland, than in the Roman Catholic bodies in the same countries.[191]

As a rhetorical device, ending the article in terms that asserted the holiness of Anglicanism and decrying the corruption of Roman Catholicism would, undoubtedly, have earned Newman the approbation of the readership of the *British Critic*. It is quite another question to answer whether he convinced himself with the jingoism of comments like: "We Englishmen like manliness, openness, consistency, truth. Rome will never gain on us till she learns these virtues, and uses them; then she may gain on us, but it will be by ceasing to be what we now mean by Rome."[192] In fact, the passage concerning sanctity makes almost no effort to demonstrate the presence of the note in the English church. Newman was clearly satisfied that this was self-evident to his readership, as was the corruption and disingenuousness of Rome. The extent to which this was a judgement not of sanctity but of culturally determined prejudice about spiritual practices is one that is a question outside the scope of this work, but, given Newman's later history in the Oratory, founded by that most Roman of Saints, with its distinctly Italianate spirituality and devotional practice, not one without a certain irony.

In order to stop the leak he had identified as being opened up in his position by Wiseman's article, Newman's response had privileged the notes of apostolicity and sanctity and had played down those of unity and catholicity. Earlier in the article, he had claimed that his purpose was to reconcile three points: "that the Church is one is the point of *doctrine*; that we are estranged from the body of the Church is the point of *fact*; and that we still have the means of grace among us, is our point of *controversy*."[193] In fact, Newman had achieved no such reconciliation. He had argued that the first was not essential, that the second was unimportant, and had offered little or no ev-

191. JHN to J. R. Bloxham, February 23, 1841, in *LD 8*, 42.
192. Newman, "Catholicity of the English Church," 88.
193. Newman, "Catholicity of the English Church," 53.

idence for the third. As with much of his ecclesiological polemic since the first days of the Oxford Movement, Newman's entire argument rested on the claim to Apostolical descent and fidelity to the Apostolic faith. Even here, however, Newman was now not so sure of his ground. After dealing with Roman developments in the article, he had considered the problem of those doctrines that were peculiar to the Church of England.

Three years earlier, as he thrashed out the theology of the *via media* in both his correspondence with the Abbé Jager and in his *Lectures on the Prophetical Office*, Newman had made much of the difference between the Episcopal or Apostolic Tradition and the Prophetical Tradition, between Articles of faith and Articles of religion. Here he has abandoned these distinctions, although it would clearly have been much simpler for the structure of his argument had he used them: the peculiar doctrines of Rome or England could have been consigned to the latter categories, considering them, as Pusey would have done, to be adiaphora. Newman had considered these doctrines and practices. He argued that while estrangement from Rome had led the Lutherans toward rationalism and the Calvinists to Socinianism, the Church of England had "endured all vicissitudes of fortune."[194] He acknowledged that the doctrinal climate "never was in so miserable case as in the reigns of Edward and Elizabeth" but that the canons of 1603, the reign of Charles I, and the Restoration Convocation of 1661 had restored true doctrine such that even the threat of relapse Newman detected in the events of 1688 could not overthrow this growth. He asserted that "as far as its formularies are concerned, it may be said all along to have grown towards a more perfect Catholicism than that with which it started at the time of its estrangement; every act, every crisis which marks its course, has been upward."[195] Once again, however, this was an assertion for which Newman offered no evidence.

Wiseman's article had, however, curtailed the force of such assertions by focusing Newman's attention on the question of just who got

---

194. Newman, "Catholicity of the English Church," 77.
195. Newman, "Catholicity of the English Church," 77.

to decide what was and what was not part of the *depositum fidei*. Newman may have felt that his response had stop the leak for the present, that the unsettling specter Wiseman had conjured up had vanished and all seemed almost as it had once been. He recalled as much in the *Apologia*,[196] and his remark in his letters to Bowden on February 21, 1840, corroborates his claim.[197] Nonetheless, the fragility of the arguments in the article was not lost on Newman, as he confessed to Bowden: "I cannot deny either of [Wiseman's] positions.... My article was to meet this—and I am glad to hear in many quarters that it has done good service. But the great speciousness of his article is one of the things which have made me despond so much."[198]

The force and effect of Wiseman's article was such that—Newman again using language strikingly similar to that which he would use in the *Essay*—it not only "pulverised the theory of the *via media*" but also provided an account of why "St. Austin or St. Basil coming among us would say at once '*That* is the Catholic Church—and *those* are heretics'—meaning Rome and us respectively."[199] The weakness of Newman's response lay precisely in the failure of his theory to give an adequate account of the status of those teachings and practices peculiar to Anglicanism. As he recalled in the *Apologia*:

> But ... the great stumbling-block lay in the 39 Articles. It was urged that here was a positive Note *against* Anglicanism: Anglicanism claimed to hold that the Church of England was nothing else than a continuation in this country ... of that one Church of which in old times Athanasius and Augustine were members. But, if so, the doctrine must be the same; the doctrine of the Old Church must live and speak in Anglican formularies, in the 39 Articles.[200]

Frank Turner, claiming to follow Stephen Thomas's line, dismissed Newman's own account.[201] Seemingly ignoring not only the correspondence, the urgent priority Newman accorded to the pro-

---

196. Newman, *Apo.*, 230.
197. JHN to J. W. Bowden, February 21, 1840, in *LD* 7, 240–42.
198. JHN to J. W. Bowden, February 21, 1840, in *LD* 7, 241.
199. JHN to J. W. Bowden, February 21, 1840, in *LD* 7, 241.
200. Newman, *Apo.*, 231.
201. Turner, *The Challenge*, 337. Cf. Thomas, *Newman and Heresy*, 220–22.

duction of the *British Critic* article, and his concessions to Wiseman's points in the article, particularly those related to want of the note of catholicity and doctrinal peculiarity, Turner argues that Newman was so distracted by "disruptive activities among young Tractarians" that the force of Wiseman's "polemic" could not have had the effect on him that Newman claimed.[202] He cites, among examples of this, Robert Williams's preoccupation with conversion to Rome,[203] Morris's preaching on fasting and "the Roman doctrine of the Mass,"[204] and Bloxam's imprudent behavior at Alton Towers. Turner characteristically exaggerates the nature of this last matter, claiming that it had been reported to Newman that Bloxam had prostrated himself at the raising of the host at Mass in Lord Shrewsbury's chapel, when, in fact, the complaint was that he had merely "bowed down."[205] The difficulty with Turner's thesis is that despite these distractions and the significant claims they made on Newman's time and energy, Newman gave priority to the production of the *British Critic* article. Turner's wider point was that the use of historical parallels, especially those of the Monophysite Heresy and Donatism, convinced nobody but Newman himself, and is reason enough to doubt Newman's own account of his reaction to those parallels. Turner held this view despite the contemporaneous evidence.[206] His reasons for

---

202. Turner, *The Challenge*, 337.
203. To which Newman's attention had been drawn by Wood. See S. F. Wood to JHN, October 29, 1839, in *LD* 7, 179–80.
204. JHN to S. F. Wood, November 10, 1839, in *LD* 7, 181.
205. The first report of the event to Newman was from William Dodsworth in his letter of November 18, 1839, in *LD* 7, 184, where the words "bowed down" are used. Bloxam's denial and his own account are contained in Newman's letter in reply on November 19; see JHN to William Dodsworth, November 19, 1839, in *LD* 7, 186–87. The controversy surrounding Bloxam's behavior dragged on until Christmas, when the Bishop of Oxford wrote to Newman substantially accepting Bloxam's account. See Richard Bagot, Bishop of Oxford to JHN, December 26, 1839, in *LD* 7, 189–90.
206. Such was Turner's determination to support his *a priori* assumption that, "It was [Newman's] peculiar argument and his alone," that the accounts of those who were profoundly unsettled by those parallels are represented as being merely 'shaken by Newman's personal doubt ... but none was drawn to the parallel itself" (Turner, *The Challenge*, 604).

Thomas's account is more nuanced than Turner gave him credit for, however. Turner claimed that Thomas shared his fundamental scepticism about Newman's account in the *Apologia* of the events of 1839, citing Thomas's argument that the 1864 account should be doubted on the grounds of "the absence of clear supporting evidence from 1839" (335).

adopting this position would appear to be derived from his attempt to demonstrate that Newman's own account of these and other events is to be dismissed as a "personally constructed conversion narrative that imposed a structure of spiritual search on what in actuality had been a series of contingent events infused with enormous personal confusion, anger, despondency, and mixture of other motives."[207] Yet the explicit remarks in, and clear inferences to be drawn from, the contemporaneous correspondence suggest that this cannot be so. Turner is, however, nearer the mark when he highlights the controversy around Tract 90. This episode was to play a central role in undermining Newman's own brittle confidence in his latest hypothesis and in focusing his mind firmly on the relationship between the authority of the church and the question of the authentication of apparent doctrinal development.

The 1840 Correspondence with Francis Newman

If the position Newman had outlined in "Catholicity of the English Church" was to hold, it would need to provide a satisfactory account of both those teachings, peculiar to Anglicanism, at least in their mode of expression, and be able to demonstrate the fidelity of the Anglican episcopate to Apostolic faith. The question of the Jerusa-

---

However, Thomas recognised that "Newman's correspondence at the time indicates strongly that he felt the pull of Wiseman's [position] and had begun to doubt his own" (Thomas, *Newman and Heresy*, 220). Thomas's argument is not that Newman did not feel the force of the Wiseman article but, rather, as has been shown, that it was Wiseman's article and the parallel with the Donatists that damaged Newman's self-confidence, not his own claimed self-realisation of the parallel with the Monophysites.

Turner, instead, chose to locate the collapse of Newman's confidence in the Tractarian conception of the Church of England not in Wiseman's article, nor in the Monophysite parallel, nor yet in the rhetorically bold but substantially fragile response of the *British Critic* article, but in the force of the argument in Keble's preface to Froude's *Remains* (339) and in the "polemical onslaught occasioned in 1841 by" Newman's own Tract 90 (334). He surely overstated the influence of the former when he claimed that: "Keble's starkly uncompromising distinction between Catholic antiquity and the Erastian Protestant Reformation, and not Wiseman's article ... baldly, perhaps fatally, posed the dilemma that would fatally disrupt Tractarianism" (339).

207. Turner, *The Challenge*, 336–37.

lem Bishopric and the reaction to what turned out to be the last of the tracts would demonstrate to Newman that his latest carefully constructed hypothesis was no more tenable than its predecessors. Yet even before these major events, as early as the summer of 1840, it became clear that Newman was far from comfortable in the position he had outlined in the *British Critic* and that he was considering a more developed hypothesis.

Newman was not alone in being concerned that one of the unintended consequences of the Oxford Movement had been, from the very beginning, the secession of individuals from Anglicanism in the direction of Rome. Writing to Keble in October 1840, with whom, as the correspondence makes clear, he had previously discussed the issue, Newman reflected on these defections and admitted that: "I fear I must allow that, whether I will or no, I am disposing them towards Rome."[208] He confessed that this was conceivably his own direction of travel and that it was a matter that had been troubling him for some time. Indeed, he had expressed the contingent nature of his position several months earlier in a letter to W. C. A. Maclaurin in July 1840: "A great experiment is going on, whether Anglocatholicism has a root, a foundation, a consistency ... or whether it be a 'sham.'"[209] Rather typically, Turner could not help but suggest that Newman's comment to Maclaurin should be set within the context of what he clearly took to be Newman's singular self-obsession, leading to "ecclesiastical and spiritual ambiguities, which Newman ... could tolerate but which proved an enormous burden to his younger followers," although it is not obvious that this was the case.[210]

In the letter to Keble, Newman commented that he had raised his concerns with Rogers a year before. This is presumably a reference to his letters to Rogers, in particular, that of September 22, 1839, in which Newman admitted to having "had the first real hit from Romanism"[211] in the form of the Wiseman article; and that of October 3, 1839, in which he explicitly confessed that: "In all this ... I assume,

208. JHN to John Keble, October 26, 1840, in *LD* 7, 417.
209. JHN to W. C. A. MacLaurin, July 26, 1840, in *LD* 7, 369.
210. Turner, *The Challenge*, 350.
211. JHN to Frederic Rogers, September 22, 1839, in *LD* 7, 154.

on the one hand, that Rome is right; on the other, that we are not bound by uncatholic subscriptions."[212] Now, despite the position that he had set out in the *British Critic* article of the previous January, to which, he maintained, he remained committed, he remarked to Keble that "I have shot my last arrow in the article on English Catholicity; and I am troubled by doubts, whether, as it is, I have not in what I have published spoken too strongly against Rome.... I begin to have suspicions about myself."[213] What those suspicions were became clearer when his thirteenth University Sermon and the correspondence of October and November 1840 with his brother Francis are considered.

Toward the end of the Trinity Term of 1840, in place of his friend and Oriel fellow R. W. Church, Newman preached his thirteenth University Sermon.[214] Given on the feast of St. Peter, June 29, Newman entitled this sermon "Implicit and Explicit Reason" and in it returned to the themes that he had touched on in two previous University Sermons.[215] The sermon takes the form of an exposition of the implications of the words of 1 Peter 3:15 (in the King James Version): "sanctify the Lord God in your hearts; and be ready always to give an answer to every man that asketh you a reason of the hope that is in you, with meekness and fear." This verse, Newman argues, gives "a clear warrant, or rather an injunction, to cast our religion into the form of Creed and Evidences."[216] He then laid out at some length the relationship of faith and reason as one where the latter, at the service of the former, has its own proper evidence, methods, and au-

212. JHN to Frederic Rogers, October 3, 1839, in *LD* 7, 160.
213. JHN to John Keble, October 26, 1840, in *LD* 7, 417.
214. John Henry Newman, "Implicit and Explicit Reason," *USS*, 251–77. He had preached his first University Sermon in 1826 and was to preach his fifteenth and last at the beginning of 1843. References in this work to the texts of the last three University Sermons are cited from the Uniform Edition of Newman's works. This departure from the practice followed with respect to Newman's other works has been taken because the original manuscript texts in the Birmingham Oratory Archives at A.9.4. are substantially identical to the published versions but lack any folio numbering, thereby making precise citation from that source difficult to achieve.
215. Specifically, in his tenth sermon, "Faith and Reason, contrasted as Habits of Mind," preached on January 6, 1839, and in *USS*, 176–201, and his eleventh, "The Nature of Faith in Relation to Reason," January 13, 1839, in *USS*, 202–21.
216. Newman, *USS*, 253.

tonomy. This structure of the relationship—reason being applied to discern the reliability of the evidences of faith—outlined by Newman sketched a notion of change and continuity that grounds the process firmly within the action of the church and in a manner which left little doubt that, although he did not use the term, his theory of the development of doctrine was, by this time, already remarkably well developed:

> And herein consists one great blessing of the Gospel Covenant, that in Christ's death on the Cross, and in other parts of that all-gracious Economy, are concentrated, as it were, and so presented to us those attributes and works which fill eternity. And with a like graciousness we are also told, in human language, things concerning God Himself, concerning His Son and His Spirit, and concerning His Son's incarnation, and the union of two natures in His One Person—truths which even a peasant holds implicitly, but which Almighty God, whether by His Apostles, or by His Church after them, has vouchsafed to bring together and methodize, and to commit to the keeping of science.[217]

Newman went on to acknowledge the inadequacy of human language and the incompleteness of the explicit expressions of hitherto implicit faith in the mysteries of the *depositum fidei*. As an explanation of apparent inconsistencies between the various doctrinal expressions over time of the truths of the Christian faith, he once more utilized the analogy of the comparison to be made between the pictures of a little child and that of the same person as an old man, an analogy which he would later return to in the *Essay*.[218] Newman was already very much aware of the prophylactic purpose of the process of making explicit that which was hitherto implicit. "Doctrinal statements may be introduced, not so much for their own sake, as because many consequences flow from them, and therefore a great variety of errors may, by means of them, be prevented,"[219] he argued, and in an acknowledgement of the apologetic purpose of theology, he explained the incompleteness and occasional particularity of the

---

217. Newman, *USS*, 269.
218. Newman, *USS*, 270.
219. Newman, *USS*, 270.

arguments used and evidence considered in those statements when he wrote: "Defenders of Christianity naturally select as reasons for belief, not the highest, the truest, the most sacred, the most intimately persuasive, but such as best admit of being exhibited in argument ... how very differently an argument strikes the mind at one time and another, according to its particular state, or the accident of the moment."[220]

In his conclusion, Newman returned to the mandate that he drew from the scriptural text and set his remarks within the context of the "real reasons" for faith:

> I have been engaged in proving the following points: that the reasonings and opinions which are involved in the act of Faith are latent and implicit; that the mind reflecting on itself is able to bring them out into some definite and methodical form; that Faith, however, is complete without this reflective faculty, which, in matter of fact, often does interfere with it, and must be used cautiously.[221]

Here Newman is explicitly talking about the faith of the individual rather than that of the whole church, but these remarks, as well as the argument of the latter part of the sermon as a whole, bear the inference that he held a more general theology of development. In the autumn of the same year, 1840, Newman was to engage in a correspondence with his brother Francis that was to leave no doubt that Newman had drawn precisely those inferences.

Francis Newman, it appeared to his elder brother, had begun to veer from his earlier, largely creedally orthodox Evangelicalism towards Unitarianism, the impetus seemingly coming from his experiences as a missionary in Persia.[222] John Henry had received a letter from Francis on October 20, 1840,[223] that he described to their brother-in-law, Thomas Mozley, as *"painful"* and "almost a confession of Unitarianism."[224] He replied at some length to Fran-

---

220. Newman, *USS*, 271.
221. Newman, *USS*, 276–77.
222. Francis William Newman, *Phases of Faith: Or, Passages from the History of My Creed* (London: J. Chapman, 1850), 16–40.
223. F. W. Newman to JHN, October 20, 1840, in *LD* 7, 408.
224. JHN to Thomas Mozley, October 21, 1840, in *LD* 7, 411.

cis on October 22, 1840,[225] and received a reply two weeks later.[226] In his further reply three days after that,[227] the elder Newman set out a comprehensive account of his own position and, in so doing, avowedly sought to make of it a 'stumbling-block" in his brother's path toward the abandonment of orthodox Christology and Trinitarian theology.[228] His account of his own position reveals just how much he had come to accept the notion of development of doctrine, how central it was to his theological preoccupations, and how sophisticated his notion of it had become by this time. It was, in fact, as both Peterburs[229] and Pereiro note, a first description of "his theory of developments."[230] The letter set out substantially what was to become the thesis of the *Essay*: that development and identity are a necessary sign of life; that the church not only grows in its ability to articulate its teachings and practices but also in its understanding of those doctrines not in spite of but because of changing historical and cultural circumstances; and that there appear to be tests by which the authenticity or otherwise of developments can be established.[231]

In the letter, Newman first stated that he believed "it to be a plain external truth that ... the Church's religion has been one and the same from first to last,"[232] and he then went on to track that religion, in a series of twelve points, in which he demonstrates that the development of the church's "doctrines and course of conduct" over time, in response to "external and internal causes,"[233] is not only observable but necessary for both the organic unity of the church itself and to ensure that its faith remains in later centuries "the same religion"

---

225. JHN to F.W. Newman, October 22, 1840, in *LD* 7, 412–15.
226. The letter does not survive, although its receipt is noted in Newman's diary for November 7, 1840, in *LD* 7, 434.
227. JHN to F. W. Newman, November 10, 1840, in *LD* 7, 436–42.
228. JHN to F. W. Newman, November 10, 1840, in *LD* 7, 442.
229. Michael Peterburs, "Newman and the Development of Doctrine," in *By Whose Authority: Newman, Manning and the Magisterium*, ed. Alan V. McClelland (Bath: Downside Abbey, 1996), 62.
230. Pereiro, "*Ethos*," 168.
231. JHN to F.W. Newman, November 10, 1840, in *LD* 7, 441.
232. JHN to F.W. Newman, November 10, 1840, in *LD* 7, 439.
233. JHN to F. W. Newman, November 10, 1840, in *LD* 7, 440.

as it professed in earlier.[234] In language that prefigures the imagery he would come to rely on in his final University Sermon and the *Essay*, he noted that "all systems which have life, have a development, yet do not cease to have an identity though they develop."[235] Furthermore, he argued that in addition to being an observable and necessary fact, there could be no objection to the development of this same religion insofar as particular "Church developments ... harmonize with its temper and principles, are consistent with the ideas from which the[y] profess to spring, and are professed unanimously by its members."[236] This was no arbitrary change but one ordered toward the unity and integrity of Christianity and one that could be tested to authenticate whether a particular development formed part of the unity and integrity: whether any particular development was "legitimate" or "doubtful."[237]

The question of how change and continuity could be reconciled had become *the* theological question for Newman, and he had come to understand that the answer would be fundamentally ecclesiological. The Church of England, if it was to sustain its claims to Newman's loyalty, would need to be able to make good its position as the branch of the Church Catholic in possession of England and her dependencies, with an explicit demonstration of its apostolicity. Until the episode of Wiseman's article, Newman had not seriously questioned whether in its teaching or in its ecclesial life the English church had remained true to this apostolical note. In the early tracts, he seemed to have treated apostolicity as the present, though often hidden, ecclesial reality of the Church of England and its teaching, and, indeed, as has been shown in the consideration of the correspondence with Jager, he simply assumed that the fidelity of the Church of England to Apostolical faith and order was a self-evident truth. Newman had admitted to his brother that there was some merit in the criticism "that I make a Church half visible, half invisible ... like a building

---

234. JHN to F. W. Newman, November 10, 1840, in *LD* 7, 441.
235. JHN to F. W. Newman, November 10, 1840, in *LD* 7, 441.
236. JHN to F. W. Newman, November 10, 1840, in *LD* 7, 441.
237. JHN to F. W. Newman, November 10, 1840, in *LD* 7, 441.

seen through a mist."[238] The extent to which Wiseman's arguments had struck home is supported by the evidence of Newman's concentration on the English church's claim to the note of apostolicity in "Catholicity of the English Church": what was once self-evident needed now to be demonstrated. The *British Critic* article had not been the place to do that, and the correspondence with his brother and with Keble had revealed the precarious nature of Newman's hold on his place in the Church of England. It was to be a process fraught with risk, one he recognized, writing: "I do not think that we have yet made a fair trial how much the English Church will bear. I know it is a hazardous experiment, like proving Cannon. Yet we must not take it for granted the metal will burst in the operation. It has borne at various times, not to say at this time, a great infusion of Catholic Truth without damage."[239]

The events of 1841 and 1842 would provide the proving ground and would make clear to him whether, despite any capacity he might or might not have had for ambiguity, the English Church would bear, in sufficient measure, the "Catholic Truth" of the role of ecclesial authority in the authentication of doctrine that Newman now believed to be a necessary mark of that Apostolical faith that he sought for so long.

Tract 90 and the Jerusalem Bishopric

If the theory of possession was to do duty in reality as a hypothesis to account for the difficulty of change and continuity and not be merely yet another paper theory, the reality of the Church of England would need to match up to the high expectations that Newman had set for it in his theory. In terms of its doctrine and its order, there would need to be sufficient correspondence between the English Church and the church of Newman's theory. In light of Newman's assertions of confidence following the *British Critic* article, it is clear that Newman expected just such a correspondence to be found in the evidence of the Church of England's life and belief. It has already

---

238. JHN to F. W. Newman, November 10, 1840, in *LD* 7, 440.
239. JHN to John Keble, November 6, 1840, in *LD* 7, 433.

been suggested that those assertions might equally be read as having something of the brittle, self-induced bravado of one who suspects that the position to which one has committed oneself might not, in fact, hold. Whatever the status of Newman's confidence, the reaction of the Bishops of the Church of England to Newman's final tract, Tract 90,[240] and the moves to establish a Lutheran-Anglican bishopric in Jerusalem, were to settle conclusively and unambiguously for Newman the question of the reality and sustainability of his latest hypothesis.

The circumstances of the generation of the Thirty-Nine Articles were such that the matter of their proper interpretation and scope would ever be likely to be a matter of debate. In their first fifty years, much of the debate was about the extent to which they bound the Church of England to an exclusively Reformed soteriology or were permissive of a rather less stringent theory which could accommodate the necessity of good works within the theology of justification. The articles "had not been intended to be rigid or exclusive upon the point,"[241] and by the first years of the reign of Charles I, they appeared to create room enough for strict Calvinist and Arminian alike to subscribe to them. In 1628, the articles had been prefaced with a declaration, almost certainly the work of Archbishop Laud, placed there on the instructions of the king with the intention of curtailing further attempts at exclusivity by closing off the mechanism for dispute as to the precise meaning of the articles. It ordered "that no man hereafter shall either print or preach to draw the Article aside any way, but shall submit to it in the plain and full meaning thereof: and shall not put his own sense or comment to be the meaning of the Article, but shall take it in the literal and grammatical sense."[242]

That such articles, sprung from the controversies of the sixteenth century and whose particular doctrinal expression had been drafted to hold a very precarious balance between competing and apparently

---

240. John Henry Newman, "Tract 90: Remarks on Certain Passages in the Thirty-Nine Articles" (J. G. F. and J. Rivington, February 27, 1841), in *Tracts 5*.

241. Owen Chadwick, *The Mind of the Oxford Movement* (London: Adam and Charles Black, 1957), 24.

242. "The King's Declaration, 1628," in Bray, *Documents of the English Reformation*, 482.

incompatible theologies, would be susceptible to be treated in accordance with such an injunction seems wishful thinking of the kind with which the history, political and ecclesiastical, of the reign of Charles I is littered. By 1643, John Bramhall, Archdeacon of Meath, a noted clerical supporter of Charles and later, after the Restoration, Archbishop of Armagh,[243] pointed out that the very nature of the articles made taking them on literal terms unrealistic. He noted that the articles contained such a range of statements, that some kind of interpretation was both essential and inevitable. They were, he wrote, of such diversity of type, that the claims to a literal reading that could be made for them, were entirely dependent upon the type of truth to which each article, itself, laid claim:

> Some of them are the very same that are contained in the Creed; some others of them are practical truths, which come not within the proper list of points or articles to be believed; lastly, some of them are pious opinions or inferior truths, which are proposed by the Church of England to all her sons, as not to be opposed; not as essentials of Faith necessary to be believed by all Christians *necessitate medii*, under pain of damnation.[244]

The genius of the articles is to be found, in part because of this diversity of type, in their ability to be held by those of widely divergent opinions. They were carefully crafted to be capable of acceptance by all but those who held to strict Anabaptist beliefs concerning the common tenure of goods or the necessity of believers" baptism, on the one hand, and the specifically Roman Catholic teachings relating to the authority of the papacy, transubstantiation, indulgences, and the invocation of saints, on the other. Henry Chadwick's description of the articles as "partly controversial"[245] has more than a hint of irony to it, but it does convey something of their mixed nature: some almost entirely uncontroversial even at the time

---

243. John Bramhall, Archbishop of Armagh (c.1594–1663), *ODNB Online*.

244. John Bramhall, "Schism Guarded," in *The Works of the Most Reverend Father in God, John Bramhall, Sometime Lord Archbishop of Armagh, Primate and Metropolitan of All Ireland: With a Life of the Author, and a Collection of His Letters*, ed. Arthur West Hadden (Oxford: John Henry Parker, 1843), 476.

245. Henry Chadwick, "Traditions, Fathers, and Councils," in Sykes, Booty, and Knight, *The Study of Anglicanism*, 105.

of their composition,[246] others speaking directly to the very issues regarding justification, ecclesial authority, and ritual practice that had been at the root of the sixteenth century's controversies. Taken as a whole, Chadwick's categorization of the articles, in that it lays out a position that "may be labelled Reformed Catholicism,"[247] is not without merit, even if it is not immediately obvious to Roman Catholic sensibilities that the articles contain much that is (or, indeed, was) distinctly Catholic. It is true that the position of the Anabaptists relating to baptism is rejected, as are opposition to private property and the taking of oaths.[248] Nevertheless, the articles' treatment of papal authority, transubstantiation, the Eucharistic Sacrifice, Purgatory, relics, and indulgences is accompanied with such condemnatory language[249] that it is hard to conclude other than that they aimed to accomplish a wholesale demolition of the apparatus and thinking behind what, then and now, was recognizably and distinctively Catholic belief and practice.

Charles I's prefatory declaration had been aimed at resolving the disputes, then current, between differing schools of Protestant thought concerning the meaning of the articles. The increasing latitude in the interpretation of the articles throughout the seventeenth and eighteenth centuries similarly provided accommodation for positions that were still distinctly Protestant. Notwithstanding Laud's attempts at ritual reform[250] and, later, the theology of the Non-jurors, such room for maneuver as there was did not extend in a Catholic direction. Insofar as there was a received reading of the articles by the

---

246. See, for example, the first five. See Bray, *Documents of the English Reformation*, 285–87.

247. Chadwick, "Traditions, Fathers, and Councils," 106.

248. Articles 27, 38, and 39, Bray, *Documents of the English Reformation*, 301, 308, respectively.

249. Articles 19, 22, 28, 31, and 37, Bray, *Documents of the English Reformation*, 296, 297, 301, 303, and 307, respectively.

250. For a largely sympathetic account, see Charles Carlton, *Archbishop William Laud* (New York: Routledge and Keegan Paul, 1987). Less sympathetic is Julian Davies, *The Caroline Captivity of the Church: Charles I and the Remoulding of Anglicanism* (Oxford: Clarendon Press, 1992), although Davies does not even attempt to approach the judgment of Patrick Collinson, who describes Laud as "the greatest calamity ever visited upon the English Church" in his *The Religion of Protestants: The Church of England 1559–1625* (Oxford: Oxford University Press, 1984), 90.

time Newman came to write Tract 90, it was a reading that permitted the Calvinist, the Arminian, the Evangelical, the old High Churchman, the Erastian, and the Latitudinarian room. Newman's "novelty" was "in his handling the articles in a Catholic direction."[251]

The tract was published on February 27, 1841, and immediately caused serious excitement. Some, such as Ward, were thrilled by its contents,[252] but the chorus of criticism was not long in coming,[253] and when it came, it was relentless and, ultimately, devastating for Newman's position within the English church. The cause of excitement for both those who thrilled to it and those who condemned it was the same: the attempt to show how those historic formularies of Anglicanism were capable of an interpretation that was both authentically Anglican and coherently Catholic. In Tract 90, in particular, Newman sought to counter the objection: "that there are in the Articles [i.e., the Thirty-Nine Articles] propositions or terms inconsistent with the Catholic faith,"[254] and he would do this, he claimed, by showing that "our Articles also . . . are, through GOD's good providence, to say the least, not uncatholic, and may be subscribed by those who aim at being catholic in heart and doctrine."[255]

Although he had earlier suggested that "tho' I believe them to be entirely scriptural, . . . I think they accidentally countenance a vile Protestantism,"[256] now Newman's conviction, expressed at the very end of Tract 90, was that the articles had been "drawn up with the purpose of including Catholics; and Catholics now will not be ex-

---

251. Chadwick, *The Mind of the Oxford Movement*, 25. Rather more harshly, Pereiro has described this as having "completed their [i.e., the Articles'] trivialization," in his "*Ethos*," 191.

252. See, for example, Rowland Edmund Prothero and George Granville Bradley, *The Life and Correspondence of Arthur Penrhyn Stanley DD, Late Dean of Westminster*, vol. 1 (London: John Murray, 1893), 292.

253. The first critical response, ostensibly from four tutors in the University of Oxford (Churton, Wilson, Griffiths, and Tait), but, in fact, largely the work of C. P. Golightly, appeared on March 8, 1841. See "From T. T. Churton and Others to the Editor of the 'Tracts for the Times,'" March 8, 1841, in *LD 8*, 59–60.

254. Newman, Tract 90, 2, in *Tracts 5*.

255. Newman, Tract 90, 4, in *Tracts 5*.

256. JHN to R. F. Wilson, May 13, 1835, in *LD 5*, 70. He was later to suggest that the Catholic sense of the articles "had never been publicly recognized, while the interpretation of the day was Protestant and exclusive." See Newman, *Apo.*, 232.

cluded."[257] Whether there was much conscious intent to be so inclusive in the middle of the controversies of the sixteenth century is, as has been shown, a matter of some debate, but it was clearly of a piece with the position of many within the Oxford Movement and with the argument Newman had put forward in "Catholicity of the English Church." Tract 90 would be an attempt to prove what he had asserted in that article, that the faith of the Church of England, insofar as it was particular to the Church of England, was a move "towards a more perfect Catholicism."[258]

Newman's stated purpose in writing Tract 90 was clear. He had felt for some time that it was necessary to offer to the members of the Oxford Movement a truly Catholic synthesis of Anglicanism's distinctive teachings, one that would act as a brake on the headlong slide toward Rome that was becoming apparent in some of the younger Tractarians. In the summer of 1840, for example, he had written to Pusey of his concerns about R. W. Williams, who had arrived at a position of appearing, to Newman, to believe that "the Roman is the Catholic Church, that therefore the Tridentine Decrees are eternal truth, that to oppose them is heresy, that all who sign the 39 articles do oppose them, and that it is a sin to be in communion with heretics."[259] Although Williams was, Newman perceived, "stationary at present,"[260] that is, in no immediate danger of secession to Rome, it was clear to him that it was his duty, and that of the other leaders of the movement, to do all they could to prevent such defections. That, at least, was the proximate cause for Tract 90.[261] Newman's need to test the Anglican synthesis against his own conception of the faith of the Old Church must, however, be counted as of more fundamentally causal importance. As Nockles accurately observes: "Without

257. Newman, Tract 90, 83.
258. Newman, "Catholicity of the English Church," 77. Cf. John Henry Newman, *Lectures on the Prophetical Office of the Church Viewed Relatively to Romanism and Popular Protestantism* (London: J. G. and F. Rivington, 1837), 20.
259. JHN to E. B. Pusey, July 28, 1840, in *LD* 7, 372.
260. JHN to E. B. Pusey, July 28, 1840, in *LD* 7, 371.
261. See also Newman's August 13, 1841, letter to Edward Pusey in *LD 8*, 242–45, and his comments in JHN to R. W. Jelf, March 13, 1841, in *LD 8*, 78.

the doubts of 1839, it probably would never have been written."[262]

Whatever his explicit or implicit motives, there are those who have argued that Newman was being deliberately antagonistic. Dean Church's recollection, one that was to become a staple of Tractarian historiography among those, Church included, who viewed Newman's eventual defection as an unqualified catastrophe for the Oxford Movement, was that from the beginning there were those, often in positions of ecclesiastical authority, who believed that Newman was being consciously "absurd, mischievous, and at length traitorous."[263] In more recent times, Paul Avis has called into question Newman's account of his purpose in publishing Tract 90, particularly the account offered in the *Apologia*. He argues that Newman must have known that the tract would have been read more widely than its ostensible target audience and that the reaction of the wider readership was entirely predictable.[264] While Newman was perfectly capable of calculated antagonism, the tone of concern Newman adopted in his correspondence about the need to provide a bulwark against conversion to Rome for the younger members of the movement is entirely consistent with the concern he had consistently displayed for those in whose pastoral charge he saw himself. This same sense of moral duty that had lain at the base of his dispute with Hawkins over the Oriel tutorship, and which, despite the admission to Wilson of their countenancing of "vile Protestantism,"[265] had him in the lists to defend retaining compulsory subscription to the articles in the University in the mid-1830s,[266] now impelled him to attempt, if at all pos-

262. Nockles, "Oxford, Tract 90 and the Bishops," 41.
263. Richard William Church, *The Oxford Movement: Twelve Years, 1833–1845* (London: Macmillan, 1891), 251.
264. Paul D. L. Avis, *Anglicanism and the Christian Church: Theological Resources in Historical Perspective* (Edinburgh: T & T Clark, 1989), 226. For rival assessments of Newman's purpose in writing Tract 90, cf. Nigel Atkinson, *Beyond the Reformation? Authority, Primacy and Unity in the Conciliar Tradition* (London: Continuum, 2006), 12–13, and John R. Connolley, *John Henry Newman: A View of Catholic Faith for the New Millenium* (Lanham, Md.: Rowman and Littlefield, 2005), 4–5.
265. JHN to R. F. Wilson, May 13, 1835, in *LD 5*, 70.
266. It was from the time of this controversy that the idea of producing a Catholic interpretation of the articles may first have come. The suggestion appears in a letter from Froude to Newman ahead of the former's intended journey to Italy with Isaac Williams: "The notion of going to Rome with Isaac is very gratifying.... It occurred to me the other

sible, a presentation which would "keep our young friends etc from stumbling at the Articles and going to Rome."[267] Newman had shown the draft tract to both Pusey and Keble before it was published, the latter commenting that he thought "it very likely to answer its purpose."[268] Neither man appears to have foreseen the storm of reaction.

Had Newman been the first to attempt a Catholic synthesis of the Thirty-Nine Articles, the very novelty of the subject matter of Tract 90 would have been enough to occasion the reaction it received. It had, however, been attempted at least three times. In the early seventeenth century, the Roman Catholic convert, Franciscan friar, and papal diplomat Christopher Davenport, under his name in religion, Francis of Santa Clara,[269] wrote a detailed examination of the articles from the perspective of Tridentine Catholicism, which aimed at securing doctrinal agreement as a prelude to formal corporate reunion.[270] Again, earlier in the nineteenth century, Samuel Wix produced another, this time from a pretractarian, High Church perspective.[271] Finally, Palmer of Worcester, in unpublished notes prepared for his students and in his *A Treatise on the Church of Christ Designed Chiefly for the Use of Students in Theology*,[272] had sought to address similar issues—although, as Nockles points out, the differ-

---

day that one might send a Latin petition to the Pope confessing one's interpretation of the 39 Articles (Which by the Jesuit Francis Santa Clara showed to be 'patient if not ambitious of a Catholic meaning' and apparently Laud did not think the interpretation over strained vid Heylin) . . . and praying that one might be allowed to communicate in their Churches" (Richard Hurrell Froude to JHN, March 4, 1835, in *LD 5*, 68). In 1877, Newman quoted Francis Santa Clara's expression "patient if not ambitious of a Catholic meaning" in the "Notice" appearing in the Uniform Edition of Tract 90, 265. Francis Santa Clara was, in fact, not a Jesuit but a Franciscan. See n. 269.

267. JHN to Thomas Mozley, March 7, 1841, in *LD 8*, 58.
268. John Keble to JHN, February 19, 1841, in *LD 8*, 39.
269. For an account of the life of this remarkable man, see John Berchmas Dockery, *Christopher Davenport: Friar and Diplomat* (London: Burns and Oates, 1960). See also "Christopher Davenport (c.1595–1680)," in *ODNB Online*.
270. Christopher Davenport, *Deus, Natura, Gratia, Sive Tractatus de Praedestinatione* (Lyon, 1634).
271. Samuel Wix, *Reflections Concerning the Expediency of a Council of the Church of England and the Church of Rome Being Holden, with a View to Accommodate Religious Differences* (London: F. C. and J. Rivington, 1818).
272. William Patrick Palmer, *A Treatise on the Church of Christ: Designed Chiefly for the Use of Students in Theology*, 2 vols. (London: J. G. and F. Rivington, 1838).

ences between the first edition of 1838 (i.e., before Tract 90) and the third edition in 1842 reveal not only something of the estrangement between Palmer and Newman over the direction of the tracts but also a difference of theological assumptions and method.[273] What distinguished these attempts from Newman's in Tract 90 was not the subject matter *per se* but Newman's controversial status and, as Nockles puts it, "the execution of the Tract, and its reasoning."[274] Gladstone observed that: "there never was an uproar, and there never were censures, which were more attributable to the manner and language of a publication as contrasted with its substance."[275] Yet the substance itself was not without responsibility for the uproar.

In deciding to tackle fourteen of the thirty-nine, Newman selected those where the popular understanding was most difficult to square with a Catholic reading. His consideration of Articles 6, 11, 12, 13, 19, 20, 21, 22, 25, 28, 31, 32, 35, and 37 covered not only those disciplinary matters where Roman and Anglican practice merely differed (such as the celibacy of the clergy) but also those that touched on the doctrinal issues that had been right at the heart of the Reformation controversies: the place of scripture, the authority of the church, the theology of justification, and the sacramental and devotional apparatus. In all of this, Newman sought to maintain a distinction between the official Roman doctrine and popular Roman belief and practice, which, he argued, allowed for an accommodation of the most of the former within a reasonable interpretation of the Thirty-Nine Articles. Although Newman's insistence on expressing himself in a manner that could easily be taken as an insinuation that he spoke on behalf of the university in some inchoate, informal, but substantially real way irritated a number of his early critics,[276] it was

---

273. Nockles, *The Oxford Movement in Context*, 140. Palmer's own account of his views about the direction the tracts had taken is given in William Patrick Palmer, *A Narrative of Events Connected with the Publication of the Tracts* (Oxford: John Henry Parker, 1843). See also Nockles, "Oxford, Tract 90 and the Bishops," 48–50.

274. Nockles, "Oxford, Tract 90 and the Bishops," 42.

275. William Ewart Gladstone, *Correspondence on Church and Religion*, ed. Daniel Connor Lathbury, vol. 1 (London: John Murray, 1910), 281.

276. Edwin Abbott, *The Anglican Career of Cardinal Newman*, vol. 2 (London: Macmillan, 1892), 95.

neither this nor the specific treatment of any particular article that gave cause for the reaction.

The principal reason that first the four tutors, then the heads of Houses, then Newman's own bishop, then wider public opinion, and, later yet, almost the whole English episcopal bench came out against Tract 90 was that, from beginning to end, it read like an attack on the entire edifice of the Thirty-Nine Articles and with it the English Church: "I do not think (to borrow Mr. Newman's illustration), that the articles are a heap of stones but a building, and he who induces himself by thirty-nine quibbles to assent to them piecemeal, and then denies them as whole, is guilty of the most hateful verbal sophistry and mental reservation."[277] Such harsh criticism from those within the university and in the public press engaged Newman's polemical interest but left him fundamentally unmoved in his ecclesial position, even if he was to comment to Maria Giberne that "a destiny hangs over us, a single step may ruin all."[278]

Newman's own bishop, Richard Bagot,[279] had expressed his reservations and requested both that there be no further tracts and that Tract 90 be withdrawn from circulation,[280] but he had not yet condemned it. Newman would still be content to write: "I consider the Church over which your Lordship presides to be the Catholic Church in this country."[281] Bagot certainly never doubted it, although it is unlikely that that is quite how he would have expressed it, unless pushed. Bagot's treatment of Newman throughout this episode was marked by a certain fatherly indulgence: he was, as Nockles says, "gentle, considerate."[282] It was a judgment with which, despite his obvious and understandable disappointment at the Bishop's eventual condemnation of Tract 90 in his charge of 1842, Newman concurred.[283] Newman took comfort that those who, in his view, stood

---

277. Robert Lowe, *Observations Suggested by "A Few More Words in Support of No.90"* (Oxford: Baxter, 1841), 18.
278. JHN to Miss M. R. Giberne, March 25, 1841, in *LD 8*, 118.
279. Richard Bagot (1782–1854), *ODNB Online*.
280. Richard Bagot, Bishop of Oxford, to JHN, March 17, 1841 in *LD 8*, 95.
281. JHN to Richard Bagot, Bishop of Oxford, March 29, 1841, in *LD 8*, 140.
282. Nockles, "Oxford, Tract 90 and the Bishops," 60.
283. "I will not imply that your Lordship can act otherwise than indulgently to any one,

in succession to the apostles had not yet formally rejected his argument. In March, he wrote to Wilberforce: "The Bishops, I trust, are likely to do nothing,"[284] and, a few weeks later, to Phillipps: "No doctrine or principle has been conceded by us, or condemned by Authority. The Bishop has but said that a certain Tract is objectionable.... I have no intention whatever of yielding any one point which I hold on conviction—And that the authorities of the Church know full well."[285] The theory of possession still held, as he reminded Phillipps: "Our Bishop is our Pope. It is our theory that each Diocese is an integral Church, intercommunion being a duty, (and the breach of it a sin) but not essential to Catholicity."[286] In a letter to Bagot, Newman could still write of the Church of England as "that favoured communion in which God's good providence has placed us."[287]

During the university's Long Vacation of 1841, Newman, resident at Littlemore, returned to his study of Athanasius in preparation for the publication of a translation of his works. Rather than a return to the tranquility of study, he later recalled that it marked a return to the unease of 1839: "The ghost had come a second time. In the *Arian History* I found the very same phenomenon, in a far bolder shape, which I had found in the Monophysite."[288] The cause of this spectral return was a historical parallel. Newman saw, once again, the similarity between the relative position of the parties in an ancient doctrinal dispute and the position of the English and Roman Catholic Churches in his own day. He now clearly saw what Wiseman had so momentously and laboriously pointed out in the *Dublin Review*

---

but certainly I did feel at the time, that in the midst of the kindness you shewed to me personally, you were exercising an anxious vigilance over my publication, which reminded me of my responsibility to your Lordship" (JHN to Richard Bagot, Bishop of Oxford, March 29, 1841, in *LD 8*, 131). Bagot's charge on Tract 90 came out in May 1842 and seemed to Newman "very favourable to us," although the wording of its treatment of the tract was cause for "delicate wording" and anxiety (JHN to John Keble, May 24, 1842, in *LD 9*, 14). The text of the charge is in *LD 9*, 605–12. Newman was later to write of Bagot's conduct regarding Tract 90: "I impute nothing whatever to him, he was ever most kind to me" (*Apo.*, 174).

284. JHN to Henry Wilberforce, March 22, 1841, in *LD 8*, 113.
285. JHN to Ambrose Lisle Phillipps, April 8, 1841, in *LD 8*, 165–66.
286. JHN to Ambrose Lisle Phillipps, April 8, 1841, in *LD 8*, 166.
287. JHN to Richard Bagot, Bishop of Oxford, March 29, 1841, in *LD 8*, 131.
288. Newman, *Apo.*, 243.

articles: that the antiquity of a doctrine is not in itself a sufficient guarantee of the doctrine's orthodoxy, and that a doctrine need not have been explicitly recognized as revealed by the Apostolic Church in order to be considered part of the Apostolic faith by the Fathers. Against this, he now had only the bulwark of his theory of possession and the security that the position he had taken in Tract 90 had, thus far, escaped formal episcopal censure.

Beginning in the summer of 1841, however, the bishops began to publish visitation charges for the clergy in their dioceses that either strongly cautioned against, or implicitly or explicitly condemned, the *Tracts for the Times*, and Tract 90, in particular.[289] It appeared to Newman that the bishops, in condemning Tract 90, were attacking the Catholic faith itself. Newman insinuated to Keble that he thought one of them, at least, John Bird Sumner of Chester,[290] was leading his diocese into schism:

> Have you seen the Bishop of Chester's charge? He seems to me, as far as in him lies, to have cut off Chester by it from the Catholic Church. In such cases I see only the alternative of obeying or of calling a bishop heretic. St. Ignatius's words about trifling with the Bishop invisible are so strong, I really see no alternative between denying he is in possession of his ... functions and obeying him.[291]

It appeared that, at least as far as Sumner was concerned, the theory of possession had broken.

Newman had, from the first, maintained a narrative in which he suggested that the bishops had, somehow, broken an implicit understanding: he would not push Tract 90, and they would not condemn it. He seems to have genuinely convinced himself, and not a few of his followers, that this was the case, although it is difficult to see how such an understanding would have manifested itself. Nonetheless, Newman was determined to fight back, writing to Maria Giberne that "I suppose it will be necessary in some shape or other to reassert

---

289. See Appendix 5, *LD 8*, 569–92; Appendix 2, *LD 9*, 605–12.

290. Sumner (1780–1862) had been appointed Bishop of Chester in 1828 and was to become Archbishop of Canterbury in 1848; John Bird Sumner, *ODNB Online*.

291. JHN to John Keble, October 24, 1841, in *LD 8*, 305–6.

Tract 90; else, it will seem, after these Bishops' Charges, as if it were silenced, which it has not been, nor do I intend it should be. I wish to keep quiet; but if Bishops speak, I will speak, too."[292] In the event, events were to intervene to make any such attempt otiose.

In 1841, the Prussian diplomat Christian Karl Josias von Bunsen[293] publicized a plan to establish a Protestant bishopric in Jerusalem. Driven by the twin desires of the Emperor Frederick Wilhelm IV to reintroduce an episcopate to the Prussian state church and counter French influence in the Near East, Bunsen's plan received early support in Britain, and by the autumn of that year, Parliament had enacted legislation that allowed for the establishment of a see, the appointment to which would alternately be made by England and Prussia.[294] Newman saw the plan as a purely opportunistic, political act, but one with far-reaching consequences for the English Church. He expressed his objections to Wood, describing the proposal as "deplorable,"[295] and observed to Maria Giberne: "What a miserable concern this Jerusalem Bishoprick [sic] is! We have not a single member of our Church there, except for travellers [sic] and officials. It is a mere political piece of business, to give our government influence in the country."[296] To Keble, he wrote that, to achieve a political end by means of "a resident religious influence" in Jerusalem, the British government was engaging in an act with profound ecclesiological consequences: "so we join with Protestant Prussia to found a sect and put a Bishop over it. Really, if one has any right to utter such a thing, considering Jerusalem is the spot, there is something awful in this."[297]

---

292. JHN to Miss M. R. Giberne, October 17, 1841, in *LD 8*, 299. See also JHN to J. R. Hope, October 17, 1841, in *LD 8*, 300–301; JHN to John Keble, October 24, 1841, in *LD 8*, 305–6; JHN to Henry Wilberforce, October 24, 1841, in *LD 8*, 307–8; and JHN to Thomas Mozley, October 29, 1841, in *LD 8*, 311–12.

293. Christian Karl Josias von Bunsen (1791–1860), *ODNB Online*.

294. For an outline of the development and implementation of the plan, see Robert William Greaves, "The Jerusalem Bishopric, 1841," *The English Historical Review* 64, no. 252 (1949): 328–52; Kathleen Curran, *The Romanesque Revival: Religion, Politics, and Transnational Exchange* (University Park: Pennsylvania State University Press, 2003), 179–84.

295. JHN to S. F. Wood, October 10, 1841, in *LD 8*, 293.

296. JHN to Miss M. R. Giberne, October 17, 1841, in *LD 8*, 299.

297. JHN to John Keble, October 24, 1841, in *LD 8*, 306.

CATHOLICISM OF THE CHURCH, 1839–1842

What he had half-suspected Sumner of having done, by virtue of his charge to the clergy of the Diocese of Chester, that is, leading the English Church into schism, he now believed Parliament, with the full support of the entire English episcopate, had done with the Jerusalem bishopric:

> Alas! I cannot deny that the outward notes of the Church are partly gone from us, and partly going; and a most fearful judgment it is.... This in good measure has fallen upon us. The Church of God is under eclipse among us. Where is our unity, for which Christ prayed? where our charity, which He enjoined? where the faith once delivered, when each has his own doctrine.[298]

Lest these words did not make sufficiently explicit Newman's concerns, when he came to publish the sermon, along with twenty-five others, in *Sermons Bearing on Subjects of the Day* in late 1843, he added two notes. For the tone as much as for the content, it is worth quoting them in full:

> 1. An allusion was here intended to the then recent appointment (1841) of an Anglican Bishop at Jerusalem, which has had a most grievous effect in weakening the argument for our church's Catholicity, and in shaking the belief in it of individualism May that measure utterly fail and come to nought, and be as though it had never been!
>
> 2. Such conversions to the Church of Rome as have occurred among us, are, for the most part, subsequent to March, 1841; from which date our Church has, in various ways, and through various of her organs, taken a side, and that the Protestant side, in a number of questions of the day. The authorities who were parties to the condemnation of No. 90 of the "Tracts for the Times," by that interposition, released the author, in his own feelings, of the main weight of a great responsibility; the responsibility, which up to that time attached to him, of inculcating religious views which, however primitive, however necessary for our Church, however sanctioned by her writers, tended, without a strong safeguard, towards the theology of Rome. Till then, whatever happened amiss in the spread of Catholic doctrine, might be supposed to flow as a direct result from that one cause which

---

298. Sermon no. 584, "Outward and Inward Notes of the Church," in *Sermons Bearing on the Subjects of the Day* (London: Longmans, Green and Co., 1902), 335, hereafter *SD*. Newman notes in his diary for December 5, 1841, "preached Number 584," *LD 8*, 363.

alone seemed in operation, the advocacy of patristical theology; and of its advocates the remedy and correction of all irregularities in the direction of Rome might fairly be demanded. But the state of the case was changed, when persons in station interfered with the work, and took the matter into their own hands. In saying this, the author has no wish at all to rid himself of such responsibility as really belongs to him. That in the course of his exposition of Anglican principles, statements or views were evolved which have become a disposing cause of certain tendencies to Rome, now existing, he does not deny; but theological principles and doctrines have little influence on the mind holding them, without the stimulus of external circumstances. Many a man might have held an abstract theory about the Catholic Church to which it was difficult to adjust our own, might have submitted a suspicion, or even painful doubts about the latter, yet never have been impelled onwards, had our rulers preserved the quiescence of former years; but it is the corroboration of a present, living, and energetic heterodoxy, which realizes and makes them practical; it has been the recent speeches and acts of authorities, who had so long been tolerant of Protestant error, which have given to inquiry and to theory its force and its edge. Such toleration of Catholic doctrine may have been impossible or wrong; that is another question, with which private persons have no right to interfere; still it may be a fact, that the want of it has been the cause of recent secessions.[299]

The theory of possession had, for Newman, been quite as pulverized as the theory of the *via media* two years previously. If the Catholicism of the church was to provide the key to the search for continuity in the face of doctrinal change, the episcopal response to Tract 90 and the lightness with which those same bishops would, as Newman saw it, lay aside their apostolical claims over the establishment of the Jerusalem bishopric, meant that it would not be found where he had thus far hoped it to be.

299. *SD*, 342.

CHAPTER 4

FROM A CATHOLICISM OF THE CHURCH TO THE CHURCH OF CATHOLICISM— 1842 TO 1845

Each of the hypotheses that Newman had proposed to account for change in Christian doctrine that might have been reconciled with his belief in its essential continuity had failed to stand up to scrutiny. Since at least as early as 1826, he had been aware of the difficulty caused by the historical evidence of doctrinal change, and he had suggested successive theories to account for this: by 1842, none still stood. The objections to each hypothesis had been sufficient to undermine Newman's capacity to reconcile his *a priori* assumption of a fixed body of divine revelation with that evidence of doctrinal change. The various hypotheses had been shown to be either insufficient explanation for what had happened or to be paper theories, untried in the real life of a Church of England unwilling to try them and decisively rejected and undermined by precisely those whose office within that church it was, Newman believed, to uphold them. This chapter examines Newman's final attempt at arriving at a real and workable hypothesis in his last University Sermon and in the *Essay*. It first surveys the background to Newman's fifteenth and final University Sermon before looking closely at the text of the sermon itself, in which the theory of development, the outlines of which were sketched out in the correspondence with his brother Francis, is first laid out in detail. The chapter then considers the full flowering of Newman's work on development in the *Essay*. It looks at the process of its production in 1844 and 1845, its structure, and its text. Examining the complete synthetic hypothesis, which preserved and incorporated many elements of his prior attempts at accounting for the difficulty of continuity and change, the chapter closes by arguing that Newman's theory of development is, in virtue of its logical structure, a fundamentally ecclesiological hypothesis to account for developments in doctrine and practice rather than an attempt to set forth a speculative, forensic method for the authentication or otherwise of particular developments in Christian doctrine in anticipation.

Background to the Final University Sermon

As has been shown in the previous chapters, Newman had long accepted that there had been a change in expressions of doctrine across time, and he had come to see that later expressions contained a complexity and richness of understanding that was not to be found in the earlier formulations of the same doctrines. Through his consideration and reconsideration of the Christological and Trinitarian controversies of the fourth and fifth centuries, over a decade or more, Newman had come to acknowledge the development of doctrinal ideas as an historical and observable fact. They were not merely changes in the doctrinal vocabulary itself, and still less were they to be explained by a growing openness of the church to speak of them. By 1842, his concern had crystalized around the need to establish a workable theological principle by which it was possible to demonstrate how those changes could be coherent and in accord with the Apostolic faith. He had first attempted to do this through considering terminological change and the *disciplina arcani*, which led him to various manifestations or iterations of a Catholicism of the Word, all of which ultimately failed to produce the account for which he was looking. This had led him to an attempt to construct a hypothesis that depended on a notion of a Catholicism of the church, an endeavor that had foundered on the rocks of Anglican *realpolitik*.

In his correspondence with the Abbé Jager, Newman had sought to subject the practical, popular (as opposed to official) doctrines and devotions of Roman Catholicism, especially those related to the veneration of the Virgin Mary, to scrutiny, and they had failed the test that he applied to them at that time. He measured them against the Vincentian Canon and found them wanting precisely because he could find no way of connecting their newness, their novelty with the ancient doctrine and practice of the church. When he attempted to justify the particular doctrinal formulations of Anglicanism in Tract 90, the reaction of his co-religionists had shown him that the problems of a hypothesis of the Catholicism of the church were practically insurmountable from within the Anglican Communion: those on whom the theory depended—the bishops—were precisely those who refused its strictures and its consequences. The effect of the Monophysite parallel and Wiseman's article on the Donatists had first suggested what the Jerusalem Bishopric and the episcopal reaction to Tract 90 had confirmed: that a Catholicism of the church could not alone provide a satisfactory account for development, not even in the attenuated form of his theory of possession and the desperate attempt to cling to the note of holiness that had characterized the article in the *British Critic*. In the letters to his brother Francis in the autumn of 1840, Newman had first explicitly, albeit privately, sketched out a synthetic system that, as this chapter will demonstrate, would provide a robust hypothesis of development that accounted for his long-lasting "difficulty." This hypothesis would draw on many elements of his earlier theories and bind them together in the ecclesial matrix of the claims of the Roman Catholic Church.

Owen Chadwick observes that Newman, "had applied the test of antiquity to the teaching and practice of the Church of England, he had pressed her to measure herself against antiquity, and the Church of England was refusing, and refusing vociferously, to be measured into the bed which he designed."[1] The immediate exterior result of

---

1. Chadwick, *From Bousset to Newman*, 120.

that procrustean struggle had been Newman's withdrawal both from controversy and from Oxford life. Chadwick argues that there was an accompanying internal result: that "between 1841 and the spring of 1843 Newman's mind ... crossed the Rubicon" with regard to the notion of the development of doctrine.[2] In support of his contention, Chadwick cites two fixed points that he takes as conclusive evidence of such a momentous change. He first notes that as late as 1841, Newman was declaring "that novelty in doctrine was heresy"[3] and, secondly, that Newman's final University Sermon, delivered on February 2, 1843, entitled "The Theory of Developments in Religious Doctrine," was his "first public utterance upon the question."[4] While both of those statements are, up to a point, correct, and the withdrawal to Littlemore a matter of record, the inference of the point in time of the internal change in Newman that Chadwick draws from them is not. The idea that Newman, in claiming that novelty in doctrine was the mark of heresy, was condemning any theory of the development of doctrine, is to misunderstand both what Newman meant by novelty and what he meant by the development of doctrine.

The lengths to which Newman had gone, both in his correspondence with Jager and in Tract 90, to distinguish between novelty and development were considerable. In the Jager correspondence, it was precisely the novelty of Roman Catholic teaching and practice that Newman criticized, but it was novelty understood in the sense of an apparent unconnected newness, incoherence, and incompatibility with antecedent, particularly patristic, expressions of Christian doctrine. Newman had presumed that the particular expression of Christian belief and practice to be found in the Church of England was capable of such a connection, although a more forensic interlocutor than Abbé Jager might have put Newman to proof on this matter, proof that the controversy around Tract 90 had shown was wanting.

In making his assertion that the Rubicon of development was crossed sometime between 1841 and 1843, Chadwick relies particularly on an interpretation of the arguments advanced by Newman

---

2. Chadwick, *From Bousset to Newman*, 120.
3. Chadwick, *From Bousset to Newman*, 120.
4. Chadwick, *From Bousset to Newman*, 120.

in a review of a series of pamphlets on the subject of conversion to Roman Catholicism, which appeared in *British Critic* in July 1841, and which came to be known by its running header, "Private Judgement."[5] Here Newman had written that

> considering, in a word, that change is really the characteristic of error, and unalterableness the attribute of truth, of holiness, of Almighty God Himself, we consider that when Private Judgment moves in the direction of innovation, it may well be regarded at first with suspicion and treated with severity. Nay, we confess even a satisfaction, when a penalty is attached to the expression of new doctrines, or to a change of communion. We repeat it, if any men have strong feelings, they should pay for them; if they think it a duty to unsettle things established, they should show their earnestness by being willing to suffer. We shall be the last to complain of this kind of persecution, even though directed against what we consider the cause of truth. Such disadvantages do no harm to that cause in the event, but they bring home to a man's mind his own responsibility; they are a memento to him of a great moral law, and warn him that his private judgment, if not a duty, is a sin.[6]

Chadwick appears to take this argument as evidence that Newman rejected the notion of development altogether, and yet Newman's point here and elsewhere in the article makes obvious the difference between those changes which were novel, relying on nothing more than private judgment, and those that represented proper developments. This is a further prefiguring of the distinction between authentic developments and corruptions, first drawn in the correspondence with his brother Francis in November of the previous year, and which he was later to repeat throughout the *Essay*. It is, of course, possible that Chadwick was unaware of the correspondence with Francis Newman, for he makes no mention of it. Nevertheless, the distinction in "Private Judgement" is clear, yet Chadwick appears not to consider it.

Immediately before the remarks in "Private Judgement" cited

---

5. John Henry Newman, "Private Judgement," *The British Critic and Quarterly Theological Review* 30 (1841): 100–134. The article is reproduced in the Uniform Edition with minor amendments in *Ess.* 1, 336–74.

6. Newman, "Private Judgement," 105.

above, Newman had already argued that "we are far indeed from saying, that it is never to advance in the direction of change or revolution, else the Gospel itself could never have been introduced; but we consider that such material changes have a *prima facie* case against them; they have something to get over, to prove their admissibility, before it can be reasonably granted."[7] Here, Newman is considering primarily the use of private judgment in justifying a change of religious confession, but he later makes clear that the same principle applies to alterations, changes, or developments in doctrine. The proper use of private judgment is, Newman maintained, not to justify which doctrines one can or cannot, should or should not assent to, but to identify who the authentic teacher of the faith is: "The great question which it [scripture] puts before private judgement is, who is God's prophet and where? Who is to be considered the voice of the Holy Catholic and Apostolic Church?"[8]

This was an argument that Newman was to repeat in his 1848 novel *Loss and Gain*, where he employs the metaphor of the use of a lamp to find one's way into a house to explain the proper use of private judgment in finding the truth:

And here we see what is meant when a person says that the Catholic system comes home to his mind, fulfills his ideas of religion, satisfies his sympathies, and the like; and thereupon becomes a Catholic. Such a person is often said to go by private judgment, to be choosing his religion by his own standard of what a religion ought to be. Now it need not be denied that those who are external to the Church must begin with private judgment; they use it in order ultimately to supersede it; as a man out of doors uses a lamp in a dark night and puts it out when he gets home. What would be thought of his bringing it into his drawing-room? ... There is no absurdity, then, or inconsistency in a person first using his private judgment and then denouncing its use. Circumstances change duties.[9]

The question for the Anglican Newman in 1841 was precisely the same as it would be for him as a Roman Catholic in 1848. It was

---

7. Newman, "Private Judgement," 104.
8. Newman, "Private Judgement," 116.
9. John Henry Newman, *Loss and Gain: The Story of a Convert*, Uniform ed. (Longmans, Green and Co., 1874), 203–4.

not: "What is the faith of the Church?" but rather, "Where was the Church of the faith?"; not "What is the Catholicism of the Church?" but rather "Where is the Church of Catholicism?"

Development for Newman, from his first, inchoate embryonic awareness of it as terminological change in the 1820s to the concrete, systematic, and fully worked out version of it as the theory of the development of doctrine in the *Essay* was not about accepting novelty in doctrine but about verifying doctrinal change as "the development being but the carrying out of an idea into its consequences."[10] The object of faith, that is, the unchanging, unalterable object of faith, remained for Newman that other "luminously self-evident being," and it was axiomatic that God does not change. Louis Allen's observation concerning Newman's position in the Jager correspondence, "that object itself remained identical and invariable,"[11] remained his position. The deposit of faith was fixed, but the truth about God was immutable.

What did change and develop, however, was the church's understanding of that immutable truth, as those proper consequences became clear under the action of prayer, reflection, and intellectual consideration, in the face of, among other things, heresy. There is no denying that between 1841 and 1843, Newman was able to bring into focus a more complete hypothesis to account for this difficulty. Nevertheless, his correspondence with his brother Francis in 1840, which was considered in the previous chapter, is persuasive evidence that what he preached in 1843 had already been substantially worked out three years earlier and, as James Pereiro argues, goes to "definitively disprove Chadwick's suggestion."[12] Newman's

10. Newman, *Dev.*, 55.
11. Allen, *Newman and Jager*, 13.
12. Pereiro, "*Ethos*," 171. The previous chapters have shown that Pereiro's own position, reliant as it is on Newman's criticisms of S. F. Wood's treatment of the subject, that "the evidence against Newman having held a theory of development before 1840 is compelling" (166) cannot withstand a scrutiny of the evidence of the link between development and principle of reserve and the unsent letter to Falconer. Furthermore, in his dismissal of Newman's own recollection of events, to his sister Jemima in 1843, that he had "now for 12 years been working out a theory" (JHN to Mrs. J. Mozley, January 23, 1843) of development, Pereiro's approach is similar to that taken by Thomas and also examined in the previous chapter. Thomas called into question Newman's recollection in the *Apologia* of the effect

attempt to grapple with doctrinal change in each of those and other episodes is entirely consonant with his claims made in letters to his sister Jemima in 1843[13] and to Mrs. William Froude in 1844.[14] What had happened, however, was that by 1844, his earlier hypotheses had each been shown to contain workable and unworkable elements: the former elements eventually coalescing into the theory that Newman had sketched for his brother and that had been shaped by the crises of the intervening years into a coherent, robust, and fundamentally ecclesiological theory of development.

"The Theory of Developments in Religious Doctrine"

While returning to the subject matter of the relationship between faith and reason under the title "Wisdom, as Contrasted with Faith and with Bigotry,"[15] Newman's fourteenth University Sermon did not take the issue of the development of doctrine significantly further forward. Echoing the impression of discomfort Newman had given when writing *The Arians*, that, to use once again Williams's apt phrase, "the advance of dogma is something almost tragic, a poign-

---

of the events of 1839, while simultaneously offering a plausible explanation of events that accorded with Newman's account. Similarly, Pereiro decides against Newman's claim in that same letter to his sister, to "have kept to the same views and arguments for 12 years" (214) while admitting that it is perfectly possible to read those words in the sense of Newman's notion "of interpreting previous steps ... by later ones" (165). Pereiro takes as decisive what he asserts to be "[t]he fact that whenever he confronted the question, whether in his 1835 controversy with Jager, in his conversations with Wood, or in the *Prophetical Office*, he resisted the principle of development and fought against it" (167).

As the examination of those episodes in the earlier chapters has shown, "the fact" is nothing of the sort. It is, rather, one reading of Newman's engagement in each of those controversies and a reading that makes the mistake of confusing Newman's rejection of what he then took to be the specifically Roman Catholic version of the idea of development with the idea of the development of doctrine *per se*.

13. JHN to Mrs. J. Mozley, January 23, 1843, in *LD 9*, 214.
14. JHN to Mrs. William Froude, July 14, 1844, in *LD 10*, 297.
15. JHN, "Sermon 14. Wisdom, as Contrasted with Faith and with Bigotry," in *USS*, 278–311. Original manuscript in A.9.4, BOA. As the fifteenth University Sermon contains, in embryo, the theory that was to be fully expatiated in the *Essay*, the fourteenth sermon contains the germ of the idea of a university. See Ker, *Newman: A Biography*, 264–66.

ant ideological puberty,"[16] he now wrote of wisdom, "that its perversions are such as love of system, theorizing, fancifulness, dogmatism, and bigotry."[17] Newman stated again what had been clear to him in the previous University Sermon and had been brought out in his correspondence with his brother:

Reason is the power of proceeding to new ideas by means of given ones. Where but one main idea is given, it can employ itself in developing this into its consequences. Thus, from scanty data, it often draws out a whole system, each part with its ascertained relations, collateral or lineal, towards the rest, and all consistent together, because all derived from one and the same origin. And should means be found of ascertaining directly some of the facts which it has been deducing by this abstract process, then their coincidence with its à priori judgments will serve to prove the accuracy of its deductions. Where, however, the facts or doctrines in question are all known from the first, there, instead of advancing from idea to idea, Reason does but connect fact with fact; instead of discovering, it does but analyze; and what was, in the former case, the tracing out of inferences, becomes a laying down of relations.[18]

It was the manner in which Newman understood that process to work that was to form the subject of his fifteenth and final University Sermon, "The Theory of Developments in Religious Doctrine," preached on the Feast of the Purification, February 2, 1843.[19]

Five days before that last sermon, the *Oxford Conservative Journal* printed the letter Newman had sent to its editor on the preceding December 12.[20] To again use Chadwick's imagery, if there was a Rubicon being crossed at this stage, this was it. As late as the *British Critic* article of January 1841, Newman's capacity for stridently crit-

16. Williams, "Newman's Arians," 270.
17. Newman, *USS*, 282.
18. Newman, *USS*, 290.
19. Newman, *USS*, 312–51. Original manuscript in A.9.4., BOA.
20. JHN to the editor of the *Oxford Conservative Journal*, December 12, 1842, in *LD* 9, 167–72. The retraction was later published in the *English Churchman* with a lengthy foreword that aimed at diffusing any intemperate reaction. For a typical reaction to Newman's retraction, see "To the Rev. J. H. Newman," a letter published in the *Oxford Herald*, March 31, 1843, from "A Member of Convocation," in *LD* 9, 296–97. The pseudonymous title of the author indicated an individual who, by virtue of holding the Master of Arts degree of the University of Oxford, was a member of the university's governing body.

ical language to describe the teachings and practices of Roman Catholicism was on display, and yet now, less than two years later, he was retracting that same anti-Catholic language. He sought to excuse himself from his previous anti-Catholic language by suggesting that he was doing no more than following "almost a consensus of the divines" of the Church of England and seeking to deflect his critics who accused him of "Romanism."[21] The more powerful reason he gave, however, was that he had believed that there had been "no other way" than to resort to such polemical language if "Rome is to be withstood" and "Anglican doctrine" affirmed as "the only possible antagonist" of the Roman Catholic system.[22] For the time being, he maintained his defense of Anglican doctrine and no longer felt that it required the support of the kind of anti-Catholic statements to which he had previously had recourse. Indeed, as Ker notes, some two years earlier, he had already expressed his "misery" at the lack of a Catholic ethos in the Church of England and had suggested to his sister that he had begun "to have serious apprehension lest any religious body is strong enough to withstand the league of evil, but the Roman Church."[23] Under the circumstances, he could no longer simply dismiss doctrines and practices peculiar to Roman Catholicism, still less do so in the pungent language to which he had previously resorted. In his final sermon, which he had prepared for the Feast of the Purification, he laid out for the first time publicly the theory that he had sketched for his brother in the 1840 correspondence. If he was right, and his hypothesis did account for the difficulty of apparent doctrinal change, the need for which he had first explicitly identified in 1826 (when, of course, he had in contemplation Rome), particularly as possibly the only strong bulwark against the league of evil of "wretched Socialists," liberal biblical critics such as Carlyle (whose name Newman misspells as "Carlile"), Arnold and Milman, "political Economists," and "Geologists,"[24] then the

---

21. JHN to the editor of the *Oxford Conservative Journal*, December 12, 1842, in *LD* 9, 171.
22. JHN to the editor of the *Oxford Conservative Journal*, December 12, 1842, in *LD* 9, 172.
23. Ker, *Newman: A Biography*, 193. See JHN to J. W. Bowden, February 21, 1840, in *LD* 7, 240, and JHN to Mrs. John Mozley, February 25, 1840, in *LD* 7, 245.
24. JHN to Mrs. John Mozley, February 25, 1840, in *LD* 7, 244–45.

Catholic Church was as entitled to have what she claimed to be her developments tested by reference to that hypothesis, as was the Church of England.

None of Newman's University Sermons are, by modern standards, brief, but the fifteenth is of a length that even he thought exceptional. As preached, "The Theory of Developments in Religious Doctrine" lasted over ninety minutes.[25] Writing to Pusey three days before he preached it, Newman had quipped that, "if any one values his Luncheon on Thursday, he must not go to hear me at St. Mary's, for my sermon is of portentous length—and my only satisfaction is that, if any persons go out of curiosity, they will be punished."[26] For their pains, his hearers heard Newman set his theory of the development of doctrine within the context of the faith of the Blessed Virgin Mary as revealed in the scriptures. Newman reminded his congregation that:

> Mary's faith did not end in a mere acquiescence in Divine providences and revelations ... she "pondered" them ... both in the reception and in the study of Divine Truth. She does not think it enough to accept, she dwells upon it; not enough to possess, she uses it; not enough to assent, she developes [sic] it; not enough to submit the Reason, she reasons upon it; not indeed reasoning first, and believing afterwards, with Zacharias, yet first believing without reasoning, next from love and reverence, reasoning after believing. And thus she symbolizes to us, not only the faith of the unlearned, but of the doctors of the Church also, who have to investigate, and weigh, and define, as well as to profess the Gospel.[27]

The sermon is an extended demonstration, in general and with reference to particular doctrines, of what Newman presented as the historical fact of the first of the themes he had identified in his letter to his brother. The relationship between life and development, and the preservation of identity through that development, is the

---

25. "On the 2nd of February 1843, the Feast of the Purification, all Oxford assembled to hear what Newman had to say.... For an hour and a half he drew out the argument," wrote John Campbell Shairp, *Studies in Poetry and Philosophy* (Edinburgh: Edmonston and Douglas, 1868), 249, cited in *LD* 9, 218, n. 1.

26. JHN to E. B. Pusey, January 20, 1843, in *LD* 9, 217.

27. Newman, *USS*, 312–13.

key idea that Newman used to account for the apparent paradox of change and continuity—his "difficulty" since 1826. This identification of the link between life, development, and identity, both necessary and observable, was neither unique nor original to Newman: Coleridge had written of something very similar in the notes to his 1812 and 1813 lectures on Shakespeare: "the organic form ... shapes as it developes [sic] itself from within, and the fullness of its development is one & the same with the perfection of its outward Form: such is the Life, such is the Form."[28]

Newman went beyond theoretical assertion, however, and argued that this relationship is an observable datum of Christian history. Christian doctrine, the "large fabric of divinity," was nothing more and nothing less than "the development of an idea, and like itself, and unlike anything else, its most widely-separated parts having relations with each other, and betokening a common origin."[29] It was, he argued, the natural "expansion of a few words, uttered, as if casually, by the fishermen of Galilee."[30] In a passage that he later noted, when preparing the sermon for publication in the Uniform Edition, owed something to his early familiarity with Bull's *Analogy* and certainly foreshadowing the "tests" of the *Essay*, Newman wrote of the Gospel:

Its half sentences, its overflowings of language, admit of development; they have a life in them which shows itself in progress; a truth, which has the token of consistency; a reality, which is fruitful in resources; a depth, which extends into mystery: for they are representations of what is actual, and has a definite location and necessary bearings and a meaning in the great system of things, and a harmony in what it is, and a compatibility in what it involves.[31]

---

28. Samuel Taylor Coleridge, *Lectures 1808–1819*, ed. R.A. Foakes (Princeton, N.J.: Routledge and Keegan Paul, 1987), 494. While there are similarities in their thought, Newman and Coleridge differed markedly on the nature of ideas; see John Coulson, *Newman and the Common Tradition: A Study in the Language of Church and Society* (Oxford: Clarendon Press, 1960), 58–63.
29. Newman, *USS*, 316.
30. Newman, *USS*, 317.
31. Newman, *USS*, 319.

Given Newman's clear explication of his purpose in preaching the sermon and the manner in which it was organized, Turner's claim that Newman's purpose was driven by a desire to defend the "Tractarian asceticism" of the "coterie" at Littlemore, to "underscore his longstanding call to a religion of obedience and ... [sustain] ... his monastic experiment," can be discounted.[32] In fact, the hypothesis of development is set out in a highly structured manner about halfway through the sermon. Newman laid out before the congregation the elements of his theory of the relationship between the idea and its doctrinal expressions in a series of points worth quoting here *in extenso*:

Now of such sacred ideas and their attendant expressions, I observe:—

(1.) First, that an impression of this intimate kind seems to be what Scripture means by "knowledge."

...

(2.) This leads me next, however, to observe, that these religious impressions differ from those of material objects, in the mode in which they are made. The senses are direct, immediate, and ordinary informants, and act spontaneously without any will or effort on our part; but no such faculties have been given us, as far as we know, for realizing the Objects of Faith.

...

(3.) Further, I observe, that though the Christian mind reasons out a series of dogmatic statements, one from another, this it has ever done, and always must do, not from those statements taken in themselves, as logical propositions, but as being itself enlightened and (as if) inhabited by that sacred impression which is prior to them, which acts as a regulating principle,

...

(4.) Again ... that Revelation itself has provided in Scripture the main outlines and also large details of the dogmatic system. Inspiration has superseded the exercise of human Reason in great measure, and left it but the comparatively easy task of finishing the sacred work.

...

(5.) Scripture, I say, begins a series of developments which it does not finish; that is to say, in other words, it is a mistake to look for every separate proposition of the Catholic doctrine in Scripture.

...

32. Turner, *The Challenge*, 501.

(6.) And here we see the ordinary mistake of doctrinal innovators, viz. to go away with this or that proposition of the Creed, instead of embracing that one idea which all of them together are meant to convey; it being almost a definition of heresy, that it fastens on some one statement as if the whole truth, to the denial of all others, and as the basis of a new faith.[33]

Here, in the sermon, Newman would develop the theory to encompass the three elements of his case to his brother: the necessary connection between life, development, and identity with respect to ideas and their expression in doctrine; growth in understanding within the church; and the existence of "tests" by which developments could be evaluated. What he would not yet attempt was to situate his theory within a definite ecclesial setting, while explicitly acknowledging the need for such. This was either because he was unclear of the answer or, as seems more likely in the light of previous admissions in correspondence, because of a prudential exercise of the principle of reserve; Newman excused himself from the task of identifying the ecclesial locus within which his theory of development was to operate. He commented: "Nor am I here in any way concerned with the question, who is the legitimate framer and judge of these dogmatic inferences under the Gospel, or if there be any. Whether the church is infallible, or the individual, or the first ages, or none of these, is not the point here, but the theory of developments itself."[34]

A striking characteristic of the sermon is how, as it progressed, Newman sought to deal with the objections to and weaknesses of the various hypotheses that he had previously proposed to account for what had appeared to him to be doctrinal change. The problem with these hypotheses, as the sermon makes clear, was that none of them could offer a sufficient account yet each of them held an element of truth, which, when taken together and combined into a composite and multifaceted theory, would do duty. Here, the linguistic development that Newman had thought some twenty years earlier could explain how the church's doctrine developed while the object of faith

---

33. Newman, *USS*, 332–37.
34. Newman, *USS*, 319–20.

remained consistent is offered not as an explanation or a rule but as an observable fact deriving from the very nature of language. As "representations of what is actual" rather than the actual thing itself, there is a natural incompleteness to them: they are not and, indeed, cannot be a complete account. As the church, like her pattern the Virgin Mary, ponders the object of faith and the terms used to represent it, in their incompleteness and contingency, those "half-sentences" and "overflowings" give way to further expressions. The objection to this facet of a theory of development of doctrine was that while it might be true that orthodox doctrine develops from this incompleteness, it was less clear from the historical record that it had done so, whereas it was clear that heresy grew in precisely this way.

In the face of this obvious shortcoming, rather than take refuge in the *disciplina arcani* as Newman had done in the early 1830s, he now proposed a series of distinguishing marks, which foreshadow the "tests" of the *Essay*. Authentic development, Newman wrote, has about these changes of linguistic expression and vocabulary the characteristics of life manifesting itself in progress, truth showing itself in consistency, reality demonstrated by its fruitfulness, and depth that leads to mystery and fits into a coherent system that has both harmony and compatibility. As Newman argued, however, although having about it the tendency to change and develop, heresy did so without these marks, substituting its own: "its dogmas are unfruitful; it has no theology; so far forth as it is heresy, it has none. Deduct its remnant of Catholic theology, and what remains? Polemics, explanations, protests.... Its *formulæ* end in themselves, without development.... It developes [sic] into dissolution."[35]

The relationship between the object of faith and the church's attempts to express it was central to Newman's argument as he set out a systematic theology of development. It is primarily a relationship that might be said to belong properly to the sphere of philosophy rather than theology. Newman explained to his listeners that it was a matter of exploring the "connexion [sic] between Faith and Dogmat-

---

35. Newman, *USS*, 318.

ic confession,"[36] the former being as distinct from the latter, as the idea is from its expression:

> Theological dogmas are propositions expressive of the judgments which the mind forms, or the impressions which it receives, of Revealed Truth. Revelation sets before it certain supernatural facts and actions, beings and principles; these make a certain impression or image upon it; and this impression spontaneously, or even necessarily, becomes the subject of reflection on the part of the mind itself, which proceeds to investigate it, and to draw it forth in successive and distinct sentences.[37]

These distinctions between the object itself, the idea of the object, and the doctrinal expression of the idea were key to the synthesis Newman was proposing in the sermon and would remain so in the *Essay*. As Terrence Merrigan notes, for Newman, "the Christian idea is Christ Himself,"[38] the divine truth, a fixed, unchanging whole; the idea, being at all times a partial and incomplete impression of that divine truth, was bound to change as the doctrinal expression of it developed through the natural—and, Newman would come to argue in the *Essay*, divinely intended—reflection upon it by the minds of those who were animated by the Holy Spirit within the communion of the church. The natural concomitant of this is that dogmatic expression might be at once both a distinct sentence, that is, a definitive expression of an idea, and yet contingent. In his consideration not of the sermon but of the *Essay*, Lash expresses this idea by observing that identity and distinctiveness are not necessarily contradictory:

> Christianity is an "idea" inasmuch as it is the human apprehension of that "fact" which is christianity [sic] considered as God's word, or self-disclosure of his will and purposes for man. The "idea" is one because the "fact" is one. The "idea" is "real" because God's revelation is an "objective fact," and not an illusion of man. The "idea" is "living" because it is God's living word.[39]

---

36. Newman, *USS*, 319.

37. Newman, *USS*, 320.

38. Terrence Merrigan, *Clear Heads and Holy Hearts: The Religious and Theological Ideal of John Henry Newman*, Louvain Theological and Pastoral Monographs 7 (Louvain: Peeters, 1991), 98.

39. Nicholas Lash, *Newman on Development: The Search for an Explanation in History* (London: Sheed and Ward, 1975), 52; Cf. Newman, *USS*, 328.

In the same way as the expression itself is distinct from the idea, understood as the judgments and impressions formed in the mind, so, too, is the object of faith distinct from the idea. In expressing the idea in "successive and distinct sentences," those expressions successively more nearly and completely approximate to the idea, and yet the idea itself is but the judgment and impression of the reality and so, under the action of ecclesial reflection, the idea itself develops. Nonetheless, because the dogmatic expression manifested itself in continuity with the underlying idea, its various expressions were themselves closely connected.

To illustrate this point, Newman utilized an analogy from St. Mark's Gospel: they were like the corn "first the blade, then the ear, after that the full corn in the ear," (4:28) each distinct, accurate, definitive and yet to be superseded not by "abrupt revolution, or reaction, or fickleness of mind" but rather as "the development, in explicit form, of what was already latent within it ... possessed, ruled, guided by an unconscious idea."[40] Neither is the lack of a public expression of a particular truth to be taken as evidence of its novelty nor yet of its suppression as part of a systematic *disciplina arcani*. Instead, Newman argued for a notion that he had most recently explored in the thirteenth University Sermon, that of a dynamic by which what was implicit became explicit: "The absence, or partial absence, or incompleteness of dogmatic statements is no proof of the absence of impressions or implicit judgments, in the mind of the Church. Even centuries might pass without the formal expression of a truth, which had been all along the secret life of millions of faithful souls."[41]

The impetus for this dynamic would be explored in much greater detail in the *Essay*, but the part that the study of heresy had played in clarifying Newman's own understanding of both the content and the proper locus of Christian doctrine provided him with at least one reason for this movement, for "when details must be drawn out, and misapprehensions anticipated," as is the case when responding to error, "we seem never to be rid of the responsibility of our

40. Newman, *USS*, 321–22.
41. Newman, *USS*, 323.

task."[42] Commenting on this, Jan Hendrik Walgrave suggested that this sermon "underestimates the part played by implicit reasoning" when compared with the *Essay*.[43] This might slightly overstate the difference between the two works, however, and Walgrave offered an alternative explanation by suggesting that this is because the sermon only "deals with the same limited question as *The Arians*, namely, the genesis of explicit dogmatic formulas, especially the Trinitarian and Christological ones, and from a definite psychological standpoint (the relations between faith and reason)."[44]

While for Newman the richness and fruitfulness were among the marks of authentic development, he was aware that he had critics who saw matters very differently. Hampden, for example, was of the view that the progressive clarification of doctrinal positions tended to diminish the underlying reality: seeking to identify as one and the same the reality with the doctrinal expression. It was in answer to this position that Newman contended that far from being an abuse of reason, the process he was outlining gave ever more fresh perspectives on that reality, or at least on the impressions of it made upon the intellect. Accordingly, the field of divinity, the apprehension of the divine reality widened under the aspect of development rather than narrowed. If anything, the process tended to broaden the understanding of the mystery of God. A natural result of this was the wide variety of the results of the process: "the great remoteness of the separate results of a common idea, or rather at first sight the absence of any connexion [sic]."[45] In fact, Newman, suggested, "we fancied our idea could be expressed in one or two sentences. Explanations grow under our hands, in spite of our effort at compression."[46]

To those others, Evangelicals and even those associated with the Oxford Movement, such as Palmer of Worcester, who sensed that

---

42. Newman, *USS*, 327.

43. Jan Hendrick Walgrave, *Newman the Theologian: The Nature of Belief and Doctrine as Exemplified in His Life and Works*, trans. A. V. Littledale (London: Geoffrey Chapman, 1960), 96.

44. Walgrave, *Newman the Theologian*, 96–97.

45. Newman, *USS*, 326.

46. Newman, *USS*, 326.

development was a "Romanizing" tendency that sought to go beyond, for the Evangelicals, the scriptural deposit and, for Palmer, "the Catholic verities [the Church] received from the Apostles,"[47] Newman's reply was that the scriptural warrant offered by the Virgin Mary's pondering and the evidence that even those "Catholic verities" had been established by precisely the process of development he was describing was answer enough. He admitted that there is a danger with this process. If one moved beyond the textual fundamentalism of a Catholicism of the Word, Newman understood that this could lead to a situation in which the church's doctrine could appear unconnected with the idea it was seeking to convey. This would be the case whether that Catholicism of the Word was one based on *sola scriptura* or on some univocal consent of antiquity. As has been shown in the second and third chapters of this work, Newman had found that neither solution was capable of providing the workable hypothesis he sought. "The difficulty, then, and hazard of developing doctrines implicitly received, must be fully allowed; and this is often made a ground for inferring that they have no proper developments at all; that there is no natural connexion [sic] between certain dogmas and certain impressions."[48]

To deal with this objection to his theory, as it lay at the time of the sermon, Newman took his listeners to the history of the changes to the church's articulation of her understanding of the Trinity and the Incarnation, but before he did so, he needed to make clearer a couple of philosophical principles that could be properly inferred from his general theory.

First, he argued:

One proposition necessarily leads to another, and a second to a third; then some limitation is required; and the combination of these opposites occasions some fresh evolutions from the original idea, which indeed can never be said to be entirely exhausted. This process is its development, and results in a series, or rather body of dogmatic statements, till what was at

---

47. Palmer, *A Narrative of Events*, 58.
48. Newman, *USS*, 328.

first an impression on the Imagination has become a system or creed in the Reason.[49]

His listeners should not expect the natural action of the human mind upon the idea, that is, the impressions it has received of a reality, particularly a divine, and thus mysterious, reality, to result in anything other than a system of doctrine for the very reason that the reality, the idea, and its expression are distinct:

> Ideas and their developments are commonly not identical, the development being but the carrying out of the idea into its consequences. Thus the doctrine of Penance may be called a development of the doctrine of Baptism, yet still is a distinct doctrine; whereas the developments in the doctrines of the Holy Trinity and the Incarnation are mere portions of the original impression, and modes of representing it.... This may be fitly compared to the impressions made on us through the senses. Material objects are whole, and individual; and the impressions which they make on the mind, by means of the senses, are of a corresponding nature, complex and manifold in their relations and bearings, but considered in themselves integral and one.[50]

Not only are the reality, the idea, and the dogma distinct, Newman reminded his listeners, but the limitations of language mean that, "particular propositions, then, which are used to express portions of the great idea vouchsafed to us, can never really be confused with the idea itself which all such propositions taken together can but reach, and cannot exceed."[51] It is the very structure of the human mind that necessitates the development of doctrine: "Creeds and dogmas live in the one idea which they are designed to express, and which alone is substantive; and are necessary only because the human mind cannot reflect upon that idea, except piecemeal, cannot use it in its oneness and entireness, nor without resolving it into a series of aspects and relations."[52]

The remainder of the sermon makes it clear that Newman was

---

49. Newman, *USS*, 329.
50. Newman, *USS*, 329–30.
51. Newman, *USS*, 331.
52. Newman, *USS*, 331–32.

aware of many of the objections to the theory he had laid out. The limitations of human reasoning and language, "immature faculties and their scanty vocabulary,"[53] mean that dogmas are expressed in words that themselves have "a very abject and human meaning."[54] Nevertheless, those limitations are transcended by the relationship between the words and the idea. Newman suggested that rather than the meaning of the technical vocabulary being primarily derived from some kind of linguistic positivism, so far as the expression of Christian doctrine was concerned, the vocabulary was defined by reference to the underlying truth of revelation that it was an attempt at expressing. Taking as his reference point some of the technical vocabulary related to the doctrines of the Trinity and Incarnation, he asserted: "there is no such inward view of these doctrines, distinct from the dogmatic language used to express them, as was just now supposed. The metaphors by which they are signified are not mere symbols of ideas which exist independently of them, but their meaning is coincident and identical with the ideas."[55]

The limitations of human (Newman uses the word "earthly") reasoning and language is to be expected as the contingent apprehends the necessary: the finite, the infinite. It is this, Newman reminded the congregation, of which St. Paul wrote when he compared "now 'seeing in a glass darkly, (*en ainygmati*), but then face to face'": then the completeness of the "Beatific Vision, or true sight of Almighty God," now "such an approximation to the truth as earthly images and figures may supply to us."[56]

In a final warning at the end of the sermon, perhaps against the Noetic attachment to intellectual brilliance ahead of faithfulness that he had experienced in the Oriel Common Room and to which he had once admitted to have been attracted, Newman cautioned his listeners: "The fault, then, which we must guard against in receiving such Divine intimations, is the ambition of being wiser than what is written; of employing the Reason, not in carrying out what is told

---

53. Newman, *USS*, 340.
54. Newman, *USS*, 338.
55. Newman, *USS*, 338.
56. Newman, *USS*, 340. See 1 Corinthians 13:12.

us, but in impugning it; not in support, but in prejudice of Faith."[57] This is a sentence that sits uncomfortably with the rest of the sermon but hints at a deficiency that Newman saw as inherent in his theory of development as it stood. Without an authoritative voice to counter the temptations to private judgment, a reductionist rationalism, and the anti-dogmatic spirit, then his theory could as easily be used in the cause of infidelity—the portmanteau term Newman had used since the beginning of the Oxford Movement for the natural, logical, and, perhaps, unavoidable outcome of these temptations—as it could to explain the apparent paradox of change and continuity in Christian doctrine. That authoritative voice, Newman already knew, was not to be found within the univocal testimony of the Fathers nor yet in the voice of the bishops of the Church of England. From the pulpit of St. Mary's, he could not go further. He could not preach what he had first suspected in the autumn of 1839 and of which the first explicit written confessions are to be found a year later in correspondence with his sister, his brother, and Keble in the autumn of 1840[58]: that the living authoritative voice to authenticate true developments of doctrine and condemn corruptions was to be found in Rome. While he held the position of vicar of the University Church, a position he had considered giving up since at least the autumn of 1840 because of the constraints it placed on his freedom of expression,[59] he could hardly voice the answer in his writings for publication, still less preach it from the university pulpit.

An Essay on the Development of Christian Doctrine

In early January 1844, Newman replied to an anonymous correspondent in terms that reveal that he was acutely aware that everything he now wrote or preached was being judged. The letter to which he was

---

57. Newman, *USS*, 351.
58. See JHN to Mrs. John Mozley, February 25, 1840, in *LD* 7, 245; JHN to F.W. Newman, October 22, 1840, in *LD* 7, 414; and JHN to John Keble, October 26, 1840, in *LD* 7, 417.
59. JHN to John Keble, November 6, 1840, in *LD* 7, 433–34.

replying does not survive, but his answer does. In it, he defended himself from the accusation of having gone "*beyond* the teaching" of the Church of England in writing of the intercession of the saints by observing that "such is our melancholy state at present that no light can be introduced without causing shadows—not a word of dogmatic truth can be uttered without giving birth to controversy."[60] Later that month, Keble wrote to Newman concerning Oakeley's plan to publish a translation of the works of the twelfth-century founder of the Cistercians, Bernard of Clairvaux.[61] Keble was clearly concerned that the increasing preoccupation with the medieval among some members of the Oxford Movement was disposing them favorably to Rome as the current expression of "Primitive Catholicity," and he suggested that "*If* the Medieval system is really the intended development of Primitive Catholicity, is it not the most natural way for the English Church to recover it *through* Primitive Catholicity."[62] While for Keble the Tractarian project of recovering the Catholic for the English Church was still a possibility, for Newman it seemed not to be. In December 1843, he had arrived at a series of resolutions[63] that revealed that he no longer felt, in light of the episcopal reaction to Tract 90, that even the imaginative conversion for which he had hoped—that which would "bring out certain truths and facts, moral, ecclesiastical, and religious, simply and forcibly,"[64] and to which his contributions to the "Lyra Apostolica" and *The Church of the Fathers* had been ordered[65]—was even possible, let alone the theological and ecclesial change he believed necessary. Replying to Keble, Newman hinted at "a steadily growing conviction about the English Church," the character of which he assumed Keble did not need to have made explicit. Newman was once again engaged in working on a new edition of *The Arians*, an edition he did not complete, and was translat-

60. JHN to an Unknown Correspondent, January 12, 1844, in *LD 10*, 87. The italics are, again, Newman's.
61. Oakeley had outlined the prospectus to Newman in a letter on January 11, 1844, in *LD 10*, 87–88.
62. John Keble to JHN, January 22, 1844, in *LD 10*, 101.
63. "MEMORANDUM," December 11, 1843, in *LD 10*, 55–56.
64. JHN to Hugh James Rose, November 26, 1832, in *LD 3*, 120.
65. As in, for example, JHN to John William Bowden, November 17, 1833, in *LD 4*, 109.

ing further works of St. Athanasius.⁶⁶ It was work of this nature that had "all along been my line of study ... this line of reading, and no other, which has lead [sic] me Romeward."⁶⁷ He still hoped that he was wrong, that by Pusey and Manning (and presumably Keble) he might "be brought back" and might "die in the English Church."⁶⁸ Nevertheless, the direction of travel was clear and was confirmed in letters to Pusey and Bowden in the next few weeks.⁶⁹

Newman was conscious of the relationship between the "growing conviction" of which he had written to Keble and the need for a thorough hypothesis relating to the development of doctrine, as his correspondence with Mrs. Froude, in the Spring and Summer of 1844 bears witness.⁷⁰ These letters to Mrs. Froude provide a detailed summary of how Newman's religious opinions had developed over the previous eleven years and are a remarkable insight into his views. The outline they provide is largely consistent with the account that he was to give twenty years later in the *Apologia*. Where they differ is that the letters are an attempt to give a dispassionate account of the intellectual positions that Newman had, successively, adopted in the face of his growing awareness of the historical record of doctrinal change.⁷¹

It was precisely within the safety of private correspondence that Newman now felt able to say what he was not yet quite ready to confess in public: that he had come to believe that, as he put it in a letter to Keble that same June, "the Roman Communion is the only true

---

66. JHN to John Keble, January 23, 1844, in *LD 10*, 102, n. 1.
67. JHN to John Keble, January 23, 1844, in *LD 10*, 101–3.
68. JHN to John Keble, January 23, 1844, in *LD 10*, 103.
69. JHN to Edward Bouverie Pusey, February 19, 1844, in *LD 10*, 126; JHN to J. W. Bowden, February 21, 1844, in *LD 10*, 129–30.
70. JHN to Mrs. W. Froude, April 3, 5, 6, and 9, May 19 and 28, June 9, and July 14, 1844, in *LD 10*, 185–88, 189–92, 195–98, 200–204, 237–44, 251, 264–66, and 297–98, respectively.
71. Gordon Harper's contention that they "give a point of view somewhat different from that of the *Apologia*" is not sustainable. See Gordon Huntingdon Harper, *Cardinal Newman and William Froude FRS: A Correspondence* (Baltimore, Md.: Johns Hopkins University Press, 1933), 30. It must be admitted that the letters lack the *post hoc* justification that, in 1864, Newman felt was needed to acquit him of Kingsley's charge of dishonesty, but it is only the attempt to furnish the history with an apologetic narrative of consistency that differentiates the later account from this correspondence.

Church."[72] To Keble, he claimed that it was his reading of the Fathers that had brought him to this point. It was, in fact, rather more complicated than that. Newman's reading of the Fathers amounted to a twenty-year search for the voice of antiquity in an attempt to provide an account for the continuity of doctrine in the face of the evidence of change. This search had convinced him that that voice was to be found not, as he had first thought, in terminological change, nor in the *disciplina arcani*, nor yet in the Vincentian Canon, but in the living authority of the church, and that church was to be found in the Roman Communion. The evidence was to be found in the historical record of the development of doctrine authenticated by the church in communion with Rome. It was this ecclesial authority that he now believed to be necessary if the truth of any doctrine was to be demonstrated and for corruptions to be refuted. Development of doctrine as *the* hypothesis to account for the "difficulty" of doctrinal change was observable in the history of the great Trinitarian and Christological controversies that he had studied so closely and, in those controversies, was intimately tied up with the claims Rome made for herself. As he wrote to Mrs. Froude on May 19, 1844:

Moreover in every case the view whether of doctrine or discipline taken by the see of Rome, ultimately prevailed, and, if success is the token of truth, is the true one. It is the Pope who has determined the rule for observing Easter, and for treating the Baptism of heretics, who has confirmed or pronounced the condemnation of Arianism, Apollinarianism, Pelagianism, and the other numerous heresies which distracted the early church. He appears to exercise an infallibility which in after ages he has more distinctly claimed.

All these things being considered, I was forced to admit that the doctrine of the papacy was a primitive one—for ... if we do not allow of developments, especially in a matter which from the nature of the case *requires* time for its due exhibition, hardly any doctrine can be proved by antiquity.[73]

---

72. JHN to John Keble, June 8, 1844, in *LD 10*, 261.
73. JHN to Mrs. W. Froude, May 19, 1844, in *LD 10*, 243. Thomas suggests that the correspondence with Mrs. Froude is further evidence that the idea of development had become, by this stage, an "*idée fixe*" for Newman. He argues that the notion of development of doctrine was being used by Newman not merely to resolve the "problem of the relation of change and continuity" but to resolve the "acute difficulties" he had in "understanding his

THE CHURCH OF CATHOLICISM, 1842–1845

Newman acknowledged that the attempt to outline his theory without adverting to its necessary ecclesiological underpinning in his final University Sermon had meant that work was unsatisfactory and, in many ways, deserving of the criticism it had received from, among others, Palmer.[74] There had been good reasons for Newman's previous reticence—fear of censure, a desire not to be seen to be leading others to Rome, even, perhaps, the principle of reserve—but these now seemed to be less important than the theory itself and the moral imperative that flowed from it. He would now need to "go the whole length of the theory"[75] and deal not only with the criticisms of Palmer, that Newman's theory appeared to suggest that "*inferences made by human reason*, are ... to be considered as articles of the

---

own identity which his obsessive concern to demonstrate consistency discloses" (Thomas, *Newman and Heresy*, 231). This argument is, of course, at the heart of Thomas's thesis. He refers to Newman's "preoccupation" with heresy which "bordered on the obsessive" in the abstract in the frontispiece, at the very beginning of his book and maintains the argument throughout it with remarkable tenacity.

As was seen in his consideration of the Monophysite parallel and the Wiseman article in the previous chapter, however, although Thomas lays out the contrary evidence, he does not appear seriously to consider the alternative constructions that such evidence might support, particularly any construction put upon it that lends credence to the account given in the *Apologia*. Here, for example, he admits that "Newman's Anglican rhetoric was always fighting off something very like the doctrine of development of the *Essay*" (231) at least since the period during which he had developed the *via media*. However, he does not take that battle and the necessarily attendant concern with heresy to be a natural corollary of Newman's concern with doctrine, that is, with those impressions upon his mind that had been so much a part of his conversion at fifteen and remained with him throughout his life. Neither does Thomas appear to give due weight to the relationship between act and belief that is at least as consistent and significant a feature of Newman's life and thought as is doctrine. Taken on the historical record, it is unarguable that Newman was preoccupied with the question of change and continuity in doctrine: he had been wrestling with precisely this difficulty for nearly twenty years. It is also clear that by the time of the correspondence with Mrs. Froude, in 1844, he was acutely seized of the personal consequences that any likely solution to the problem would have for him. In the midst of the correspondence, he notes in his diary both his intellectual convictions and their attendant consequences. Furthermore, it has been shown that Newman had attempted to posit a number of solutions to the question since first he had become aware of its existence. Therefore, to characterize as "obsessive" the care for consistency and attention to detail which marks Newman's consideration of the subject throughout the period since 1839 and particularly in the period from the final University Sermon to the publication of the *Essay* might be seen as a rather forced attempt to make the evidence fit the theory rather than the reverse.

74. JHN to Mrs. W. Froude, July 14, 1844, in *LD 10*, 297.
75. JHN to Mrs. W. Froude, July 14, 1844, in *LD 10*, 297.

Catholic Faith" such that "the doctrine of Purgatory, as a *development*, must be as binding as that of the Trinity,"[76] but also with those particular considerations that weighed on him. Those considerations certainly show Newman's awareness of the personal consequences that the answer to the difficulty contained. Nonetheless, they are fundamentally theological concerns rather than existential; still less are they evidence of a psychopathology. The structure of his answer to these concerns that he provided in the *Essay* was to be determined by his need to satisfy himself with regard to those "particular considerations," and they were to prove of such governing significance in the *Essay* that they justify being quoted in full:

1. I am far more certain (according to the Fathers) that we *are* in a state of culpable separation *than* that developments do *not* exist under the gospel, and that the Roman developments are *not* true ones.

2. I am far more certain that *our* (modern) doctrines are wrong, *than* that the *Roman* (modern) doctrines are wrong.

3. Granting that the Roman (special) doctrines are not found drawn out in the early Church, yet I think there is sufficient trace of them in it, to recommend and prove them, *on the hypothesis*, of the Church having a divine guidance, though not sufficient to prove them by itself. So that the question simply turns on the nature of the promise of the Spirit made to the Church.

4. The proof of the *Roman* (modern) <special> doctrines is as strong <(or stronger)> in Antiquity, as that of certain doctrines which *both we and the Roman* hold.

5. The Analogy of the Old Testament and the New leads to acknowledgement of doctrinal developments.[77]

The structure of the *Essay* would be determined by the need to fully explore the three underlying principles that Newman had first sketched out in the 1840 correspondence with his brother, as shown in the previous chapter, as necessary components of a theory of the development of doctrine. Those principles being that: (1) "all systems which have life, have a development, yet do not cease to have an

---

76. Palmer, *A Narrative of Events*, 170.
77. JHN to Mrs. W. Froude, July 14, 1844, in *LD 10*, 297–98. It is not clear when Newman's later interpolations, which are shown in the published edition and cited here within angular brackets, thus <....>, were added to the manuscript.

identity though they develop";[78] (2) development includes growth in the church's ability to express its doctrines more accurately through time by the action of its interaction with historical and cultural phenomena; and (3) that there are tests by which developments can be tested. It was the "particular considerations" however, that would determine the manner in which that structure would be filled, the examples from history chosen, and the apologetic flavor of the *Essay* determined.

It has already been noted that Newman had started to keep a notebook of his thinking related to the theory of development in March 1844. Throughout the rest of that year, his correspondence and journals indicate that he was much taken up with both his own weakening hold on his position within the Church of England[79] and that of others,[80] his involvement in the ongoing fallout from both the "row"[81] over Tract 90, and other controversies, most notably that which related to Ward. It is clear from the notebook and the other papers related to the development of doctrine that have survived, however, that he was becoming ever more conscious of the urgent need to set down a complete account of his theory of development of doctrine.[82]

Newman had finished his translation of Athanasius in January 1845,[83] and the *dénouement* of the controversies concerning Tract 90 and Ward occurred in Oxford University's convocation on February 13, 1845. Ward's book was condemned, and he was deprived of his degrees and, accordingly, his Balliol fellowship: Newman's tract was saved from formal censure only by the action of the proctors, one of

---

78. JHN to F. W. Newman, November 10, 1840, in *LD* 7, 441.

79. JHN to Henry Wilberforce, July 17, 1844, in *LD* 10, 299. In this letter, Newman doubted even "the lawfulness" of his remaining within the Church of England, given the position at which he has arrived.

80. See, for example, JHN to Robert Francis Wilson, April 11, 1845, in *LD* 10, 623. Newman admitted to having had, for six years, "the gravest suspicions that the English Church is in schism."

81. February 27, 1841, in *LD* 8, 45.

82. JHN, *Copybook on Development*, n.d., and *1844–5 Papers and Fragments on Development*, both in B.2.8, BOA.

83. JHN to Maria Giberne, January 8, 1845, in *LD* 10, 484.

whom, the junior proctor, was his friend R. W. Church, whose *non placet* vetoed the motion.[84] It seems likely that Newman began work on the *Essay* almost immediately after this hiatus, and he was certainly "immersed" in it by the beginning of April.[85] On October 6, 1845, he laid down the manuscript,[86] not finished but sufficiently complete to have both settled the question of his own position and to have set out his theory of development in Christian doctrine.

Coming from a man so grounded in an apologetic aimed at justifying his own religious opinions, the closing words of the advertisement at the front of the 1845 edition of Newman's *Essay* come as something of a shock. He prefaces his 453-page argument relating to the theory of development in doctrine with the following words: "It is scarcely necessary to add that he now submits every part of the book to the judgement of the Church, with whose doctrine, on the subjects of which it treats, he wishes all his thoughts to be coincident."[87] It was a statement that he was able to make only because the argument of the essay itself had proved to Newman's own personal satisfaction that the "church" of which he spoke, the Roman Catholic Church, was one and the same as the church of antiquity whose voice he had sought for nearly thirty years, throughout his studies of the early Christian doctrine. Not only was the Roman Communion that self-same church, Newman now believed, but he had argued himself into a position whereby, as the *Essay* demonstrates, he now believed it to be the authentic teacher of the faith, the living organ which was the only guarantee of Catholic and Apostolic truth. As Newman had come to see the need for a Catholicism of the church, he had arrived at the belief that, as David Nicholls and Fergus Kerr observe: "the Catholic position is distinguished from the Protestant in being concerned not with a judgment about the content of Revelation, but

---

84. "Declaration of Thanks to the Proctors," in *LD 10*, 551–55. Cf. Mary C. Church and Francis Paget, eds., *Life and Letters of Dean Church* (London: Macmillan, 1894), 54–56; Rowland Edmund Prothero and George Granville Bradley, *The Life and Correspondence of Arthur Penrhyn Stanley DD, Late Dean of Westminster*, vol. 1 (London: John Murray, 1893), 339–42.
85. Newman, *LD 10*, 614, n. 2.
86. Newman, *LD 10*, 780, n. 8.
87. Newman, *Dev.*, advertisement.

about who is the accredited teacher: whose voice is to be followed."[88] Nicholas Lash puts it somewhat differently:

> It seemed obvious to [Newman], not so much that Roman catholic [sic] doctrine corresponded most closely to the teaching of the apostolic church, but rather that the complex concrete reality of the Roman catholic [sic] church as he envisaged it ... corresponded more closely than any other claimant to the concrete reality of the church of the fathers.[89]

In October 1845, Newman had come to the firm conviction that the Roman Church, against whom he had once fulminated in language he had only lately abjured, was the voice to be followed.

The *Essay* begins with an introduction that runs to twenty-nine pages[90] and is then followed by the first chapter, "On the Development of Ideas," which outlines over the following sixty-four pages the essential elements of the theory in its entirety in such a way as to set out explicitly the three elements that were found in the correspondence with Francis and in the final University Sermon. The chapter starts with a section called "On the Process of Development of Ideas"[91] before moving on to a consideration of the kinds of development in ideas[92] and then to a section "On the Corruption of an Idea," in which Newman explicitly defines, for the first time, what he means by the developments of an idea: "nothing else than its adequate representation and its fulfilment, in its various aspects, relations, and consequences."[93] This final section of the first chapter laid out Newman's views on what he referred to as the "Distinctive Test between Development and Corruption"[94] and proposed seven "tests of a true development" by which any change could be accepted as an authentic development or rejected as a corruption of the previous doctrine: "Preservation of Type or Idea," "Continuity of Principles," "Power of Assimilation," "Early Anticipation," "Logical

---

88. David Nicholls and Fergus Kerr, *John Henry Newman: Reason, Rhetoric and Romanticism* (Bristol, Mich.: Bristol Press, 1991), 202.
89. Lash, *Newman on Development*, 9.
90. Newman, *Dev.*, 1–29.
91. Newman, *Dev.*, 30–43.
92. Newman, *Dev.*, 43–57.
93. Newman, *Dev.*, 57–93.
94. Newman, *Dev.*, 57.

Sequence," "Preservative Additions," and "Chronic Continuance."[95]

The second chapter of the *Essay* concerns the development of Christian ideas, as Newman put it, "antecedently considered,"[96] divided into sections "On the Probability of Developments in Christianity"[97] and "On the Probability of a Developing Authority in Christianity."[98] The third chapter, "On the Nature of the Argument in Behalf of the Existing Developments of Christianity,"[99] provides an historiographic rationale for development before Newman devoted the remaining five chapters to illustrations of his rationale by reference to specific doctrinal developments considered under the aspect of each of his seven tests.

The fourth chapter[100] considered the application of the first test to the developments of Christianity by reference to the church of the first century and fourth centuries and the fifth chapter to the church of the fifth and sixth centuries.[101] The sixth chapter contained illustrations of the application of the second and third tests,[102] and in chapter seven those that Newman suggested illustrated the fourth test.[103] The final chapter, concluded Newman's illustrations by considering examples of the remaining three tests.[104]

A striking feature of this structure is the balance between the various chapters and sections, and between the length of the consideration given to each of the tests. The chapters dealing with the theory in principle accounted for over two hundred pages of the first edition, those concerning illustrations related to the first test of fidelity covered 113, and the second and third only fifty pages. The exposition of the fourth test took twenty-seven pages, and thirty-one pages were needed to illustrate the fifth, with the sixth and seventh test being given seventeen and seven pages, respectively. In this dis-

95. Newman, *Dev.*, 64–93.
96. Newman, *Dev.*, 94–130.
97. Newman, *Dev.*, 94–114.
98. Newman, *Dev.*, 114–30.
99. Newman, *Dev.*, 131–202.
100. Newman, *Dev.*, 203–69.
101. Newman, *Dev.*, 270–317.
102. Newman, *Dev.*, 318–68.
103. Newman, *Dev.*, 369–96.
104. Newman, *Dev.*, 397–453.

tribution, there is an unavoidable sense of acceleration, if not quite impatience. When Newman outlined the tests in principle, the care taken to spell them out does not vary nearly so much: the first test taking no longer to describe than the eighth; yet when he came to illustrate them, it becomes obvious that he was progressively less and less concerned with demonstrating them in practice, since he apparently felt he had proved his case.

Chadwick observes that the "tests which convinced no one and which he himself once admitted to be incapable of performing their ostensible purpose" were not at the heart of the purpose of the essay, which he claims were the "momentous" feature that it was concerned less with the development of particular doctrines than with determining the identity of the present church "upon a historical inquiry into the ancient Church."[105] Nevertheless, having claimed for them a scientific rather than practical character, Newman immediately asserted their utility as "instruments rather than warrants of right decisions."[106] Indeed, that they were precisely intended by Newman to have a practical character is clear from his remarks that the tests were "required to distinguish legitimate developments from those which are not such,"[107] a point he stated yet more clearly in the third edition of the *Essay*:

> This is what may be said, and I acknowledge its force: it becomes necessary in consequence to assign certain characteristics of faithful developments, which none but faithful developments have, and the presence of which serves as a test to discriminate between them and corruptions. This I at once proceed to do, and I shall begin by determining what a corruption is, and why it cannot rightly be called, and how it differs from, a development.[108]

---

105. Chadwick, *From Bousset to Newman*, 143–44. While the ecclesiological point is well made, Chadwick offers no evidence to support his contention that Newman was unconvinced by the utility of the tests themselves. It is possible that Chadwick is relying on Newman's remark, that the tests "are insufficient for the guidance of individuals in the case of so large and complicated a problem as Christianity," and that they are "of a scientific and controversial, not of a practical character" (*Dev.*, 117).
106. Newman, *Dev.*, 117.
107. Newman, *Dev.*, 58.
108. Newman, *Dev.*, 170.

Newman repeated the same point, in striking language, in a letter of 1861, which makes clear not only the practical nature of the tests but that he believed that they did, indeed, provide the continuity he sought in the face of the evidence of change: "I lay down, that no one can religiously speak of development, without giving the *rules* which keep it from extravagating endlessly. And I give seven tests of a true development, founded on the nature of the case. These tests secure the substantial immutability of Christian doctrine."[109]

The introduction to the *Essay* begins with the assertion that, because Christianity is an historical fact, and its then–1,800-year history of doctrine a matter of record, the very fact of that history requires a theory to account for the continuity of Christianity given the claim that Christianity is not, in Newman's day, a different religion from that of the Apostles.[110] What Newman had set out to prove was that, in any century, what was believed by the Catholic Church can be seen to be the logical and necessary outgrowth and deeper understanding of what was believed in the century before: that there was both change and continuity, and that these were not merely accidental but to be expected and intimately connected. If examined in sequence, Newman would claim, it was possible to see a natural progression, a true growth in doctrine. There was no observable change of course, but rather a continuation along a single track. An aspect of doctrine is clarified in one century and in the next that clarification is investigated and built on so that further clarification is produced. That which had been determined with finality in the past by the voice of the church was kept in later centuries. Old doctrines were not overthrown to make way for new ones; instead, the church's understanding of those older doctrines was made more explicit, new aspects of the same truth were added, and so, by stages, a fuller expression of the truth was possible. In tracing this, he believed, the question of the identity of the church would become apparent, indeed, obvious.

Newman outlined not only that this happens but also why it is

---

109. JHN to Cowley Fisher, October 14, 1861, in *LD 20*, 54.
110. Newman, *Dev.*, 1–2.

important to understand the reason for and process by which it happens. The "difficulty" is that Christianity has changed so much over the centuries that it is not obvious that there is "real continuity of doctrine" since the Apostolic era, he noted, and so the theory he was to enunciate would have to demonstrate that there was such continuity in the face of the observable change. One thing was obvious to Newman at this stage: that, in what Chadwick rather superciliously calls "typically loose use of words,"[111] whatever be historical Christianity, it is not Protestantism. If ever there were a safe truth, it is this."[112]

The introduction begins with an assertion of the objective, factual nature of the Christian religion. This is not to claim that, for Newman, matters relating to faith are not matters of opinion but that what he understood to be the liberal contention about Christianity, that it "is to each man what each man thinks it to be, and nothing else,"[113] is simply not true. Newman was aware that the wide range of views and practices claiming to be Christian could easily give the appearance that Christianity was "a mere name for a number of different religions altogether, and, at variance with one another, and claiming the same appellation"[114] simply as a result of there being some points of common agreement. He also wished to discount the view that none of the present manifestations of Christianity "represent it as taught by Christ and his apostles." As he was later to observe, the *Essay* "starts with assuming the historical identity of the present and the past Church" and "with the infallibility of the former."[115] Newman, instead, proposed to consider Christianity as "the society of Christians which the apostles left on earth ... the internal continuity of name, profession, and communion."[116] That was, in his view, both an observable datum of the historical record and "a *prima facie* argument for a real continuity of doctrine."[117] As he put it quite

111. Chadwick, *From Bousset to Newman*, 140.
112. Newman, *Dev.*, 5.
113. Newman, *Dev.*, 2.
114. Newman, *Dev.*, 2.
115. JHN to Catherine Ward, November 18, 1848, in *LD* 12, 333.
116. Newman, *Dev.*, 2.
117. Newman, *Dev.*, 2.

straightforwardly, "the Christianity of the second, fourth, seventh, twelfth, and sixteenth, and intermediate centuries is in its substance the very religion which Christ and his apostles taught in the first."[118]

Newman understood that whatever theory, mechanism, or hypothesis he was to propose would have to offer an account of those changes, observable clearly from the record or otherwise, in Christianity that "for good or evil ... lapse of years, or the vicissitudes of human affairs have impressed upon it."[119] Newman admitted that there were those who took this as evidence that "it is useless, in fact, to seek in history the matter of that Revelation which has been vouchsafed to mankind":[120] Christianity, it would appear, is anything but consistent and continuous. Quoting the Caroline Divine, William Chillingworth, whose history of conversion to Roman Catholicism and later reversion to the Established Church makes him an interesting character for Newman to have quoted at this point in his own religious journey.[121] Newman reminded his readers that the history of Christianity gives witness to: "popes against popes, councils against councils, some fathers against others, the same fathers against themselves, a consent of fathers of one age against a consent of fathers of another age, the Church of one age against the Church of another age."[122]

This had been precisely Newman's own observation when he had written *The Arians*. It was the witness of history that his correspondence with the Abbé Jager had put so clearly before him and in answer to which he had developed the notion of prophetical tradition. It was this that had appeared so powerfully to him in his research into Apollinarianism and the Monophysite crisis and, most forcefully of all, which Wiseman's article had driven home so insistently. If Newman was not to abandon the conviction that Christianity was one and the same religion then as it had been at first, he would have to describe a theological principle that could hold together the change

118. Newman, *Dev.*, 3.
119. Newman, *Dev.*, 4.
120. Newman, *Dev.*, 3.
121. William Chillingworth (1602–1644) in *ODNB Online*.
122. Newman, *Dev.*, 4.

and the continuity. Newman argued that it is not to history *per se* or to any historiographical principles that the enquirer should look to solve this inconsistency. Rather, he contended that, while taking seriously the historical record and so writing historically, it was possible to observe, not merely to propose, a theological principle at work that would allow the Christianity of history to be identified. While asserting "that Protestantism, then, is not the Christianity of history,"[123] for Newman, the task of finding, let alone proving, the identity of that Christianity of history was now of urgent, critical importance.

The first hypothesis he analyzed in the introduction brought him onto the grounds of the controversies of the first years of the Oxford Movement. He admitted that seeking for a workable theory, as he had sought to do in the 1830s, in what he now referred to as "the celebrated dictum of Vincentius," was no longer satisfactory.[124] Although Newman admitted that St. Vincent of Lérins' Canon might well provide "a short and easy method for reconciling the various informations of ecclesiastical history" and allowed that it contains "a majestic truth . . . offers an intelligible principle, and wears a reasonable care," he observed that it works better at "determining what is not, than what is Christianity."[125] His own experience of attempting to work with the Vincentian Canon as he had attempted to construct his Catholicism of the Word several years earlier had revealed to Newman that if used:

for the purpose of disproving the catholicity of the Creed of Pope Pius, it becomes also an objection to the Athanasian; and if it be relaxed to admit the doctrines retained by the English church, it no longer excludes certain doctrines of Rome which that Church denies. It cannot at once condemn St. Thomas and St. Bernard and defend St. Athanasius and St. Gregory Nazianzen.[126]

What he had sought to do with the rule in first attacking what he supposed were Roman Catholic doctrines and practices in the Jager

---

123. Newman, *Dev.*, 7.
124. Newman, *Dev.*, 7.
125. Newman, *Dev.*, 8.
126. Newman, *Dev.*, 9.

correspondence and then in giving an account of Anglican formularies as being conformable with the Tridentine decrees in Tract 90 is now admitted as impossible. To illustrate this further, Newman then spent several pages examining the development of the doctrine of the Holy Trinity, with which he was very familiar as a result of his systematic reading of the Fathers and his familiarity with Christian antiquity. The survey further demonstrated what those earlier controversies had shown: that the Vincentian rule could not provide an adequate hypothesis to account for the development of church doctrine, from what was known of the ante-Nicene faith through to the confirmed Nicene faith and the post-Nicene developments. The same is apparent in his presentation of the doctrines of purgatory and original sin, the latter, as he noted, appearing "neither in the apostles nor the Nicene creed."[127] Such is the character of the Vincentian Canon that, Newman observed in a pun, conscious or otherwise, if it were to work at all, it would only do so as a "Lesbian Rule."[128] The same point is made with regard to the doctrine of the real presence of the Eucharist or the doctrine of papal supremacy. Newman argued that if the Vincentian Canon were to be the rule, the church's belief in the real presence rested on far more slender historical evidence than it did for the doctrine of papal supremacy. Having sought for so long and in the face of such controversy to maintain that "Christianity is what has been held always, everywhere and by all,"[129] Newman abandons it as a tool of practical use:

It does not seem possible, then, to avoid the conclusion that, whatever the proper key for harmonizing the records and documents of the early and later Church, and true as the dictum of Vincentius must be considered in the abstract, and possible as its application might be in his own age, when he

---

127. Newman, *Dev.*, 19.
128. Newman, *Dev.*, 17. This was the name given historically to the flexible mason's rule, usually made of lead, that could be bent to the curves of a molding and used to measure or reproduce irregular curves. Its name derives from Aristotle's *Nichomachean Ethics* (*The Complete Works of Aristotle: The Revised Oxford Translation*, ed. Jonathan Barnes, vol. 2, Bollingen Series, 71:2 [Princeton, N.J.: Princeton University Press, 1984], bk. 5, ch. 10, 1137b), where it is used to describe the flexibility required of systems of justice if they are to operate equitably. See the "Lesbian Rule" in *Oxford English Dictionary Online*.
129. Newman, *Dev.*, 8.

might almost ask the primitive centuries for their testimony, it is hardly available now or effective of any satisfactory result. The solution it offers is as difficult as the original problem.[130]

Having laid aside the claims of the Vincentian Canon, Newman next considered what he referred to as a "far more widely adopted, not less plausible, and in a certain measure irreconcilable with the former" hypothesis, namely that early Christianity was corrupted by external influences such that whatever we today call Christianity is simply irreconcilable with the original form of the religion.[131] While, he acknowledged, this hypothesis perfectly well accounts for variations "in doctrine and practice, and for the growth of opinion on particular points,"[132] he was simply not convinced of it. In fact, his first test of "fidelity in development" is designed, as will be shown, to disprove even the possibility of any such suggestion.

Newman then considered a third hypothesis. Here he was back on the territory of *The Arians* and Bishop Kaye's criticism of it: the *disciplina arcani*. Ascribing the theory here, perhaps slightly disingenuously given the reliance he had himself placed upon it a dozen years previously, to "divines of the Church of Rome,"[133] he argued that it was the case that "it is certain that portions of the church system were held back in primitive times."[134] Nonetheless, he now argued, as an hypothesis to account for doctrinal change and continuity, it will not serve because it is an hypothesis that, while providing a reasonable explanation for the principle of reserve during periods of persecution, once toleration is granted, its *raison d'être* disappears, and, after a short time, even the habit of the *disciplina arcani* would fall into desuetude, its utility gone once the faith could be openly practiced and taught. Since the development of doctrine appeared to have extended beyond the period of persecution, to a time when it could be demonstrated from the written record that there was no continuing progressive revealing of previously hidden teaching, this

130. Newman, *Dev.*, 24.
131. Newman, *Dev.*, 24.
132. Newman, *Dev.*, 24–25.
133. Newman, *Dev.*, 25.
134. Newman, *Dev.*, 26.

was conclusive evidence that the hypothesis of the *disciplina arcani* did not adequately account for the difficulty.

Having dismissed these three possible hypotheses to account for the development of doctrine, Newman reasserted that the essay "is directed towards a solution of the difficulty" that accords with "the testimony of . . . the history of 1800 years."[135] He claimed that what he proposed to describe was a "theory of development" that "has at all times, perhaps, been implicitly adopted by theologians."[136] The theory, put simply by Newman, was that:

> The increase and expansion of the Christian creed and ritual, and the variations which have attended the process in the case of individual writers and Churches, are the necessary attendants on any philosophy or polity which takes possession of the intellect and heart and has had any wide or extended dominion; that from the nature of the human mind, time is necessary for the full comprehension and perfection of great ideas; and that the highest and most wonderful truth, though communicated to the world once for all by inspired teachers, could not be comprehended all at once by the recipient, but was received and transmitted by minds not inspired and through the media which were human, have required only the longer time and deeper thought for their full elucidation.[137]

Newman concluded the introduction with two significant observations that hinted at the tentative nature of what otherwise might have looked like a characteristically robust piece of controversial writing. First, Newman made clear that the theory of development that he was proposing was, in language he had been using for nearly twenty years, "an hypothesis to account for a difficulty."[138] In the same way as the theories of Ptolemy and Newton seem to account for "the apparent motions of heavenly bodies," he believed the hypothesis to be an explanation which fitted the observable data insofar as it "rests upon facts as well as accounts for them."[139] It was not a universal scientific law but a hypothesis that would have to be

---

135. Newman, *Dev.*, 27.
136. Newman, *Dev.*, 27.
137. Newman, *Dev.*, 27
138. Newman, *Dev.*, 27.
139. Newman, *Dev.*, 27–28.

tested. Secondly, he argued, the theory itself could provide no "direct justification" for the adoption of "Roman Catholic doctrine," even if it does, in fact, indirectly "vindicate the reasonableness of" that doctrine.[140] These observations are important, self-imposed limitations that should be borne in mind when analysing Newman's use of the hypothesis in the *Essay* in its first edition, the amendments he made to the *Essay* for the Uniform Edition, and subsequent attempts by theologians, Roman Catholic and others, to put Newman's theory of development to forensic use.

If Newman was to describe the process of development of ideas, it was important that he first set out what he meant by the term idea. The first section of the first chapter of the *Essay* was devoted to this task. Ideas were, Newman wrote, "habitual judgments" made by the human mind "on the things which come before them."[141] Such ideas may be more than mere subjective opinions, indeed, they may approximate to the status of being objective truths when:

> held by persons who are independent of each other, and are variously circumstanced, and have possessed themselves of it by different ways, and when it presents to them under very different aspects, without losing its substantial unity and its identity, and when it is thus variously presented, yet recommended to persons similarly circumstanced; and when it is presented to persons variously circumstanced, under aspects, discordant indeed at first sight, but reconcilable after such explanations as their respective states of mind require.[142]

Newman was keen to remind his readers that "ideas are not ordinarily brought home to the mind, except through the medium of a variety of aspects"; they constituted the "objects of faith" and are themselves aspects of the divine. Thomas Norris observes that: "The abiding core of Christianity for Newman is Christ, or rather the "idea" or image of Christ impressed upon the collective mind of believers."[143] Newman used the analogy of material objects viewed

---

140. Newman, *Dev.*, 29.
141. Newman, *Dev.*, 30.
142. Newman, *Dev.*, 31–32.
143. Thomas Norris, "The Development of Doctrine: A Remarkable Philosophical Phenomenon," *Communio* 22, no. 3 (1995): 483.

from different points to illustrate what he meant by this. The connection between the idea and the object that it represents or seeks to convey, is, Newman wrote, that the idea is "practically identical" with the particular aspects of the object of which it speaks. Accordingly, it becomes more complete as different aspects are expressed: "They introduce us to that idea from which they are derived, and, so far as they seem to oppose, they correct each other and serve to impress a fuller and more exact representation of their original upon the mind."[144]

Newman then claimed that ideas have a life "in the mind which is the recipient" if the idea "is of a nature to interest and possess the mind." He drew a distinction between, on the one hand, the ideas of mathematics, which, he observed, "real as they are, cannot be called living, for they have no influence and lead to nothing," and, on the other, to those that amount to "some great enunciation, whether true or false, about human nature, or present good, or government, or duty, or religion." This second class of idea, he argued, is capable of being "not only passively admitted in this or that form into the minds of men, but it becomes a living principle within them, leading them to an ever-new contemplation of itself, an acting upon it and a propagation of it."[145] So, he contended, ideas develop as "new lights [are] brought to bear upon the original idea" and "aspects ... multiply, and judgements ... accumulate."[146] It is this process that Newman sought to describe and to name as the theory of development: the "germination, growth, and perfection of some living, that is, influential truth, or apparent truth, in the minds of men during a sufficient period."[147]

Newman admitted that this process of development is inherently risky but that the "risk of corruption from intercourse with the world around it"[148] is necessary if the idea is to struggle to perfection, and such a struggle to perfection is precisely what the process of devel-

144. Newman, *Dev.*, 34.
145. Newman, *Dev.*, 35.
146. Newman, *Dev.*, 36.
147. Newman, *Dev.*, 37.
148. Newman, *Dev.*, 38.

opment tends toward. Here, Newman introduced one of the most powerful analogies from nature in the entire essay: that of the image of the stream, which, he observed, is not "clearest near the spring" but "on the contrary, is more equable, and purer, and stronger, when its bed has become deep, and broad, and full."[149] It is in its lower reaches, far from the source, that the stream reveals its "capabilities" and 'scope": so, too, with ideas. As they develop, they reveal their fullness. Under the action of external factors and causes, the stream changes and adapts in order to retain its identity, in order that it remains the same stream.

The analogy ends with perhaps Newman's most frequently quoted expression. Used by Newman to convey the need of change in order to maintain identity, to manifest continuity, and not as a justification of any change for its own sake, he wrote: "it changes with them"—that is, those external stimuli—"in order to remain the same. In a higher world it is otherwise; but here below to live is to change, and to be perfect is to have changed often."[150] It is clear, from the preceding sentence that Newman's purpose here is to set change at the service of continuity. Unfortunately, so quotable is the expression that, shorn of its preceding sentence and quoted entirely out of context, it is most often used to justify change almost for its own sake or in the service of some other progressivist conception, inverting almost completely Newman's intended sense.[151]

Having established what he meant by "idea" and demonstrated that ideas are subject to development without losing their practical identity with the object which they express, in the second section of the first chapter, Newman gave consideration to the fact that ideas might well develop but that such developments could be of a number of different kinds. He considered at length a wide range of devel-

149. Newman, *Dev.*, 38.
150. Newman, *Dev.*, 39.
151. See, for example, Neil Ormerod, "'The Times They Are a Changin': A Response to O"Malley and Schoessler," *Theological Studies* 67, no. 4 (2006): 834–855, where the author misquotes this line as "and to be perfect is to change often," using it as the motif at the head of an article in which he argues "for the need to develop a historical ecclesiology grounded in the systematic of history" (835).

opments, from the mathematical to the metaphysical, each differing from the other by virtue of the nature of the field: mathematical and logical developments proceeding by strict demonstration but political and metaphysical by contemplation and argument. The specific characters of these classes and the description of them that Newman gave are not germane to the current work, but Newman's consideration that developments might be "true or not true, (that is, faithful or unfaithful to the ideas from which it started)" [152] certainly is. Newman was concerned to show how those developments that were "false or unfaithful developments," and thereby "called a corruption,"[153] were to be distinguished from those true, faithful, and properly so-called developments. It is to the outline of how this task might be accomplished that the final section of the first chapter of the *Essay* was devoted. As Newman put it:

Since the developments of an idea are nothing else than its adequate representation and fulfilment, in its various aspects, relations, and consequences, and since the causes which stimulate may also distort its growth, as is seen in the corruptions of truth with which the world abounds, rules are required to distinguish legitimate developments from those which are not.[154]

Taking as his analogy "physical growth" in the animal world, Newman suggested that the "most obvious characteristic of a faithful development" was "unity in type," while not excluding "all variation, nay, considerable alteration of proportion and relation, in the development of the parts or aspects of an idea."[155] He illustrated what he meant by this with reference first to developments in the natural world, using as an analogy of the bodily resurrection these images: "the fully fledged bird differs from the egg. The butterfly is the development, but not in any sense the image of the grub."[156] Similarly, in the case of the development of the doctrine of the Holy Trinity, he argued, appealing to the authority of Petavius, that the doctrine of

152. Newman, *Dev.*, 44.
153. Newman, *Dev.*, 44.
154. Newman, *Dev.*, 57–58.
155. Newman, *Dev.*, 58.
156. Newman, *Dev.*, 58.

the three persons more readily witnesses to the truth "that God is One and most Simple."[157] British political economy provided Newman with a further example of this unity in type in spite of variation. He observed that individuals, political movements, or, indeed, national character, might change in ways which might appear to "be in themselves irreconcilable" and yet "be acquitted of inconsistency" since they "may be nothing more than accidental instruments or expressions of what [they are] inwardly from first to last."[158] These, and a further illustration from the history of the Jewish people, led him to observe that the problem with unity in type is that "it may happen that a representation which varies from its original may be felt as more true and faithful than one which has more pretensions to be exact."[159] Furthermore, this was, Newman noted, also true not only of authentic developments but "real diversions and corruptions," in that they "are often not so unlike externally to the doctrine to which they belong, as are changes which are consistent with it and true developments."[160]

If Newman were to be able to make a proper distinction between authentic developments and corruptions, using his theory, then the cause of "corruption in religion" would need to be identified. The first cause he identified, one that underlay several of his seven tests, which he had encountered throughout his reading of antiquity and now saw exhibited in the search for primitive Christianity among Protestants, was "the refusal to follow the course of doctrine as it moves on, and an obstinacy in the notions of the past."[161] In illustration of this, having considered the evidence of scripture, in particular, the case of the Sadducees, and after a short discussion regarding the "literal meaning of the word corruption, as used by material substances,"[162] Newman argued that unity in type can be used in "draw-

---

157. Newman, *Dev.*, 58–59. The quote from Petavius cited in the *Essay* is from his *De Deo*, ii, 4, n. 8.
158. Newman, *Dev.*, 59.
159. Newman, *Dev.*, 60.
160. Newman, *Dev.*, 61.
161. Newman, *Dev.*, 61.
162. Newman, *Dev.*, 62.

ing the line between a development and a corruption.[163] Any development, he argued, "is to be considered a corruption which *obscures or prejudices its essential idea*, or which *disturbs the laws of development* which constitute its organisation, or which *reverses its course of development.*" Whereas, he continued, "that is *not* a corruption which is *both a chronic and an active state* or which is *capable of holding together* the component parts of the system."[164]

The result of this twofold test of unity in type allowed Newman to set forth the seven tests of a development that, he admitted from the first, are of "varying cogency and independence."[165] As has already been observed, much of the *Essay* is given over to a discussion of the application of these seven tests to developments of doctrine, with explanations and historical illustrations of varying cogency and independence, not to mention length. Newman admitted, at the end of the first chapter, that these "criteriae ... are only of a practical character, and not determined on any logical principle of division."[166] He appeared, implicitly, to recognize that the tests themselves point to or beg two important questions: (1) is it probable that there would be a development of ideas in Christianity, and (2), arising from the nature of the criteria, would there be an authority within Christianity to which the believer could turn for an authoritative determination as to whether a particular change was an authentic development or a corruption? That there should be tests, and what they might be, had been a consistent feature of Newman's development of this hypothesis, as has been related, since he first began to outline it to his brother Francis in November 1840. These tests are not unimportant, but they are not, in themselves, constitutive of the theory of development in the *Essay*. Nevertheless, they do provide "interpretative assistance" to Newman's primary task.[167] They are illustrations of change in continuity considered under different aspects and subject to the judgment of the church. They were, as John T. Ford claims,

163. Newman, *Dev.*, 63.
164. Newman, *Dev.*, 63–64.
165. Newman, *Dev.*, 64.
166. Newman, *Dev.*, 93.
167. Nichols, *From Newman to Congar*, 51.

expected by Newman to serve to confirm that the hypothesis of development he had proposed would demonstrate that the church was what he had hitherto called the Roman Communion.[168]

The seven tests are, therefore, of secondary significance when compared with the answers to these two questions, which would point Newman conclusively in the direction of an enduring and fundamentally ecclesial hypothesis that, he now believed, could provide the practical solution to his long-lasting difficulty. Nevertheless, before considering the answers Newman provided to those two important questions, it is necessary to examine briefly the nature and character of each of the tests since they play such an important part in illustrating how the answers to those two questions have, in fact, operated in the history of Christianity and illuminate how the theory proper was seen by Newman to have worked in practice.

The first "Test of a True Development" that Newman described was the test of the preservation of type, or idea.[169] It was the test that he gave more space to in the *Essay* than any other. Over one-third of the pages considering the tests were given over to illustrations of the application of the tests to particular historical examples of the development of doctrine that concern preservation of type. Notwithstanding the point about the acceleration of the argument of the *Essay* made earlier, it is reasonable to assume that Newman considered it to be the most significant of the tests. Newman's definition of this note savors of a particularly platonic note. He wrote: "That the essential idea or type which a philosophical or political system represents must continue under all its developments, and that its loss is tantamount to the corruption of the system, will scarcely be denied."[170] What such an "essential idea or type" might be, however, escaped such straightforward definition, and Newman recognized that this made it not "easy of application in particular cases."[171] He offered the analogy from nature of the growth of a plant, changing as

168. John T. Ford, "Faithfulness to Type in Newman's: 'Essay on Development,' in *Newman Today*, ed. Stanley L. Jaki (San Francisco: Ignatius Press, 1989), 19.
169. Newman, *Dev.*, 64–66.
170. Newman, *Dev.*, 64.
171. Newman, *Dev.*, 65–66.

it grows, yet remaining the same plant. Rather than provide a concise definition, however, the idea being, in his view, "too obvious and too close upon demonstration,"[172] Newman chose instead to give examples later in the essay of where this test could be shown to be at work. Two of those examples will serve to demonstrate what Newman meant.

Newman's familiarity with the controversies and characters of the fourth century meant that he felt that he was on particularly sound territory when he considered the events of the period immediately after the first Nicene Council: "How," in such turbulent times, "was the man to guide his course who wished to join himself to the doctrine and fellowship of the Apostles?"[173] The answer that he came to, after surveying the Christian *orbis terrarum*, was to cite the unity of the title "Catholic," which, in opposition to the various heresies, was everywhere applied to those churches that were united one with another, exclusive of those ideas and sects that have come to be called heretical, but, crucially, as he now recognized "denoted by the additional title of 'Romans.'"[174] The ecclesiological idea or type to be preserved, then, was of a church identified by its Catholic unity in communion with the Bishop of Rome, as distinguished from those known for their disunity as polities the one with another and their lack of shared faith and communion.

In the field of doctrine, Newman chose as one example, among others: "the definition passed at Chalcedon."[175] Again on territory that he might reasonably have claimed to have made his own, the history of the Monophysite crisis, this time Newman tackled the apparent discontinuity of the Christological definition of this council with the Niceno-Constantineapolitan Symbol. The Chalcedonian definition, Newman claimed, was "the Apostolic Truth once delivered to the Saints... in simple accordance with the faith of St. Athanasius, St. Gregory Nazianzen, and all the other Fathers."[176] Newman

---

172. Newman, *Dev.*, 65.
173. Newman, *Dev.*, 242–43.
174. Newman, *Dev.*, 276.
175. Newman, *Dev.*, 307.
176. Newman, *Dev.*, 307.

baldly claimed that his account "will be evident to the theological student."[177] Despite this assertion, it is far from clear that it was so obvious. Newman admitted that the Chalcedonian definition was "a doctrine which the Creed did not declare, which the Fathers did not unanimously witness" but rather was a doctrine necessarily imposed upon all "under sanction of anathema," and, let it not be forgotten, he wrote, made obligatory because of the "resolution of the Pope of the day." This was, Newman believed, because the definition was necessary to preserve the idea of the Incarnation in its entirety as the church had conceived it, against those who would corrupt it into something that it had not been.[178]

The second test, given the name "continuity of principles"[179] by Newman, was more readily defined. "Doctrines are developed by the operation of principles, and develop differently according to those principles."[180] If those principles alter, then the doctrine itself will alter, Newman argued, and those developments, "if they really deserve the name," rather than being called corruptions, "must be conducted all along on definite and continuous principles, which determine their course."[181] By way of illustrating how this had operated in the history of the Christian idea, Newman looked at the consistent use by the church throughout history of the mystical sense in the understanding of the meaning of sacred scripture. He argued that while "the Jews clung to the literal sense of the Old Testament and rejected the Gospel; the Christian Apologists proved its divinity by means of the allegorical."[182] In the same way, St. Methodius had sought to "enforce vows of celibacy" by appeal to the mystical sense of the Book of Numbers, St. Irenaeus had proclaimed "the dignity of St. Mary" by seeing in an allegorical reading of Genesis the words of St. Luke's Gospel, and so on, up and until the present, with those particular Roman doctrines, such as that of purgatory, resting on precisely the

177. Newman, *Dev.*, 307.
178. Newman, *Dev.*, 307.
179. Newman, *Dev.*, 71.
180. Newman, *Dev.*, 71.
181. Newman, *Dev.*, 319.
182. Newman, *Dev.*, 324.

same principle for the interpretation of sacred scripture.[183] He further illuminated his meaning with the illustrations he gave to show the continuity of the principle of the supremacy of faith, particularly with regard to reason. He was, here, rehearsing the arguments of his later University Sermons, particularly the tenth and eleventh, that it is "the teaching of the Ancient Church" as much of the "modern schools" that the continuous principle that forces doctrines to develop is that faith "corrects that perplexity of doubts" that arises from the exercise of reason alone.[184]

The power of assimilation is, Newman claimed, a further test: "The idea never was that throve and lasted, yet ... incorporated nothing from external sources."[185] Once again, Newman used an analogy from natural science, observing that "whatever has life ... grows by taking into its own substance external materials" by way of nourishment.[186] The adoption of ideas from pagan philosophy, for example, those from Greek philosophy that made possible the development of the "Dogmatic and Sacramental" principles, are illustrations offered by Newman as examples of this test.[187]

The fourth test is that of the early anticipation of a later development in the history of an idea. Newman wrote that "since developments are in great measure only aspects of the idea from which they come ... it is no wise strange that here and there definite specimens should very early occur, which, in the historical course are not found till a late day."[188] He gave several, almost trivial, examples of this from Christian and "profane" history, such as the election of St. Athanasius as a bishop by his childhood "playfellows," or the early intimations of eighteenth-century cabinet government in King James VI and I's attempts at managing the business of the House of Commons.[189] He was to give more extensive examples of the application of this test, however, to a number of particular aspects of later Roman Cathol-

183. Newman, *Dev.*, 320–21.
184. Newman, *Dev.*, 332–33.
185. Newman, *Dev.*, 75.
186. Newman, *Dev.*, 73.
187. Newman, *Dev.*, 339–45.
188. Newman, *Dev.*, 77.
189. Newman, *Dev.*, 78.

icism in the seventh chapter of the *Essay*. The doctrines and practices—those "specimens of Theological Science"[190] relating to relics, the cult of the saints, celibacy, the Blessed Virgin Mary, and the dogmatic system—were ones that came in for particular criticism from Protestants, and which Newman and the other Tractarians had been compelled by their various interlocutors to deal. In the *Essay*, Newman examined the history of each of these doctrines or practices in turn and, instead of attempting lengthy apologetic or even correction of misapprehension, concluded that the historical record provided "proof of the existence from the first ... of those doctrinal developments which afterwards became recognised portions of the Church's Creed."[191]

For all his desire to maintain the superiority of faith over reason, as was observed when we considered his thirteenth University Sermon in the previous chapter, Newman had very high regard for reason. His fifth note, logical sequence, gave voice to this regard: "An idea grows in the mind by remaining there; it becomes familiar and distinct, and is viewed in its relations; it suggests other ideas, and these again others, subtle, recondite, original."[192] Newman's definition of logic, at least for the purposes of the *Essay*, is wider than might normally be applied, as Chadwick notes.[193] It is, nevertheless, recognizably coherent with the sense of sequential and reconcilable reasoning from one truth to another. Both the cult of the saints and of the Blessed Virgin Mary as logical developments from the doctrine of the divinity of Jesus and the Sacrament of Penance, the doctrine of Purgatory and the practice of Monasticism as logical developments from the doctrine of baptism (and their corruptions as illogical), are cited as examples of the illustration of this test at work in the history of the church.[194]

Newman called his sixth test one of "preservative additions": the notion that developments that preserve or strengthen the earlier

190. Newman, *Dev.*, 388.
191. Newman, *Dev.*, 396.
192. Newman, *Dev.*, 81.
193. Chadwick, *From Bousset to Newman*, 157.
194. Newman, *Dev*, 397–429.

ones enjoy "a fair presumption in their favour, so those which do not ... are certainly corrupt."[195] He was later to describe this test as being that of "conservative action upon its past."[196] The most significant of the illustrations of the sixth test that he offered was that of "whether the honours paid to St. Mary, which have grown out of devotion to her Almighty Lord and Son, do not, in fact, tend to weaken that devotion?"[197] On more than one occasion in his writings critical of Catholic devotion, Newman had contended that they did precisely this, most recently in the *British Critic* article of 1840:[198] he was now to argue that it was not the case. He asserted that the title given the Blessed Virgin at the Council of Ephesus, θεοτοκος, or Mother of God, is itself "sanction" for devotion to Mary as preservative of the doctrine of her son's divinity:[199] so, too, is the tone of that devotion, distinct as it is, from that paid to the Trinity.[200]

The seventh, final test Newman proposed was that of "chronic continuance." "Corruption cannot," he asserted, "be of long standing" because it leads briefly and rapidly to dissolution.[201] Authentic development, however, is characterised by "*duration*,"[202] because the ideas it relates to live "in men's minds" and hence are "ever enlarging into fuller development."[203] Newman's illustration of this is to contrast the long duration of the "Catholic system" in the face of "the severity of the trials it has undergone" with the fate of the various heresies with which it has had to contend,[204] although the briefest of his descriptions and illustrations of the tests, this seventh, the detailed examination of which concludes the *Essay*, brought Newman to the notion of what might be described as the "metatest": the Catholic Church.

195. Newman, *Dev.*, 86.
196. The name he was to give this test as his sixth "note" in the Uniform Edition. See Newman, *Dev.* (1878), 199.
197. Newman, *Dev.*, 435.
198. Newman, "Catholicity of the English Church," 40–88.
199. Newman, *Dev.*, 436.
200. Newman, *Dev.*, 436–41.
201. Newman, *Dev.*, 90.
202. Newman, *Dev.*, 91.
203. Newman, *Dev.*, 90.
204. Newman, *Dev.*, 446.

Newman had begun the second chapter of the *Essay*, "On the Development of Christian Ideas Antecedently Considered," by once again asserting the factual character of Christianity, and that the facts about its doctrines and practices could be made the "subject matter of exercises of the reason, and impressed an idea on our minds."[205] He also repeated his assertion that "it is the peculiarity of the human mind that it cannot take in an object that is submitted to it, simply and integrally," but instead requires "a number of statements, strengthening, interpreting, correcting each other, and with more or less exactness approximating, as they accumulate, to a perfect image" of the object."[206] Given these two considerations, Newman argued that it was, indeed, probable that "Christianity, as a doctrine and worship, will develop in the minds of recipients."[207]

The fact that Christianity is not confined to specific times or localities, Newman suggested, was further evidence of the probability of its development. Here Newman came to a consideration of the place of heresy in the development of doctrine. Given the importance the study of heresy had been in Newman's intellectual history, his remarks are both to be expected and also of some significance. Rather than choosing to locate his comments in a consideration of the Trinitarian and Christological controversies of Christian late antiquity, he chose instead to examine the Council of Trent's treatment of Luther's view of the doctrine of justification, which provided at least as good an example of what he wanted to show. Newman's words could, however, have been equally applied to any of the disputes of the early centuries that he had earlier considered in such detail: "The refutation and remedy of errors cannot precede their rise; and thus the fact of false developments or corruptions involves the correspondent manifestation of true ones."[208] Here, in the definitive formulation of his theory of the development of doctrine, was the proper explanation for Newman's concern with heresy. Notwithstanding Thomas's thesis, it was not an obsession with heresy, either for its own sake

205. Newman, *Dev.*, 94.
206. Newman, *Dev.*, 94.
207. Newman, *Dev.*, 96.
208. Newman, *Dev.*, 96–97.

or for some darkly hinted at but never made explicit psychological deficiency, but rather a proper concern to establish an hypothesis to account for the difficulty of change of doctrine in continuity with antecedent teaching that explains why Newman had spent so much time considering the history of Christian heresy. It was clear to him that the only conceivable explanation for many Christian doctrines that had appeared throughout the 1,800-year history of the religion was that untruths had developed from truths against which further explicit developments of the truth were necessary in order to guard and guarantee the continuity of the later doctrine with the earlier and overcome or refute the intervening heresy.

Even the structure of sacred scripture suggested to Newman an antecedent probability of development. He had previously argued that the fulfilment of earlier prophecies in later teachings or events in sacred scripture, particularly those of the Old Testament in the New, demonstrated that scripture itself presumes development. Now he argued that even the concept of an argument in favor of a doctrine or practice from scripture itself is an example of development, since it "implies deduction, that is, development."[209] Far from diminishing the role of scripture, as Turner, following George Stanley Faber, argued,[210] this accords it a role that is not easily diluted by the findings or, more properly, the claims of liberal-Protestant biblical criticism.

Newman argued, furthermore, that in making such deductions, the Catholic relying upon an *"ex cathedrâ"* judgement of the pope, and the Protestant relying on his or her private judgement, were relying on the same "claim of authority" to determine the veracity of a particular development.[211] Whether considered as the action of the mind of the whole church or the action of individual minds, the conscious or "unconscious growth of ideas habitual to the mind"[212] or the "slow process of thought, the influence of mind upon mind, the issues of controversy, and the growth of opinion are ... an ob-

---

209. Newman, *Dev.*, 97.
210. Turner, *The Challenge*, 569.
211. Newman, *Dev.*, 97.
212. Newman, *Dev.*, 97.

servable and natural part of Christianity," Newman argued.[213] On the one hand, doctrines such as the baptism of children were, he maintained, evidence of this historically observable truth and evidence of the fulfilment of sacred scripture. On the other hand, however, the development of the idea of Christianity was intended by God himself:

> Thus vast developments of Christianity are proved to have been in the contemplation of its Divine Author, by an argument parallel to that by which we infer intelligence in the system of the physical world. In whatever sense the need and its supply are proof of design in the visible creation, in the same do the gaps, if the word may be used, which occur in the structure of the original creed of the Church, make it probable that those developments, which grow out of the truths which lie around them, were intended to complete it.[214]

It was Newman's case that even the method of revelation underlying the scriptural texts is proof of the probability of developments in Christianity. Prophecy, for example, is predicated on the notion of a developing revelation, since individual prophecies "are pregnant texts out of which the succeeding announcements grow," and, Newman maintained, what is true of prophecy is true also of the "injunctions of doctrine."[215] These are expressions the meanings of which are not immediately apparent but that "have the same structure" as prophecies and, therefore, "should admit the same expansion."[216] In support of his argument, Newman quoted at some length from his *Lectures on the Prophetic Office*, in which he had examined several of Jesus' teachings in passages in the New Testament and found them to be what he now called "pregnant texts."[217] The parables and often the actions of Jesus, such as washing his disciples feet and paying tribute, are, Newman wrote, "instances of a similar peculiarity," that peculiarity being "developments of revelation" that had "preceded all through the old dispensation down to the very end of our Lord's

---

213. Newman, *Dev.*, 99.
214. Newman, *Dev.*, 101–2.
215. Newman, *Dev.*, 102–3.
216. Newman, *Dev.*, 104.
217. Newman, *Dev.*, 102–3. See also Newman, *VM 1*, 356–61.

ministry."[218] What is more, in the period immediately after that recorded in the New Testament, that is, in "the beginnings of apostolic teaching,"[219] this continued. No matter how hard we try, Newman observed, "we shall find ourselves unable to fix an historical point at which the growth of doctrines ceased, and the rule of faith was once for all settled."[220]

What Newman claimed to have observed in the development of the church's teaching, he also claimed to be able to observe in the development of ecclesial structures, or the "political development" of Christianity. This was a crucial point if he was to find justification for the development of the authority structure, particularly the office of the papacy, to the point it stood as he wrote. He felt able to conclude that: "From the necessity, then, of the case, from the history of all sects and parties in religion, and from the analogy and example of Scripture, we may fairly conclude that Christian doctrine admits of formal, legitimate, and true developments, or of developments contemplated by its divine author."[221]

Having made the case that it was probable that there would be developments in the Christian faith, Newman had then to consider the question of what: "rule is necessary for arranging and authenticating these various expressions and results of Christian doctrine ... how are we to discriminate the greater from the less, the true from the false."[222] It was at this point in the *Essay* that Newman admitted that the seven tests that he had set out were "insufficient" since they were "of a scientific and controversial, not a practical character, and are instruments rather than warrants of right decisions."[223] The want of such a mechanism, the need for which had been obvious to Newman since he first had read St. Augustine's "palmary words," meant that his tests of true development were not of the desired practical character: at least not as a simple binary test by which any single devel-

218. Newman, *Dev.*, 107.
219. Newman, *Dev.*, 107.
220. Newman, *Dev.*, 107.
221. Newman, *Dev.*, 113.
222. Newman, *Dev.*, 116.
223. Newman, *Dev.*, 117.

opment (still less prospective development) could be immediately identified as either authentic or corrupt.

Newman held that it was antecedently probable, that is, it is likely from the character of the Christian idea and its propensity to develop, that an authority to provide the warrant, the practical mechanism, would itself develop. Of course, such a warrant "must of necessity be external to the developments themselves,"[224] in order that it might be the judge of them. It was his case that, insofar as it is probable that Christian doctrine would develop, "and in proportion" to that probability, it was similarly probable that there should be a "scheme of an external authority to decide upon [those developments].... This is the doctrine of the infallibility of the church."[225]

Newman appreciated that this claim to an infallible teaching authority was not uncontroversial. He argued that the fact that Christian doctrine, as first imparted by Christ and the Apostles, "admits of true and important developments" was "a strong antecedent argument in favour of a provision in the Dispensation for putting a seal of authority upon those developments."[226] He took as a matter of fact that Christ and the Apostles were infallible teachers of that doctrine. Newman maintained these positions while also acknowledging that there were a number of objections to them, such as the common Protestant criticism of "Romanists" that the church's claim to infallibility is, in fact, circular and, as his own argument was constructed, at best, only probable. It was circular because it rested on the claim of infallibility in deciding the meaning of both scriptural texts and the development of that notion of infallibility, and it was only probable because, as Newman had demonstrated, the only grounds other than the scriptural that could justify the development of an infallible authority was from the antecedent probability that the structure of Christian doctrine regarding development required such an authority.[227] Yet, Newman argued that probability rather than demonstrable certainty is in the very nature of faith, and that any exercise of faith

224. Newman, *Dev.*, 117.
225. Newman, *Dev.*, 117.
226. Newman, *Dev.*, 118.
227. Newman, *Dev.*, 120.

involves the acceptance on trust of claims about which it is possible to claim nothing more than probability. Neither does the existence of such an authority remove free will, as was commonly claimed in objection to the idea of infallibility, either of the pope or the church as a whole: it merely narrowed the subject matter to which the free exercise of private judgment was to be applied, and this, too, was to be expected on grounds of antecedent probability:

> A Church, or a Council, or a Pope, or a Consent of doctors, or a Consent of Christendom, limits the enquiries of the individual in no other way than Scripture limits them: it does limit them; but while it limits their range, it preserves intact their probationary character; we are tried as really, though not on so large a field. To suppose that the doctrine of a permanent authority in matters of faith interferes with our freewill and responsibility is, as before, to forget that there were infallible teachers in the first age, and heretics and schismatics in the ages subsequent.[228]

In the end, for Newman, the argument came down to this issue, or, as he put it:

> The case then stands thus: ... as the essence of all religion is authority and obedience, so the distinction between natural religion and revealed lives in this, that one has a subjective authority, and the other an objective. Revelation consists in the manifestation of the invisible divine power, or in the substitution of the voice of a lawgiver for the voice of conscience. The supremacy of conscience is the essence of natural religion; the supremacy of apostle, or Pope, or church, or Bishop, is the essence of the revealed; and when such external authority is taken away, the mind falls back again upon that inward guide which it possessed even before revelation was vouchsafed. Thus what conscience is in the system of nature, such is the voice of Scripture, or of the church, or of the Holy See, as we may determine it, in the system of Revelation.[229]

The mention of conscience appears to have encouraged Newman to engage in a short excursus. He admitted that conscience is not infallible but yet notes the universal consensus in favor of obeying it. He pointed out that, as Robert Bellarmine had observed, popes, too,

---

228. Newman, *Dev.*, 121.
229. Newman, *Dev.*, 124.

can err "in particular controversies of fact, which chiefly depend on human information and testimony."[230] Nevertheless, he maintained, the analogy with conscience supports obedience to even erroneous papal judgments on moral grounds. He quoted and developed Bellarmine:

"All Catholics agree in two other points ... first, that the Pope with general counsel cannot err, either in framing decrees of faith or general precepts of morality; secondly, that the Pope, when determining anything in their doubtful matter, whether by himself or with his own particular Council, *whether it is possible to him to or not, is to be obeyed* by all the faithful." And as obedience to conscience, even supposing conscience ill-formed, tends to the improvement of our moral nature, and ultimately of our knowledge, so obedience to our ecclesiastical superior may subserve our growth in illumination and sanctity, even though he should command what is extreme or inexpedient, or teach what is external to his legitimate province.[231]

It was a position that he was to maintain, even when invited by others to depart from it in the wake of the definition of the dogma of papal infallibility at the First Vatican Council a quarter of a century later, when he wrote: "Unless a man is able to say to himself, as in the Presence of God, that he must not, and dare not, act upon the Papal injunction, he is bound to obey it."[232]

Newman was now close to what had become the unavoidable question. He believed that it was possible to prove that Christian doctrine did develop and that it was probable that this was a constituent element of it. He believed, too, that there was an external authority capable of providing a warrant, authenticating such developments. He now needed to identify what that authority was and where its voice was to be heard. He would do this by following the same principles that he had followed in determining whether or not doctrine would develop or that there would be an authority for authenticating it: by the use of historical analysis to determine what

---

230. Newman, *Dev.*, 125.
231. Newman, *Dev.*, 125.
232. John Henry Newman, *Conscience and Papacy, Letter to the Duke of Norfolk* (New Hope, Ky.: Real View Books, 2002), 258.

was both antecedently probable and what had developed. Scriptural considerations had pointed Newman in the direction of the church as the authority, but the identity of the church had for so long been an issue to him. Now he was to suggest, in the third chapter of the *Essay*, entitled "On the Nature of the Argument in behalf of Existing Development of Christianity," that only a church that claims to be an infallible judge could, as a matter of logic, be such. Together with a claim "of an infallible sanction—a claim, the existence of which, in some quarters or other of the Divine Dispensation, is, as we have already seen, antecedently probable,"[233] Newman asserted that the Roman Catholic Church's claim to be that infallible guide is supported by "the argument which arises from the coincidence of their consistency and permanence," that is, the consistency and permanence of Catholic doctrines.[234]

Newman then returned to the argument which had dominated the consideration of the rival claims of the English Church and the Roman in his *British Critic* article of January 1840, that is, the creedal notes of the church: unity, holiness, catholicity, and apostolicity. Departing from the theory of possession and the self-consciously anti-Catholic rhetoric, which he had so lately and publicly abjured, concerning want of holiness in the Roman Communion in the article, Newman now argued that unity, catholicity, and apostolicity are intimately related, cannot but exist together, and are to be found within the Roman Catholic communion. He wrote, using an illustration that may have suggested itself to him from one used by Miss Mary Holmes in correspondence with him in November 1844,[235] that

did St. Athanasius or St. Ambrose come suddenly to life, it cannot be doubted what communion they would mistake for their home. All differences of opinion, whatever protests, if we will, would find themselves more at home with such men as St. Bernard or St. Ignatius Loyola, all with the lonely priest in his lodging, or the holy sisterhood of mercy, or the unlettered crowd be-

---

233. Newman, *Dev.*, 136.
234. Newman, *Dev.*, 136.
235. Miss Mary Holmes to JHN, November 30, 1844, in *LD 10*, 441–42.

fore the altar, than with the rulers or members of any other religious community.[236]

This was Newman at his controversialist best, but the audience here was not those with whom he was or had been engaged in the various ecclesial controversies of the last decade and more, so much as himself. In a purple passage, he drove home the point:

And may we not add, that were the two Saints, who once sojourned in exile or on embassage, at Treves, to come more northward still, and to travel until they reached another fair city, seated among groves, green meadows, and calm streams, the holy brothers would turn from many a high aisle and solemn cloister which they found there, and ask the way to some small chapel where mass [sic] was said in the populous alley or forlorn suburb? And on the other hand, can anyone who has but heard his name, and cursorily read his history, doubt for one instant, how, in turn, the people of England ... would deal with Athanasius—Athanasius who spent his long years in fighting against Kings for theological term?[237]

Newman had discovered his Church of Catholicism; he had found his infallible guide; he had his external authority to decide between authentic developments and corruptions. He would use the rest of the *Essay* to illustrate how this Church of Catholicism, the Roman Catholic Church (although, as he was later to note, he now "boldly" referred to it simply as the Catholic Church)[238] was able to determine with authority the development of

doctrines [which] come to us, professing to be Apostolic, and possessed of such high antiquity that, though we are only able to assign the date of their formal establishment to the fourth or fifth or eighth or thirteenth century, as it may happen, yet their substance may, for what appears, be coeval with the apostles, and be expressed or implied in texts of Scripture.[239]

    236. Newman, *Dev.*, 138. Cf. The JHN letter at n. 235. Miss Holmes wrote: "Could St. Thomas of Canterbury, St. Anselm and the Venerable Bede rise from their graves, can you doubt an instant which side they would take? Would they submit to Dr. Wiseman or to the Bishop (so called) of Oxford? Would St. Stephen Harding and St. Bernard have any fellowship with a Church founded by Cranmer, and Henry 8th?" (Miss Mary Holmes to JHN, November 30, 1844, in *LD 10*, 442).
    237. Newman, *Dev.*, 138–39.
    238. Newman, *Apo.*, 388.
    239. Newman, *Dev.*, 146.

Here, then, was Newman's theory of development in its three aspects. First, because the idea of Christianity lives in the minds of men and women, it has a development that preserves the identity of the idea. Second, development involves the progressive and more accurate enunciation of the idea in doctrines and practices through their engagement with historical and cultural frameworks. Finally, there are tests, or perhaps they might better be termed "indications" or even "notes," as Newman would come to call them in the Uniform Edition, that, subject to the infallible judgment of the Roman Catholic Church, might be used to determine whether a particular change is a development or a corruption. The metatest, however, was the living authority of the Catholic Church:

> It is true, there have been seasons when, from the operation of external or internal causes, the church has been thrown into what was almost a state of *deliquium*; but her wonderful revivals, while the world was triumphing over her, is a further evidence of the absence of corruption, in the system of doctrine and worship into which she has developed. If corruption be an incipient disorganisation, surely an abrupt and absolute recurrence to such a state, after an interval during which it has ceased to be, is even less conceivable than its sustained existence. Now this is the case with the revivals I speak of. After violent exertion men are exhausted and fall asleep; they await the same as before, refreshed by the temporary cessation of their activity; and such has been the slumber and such the restoration of the church. She pauses in her course, and almost suspends her functions; she rises again, and she is herself once more; all things are in their place and ready for action. Doctrine is where it was, and usage, and precedents, and principle, and policy; there may be changes, but they are consolidations or adaptations; all is unequivocal and determinate, with an identity which there is no disputing. Indeed, it is one of the most popular charges against the Catholic Church at this very time, that she is "incorrigible"—change she cannot, if we listen to St. Athanasius or St. Leo; change she never will, if we believe the controversialist or alarmist of the present day.[240]

This Catholic Church, changed in appearance, but yet having the same identity as the Church of the Fathers which Newman had

---

240. Newman, *Dev.*, 452–53.

sought since the summer of 1816, was the arbiter of change in continuity; it was the living organ necessary to verify development; it was the Church of Catholicism; it was the keystone of the hypothesis to account for the difficulty of which he had been aware for so long; it was, Newman now believed, the Roman Catholic Church.

CONCLUSION

When he published his *Essay*, John Henry Newman did more than set out an intellectual theory: he addressed a question that had posed for him a serious existential difficulty for a very considerable period of time. The intensity with which he addressed that difficulty had grown to such significance that the answer could not but leave him utterly changed. His theory of the development of doctrine provided him his long-sought solution and was arguably his most significant contribution to theology.

The remote origins of this solution were in the intense religious experience of the autumn of 1816 and in the books he read in the months before he first went to Oxford the following year. The need for a theory of the development of Christian doctrine gradually and haltingly emerged, yet it had become explicit enough by the mid-1820s for Newman to begin to frame the question in precisely the language he would use for the next twenty years. In the intervening years, and in response to the specific circumstances of various occasions, Newman proposed a series of theories, more or less complete depending upon the nature of the occasion, to account for the paradox of a fixed deposit of faith and a changing doctrinal expression. Under testing, these successive theories failed, revealed as unreal, unworkable, or failing to correspond with the historical data.

The first hypothesis, that of the principle of reserve protected by a *disciplina arcani*, proposed that the terminological changes that could be observed in the expressions of the church's doctrine in the early centuries were, in fact, the gradual lifting of a veil of secrecy that had kept the teaching from public view in times of persecution. The weakness of this theory was two-fold: first, the historical record contained no evidence to support the contention that the early church was conscious of a need to maintain a strict distinction between the exoteric and esoteric expressions of her doctrine and so practice a *disciplina arcani* before the fourth century, yet Newman was faced with evidence of at least the language of doctrine changing well before that; secondly, this theory provided no tool for distinguishing between changes that had come to be seen as orthodox expressions of faith and those judged to be heresy. By appending the Vincentian Canon to his theory, Newman initially believed he had solved the latter difficulty and, by appealing to an unauthoritative tradition to facilitate the collecting of the sense of scripture in understanding the church's doctrine, considered that he had sidestepped the inconvenience of the former.

Newman's own research into the controversies of the fourth and fifth centuries repeatedly drew his attention to the contradictions between the teachings, not just of those early Christian writers who had come to be called heretics but also of the orthodox Fathers. In the light of this, the need for a hypothesis that would stand up to the evidence in the historical record was increasingly obvious. Although he claimed at the time that its immediate effect was negligible, Newman's correspondence with the Abbé Jager and the *Lectures on the Prophetical Office*, which were among its products, demonstrated the need for an authoritative rule against which competing claims could be measured. The hoped-for stronghold in what has been called a Catholicism of the Word proved to be illusory: the lack of consensus as to if and where such a univocal patristic voice was to be found fatally undermined it. For a time, Newman believed that the authoritative note of Apostolical faith could be found in the voice of the Church of England and its adherence to a *via media* between Protestant infidelity and Roman corruption. Even this hypothesis, however, was to crumble in the face of its own essentially untried and theoretical nature, the refusal of Anglican bishops to behave as guardians of that Apostolical faith to Newman's satisfaction, and the historical parallels between the position of the Church of England and various heretical sects in the early church that, as Wiseman made explicit, forced themselves upon Newman as he continued his study of the Fathers.

CONCLUSION

As Newman's confidence in the position of the Church of England, and his place in it, faltered in the early 1840s, he came to the lasting conviction that only a dynamic and organic authority could provide the locus for the resolution of the difficulty. In the *Essay* of 1845, Newman both outlined a theory of the theology of development that he believed accounted for the difficulty in a manner that did not contain the same flaws of his earlier theories and provided justification for his conclusion that the necessary dynamic and organic authority was to be found in the Roman Catholic Church. The theory itself, and its ecclesial consequences for Newman, involved a delicate, even "precarious balancing act,"[1] between those "impressions of dogma, which, through God's mercy, have never been effaced or obscured,"[2] of the summer of 1816, on the one hand, and the story of the intervening twenty-nine years, on the other. It was one that, as Merrigan has noted, was "inspired not simply by the concern to reconcile a theological datum (the definitiveness of revelation in Christ) with the facts of history, but by the attempts to develop an adequate science (or theology) of the Living Word."[3]

Newman's polemical Tractarian co-conspirator and almost contemporary fellow-convert to Roman Catholicism, William Ward, anticipated Newman's adoption of a theory of development when, a year before the *Essay*, he boasted: "My difficulty in defending this doctrine of development arises from my inability to conceive how anyone can have, for a single day, pursued a course of moral and religious action, and yet deny it."[4]

What Ward claimed to see with such clarity, Newman came to with a characteristic suspicion of his own motives and a desire to ensure that the hypothesis was, indeed, equal to the task. The history of his own engagement with the difficulty of continuity and change meant that the theory of development that he described was both subtle and

---

1. Merrigan, *Clear Heads and Holy Hearts*, 97.
2. Newman, *Apo.*, 58.
3. Merrigan, *Clear Heads and Holy Hearts*, 97.
4. William George Ward, *The Ideal of a Christian Church Considered in Comparison with Existing Practice: Containing a Defence of Certain Articles in the British Critic in Reply to Remarks on Them in Mr. Palmer's "Narrative"* (London: James Toovey, 1844), 547.

robust. It had to be subtle enough to address the short comings of the simpler, more obvious solutions that he had previously adopted, and yet robust enough to stand up to the scrutiny of being not merely a "paper theory" but a reality of ecclesial life. Ward's bombast scarcely outlasted his conversion to Roman Catholicism, replaced with an extreme, almost caricatured, Ultramontanist positivism not unlike that which Newman had mistakenly believed to be the Roman Catholic doctrine at the time of his correspondence with Jager. Newman's theory remained largely unaltered, not least because the difficulty to which it was addressed remained the same.[5] That it did remain so in the difficult period around and after the First Vatican Council, when, in the wake of the definition of papal infallibility a Ward-like Ultramontanism seemed triumphant, is testament to its robustness and Newman's tenacity in holding to it.

This work has looked closely at the detailed history of Newman's attempt to account for both continuity and change in Christian doctrine in the period until his seceding from the Church of England and his submission to the authority and communion of the Roman Catholic Church in October 1845. It has provided an analysis of the structure of the theory as it was expressed by Newman in the first edition of his *Essay*, which appeared in November 1845, identifying those elements of the theory that answered the specific problems that had arisen with those earlier, failed hypotheses. It has neither attempted a systematic, theological analysis of Newman's theory of development nor to assess the theory's utility as a tool for the forensic assessment of the status—whether authentic development or corruption—of any particular contemplated change in doctrine. Nevertheless, it is clear that, as the International Theological Commission observed, the tests or notes it proposes constitute "a criteriology for the development of dogma, which ... can be applied in proper proportions to ... further interpretation of dogmas aimed at giving them contemporary relevance."[6] Even if the theory did not

---

5. Wilfrid Philip Ward, *Life of John Henry Cardinal Newman Based on His Private Journals and Correspondence*, vol. 2 (London: Longmans, Green and Co., 1912), 212.

6. International Theological Commission, *The Interpretation of Dogma*, 1989,

take shape in order to undertake such a task, when it has been used in such a way, by, for example, O'Collins in his consideration of the Resurrection or by Ker in an analysis of the development of the Roman Catholic theology of religious liberty at Vatican II, its utility is beyond doubt.[7]

The postpublication histories of the *Essay* and Newman's engagement with his own theory of development are also beyond the scope of this present work. His ideas did not find immediate universal and unqualified endorsement in his new communion, where the criticisms of his critics were often heard more insistently than Newman's own arguments. Newman's eventually creative engagement with the eminent Roman Jesuit, Giovanni Perrone, and the outright attack on his work by the American Orestes Brownson, marked his first years as a Roman Catholic. Whereas Brownson rejected Newman's arguments out of hand, Perrone's response was much more positive. Indeed, as C. Michael Shea has repeatedly demonstrated, in its influence on Perrone, the *Essay* has "an overlooked legacy."[8] There were, undoubtedly, those of the Roman School who suspected Newman of heresy, yet his reception by Perrone, others in Rome, and elsewhere who saw the value in Newman's arguments, show that the picture was far more complex than once was commonly accepted. Whereas once any argument that the opinion of an "inopportunist" such as Newman would have echoed in the minds of the framers of *Pastor Aeternus* would have been discounted, this view is itself developing. Shea, for example, has argued persuasively for its not insig-

---

http://www.vatican.va/roman_curia/congregations/cfaith/cti_documents/rc_cti_1989_interpretazione-dogmi_en.html.

7. See Gerald O'Collins, "Newman's Seven Notes: The Case of the Resurrection," in *Focus on Jesus: Essays in Christology and Soteriology*, ed. Gerald O'Collins and Daniel Kendall (Leominster: Gracewing, 1996), 135–48; Ian Turnbull Ker, "Is Dignitatis Humanae a Case of Authentic Doctrinal Development," *Logos* 11, no. 2 (2008): 149–57.

8. C. Michael Shea, "Father Giovanni Perrone and Doctrinal Development in Rome: An Overlooked Legacy of Newman's Essay on Development," *Journal for the History of Modern Theology / Zeitschrift Für Neuere Theologiegeschichte* 20, no. 1 (2013): 85–116; *Newman's Early Roman Catholic Legacy 1845–1854*, 1st ed. (Oxford: Oxford University Press, 2017); and his chapter on "Doctrinal Development," in *The Oxford Handbook of John Henry Newman*, eds. Frederick D. Aquino and Benjamin Kings, 1st ed. (Oxford: Oxford University Press, 2018). Mark McInroy's essay "Catholic Receptions," 495–99, in the same volume, is also helpful.

nificant influence on the definition of papal infallibility at the First Vatican Council in 1870.[9]

What emerged in his 1868 *Unpublished Paper on the Development of Doctrine*[10] and in the reworked text of the *Essay* for its third edition in 1878 was, if anything, a stronger attachment to the theory of 1845. In the *longue durée*, Newman's influence has eclipsed his contemporary critics, and a thoroughgoing appraisal of his impact on the major theologians of the twentieth century can only be assisted by a detailed explanation of the origins of the *Essay*.

On receiving a copy of the third edition of the *Essay*, Newman's once-devout disciple, Mark Pattison, surely did not exaggerate when he wrote to him, to say: "Is it not a remarkable thing that you should have first started the idea—the word—Development, as the key to the history of church doctrine, and since then it has gradually become the dominant idea of all history, biology, physics, and in short has metamorphosed our view of every science, and of all knowledge."[11]

Theology has been altered utterly by the notion of development. Since the Second Vatican Council, the Roman Catholic Church has seen a curious inversion of the Ultramontanist positivism with which Newman had to contend in his later years. While Newman had to engage with a tendency to invest excessive authority in any and all papal pronouncements, often in an almost reflexively obscurantist attempt to deny the possibility of development, the post–Vatican II period has seen a manifestation of the same positivist tendency now deployed in support of innovations and changes justified simply by

---

9. C. Michael Shea, "Newman's Theory of Development and the Definition of Papal Infallibility," in *Authority, Dogma, and History: The Role of the Oxford Movement Converts in the Papal Infallibility Debates*, ed. Kenneth L. Parker and Michael J. G. Pahls (Palo Alto, Calif.: Academica Press, 2009), 77–93. That this might be so had been foreseen by Bishop David Moriarty of Kerry—who had conspicuously sided with Newman against Cullen during the dispute over the establishment of the Catholic University in Dublin in the 1850s—who wrote to Newman during the council, saying: "If ever this definition comes, you will have contributed much towards it. Your treatise on development has given the key." See *LD 25*, 58, n. 2.

10. John Henry Newman, "Unpublished Paper on the Development of Doctrine," in Hugo de Archaval, "An Unpublished Paper by Cardinal Newman on the Development of Doctrine," *Gregorianum* 39, no. 3 (1958): 585–96.

11. Mark Pattison to JHN, April 5, 1878, in *LD 28*, 339, n. 3.

CONCLUSION

an appeal to authority in either to what the documents of the council are thought to say or, more often, to a *soi-disant* "Spirit of Vatican II." Engaging with the question of how Newman searched for continuity in the face of change offers the prospect of an answer to the question of development identified by John Courtney Murray in January 1965 that goes beyond such naivety.

Furthermore, this revival of Ultramontanism has not been the preserve of one "party" or another in the contemporary church. The dismantling of devotional culture, the revision of the liturgy, and the reordering of churches in the immediate postconciliar period was often imposed upon and justified to a bewildered but naturally obedient faithful in the name of arguments from precisely this authority.[12] Under the papacies of St. John Paul II and Benedict XVI, such appeals to authority were deployed in what might be called a more "conservative" direction, but these appeals were often made without acknowledging the complexity and far-from-univocal voice of tradition. Those whose Ultramontanist instincts served more "progressive" causes were prone to the same error—especially when claiming the warrant of the early church in support—but did and continue to do so without any serious consideration of the extent to which such innovations and changes are consistent and cohere with the antecedent teaching or practice. This approach, when yoked to a mentality that is inclined to see progress as an unalloyed good in and of itself, appears to contain an "almost naïve progressivist optimism which [seems] unaware of the ambivalence of all external progress."[13]

These simmering tendencies have been brought to a boil during the pontificate of Pope Francis, which indicates that the issue of doctrinal development is no less relevant in the twenty-first century than it was in the nineteenth. The most obvious example, for which

---

12. See, for example, Louis Bouyer's account of how certain proposed changes to the liturgy were presented and justified to (and passively accepted by) the *Consilium ad exsequendam Constitutionem de Sacra Liturgia* by its secretary, Fr. Annibale Bugnini, CM, on the sole criterion that "the Pope wills it!" See Louis Bouyer, *Memoirs*, trans. Anne Englund Nash (San Francisco: Ignatius Press, 2015), 224–25.

13. Joseph Ratzinger, *Theological Highlights of Vatican II* (Mahwah, N.J.: Paulist Press, 2009), 227.

CONCLUSION

the Congregation of the Doctrine of the Faith explicitly invoked the notion of doctrinal development, is the latest change to the *Catechism of the Catholic Church* on the death penalty. The church's teaching on the death penalty had until the last decade of the twentieth century long been considered a settled matter. In certain circumstances (which included the gravity of the offense and protection of society), it was permissible, and, indeed, as recently as the 1940s and 50s, Pope Pius XII had taught that it might even be required on grounds of justice.[14] But the 1995 promulgation of Pope St. John Paul II's vigorous encyclical letter on the defense of human life, *Evangelium vitae*, signaled a change regarding the death penalty, in which he sought severely to restrict its morally licit use. This new approach was codified in the pontiff's personal revisions to the *Catechism of the Catholic Church* in 1997, which states in its paragraph 2267, that although "the traditional teaching of the Church does not exclude recourse to the death penalty, if this is the only possible way of effectively defending human lives against the unjust aggressor.... If, however, non-lethal means are sufficient to defend and protect people's safety from the aggressor, authority will limit itself to such means, ... the cases in which the execution of the offender is an absolute necessity are very rare, if not practically non-existent."[15]

That this paragraph excluded any consideration of the magisterial claims of the appropriateness, even necessity, on grounds of justice, was itself noteworthy. Rather than appearing to contradict even his recent predecessors (not to mention the prescriptions of sacred scripture), Pope John Paul II side-stepped the issue and cast the question entirely in terms of the defense of human life against an unjust aggressor and the prudential judgement about absolute necessity. The weakness of this teaching, however, was that by grounding itself in prudential judgment, it allowed Catholics and others to

---

14. For the Pian teaching, see Pope Pius XII, *Ai Partecipanti al I Congresso Nazionale Dell'Unione Giuristi Cattolici Italiani*, November 6, 1949, http://w2.vatican.va/content/pius-xii/it/speeches/1949/documents/hf_p-xii_spe_19491106_giuristi-cattolici.html and *Discorso Di Sua Santità Pio PP. XII Ai Partecipanti al VI Congresso Internationale de Diritto Penale*, October 3, 1953, http://w2.vatican.va/content/pius-xii/it/speeches/1953/documents/hf_p-xii_spe_19531003_diritto-penale.html.

15. *Catechism of the Catholic Church* (London: Geoffrey Chapman, 1992), para. 2267.

dissent from it on the established moral grounds that no man's prudential judgment is absolutely binding in faith upon another. The validity of the judgment is dependent upon the underlying factual matrix: if it could be argued that, in the specific circumstances under consideration, it was the only possible way of effectively defending human lives against the unjust aggressor, or that nonlethal means are insufficient to defend and protect people's safety from the aggressor, or even that the possibilities which the state has in a particular location, time, context, for effectively preventing crime, do not render one who has committed an offense incapable of doing harm, then it was permissible to come to a different judgement than the pope had.

Pope Francis, in turn, has sought to further advance and strengthen Catholic opposition to the death penalty, citing the confused witness to the dignity of human life that was caused when Catholics sought, on the one hand, to protect the life of those as yet unborn or those incapacitated by age or medical and psychological decay, while on the other continuing to support the use of the death penalty, as the reason that the change was necessary. In May 2018, Pope Francis instructed that paragraph 2267 be amended such that it now reads: "the death penalty is inadmissible because it is an attack on the inviolability and dignity of the person, and she [the Church] works with determination for its abolition worldwide."[16] Whether one welcomes this change or not, that it marks a distinct movement beyond the already novel position adopted by John Paul II is beyond doubt. It is certainly difficult to cast this as merely a papal observation on a matter of prudential judgement, particularly when the Prefect of the Congregation for the Doctrine of the Faith explicitly described the change in terms of doctrinal development, even while neatly avoiding the question of how it can be shown to be a development in continuity with the teaching expressed by Pius XII.[17]

---

16. "New revision of number 2267 of the Catechism of the Catholic Church on the death penalty – Rescriptum 'ex Audentia SS.mi,'" August 2, 2018, at https://press.vatican.va/content/salastampa/en/bollettino/pubblico/2018/08/02/180802a.html, accessed August 9, 2020.

17. Congregation of the Doctrine of the Faith, *Letter to the Bishops Regarding the New*

CONCLUSION

If the change to the *Catechism* on the death penalty was explicitly cast as a development whose ramifications are as yet unknown, a second change ushered in by Pope Francis has caused even more uncertainty and tension within the church, even as it was initially defended as requiring no change in doctrine at all. This change was derived, of course, from controversies that began with the 2014 Extraordinary and 2015 Ordinary Synods on the Family, after which came the publication of the Post-Synodal Exhortation *Amoris laetitia* in March 2016.[18] At first, it seemed that the more radical proposals suggested at the synods—such as allowing communion to the divorced and civilly remarried—did not find support in the pope's official document. However, a single, ambiguous footnote (351) in chapter 8 gave rise to some ecclesial bodies revising the previous practice of requiring divorced and civilly remarried Catholics to have their previous marriages declared null or refrain from "marital relations" in order to receive communion, while others interpreted the document as requiring or authorizing no such change. Only over time did Pope Francis's own position become clearer, which culminated with the insertion into the *Acta Apostolicae Sedis* of a set of pastoral guidelines adopted by the Bishops of the Pastoral Region of Buenos Aires concerning the application of *Amoris laetitia*,[19] together with an endorsement by Pope Francis in what was originally a private letter with the expression, "there is no other interpretation."[20]

While it may seem that the pastoral question at issue—the pro-

---

Revision of Number 2267 of the Catechism of the Catholic Church on the Death Penalty, August 1, 2018, http://press.vatican.va/content/salastampa/en/bollettino/pubblico/2018/08/02/180802b.html., accessed August 9, 2020.

18. Pope Francis, Post-Synodal Apostolic Exhortation *Amoris laetitia* (March 19, 2016), http://w2.vatican.va/content/francesco/en/apost_exhortations/documents/papa-francesco_esortazione-ap_20160319_amoris-laetitia.html.

19. "Criterios básicos para la aplicacíon del capitulo VIII de Amoris Laetitia," in Pope Francis, *Epistula Apostolica Ad Excellentissimum Dominum Sergium Alfredum Fenoy, Delegatum Regionis Pastoralis Bonaërensis, Necnon Adiunctum Documentum (de Praecipuis Rationibus Usui Capitis VIII Adhortationis Post-Synodalis "Amoris Laetitia")*, September 5, 2016, in *AAS*, vol. 108 (10) (2016): 1071–74.

20. "No hay otras interpretaciones," in response to the text in the *Criterios básicos*, referred to in the immediately preceding footnote, which appeared to permit the admission to Holy Communion of individuals who were in second unions lived *more uxorem* while still bound by the obligations of a prior union (*AAS*, vol. 108 (10): 1071).

CONCLUSION

vision of the Eucharist to a subset of the faithful—affects only that subset of the church, to allow such a practice seems logically to require the suspension of one or another of the principles previously established by the Magisterium. As the various interpretations of different Bishops developed, without clear guidance from the pope, serious theological questions concerning the presupposed doctrinal change began to be asked by theologians, other scholars, and pastors—not only about one footnote but the approach of the entire chapter 8, which seemed at odds with Pope John Paul II's reiteration of the existence of intrinsically immoral actions in the encyclical *Veritatis splendor*.[21] The theological concerns were sufficiently serious for four members of the College of Cardinals to submit formal questions, or *dubia*, to the Holy Father—questions that were, at least on the Cardinals' own accounts, entirely concerned with establishing what the doctrinal content of *Amoris laetitia* was and how any changes from the previous settled teaching could be reconciled or made to cohere with it.[22]

Whatever one's views of the wisdom of the formulation of the questions in the *dubia*, of sending them, or still less of later publishing them, they were manifestly concerned with the nature of the development of doctrine in the document. Defenders of the changes sought to sidestep these concerns with the distinction between "doctrine" and "practice"—that is, to explain any change that there might have been by suggesting that the doctrine remains unchanged, even though the practice has changed. While the distinction between πρᾶξις, praxis (doing),[23] and its proper relations to and interactions

---

21. Although the validity of those concerns is not within the scope of this book, I acknowledge that I was one of the forty-five or so signatories to a letter to the Cardinals and Patriarchs asking them to urge the Holy Father to clarify certain potentially problematic positions and practices that claimed to find either their origin or magisterial justification in that document and its footnotes. For clarity on the reader's part, I did not sign a subsequent letter positively accusing the Holy Father of formal heresy; the clarification letter was a prior initiative.

22. Edward Pentin, "Full Text and Explanatory Notes of Cardinals' Questions on 'Amoris Laetitia,'" *National Catholic Register*, accessed July 21, 2019, http://www.ncregister.com/blog/edward-pentin/full-text-and-explanatory-notes-of-cardinals-questions-on-amoris-laetitia.

23. Aristotle, *Nicomachean Ethics*, VI, 5, 1140b.

with θεορια, theoria (thinking) and ποιησις, poesis (making) goes back to Aristotle, it has been dramatically transformed, first by Hegelian and then by specifically Marxist thinkers, such that it is now difficult to posit a useful distinction between the two.[24] Whatever *praxis* is, it is not a properly robust theological methodology that can be used to assess whether a change is an authentic development of an antecedent doctrine or a corruption of it.

In any event, when the controversy erupted, the Holy See chose Christoph Cardinal Schönborn, Archbishop of Vienna, to field questions, and it was Schönborn who explicitly cast the change wrought through *Amoris laetitia* in the language of the development of doctrine and even cited Newman as proof that this was perfectly in order. Just as with the later death penalty change, the cardinal offered no explanation as to how the perceived changes in, and even contradictions with, former doctrine could be made to cohere with the theology of the development of doctrine proposed by Newman. In the years since the cardinal's press conferences, there have been no further clarifications from the pope or other magisterial sources to affirm or defend this contention.

It remains to be seen the extent to which Newman's theory will be able to demonstrate that these and other changes initiated by Pope Francis since his election in 2013[25] represent authentic develop-

---

24. The influences on the Catholic Church of both the cultural Marxism of the Italian Antonio Gramsci and the thinking of Frankfurt School Marxists are outside the present study, but given the historical and contemporary evidence of the use of changing praxis to facilitate changing doctrine—at least at the level of what is commonly, if not authoritatively taught—is so overwhelming, it is no longer in doubt that "action oriented to changing society," to use Cieszkowski's definition of *praxis* (August von Cieszkowski, *Prolegomena Zur Historiosophie* [Berlin: Bei Veit und Comp., 1838]) is a process observably at work in the church, whether this process is deliberate or inadvertent.

25. For example, his repeated calls for the sharing of the *munus regendi* with those—particularly women—neither in priestly nor episcopal orders, or his apparent endorsement of the claim in the Abu Dhabi Declaration that God wills a plurality of religions. For the latter, see Pope Francis and the Grand Imam of Al-Azhar Ahmad Al-Tayyeb, *A Document on Human Fraternity for World Peace and Living Together*, February 4, 2019, at http://www.vatican.va/content/francesco/en/travels/2019/outside/documents/papa-francesco_20190204_documento-fratellanza-umana.html, accessed August 9, 2020. It is, of course, perfectly possible to interpret this as merely a recognition of the action of the divine permissive will. Whether the context of the document lends itself to such an interpretation is open to question: nevertheless, if anyone is entitled to the presumption of orthodoxy, it must be the pope.

ments of the church's doctrine, that is, of what Newman understood in terms of the faith once committed to the Apostles, or corruptions of it. But perhaps the failure of the Magisterium to defend its own actions—to invoke Newman and leave it to theologians to work out an intellectually satisfying response to the question (pro or con) is a blessing in disguise. What is certain is that the church urgently needs a theology of development that commands widespread agreement: one which does not rely entirely on an overblown, creeping extension of the dogma of papal infallibility. To settle for such an argument from authority would, indeed, be the "nothing else than shooting Niagara" that Newman so feared would follow the definition of that dogma at Vatican I.[26]

Newman found a lasting hypothesis to account for the difficulty of doctrinal development in the living authority of the Roman Catholic Church and not in the *disciplina arcani*, nor the univocal voice of Vincentian antiquity, nor yet in a *via media*, nor yet a Catholicism of the Word, guaranteed by a theory of *de facto* ecclesial possession. To this extent, he seems to provide theological support to a new generation of Ultramontanist positivism—this is, however, to fail to understand what the voice of the living authority exists to do. The voice of the living authority of the Roman Catholic Church, and particularly of the Roman Pontiff, is not—in Newman's *Essay*—a new source of revelation, handing down new truths as if upon Mount Sinai (still less in a footnote to an Apostolic exhortation, an answer to a journalist's question on an airplane, or a private conversation or telephone call). When considering the response of the Fathers at Chalcedon to Leo the Great's *Tome*, Newman noted that this pope's authority was "as great as he claims now almost."[27] Yet he perceived that authority as acting primarily in a negative manner. As he was to put it in his answer to Charles Kingsley:

It is hardly necessary to argue out so plain a point. It is individuals, and not the Holy See, that have taken the initiative, and given the lead to the Catholic mind, in theological inquiry. Indeed, it is one of the reproaches

---

26. Newman, *LD* 25, 262.
27. JHN to Frederic Rogers, July 12, 1839, in *LD* 7, 105.

urged against the Roman Church, that it has originated nothing, and has only served as a sort of *remora* or break in the development of doctrine. And it is an objection which I really embrace as a truth; for such I conceive to be the main purpose of its extraordinary gift.[28]

The key to understanding the voice of living authority for Newman and, perhaps, for the church at this moment, is to conceive of that living authority operating in its proper context: that is, in relation to the development of the idea of Christianity. The idea of Christianity was, in Newman's thinking, Christ Himself:[29] God made Man for our Salvation. Because this idea lives in the minds of men and women its authentic development, our ever more perfect understanding of it must preserve its identity through progressive and more accurate enunciation of the idea in doctrines and practices through engagement with historical and cultural frameworks. Newman showed in the *Essay* that there are indicators, his "tests" or "notes," that might be used to indicate whether any particular change does that or not. It is the conclusions drawn from those notes that, for Newman, were the proper subject of the infallible judgment of the church.

This book was written in the confident belief that the needed theology of development is to be found in Newman's *Essay*. Following his October 13, 2019, canonization, it is certainly to be hoped that the higher prominence in the Universal Church of not just the person of the now St. John Henry Newman but also the attention given to his lasting contribution to Catholic theology will mean that his theory of development becomes better known, more thoroughly understood, and widely adopted as means of answering questions related to change and continuity, authentic development, and corruption of doctrine. Regardless of whether that happens, it is undeniable that Newman's own cautious approach to judging developments of doctrine would have required a great deal more measured a response than the bald assertions that have so far been made by those who would seek to dismiss the very propriety of asking the question, nor

---

28. Newman, *Apo.*, 407.
29. Merrigan, *Clear Heads and Holy Hearts*, 98.

CONCLUSION

yet the failure to acknowledge that it has been asked. It is beyond doubt that these matters would have exercised Newman today as much as the developments in historic Christianity and those in his own lifetime did. They would have required of him that he took seriously the authoritative testimonies of the past as the context for understanding if, when, and how that living authority has made its voice heard in the present. In beginning to do that in the current *status ecclesiae*, Newman's *Essay* might well serve as a sensible point of departure and, that being so, its genesis, structure, and purpose need properly to be considered and understood. This book is intended as a modest contribution to that preparatory task.

BIBLIOGRAPHY

Works by John Henry Newman
Manuscript Sources

Newman, John Henry. "Apollinarianism," 1835. B.2.9.a, Birmingham Oratory Archives.
———. "Apollinaris" History," 1835. B.2.5, Birmingham Oratory Archives.
———. "Copybook on Development," n.d. B.2.8, Birmingham Oratory Archives.
———. "The Monophysite Heresy," August 23, 1839. B.2.9, Birmingham Oratory Archives.
———. "Papers and Fragments on the Development of Christian Doctrine," Various dates. B.2.8, Birmingham Oratory Archives.
———. "Preparatory Notes for the 3rd Edition of Development," n.d. D.7.6, Birmingham Oratory Archives.
———. "Various Sermons," n.d. B.3.4, Birmingham Oratory Archives.

Published Sources

Newman, John Henry. *Addresses to Cardinal Newman with His Replies Etc. 1879–1881*. Edited by W. P. Neville. London: Longmans, Green and Co., 1905.
———. *A Letter to the Rev. Godfrey Faussett, D.D., Margaret Professor of Divinity, on Certain Points of Faith and Practice*. Oxford: John Henry Parker, 1838.
———. *An Essay on the Development of Christian Doctrine*. London: James Toovey, 1845.
———. *An Essay on the Development of Christian Doctrine*. London: Longmans, Green and Co., 1909.
———. *An Essay on the Development of Christian Doctrine*. Edited by Ian Turnbull Ker. Notre Dame, Ind.: University of Notre Dame Press, 1989.
———. *An Essay on the Development of Christian Doctrine, New Edition*. Edited by Charles Frederick Harrold. New York: Longmans, Green and Co., 1949.
———. *An Essay on the Development of Christian Doctrine: The Edition of 1845*. Edited by James M Cameron. London: Penguin, 1974.
———. "Apollonius of Tyanaeus." In *Encyclopedia Metropolitana*, 619–44. London: Mawman, 1826.

BIBLIOGRAPHY

———. *Apologia Pro Vita Sua*. Edited by Martin Svaglic. Oxford: Clarendon Press, 1974.

———. *Apologia Pro Vita Sua*. Edited by Ker and Ian Turnbull. London: Penguin, 1994.

———. *Apologia Pro Vita Sua and Six Sermons*. Edited by Frank Miller Turner. New Haven, Conn.: Yale University Press, 2008.

———. *Apologia Pro Vita Sua: Being a History of His Religious Opinions*. Uniform Edition. London: Longmans, Green and Co., 1908.

———. *Apologia Pro Vita Sua: Being a Reply to a Pamphlet Entitled "What Then Does Dr Newman Mean?"* 1st ed. London: Longmans, Green and Co., 1864.

———. *Autobiographical Writings*. Edited by Henry Tristram. London: Sheed and Ward, 1957.

———. "Book Review." *The British Critic, and Quarterly Theological Review* 30 (1841): 100–134.

———. "Catholicity of the English Church." *The British Critic, and Quarterly Theological Review* 27 (1840): 40–88.

———. *Certain Difficulties Felt by Anglicans in Catholic Teaching*. 2 vols. London: Longmans, Green and Co., 1901.

———. *Conscience and Papacy, Letter to the Duke of Norfolk*. Pinckney, Mich.: Real View Books, 2002.

———. *Discussions and Arguments on Various Subjects*. 2nd ed. London: Basil Pickering, 1873.

———. *Essays Critical and Historical*. 2 vols. London: Longmans, Green and Co., 1907.

———. *Fifteen Sermons Preached before the University of Oxford between AD 1826 and 1843*. London: Longmans, Green and Co., 1909.

———. *Historical Sketches*. 3 vols. London: Longmans, Green and Co., 1906.

———. *John Henry Newman: Autobiographical Writings*. Edited by Henry Tristram. New York: Sheed and Ward, 1956.

———. *Lectures on the Doctrine of Justification*. London: Longmans, Green and Co., 1908.

———. *Lectures on the Prophetical Office of the Church Viewed Relatively to Romanism and Popular Protestantism*. London: J. G. and F. Rivington, 1837.

———. "Letters on the Church Fathers: Letters XVI." *British Magazine*, no. 10 (1 July 1836).

———. *Loss and Gain: The Story of a Convert*. Uniform Edition. Longmans, Green and Co., 1874.

———. "Marcus Tullius Cicero." In *Encyclopedia Metropolitana*, 279–94. London: Mawman, 1824.

———. *Newman's Apologia Pro Vita Sua. The Two Versions of 1864 and 1865, Preceded by Newman's and Kingsley's Pamphlets, Introduced by Ward and Wilfred*. London: Oxford University Press, 1913.

BIBLIOGRAPHY

———. "Notice of Books." *The British Critic, and Quarterly Theological Review* 24 (1838): 230–38.

———. "On Consulting the Faithful in Matters of Doctrine." *The Rambler*, 3 July 1859, 189–230.

———. "On the Inspiration of Scripture." In *The Nineteenth Century* 15 (1884):185–99.

———. *Parochial and Plain Sermons*. 8 vols. London: Longmans, Green and Co., 1907.

———. "Preface to the Catechetical Lectures of St. Cyril of Jerusalem, in R.R. Church, Library of the Fathers." Vol. 2. Oxford: J. G. and F. Rivington, 1839.

———. "Records of the Church Nos. I–XVIII." Oxford: Messrs. Rivington's, 11 November 1833.

———. "Records of the Church, Nos. XIX–XXV." Oxford: Messrs. Rivington's, 11 November 1833.

———. *Select Treaties of S. Athanasius*. Oxford: James Parker and Company, 1877.

———. *Sermons 1824–1843*. Edited by Vincent Blehl, SJ, and Paul Murray. Vol. 2. Oxford: Clarendon Press, 1991.

———. *Sermons Bearing on Subjects of the Day*. London: J. G. F. and J. Rivington, 1843.

———. *Sermons Bearing on the Subjects of the Day*. London: Longmans, Green and Co., 1902.

———. *Sermons Preached on Various Occasions*. London: Longmans, Green and Co., 1908.

———. *The Arians of the Fourth Century*. Uniform Edition. London: Longmans, Green and Co., 1908.

———. *The Arians of the Fourth Century: Their Doctrine, Temper and Conduct Chiefly as Exhibited in the Councils of the Church between A.D. 325 & A.D. 381*. 1st ed. London: J. G. and F. Rivington, 1833.

———. "'The Brothers' Controversy, Being a Genuine Correspondence between a Clergyman of the Church of England and a Layman of Unitarian Opinions." *British Critic, and Quarterly Theological Review* 20 (1836): 166–99.

———. *The Idea of a University: Defined and Illustrated*. London: Longmans Green and Co., 1873.

———. *The Letters and Diaries of John Henry Newman*. Edited (variously) by Charles Stephen Dessain, Edward E. Kelly, Ian Turnbull Ker, Francis J, McGrath, and Gerard Tracey. Vols. 1–10, Oxford: Clarendon Press, 1978–2006; Vols. 11–22, London: Thomas Nelson, 1961–1972; Vols. 23–32, Oxford: Clarendon Press, 1973–1977; and Vol. 32 Supplement, Oxford: Oxford University Press, 2008.

BIBLIOGRAPHY

———. *The Via Media of the Anglican Church*. Uniform Edition. 2 vols. London: Longmans, Green and Co., 1885.

———. *The "Via Media" of the Anglican Church*. Edited by H. D. Weidner. Oxford: Clarendon Press, 1990.

———. *The Via Media of the Anglican Church: Illustrated in Lectures, Letters and Tracts Written between 1830 and 1836*. Vol. 1. London: J. F. and G. Rivington, 1836.

———. *The Via Media of the Anglican Church: Illustrated in Lectures, Letters and Tracts Written between 1830 and 1841*. Vol 2. London: Pickering, 1877.

———. *The Via Media of the Anglican Church: Illustrated in Lectures, Letters and Tracts Written between 1830 and 1841*. Uniform Edition. Vol. 1. London: Longmans, Green and Co., 1878.

———. *The Via Media of the Anglican Church: Illustrated in Lectures, Letters and Tracts Written between 1830 and 1841*. Uniform Edition. Vol. 2. London, New York, Bombay, and Calcutta: Longmans, Green and Co, 1882.

———. "Tract 1: Thoughts on the Ministerial Commission Respectfully Addressed to the Clergy." Oxford: Messrs. Rivington's, 9 September 1833.

———. "Tract 8: The Gospel a Law of Liberty." Oxford: Messrs. Rivington's, 31 October 1833.

———. "Tract 11: The Visible Church (In Letters to a Friend)." Oxford: Messrs. Rivington's, 11 November 1833.

———. "Tract 19: On Arguing Concerning the Apostolical Succession. On Reluctance to Confess the Apostolical Succession." Oxford: Messrs. Rivington's, 23 December 1833.

———. "Tract 20: The Visible Church, Letter III." Oxford: Messrs. Rivington's, 24 December 1833.

———. "Tract 34: Rites and Customs of the Church." Oxford: Messrs. Rivington's, 1 May 1834.

———. "Tract 38: Via Media No. I." Oxford: Messrs. Rivington's, 25 July 1834.

———. "Tract 41: Via Media No. II." Oxford: Messrs. Rivington's, 24 August 1834.

———. "Tract 45: The Grounds of Our Faith." Oxford: Messrs. Rivington's, 18 October 1834.

———. "Tract 71: On the Mode of Conducting the Controversy with Rome." London and Oxford: J. G. F. and J. Rivington and J. H. Parker, 1 January 1836.

———. "Tract 83: Advent Sermons on Anti-Christ." London and Oxford: J. G. F. and J. Rivington, 1838.

———. "Tract 85: Lectures on the Scripture Proofs of the Doctrines of the Church." London and Oxford: J. G. F. and J. Rivington, 1838.

———. "Tract 90: Remarks on Certain Passages in the Thirty-Nine Articles." London and Oxford: J. G. F. and J. Rivington, 27 February 1841.

BIBLIOGRAPHY

———. *Tracts Theological and Ecclesiastical*. Uniform Edition. London, New York, Bombay, and Calcutta: Longmans, Green and Co., 1908.
———. *Tracts, Theology and Ecclesiastical*. Palala Press, 2016.
———. *Two Essays of Biblical and Ecclesiastical Miracles*. London: Longmans, Green and Co., 1907.
———. "Utrum Profecerit Ecclesia Catholica in Cognitione Sua Fidei Semel Sibi Ab Apostolis Traditae [1847]." In Thomas Lynch, *The Newman-Perone Paper of Development*. Gregorianum. Vol. 16, 402–47. Rome: Pontificia Università Gregoriana, 1935.
———. "Wiseman's Lectures on the Church." *British Critic, and Quarterly Theological Review* 20 (1836): 373–403.
———. "X. Catholicity of the English Church." In *Essays Critical and Historical 2*. London, New York, Bombay, and Calcutta: Longmans, Green and Co., 1910.
Newman, John Henry et al. *Extracts from the Tracts for the Times, the Lyra Apostolica and Other Publications; Showing That to Oppose Ultra-Protestantism Is Not to Favour Popery*. London: J. G. and F. Rivington, 1839.

Other Authors

Abbott, Edwin. *The Anglican Career of Cardinal Newman*. 2 vols. London: Macmillan, 1892.
Abraham, Charles John. *Mithridates: Or, Mr. Newman's Essay on Development Its Own Confutation, by a Quondam Disciple*. London: J. W. Cleaver, 1846.
Alberigo, Giuseppe, and Joseph Andrew Komonchak. *History of Vatican II*. 5 vols. Leuven: Peeters, 1995.
Allen, Louis. *John Henry Newman and the Abbé Jager: A Controversy on Scripture and Traditon (1834–1836)*. London: Oxford University Press, 1975.
Allen, W. "Newman's Model of the Church." In *A Thankful Heart and a Discerning Mind: Essays in Honour of John Newton*, edited by John A Newton and Mervyn Davies. London: Lonely Scribe, 2010.
Andrewes, Lancelot. *The Pattern of Catechistical Doctrine at Large: Or a Learned and Pious Exposition of the Ten Commandments*. London: Roger Norton and George Badger, 1650.
Anonymous ("M. A."). *Mr. Ward and the New Test, Or, Plain Reasons Why Those Who Censure Mr. Ward Should Not Vote for the New Statute, Which Limits the Thirty Nine Articles: In a Letter to a Friend*. Oxford, 1844.
Aquino, Frederick D., and Benjamin J. King, eds. *Receptions of Newma*. Oxford: Oxford University Press, 2015.
———. *The Oxford Handbook of John Henry Newman*. 1st ed. Oxford: Oxford University Press, 2018.
Archaval, Hugo de. "An Unpublished Paper by Cardinal Newman on the Development of Doctrine." *Gregorianum* 39, no. 3 (1958): 585–96.

BIBLIOGRAPHY

Archaval, Hugo de, and Derek J. Holmes, eds. *The Theological Papers of John Henry Newman on Faith and Certainty*. Oxford: Clarendon Press, 1976.

Arnold, Thomas. *Sermons, Preached Mostly in the Chapel of Rugby School, 1835–1840*. 4 vols. London: Longmans, Green and Co., 1878.

Artz, Johannes. Preface to *Newman and His Theological Method*, by Thomas Norris, xi–xiv. Leiden: Brill, 1977.

Aston, Nigel. *Christianity and Revolutionary Europe, c. 1750–1830*. Cambridge: Cambridge University Press, 2002.

Asveld, Paul. "Saint Vincent de Lérins Dans La Discussion Entre Newman et l'Abbé Jager." In *Newman et L"Histoire: Actes Du Colloque 1990 de L"Association Français Des Amis de John Henry Newman*, edited by Claude Lepelley and Paul Veyiras, 169–88. Lyon: Presses Universitaires de Lyon, 1992.

Atkinson, Nigel. *Richard Hooker and the Authority of Scripture, Tradition and Reason*. London: Paternoster Press, 1997.

———. *Beyond the Reformation? Authority, Primacy and Unity in the Conciliar Tradition*. London: Continuum, 2006.

Avis, Paul D. L. *Anglicanism and the Christian Church: Theological Resources in Historical Perspective*. Edinburgh: T & T Clark, 1989.

Baker, W. J. *Beyond Port and Prejudice: Charles Lloyd of Oxford 1784–1829*. Orono: University of Maine at Orono Press, 1981.

Barbeau, Jeffrey W. "Newman and the Interpretation of Inspired Scripture." *Theological Studies* 63, no. 1 (2002): 53–67.

Baring-Gould, Sabine. *The Church Revival: Thoughts Thereon and Reminiscences*. London: Methuen, 1914.

Barnes, Jonathan. *The Complete Works of Aristotle: The New Oxford Translation*. 2 vols. Princeton, N.J.: Princeton University Press, 1984.

Bebbington, David William. *Evangelicalism in Modern Britain: A History from the 1730s to the 1980s*. London: Unwin Hyman, 1989.

Bebbington, David William, Mark A. Noll, and George A. Rawlyk, eds. *Evangelicalism: Comparative Studies of Popular Protestantism in North America, the British Isles, and Beyond, 1700–1990*. Oxford: Oxford University Press, 1994.

Bellenger, Dominic Aiden. *The French Exiled Clergy in Great Britain after 1789: A Working List*. Bath: Downside Abbey, 1986.

Bennett, Gareth Vaughan. "King William III and the Episcopate." In *Essays in Modern Church History in Memory of Norman Sykes*, edited by Gareth Vaughan Bennett and John D. Walsh. London: Adam and Charles Black, 1966.

———. "Patristic Tradition in Anglican Thought 1660–1900." In *Tradition in Luthertum and Anglikanismus: OEcumenica 1971/71*, edited by Gunther Grassman and Vajta Vilmos, 63–76. Güttersloh: Mohr, 1972.

Benson, Christopher. *Discourses upon Tradition and Episcopacy*. London: Parker, 1839.

Beveridge, William. *Ecclesia Anglicana Ecclesia Catholica; Or, The Doctrine of the*

BIBLIOGRAPHY

Church of England Consonant to Scripture, Reason and Fathers. Oxford: John Henry Parker, 1840.

Biemer, Günter. *Newman on Tradition*. New York: Herder and Herder, 1967.

———. "Newman's View of Liberalism in Religion: An Historical Introduction to a Relevant Problem." In *Sorgfalt Des Denkens: Wege Des Glaubens Im Spiegel von Bildung Und Wissenschaft: Ein Gespräch Mit John Henry Newman*, edited by Roman R. Siebenrock and Wilhem Tolksdorf, 197–213. Frankfurt am Main: Peter Lang, 2006.

Blehl, Vincent Ferrer. *John Henry Newman: A Bibliographical Catalogue of His Writings*. Charlottesville: University Press of Virginia, 1978.

———, ed. *John Henry Newman: Sermons, 1824–1843*. 5 vols. Oxford: Oxford University Press, 1991.

Bloch, R. H. *God's Plagiarist: Being an Account of the Fabulous Industry and Irregular Commerce of the Abbe Migne*. Chicago: University of Chicago Press, 1994.

Boekraad, Adrian J. *The Personal Conquest of Truth according to J. H. Newman*. Louvain: Nauwelaerts, 1955.

Bokenkotter, Thomas. *Cardinal Newman as an Historian*. Louvain: Publications Universitaires, 1959.

Booty, John. "Standard Divines." In *The Study of Anglicanism*, edited by John Booty, Stephen Sykes, and Jonathan Knight, part 4, chap. 5. London: SPCK, 1998.

Bossuet, Jacques-Bénigne. *Exposition de Le Foi Catholique*. Paris, 1671.

———. *Histoire Des Variation Des Églises Protestantes*. Paris: Charpentier, 1844.

Bossy, John. *The English Catholic Community, 1570–1850*. London: Darton, Longman and Todd, 1975.

Bouyer, Louis. *Newman: His Life and Spirituality*. London: Burns and Oates, 1958.

Bramhall, John. "Schism Guarded." In *The Works of the Most Reverend Father in God, John Bramhall Sometime Lord Archbishop of Armagh, Primate and Metropolitan of All Ireland: With a Life of the Author, and a Collection of His Letters*, edited by Arthur West Hadden. Oxford: John Henry Parker, 1843.

Bray, Gerald Lewis, ed. "The Thirty-Nine Articles, 1571." In *Documents of the English Reformation*, 285–309. Cambridge: James Clarke and Co, 2004.

Breisach, E. *Historiography: Ancient, Medieval and Modern*. Chicago: University of Chicago Press, 2007.

Brose, Olive J. "The Irish Precedent for English Church Reform: The Church Temporalities Act of 1833." *Journal of Ecclesiastical History* 7, no. 2 (1956): 204–25.

———. *Church and Parliament: The Reshaping of the Church of England, 1828–1860*. Stanford, Calif.: Stanford University Press, 1959.

Brotherton, Joshua R. "Development(s) in the Theology of Revelation: From Francisco Marin-Sola to Joseph Ratzinger: Development(s) in the Theology of Revelation." *New Blackfriars* 97, no. 1072 (November 2016): 661–76.

BIBLIOGRAPHY

Brown, David, ed. *Newman: A Man for Our Time, Centenary Essays*. London: SPCK, 1990.

Brown, Ralph. "Victorian Anglican Evangelicalism: The Radical Legacy of Edward Irving." *Journal of Ecclesiastical History* 58, no. 4 (2007): 675–504.

Brown, Stewart J. *The National Churches of England, Ireland and Scotland 1801–1846*. New York: Oxford University Press, 2001.

Brownson, Orestes A. "Doctrinal Developments." *Brownson's Quarterly Review* 1, no. 2 (1854): 525–39.

———. "The Mercersburg Hypothesis." *Brownson's Quarterly Review* 3, no. 2 (1854): 253–65.

———. "Newman's Development of Christian Doctrines." In *The Works of Orestes A. Brownson*, edited by H. F. Brownson, 1–28. New York: AMS Press, 1966.

Bull, George. *Defensio Fidei Nicaenae, Ex Scriptis, Quae Exstant, Catholicorum Doctorum Qui Intra Tria Prima Ecclesiae Christianae Saecula Floruerunt. In qua Obiter Quoque Constantinopolitana Confessio, de Spiritu Sancto, Antiquiorom Testimoniis Adstritur*. Oxford, 1685.

Burke, Patrick. *Reinterpreting Rahner: A Critical Study of His Major Themes*. New York: Fordham University Press, 2002.

Butler, Joseph. *The Analogy of Religion, Natural and Revealed, the Constitution and Course of Nature*. 2nd ed. London: James, John and Paul Knapton, 1736.

Butler, Perry. *Gladstone: Church, State Tractarianism: A Study of His Religious Ideas and Attitudes, 1809–1859*. Oxford: Clarendon Press, 1982.

Butler William Archer. *Letters on the Development of Christian Doctrine, in Reply to Mr. Newman's Essay*. Edited by T. Woodward. Dublin: Hodges and Smith, 1850.

Cameron, Euan. *Interpreting Christian History: The Challenge of the Churches' Past*. Oxford: Blackwell, 2005.

Carlton, Charles. *Archbishop William Laud*. New York: Routledge and Keegan Paul, 1987.

Carpenter, Spencer Cecil. *Church and People, 1789–1889: A History of the Church of England from William Wilberforce to "Lux Mundi."* London: SPCK, 1933.

Carr, Thomas K. *Newman and Gadamer: Towards a Hermeneutic of Religious Knowledge*. Atlanta: Scholars Press, 1996.

Carroll, Lewis. *Alice's Adventures in Wonderland*. London: Macmillan and Company, 1865.

———. *Through the Looking Glass and What Alice Found There*. London: Macmillan and Company, 1871.

Catechism of the Catholic Church. London: Geoffrey Chapman, 1992.

Catholic Hierarchy. "Bishop Jean-François-Marie Le Pappe de Trévern." Accessed February 29, 2020. http://www.catholic-hierarchy.org/bishop/blpdt.html.

Chadwick, Henry. "Newman's Significance for the Anglican Church." In *Newman: *A Man for Our Time, Centenary Essays*, edited by David Brown, 52–74. London: SPCK, 1990.

———. "Traditions, Fathers, and Councils." In *The Study of Anglicanism*, edited by Stephen Sykes, John Booty, and Jonathan Knight, 100–115. London: SPCK, 1998.

Chadwick, Owen. *From Bousset to Newman*. 1st ed. Cambridge: Cambridge University Press, 1957.

———. *The Mind of the Oxford Movement*. London: Adam and Charles Black, 1957.

———. *From Bousset to Newman*. 2nd ed. Cambridge: Cambridge University Press, 1987.

———. *The Secularization of the European Mind in the Nineteenth Century: The Gifford Lectures in the University of Edinburgh for 1973/74*. Cambridge: Cambridge University Press, 1975.

———. "A Consideration of Newman's Apologia Pro Vita Sua." In *From Oxford to the People: Reconsidering Newman and the Oxford Movement*, edited by P. Vaiss. Leominster: Gracewing, 1996.

Chandler, Michael. *An Introduction to the Oxford Movement*. London: SPCK, 2003.

Chapman, Mark D. "John Keble, National Apostasy, and the Myths of 14 July." In *John Keble in Context*, edited by Kirstie Blair, 47–58. London: Anthem Press, 2004.

———. "Why Do We Still Recite the Nicene Creed at the Eucharist?" *Anglican Theological Review* 87, no. 2 (2005): 207–23.

———. *Bishops, Saints and Politics: Anglican Studies*. London: T & T Clark, 2007.

———. "A Catholicism of the Word and a Catholicism of Devotion: Pusey, Newman and the First Eirenicon." *Journal for the History of Modern Theology* 14, no. 2 (2007): 167–90.

———. *Anglican Theology*. London: Continuum, 2012. See especially "The Theology of Richard Hooker," 103–25.

———. *The Theology of Richard Hooker*. London: Continuum, 2012.

———. "Temporal and Spatial Catholicism: Tensions in Historicism in the Oxford Movement." In *The Shaping of Tradition: Context and Normativity*, edited by Colby Dickinson, with Lieven Boeve and Terrence Milligan, 17–26. Leuven: Peeters, 2014.

Christie, Robert. "The Logic of Conversion: The Harmony of Heart, Will, Mind and Imagination in John Henry Newman." PhD diss., Fordham University, 1997.

Church, Mary C., and Francis Paget, eds. *Life and Letters of Dean Church*. London: Macmillan, 1894.

Church, Richard William. *The Oxford Movement: Twelve Years, 1833–1845*. London: Macmillan, 1891.

BIBLIOGRAPHY

Churton, Edward, ed. *Memoir of Joshua Watson.* 2 vols. Oxford: John Henry and James Parker, 1861.

Cieszkowski, August von. *Prolegomena Zur Historiosophie.* Berlin: Bei Veit und Comp., 1838.

Clark, Jonathan C. D. *English Society 1688–1832: Ideology, Social Structures and Political Practice during the Ancien Regime.* Cambridge: Cambridge University Press, 1985.

Coburn, Kathleen, ed. *The Notebooks of Samuel Taylor Coleridge.* Vol. 1. London: Routledge, 1957.

Coleridge, Samuel Taylor. *The Friend.* Edited by Barbara E. Rooke. Vol. 4 of *The Collected Works of Samuel Taylor Coleridge.* Princeton, N.J.: Routledge and Keegan Paul, 1969.

———. *Lay Sermons.* Edited by R. J. White. Princeton, N.J.: Routledge and Keegan Paul, 1972.

———. *On the Constitution of the Church and State According to the Idea of Each.* Edited by John Colmer. Princeton, N.J.: Routledge and Keegan Paul, 1976.

———. *Lectures 1808–1819.* Edited by R. A. Foakes. 2 vols. Princeton, N.J.: Routledge and Keegan Paul, 1987.

———. *Aids to Reflection.* Edited by John Beer. Princeton, N.J.: Routledge and Keegan Paul, 1993.

———. *Marginalia.* Edited by H. J. Jackson and George Whalley. 5 vols. Princeton, N.J.: Routledge and Keegan Paul, 2000.

Collinson, Patrick. *The Religion of Protestants: The Church of England 1559–1625.* Oxford: Oxford University Press, 1984.

Congar, Yves. *Tradition and Traditions.* Translated by Michael Naseby and Thomas Rainborough. London: Burns and Oates, 1966.

———. *A History of Theology.* New York: Doubleday, 1968.

———. *The Meaning of Tradition.* San Francisco: Ignatius Press, 2004.

Conn, Walter E. "From Oxford to Rome: Newman's Ecclesial Conversion." *Theological Studies* 68, no. 3 (2007): 595–617.

Connolley, John R. *John Henry Newman: A View of Catholic Faith for the New Millennium.* Lanham, Md.: Rowman and Littlefield, 2005.

Cornwell, James. *Newman's Unquiet Grave: The Reluctant Saint.* London: Continuum, 2012.

Cosin, John. *A Scholastic History of the Canon of the Holy Scripture.* London: Roger Norton and Timothy Garthwait, 1658.

Coulson, John. *Newman and the Common Tradition: A Study in the Language of Church and Society.* Oxford: Clarendon Press, 1960.

———. "Newman's Idea of the Church and Its Kinship with Similar Ideas in Coleridge and F. D. Maurice." PhD diss., University of Oxford, 1968.

———. *Religion and Imagination: "In Aid of a Grammar of Assent."* Oxford: Clarendon Press, 1981.

BIBLIOGRAPHY

Coulson, John, and Arthur Macdonald (Douglas) Allchin. *The Rediscovery of Newman: An Oxford Symposium*. London: SPCK, 1967.

Cragg, Gerald Robertson. *The Church and the Age of Reason, 1648–1789*. Harmondsworth: Penguin Books, 1966.

Crowley, Paul G. "Dogmatic Development after Newman: The Search for a Hermeneutical Principle in Newman, Marin-Sola, Rahner and Gadamer." Ann Arbor, Mich.: Graduate Theological Union, 1984.

Curran, Kathleen. *The Romanesque Revival: Religion, Politics, and Transnational Exchange*. University Park: Penn State University Press, 2003.

Daley, Brian. "Newman and the Alexandrian Tradition." In *Newman and Truth*, edited by Ian Turnbull Ker and Terrence Merrigan, 147–88. Louvain: Peeters, 2008.

Daly, Gabriel. "Newman, Divine Revelation and the Catholic Modernists." In *Newman and the Word*, edited by Terrence Merrigan and Ian Turnbull Ker, 49–68. Louvain: Peeters, 2000.

D'Arcy, Eric. "The New Catechism and Cardinal Newman." *Communio: International Catholic Review* 20 (Fall 1993): 485–502.

Davenport, Christopher. *Deus, Natura, Gratia, Sive Tractatus de Praedestinatione*. Lyon, 1634.

Davies, Julian. *The Caroline Captivity of the Church: Charles I and the Remoulding of Anglicanism*. Oxford: Clarendon Press, 1992.

Davis, H. Francis. "Newman and the Theology of the Living Word." *Newman Studien* 6 (1964): 167–77.

De Mattei, Roberto. *Il Concilio Vaticano II. Una Storia Mai Scritta*. Turin: Lindau, 2010.

Denzinger, Heinrich. *Enchiridion Symbolorum, Definitionum et Declarationum de Rebus Fidei et Morum*. Edited by Peter Hünermann, Robert Fastiggi, and Anne Eglund Nash. 43rd ed. San Francisco: Ignatius Press, 2012.

Dessain, Charles Stephen. "An Unpublished Paper by Cardinal Newman on the Development of Doctrine." *Journal of Theological Studies* 9, no. 2 (1958): 324–35.

———. *John Henry Newman*. Oxford: Oxford University Press, 1980.

Dick, Klaus. "Das Analogieprinzip bei J. H. Newman und seine Quelle in J. Butlers Analogy." *Newman Studien* 5 (1962): 9–228.

Dietz, Kathleen. "John Henry Newman and the Fathers of the Church: The Birth of an Ecclesiology." STD diss., Pontifical University of St. Thomas, Rome, 2007.

Dockery, John Berchmas. *Christopher Davenport: Friar and Diplomat*. London: Burns and Oates, 1960.

Drey, Johann Sebastian von. *Apologetik Als Wissenschaftliche Nachweisung Der Göttlichkeit Des Christentums in Seiner Escheinung*. 2nd ed. 3 vols. Mainz: Florian Kupferberg, 1844.

BIBLIOGRAPHY

———. "Ideen Zur Geshichte Des Katholischen Dogmensystems." In *Geist Des Christentums Und Des Katholizimus. Ausgewählte Schriften Katholischer Theologie Im Zeitalter Des Deutschen Idealismus under Der Romantik*, edited by J. R. Geiselmann, 235–331. Mainz: Florian Kupferberg, 1940.

Dudley, Robert. *Newman at Oxford: His Religious Development*. Oxford: Oxford University Press, 1950.

Duffy, Eamon. "The Reception of Turner's *Newman*: A Reply to Simon Skinner." *Journal of Ecclesiastical History* 63, no. 3 (2012): 534–48.

Dulles, Avery. "From Images to Truth: Newman on Revelation and Faith." *Theological Studies* 51, no. 2 (1990): 252–67.

———. "The Threefold Office in Newman's Ecclesiology." In *Newman after a Hundred Years*, edited by Alan G. Hill and Ian Turnbull Ker, 375–99. Oxford: Clarendon Press, 1990.

———. "Newman: The Anatomy of a Conversation." In *Newman and the Conversion*, edited by Ian Turnbull Ker. Edinburgh: T & T Clark, 1997.

———. *Newman*. London: Continuum, 2002.

Dupré, Louis K. *The Enlightenment and the Intellectual Foundations of Modern Culture*. London: Yale University Press, 2004.

Earnest, James David. "A Study of John Henry Newman's Oxford University Sermons." PhD diss., Yale University, 1978.

Egan, Philip Anthony. "Lonergan on Newman's Conversion." *The Heythrop Journal* 37, no. 4 (1996): 437–55.

———. "Newman, Lonergan and Doctrinal Development." PhD diss., Birmingham University, 2004.

Every, George. *The High Church Party 1688–1718*. London: SPCK, 1956.

Faber, Geoffrey Cust. *Oxford Apostles: A Character Study of the Oxford Movement*. London: Faber & Faber, 1933.

Faber, George Stanley. *The Apostolicity of Trinitarianism*. 2 vols. London: J. G. and F. Rivington, 1832.

Faggioli, Massimo. *Vatican II: The Battle for Meaning*. Mahwah, N.J.: Paulist Press, 2012.

Fergusson, David. *The Blackwell Companion to Nineteenth-Century Theology*. Oxford: Blackwell, 2010.

Fergusson, Thomas. "The Enthralling Power: History and Heresy in John Henry Newman." *Anglican Theological Review* 85, no. 4 (2003): 641–62.

Ffoulkes, Edmund S. *A History of the Church of St. Mary the Virgin, Oxford: The University Church: From Doomsday to the Installation of the Duke of Wellington, Chancellor of the University*. London: Longmans, Green and Co., 1892.

Foot, Sarah. "Has Ecclesiastical History Lost the Plot?" In *The Church on Its Past*. Vol. 49 of *Studies in Church History*, 1–25. Cambridge: Cambridge University Press, 2013.

———. "Thinking with Christians: Doing Ecclesiastical History in a Secular

Age." http://podcasts.ox.ac.uk/thinking-christians-doing-ecclesiastical-history-secular-age-audio.

Ford, John T. "Faithfulness to Type in Newman's: 'Essay on Development.'" In *Newman Today*, edited by Stanley L. Jaki. San Francisco: Ignatius Press, 1989.

Forster, Charles, ed. *Thirty Years Correspondence between John Jebb and Alexander Knox*. London: James Duncan, 1834.

Fothergill, Brian. *Nicholas Wiseman*. London: Faber & Faber, 1963.

Fuller, Reginald. "The Classic High Church Reaction to the Tractarians." In *Tradition Renewed: The Oxford Movement Conference Papers*, edited by Geoffrey Rowell, 51–63. London: Darton, Longman and Todd, 1986.

Gallagher, Michael Paul. "Newman: Sulla Disposizione per La Fede." *La Civiltá Cattolica* (2001): 452–63.

Gee, Henry, and William Hardy, eds. *Documents Illustrative of English Church History*. London and New York: Macmillan, 1896.

Geiselmann, J. R. *The Meaning of Tradition*. London: Burns and Oates, 1966.

George, IV. Catholic Relief Act, Pub. L. No. 10, § 7 (1829).

Gherardini, Brunero. *Concilio Ecumenico Vaticano II: Un Discorso Da Fare*. Turin: Lindau, 2009.

———. *Concilio Ecumenico Vaticano II: Il Discorso Mancato*. Turin: Lindau, 2011.

Gilley, Sheridan. *Newman and His Age*. London: Darton, Longman and Todd, 1990.

Gladstone, William Ewart. *The State in Its Relations with the Church*. London: John Murray and Hatchard and Sons, 1838.

———. *Church Principles Considered in Their Results*. London: John Murray and Hatchard and Sons, 1840.

———. *Correspondence on Church and Religion*. Edited by Daniel Connor Lathbury. Vol. 1. London: John Murray, 1910.

Glover, George. *Remarks on the Bishop of Peterborough's "Comparative View of the Churches of England and Rome."* London, 1821.

Greaves, Robert William. "The Jerusalem Bishopric, 1841." *The English Historical Review* 64, no. 252 (1949): 328–52.

Guitton, Jean. *La Philosophie de Newman: Essai Sur l"idée de Développment*. Paris: Boivin, 1933.

———. *L"Église et Les Laïcs*. Paris: Desclée de Brouwer, 1963.

Gunton, Colin. "Newman's Dialectic: Dogma, Revelation and Reason in the Seventy-Third Tract for the Times." In *Newman after a Hundred Years*, edited by Alan G. Hill and Ian Turnbull Ker, 309–22. Oxford: Clarendon Press, 1990.

Hall, Joseph. "Bishop Hall's Latin Theology, with Translations." In *The works of Joseph Hall, D.D., successively Bishop of Exeter and Norwich : with some account of his life and sufferings*. Vol. 9. Oxford: Talboys, 1839.

BIBLIOGRAPHY

Hammond, David. "Imagination and Hermeneutical Theology: Newman's Contribution to Theological Method." *The Downside Review* 106, no. 362 (1988): 17–34.

Hammond, Jay. "Interplay of Hermeneutics and Heresy in the Process of Newman's Conversion from 1830–1845." In *Authority, Dogma, and History: The Role of Oxford Movement Converts on the Papal Infallibility Debates*, edited by Kenneth Parker and Michael J. G. Pahls. Palo Alto, Calif.: Academica Press, 2009.

Hanson, Ellis. *Decadence and Catholicism*. Cambridge, Mass.: Harvard University Press, 1988.

Hare, Julius Charles. *Charges to the Clergy of the Archdeaconry of Lewes, Delivered at the Ordinary Visitations from the Year 1840 to 1854*. 3 vols. Cambridge: Macmillan and Company, 1856.

Harper, Gordon Huntington. *Cardinal Newman and William Froude FRS: A Correspondence*. Baltimore, Md.: Johns Hopkins University Press, 1933.

Harrison, Benjamin. "Tract 16: Advent." Messrs Rivington's, 17 December 1833.

———. "Tract 17: The Ministerial Commission: A Trust from Christ for the Benefit of His People." Messrs Rivington's, 20 December 1833.

———. "Tract 24 The Scripture View of the Apostolical Commission." Messrs Rivington's, 25 January 1834.

———. "Tract 49: The Kingdom of Heaven." Messrs Rivington's, 25 December 1834.

Hawkins, Edward. *A Dissertation upon the Use and Importance of Unauthoritative Tradition, as an Introduction to the Christian Doctrines; Including the Substance of a Sermon upon 2 Thess. Ii, 15*. London: J. Parker and F. C. and J. Rivington, 1819.

Hedley, Douglas. "Participation in the Divine Life: Coleridge, the Vision of God and the Thought of John Henry Newman." In *From Oxford to the People: Reconsidering Newman and the Oxford Movement*, edited by P. Vaiss, 238–51. Leominster: Gracewing, 1996.

———. *Coleridge, Philosophy, and Religion: Aids to Reflection and the Mirror of the Spirit*. Cambridge: Cambridge University Press, 2000.

Henry, Lawrence Joseph. "Newman and Development: The Genesis of John Henry Newman's Theory of Development and the Reception of His Essay on the Development of Christian Doctrine." PhD diss., University of Texas, 1973.

Herring, George. *What Was the Oxford Movement?* London: Continuum, 2003.

Hole, Robert. *Pulpits, Politics and Public Order in England, 1760–1832*. Cambridge: Cambridge University Press, 1989.

Hollingsworth, Arther George Harpur. *The Folly of Going to Rome for a Religion, in Two Letters to a Friend*. London: John Hatchard, 1846.

BIBLIOGRAPHY

Holmes, Derek J., ed. *The Theological Papers of John Henry Newman on Faith and Certainty*. Oxford: Clarendon Press, 1976.

Hooker, Richard. "Of the Laws of Ecclesiastical Polity: Book 1, Chapter XIV." In *The Works of That Learned and Judicious Divine, Mr. Richard Hooker: With an Account of His Life and Death*, edited by John Keble. Oxford: Clarendon Press, 1876.

Horne, Brian. "Church and Nation: Newman and the Tractarians." *International Journal for the Study of the Christian Church* 5, no. 1 (2005): 25–40.

Imburg, Rune. *In Quest of Authority: The "Tracts for the Times" and the Development of the Tractarian Leaders 1833–1841*. Lund: Lund University Press, 1987.

Irons, William Josiah. *The Theory of Development Examined: With Reference Specially to Mr. Newman's Essay, and to the Rule of St. Vincent of Lerins*. London: Francis and John Rivington, 1846.

Israel, Jonathon Irvine. "William III and Toleration." In *From Persecution to Toleration: The Glorious Revolution and Religion in England*, edited by O. P. Grell, J. I. Israel, and N. Tyacke, 129–70. Oxford: Clarendon Press, 1991.

Jager, Jean-Nicholas. *Le Protestantisme Aux Prises Avec La Doctine Catholique, Ou Controverses Avec Plusiers Ministres Anglicanes, Membres de l"Université d"Oxford*. Paris: Débécourt, 1836.

Jaki, Stanley L. *Newman's Challenge*. Grand Rapids, Mich.: Eerdmans, 2000.

———. Introduction to *An Essay of the Development of Christian Doctrine* [*1845*]. Pickney, Mich.: Real View Books, 2003.

Jaki, Stanley L., ed. *Newman Today*. San Francisco: Ignatius Press, 1989.

Jebb, John. *Sermons, on Subjects Chiefly Practical, with Illustrative Notes and an Appendix, Relating to the Character of the Church of England, as Distinguished Both from Other Branches of the Reformation, and from the Modern Church of Rome*. 1st ed. London: Cadell & Davies, 1815.

———. *Sermons, on Subjects Chiefly Practical, with Illustrative Notes and an Appendix, Relating to the Character of the Church of England, as Distinguished Both from Other Branches of the Reformation, and from the Modern Church of Rome*. 3rd ed. London: Cadell & Davies, 1831.

Jelf, Richard William. *Grounds for Laying Before the Council of King's College, London, Certain Statements Contained in a Recent Publication, Entitled, "Theological Essays, by the Rev. F. D. Mauric, M. A. Professor of Divinity in King's College."* 2nd ed. Oxford: John Henry Parker, 1853.

Kater, John L., Jr. "Whose Church Is It Anyway? Anglican 'Catholicity' Re-Examined." *Anglican Theological Review* 76, no. 1 (1994): 44–60.

Kaye, John. *The Ecclesiastical History of the Second and Third Centuries, Illustrated from the Writings of Tertullian*. Cambridge: J. Deighton and Son, 1826.

———. *Some Account of the Writings and Opinions of Clement of Alexandria*. London: J. G. and F. Rivington, 1835.

BIBLIOGRAPHY

Keaty, Anthony W. "Newman's Account of the Real Apprehension of God: The Need for a Subjective Context." *Downside Review* 114, no. 394 (1994): 1–18.

Keble, John. *The Christian Year*. London: C. and J. Rivington, 1827.

———. *National Apostasy: Considered in a Sermon Preached in St. Mary's Church, Oxford before His Majesty's Judges of Assize on Sunday July 14th 1833*. Abingdon: Rocket Press, 1983.

Ker, Ian Turnbull. "Newman's Theory: Development or Continuing Revelation." In *Newman and Gladstone: Centennial Essays*, edited by James D. Bastable, 145–59. Dublin: Veritas, 1978.

———. *John Henry Newman: A Biography*. 1st ed. Oxford: Oxford University Press, 1988.

———. *Newman after a Hundred Years*. Edited by Alan G. Hill. Oxford: Clarendon Press, 1990.

———. *Newman on Being a Christian*. London: Harper Collins, 1990.

———. *Newman the Theologian: A Reader*. Notre Dame, Ind.: University of Notre Dame Press, 1990.

———. *Newman and the Fullness of Christianity*. Edinburgh: T & T Clark, 1993.

———. *Healing the Wound of Humanity*. London: Darton, Longman and Todd, 1993.

———, ed. *Newman and Conversion*. Edinburgh: T & T Clark, 1997.

———. "Slow Road to Rome." *Times Literary Supplement*, December 6, 2002, 32.

———. *Newman and Faith*. Edited by Terrence Merrigan. Louvain: Peeters, 2004.

———. "Newman, Councils and Vatican II." In *Newman and Faith*, edited by Ker and Terrence Milligan. Louvain: Peeters, 2004.

———. "Is Dignitatis Humanae a Case of Authentic Doctrinal Development?" *Logos* 11, no. 2 (2008): 149–57.

———. *John Henry Newman: A Biography*. Revised. Oxford: Oxford University Press, 2010.

King, Benjamin John. *Newman and the Alexandrian Fathers: Shaping Doctrine in Nineteenth-Century England*. Oxford: Oxford University Press, 2009.

Komonchak, Joseph A. "John Henry Newman's Discovery of the Visible Church 1816–1828." PhD diss., Union Theological Seminary, 1976.

Lamb, Matthew, and Matthew Levering, eds. *Vatican II: Renewal within Tradition*. Oxford: Oxford University Press, 2008.

Lash, Nicholas. "The Notions of "Implicit" and "Explicit" Reason in Newman's University Sermons: A Difficulty." *The Heythrop Journal* 11, no. 1 (1971): 48–54.

———. "Faith and History: Some Reflections on Newman's 'Essay of the Development of Christian Doctrine.'" *Irish Theological Quarterly* 38, no. 3 (1971): 224–41.

BIBLIOGRAPHY

———. *Change in Focus: A Study in Doctrinal Change and Continuity*. London: Sheed and Ward, 1973.
———. *Newman on Development: The Search for an Explanation in History*. London: Sheed and Ward, 1975.
———. "Was Newman a Theologian?" *The Heythrop Journal* 17, no. 3 (1976): 322–25.
———. "Tides and Twilight: Newman since Vatican II." In *Newman After a Hundred Years*, edited by Ian Turnbull Ker and Alan G. Hill, 447–64. Oxford: Clarendon Press, 1990.
Le Pappe de Trévern, Jean-François-Marie. *Discussion Amicale Sur l"établissement et La Doctrine de l"Église Anglicane et En Genéral Sur La Réformation*. 2 vols. London, 1817.
Lease, Gary. *Witness to the Faith: Cardinal Newman on the Teaching Authority of the Church*. Shannon: Irish University Press, 1971.
Liddell, Henry, and Robert Scott. *A Greek-English Lexicon*. Oxford: Clarendon Press, 1843.
Liddon, Henry. "Correspondence of Dr Pusey, Liddon Bound Volumes," n.d. Dr. Pusey's Library, Pusey House.
Liddon, Henry Parry. *Life of Edward Bouverie Pusey*. 3 vols. London: Longmans, Green and Co., 1893.
Linnan, John E. "The Evangelical Background of John Henry Newman 1816–1826." STD diss., Katholieke Universiteit Leuven, 1965.
Longley, Charles Thomas, and Richard Davenport. *"The Brothers" Controversy: Being a Genuine Correspondence between a Clergyman of the Church of England and a Layman of Unitarian Opinions: Chiefly on the Questions How Far Belief Is an Act of the Will; on the Use of Reason in the Study of the Bible; and How Far It Is the Duty of Unlearned Christians to Examine or Implicitly Abide by the Religion of Their Education*. London: Fellowes, 1836.
Lovegrove, Deryek. *Established Church, Sectarian People: Itinerancy and the Transformation of English Dissent, 1780–1830*. Cambridge: Cambridge University Press, 1988.
Lowe, Robert. *Observations Suggested by "A Few More Words in Support of No.90."* Oxford: Baxter, 1841.
Lubac, Henri de. *A Brief Catechesis on Nature and Grace*. Translated by R. Arnandez. San Francisco: Ignatius Press, 1984.
———. "The Problem of the Development of Dogma." In *Theology in History*. Translated by Anne Englund Nash. San Francisco: Ignatius Press, 1996.
———. *The Mystery of the Supernatural*. Translated by R. Sheed. New York: Herder and Herder, 1998.
Lynch, Thomas, ed. "The Newman-Perrone Paper on Development." *Gregorianum* 16 (1935): 402–47.

BIBLIOGRAPHY

Macaulay, Ambrose. *Dr Russell of Maynooth*. London: Darton, Longman and Todd, 1983.

MacCulloch, Diarmaid. "Richard Hooker's Reputation." *The English Historical Review* 117, no. 473 (2002): 773–812. http://www.literaryreview.co.uk/macculloch_06_10.html.

———. *Christianity: The First Three Thousand Years*. London: Penguin, 2009.

———. "A Different Cloth." Review of *Newman's Unquiet Grave: The Reluctant Saint*, by John Cornwell. *Literary Review* (June 2010).

Machin, G., and Ian Turnbull Ker. *The Catholic Question in English Politics, 1820–1830*. Oxford: Clarendon Press, 1964.

Magill, Gerard, ed. *Discourse and Context: An Interdisciplinary Essays on John Henry Newman*. Carbondale, Ill.: Southern Illinois University Press, 1993.

———, ed. *Personality of Belief: Interdisciplinary Essays on John Henry Newman*. Lanham, Md.: University Press of America, 1995.

Maistre, Joseph de. "Du Pape," (Originally Published Paris 1819). In *Ouevres Complètes de J"DeMaistre*. Paris: Vitte, 1928.

Mandle, W. F. "Newman and His Audiences: 1825–1845." *Journal of Religious History* 24, no. 2 (2000): 143–58.

Mannion, Gerard. Review of *History of Vatican II*, edited by Giuseppe Alberigo and Joseph A. Komonchak. *International Journal of Systematic Theology* 12, no. 4 (2010): 478–84.

Marchetto, Agostino. *The Second Vatican Ecumenical Council: A Counterpoint for the History of the Council*. Edited by Kenneth D. Whitehead. Scranton, Pa.: University of Scranton Press, 2010.

Marin-Sola OP, Francisco. *La Evolución Homogénea Del Dogma Católico*. Biblioteca de Tomistas Españoles 1. Madrid: Valencia La Ciencia Tomista Real Convento de Predicadores, 1923.

Mazich, Edward. "Ideas and Authority: F. D. Maurice's Critique of John Henry Newman's 'Essay of the Development of Christian Doctrine.'" DPhil diss., University of Oxford, 2009.

McCarren, Gerard. "Tests or Notes? A Critical Evaluation of the Criteria for Genuine Doctrinal Development in John Henry Newman's *Essay on the Development of Christian Doctrine*." STD diss., Catholic University of America, 1998.

McClelland, Alan V., ed. *By Whose Authority? Newman, Manning, and the Magisterium*. Bath: Downside Abbey, 1996.

McCormack, Edward. "The Development of John Henry Newman's View of the Christian Life in His Anglican Sources." PhD diss., Catholic University of America, 2001.

McGrath, Francis. *John Henry Newman: Universal Revelation*. Tunbridge Wells: Burns and Oates, 1997.

BIBLIOGRAPHY

———. "John Henry Newman and the Dispensation of Paganism." *International Journal for the Study of the Christian Church* 1, no. 1 (2001): 26–42.

McKeon, Richard. *The Basic Works of Aristotle*. New York: Random House, 1941.

Merrigan, Terrence. "Newman on the Practice of Theology." *Louvain Studies* 14, no. 3 (1989): 260–84.

———. *Clear Heads and Holy Hearts: The Religious and Theological Ideal of John Henry Newman*. Louvain Theological and Pastoral Monographs 7. Louvain: Peeters, 1991.

———. "Newman's Catholic Synthesis." *Irish Theological Quarterly* 60, no. 1 (1994): 39–48.

———. "The Anthropology of Conversion: Newman and the Contemporary Theology of Religions." In *Newman and Conversion*, edited by Ian Turnbull Ker, 117–44. Edinburgh: T & T Clark, 1997.

———. "The Image of the Word: Faith and Imagination in John Henry Newman and John Hick." In *Newman and the Word*, edited by Terrence Merrigan and Ian Turnbull Ker, 5–47. Leuven: Peeters Press, 2000.

Merrigan, Terrence, and Ian Turnbull Ker. *Newman and the Word*. Leuven: Peeters Press, 2000.

Meszaros, Andrew. *The Prophetic Church: History and Doctrinal Development in John Henry Newman and Yves Congar*. 1st ed. Oxford: Oxford University Press, 2016.

Middleton, Arthur Pierce. *Fathers and Anglicans: The Limits of Orthodoxy*. Leominster: Gracewing, 2001.

Migne, Jacques-Paul. Patrologiae Cursus Completus. Series Latina. Vol. 43. Paris, 1848.

Miller, Jeremy Edward. "The Idea of the Church in Correspondence of John Henry Newman." PhD diss., Université Catholique de Louvain, 1975.

Milman, Henry Hart. "Newman on the Development of the Christian Doctrine." *The Quarterly Review* 7 (1846): 404–65.

Milner, Joseph. *History of the Church of Christ*. 5 vols. London, 1794.

———. *The End of Religious Controversy, in a Friendly Correspondence between a Religious Society of Protestants and a Roman Catholic Divine. Addressed to the Bishop of St. David's, in Answer to His Lordships Protestant Catechism*. London: Thomas Burgess, 1824.

Misner, Paul. "Newman's Concept of Revelation and the Development of Doctrine." *The Heythrop Journal* 11, no. 1 (1970): 32–47.

Moberly, George. *The Proposed Degradation and Declaration, Considered in a Letter Addressed to the Rev. The Master of Balliol College*. Oxford: John Henry Parker, 1845.

———. *The Sayings of the Great Forty Days, between the Resurrection and Ascension, Regarded as the Outlines of the Kingdom of God: In 5 Sermons. With an

Examination of Mr. Newman's Theory of Developments. London: Francis and John Rivington, 1846.

Morris, Jeremy. "Newman and Maurice on the Via Media of the Anglican Church: Contrasts and Affinities." *Anglican Theological Review* 85 (2003): 623–40.

Mozley, Anne, ed. *Letters and Correspondence of John Henry Newman During His Life in the English Church: With a Brief Auto Biography*. 2 vols. London: Longmans, Green and Co., 1891.

Mozley, James Bowling. *The Theory of Development, a Criticism of Dr. Newman's Essay of the Development of Christian Doctrine*. London: Francis and John Rivington, 1878.

Mozley, Thomas. *Reminiscences Chiefly of Oriel College and the Oxford Movement*. Vol. 1. London: Longmans, Green and Co., 1882.

Murray, John Courtney. "The Matter of Religious Freedom." *America* (January 9, 1965): 40–43.

Newman, Francis William. *Phases of Faith: Or, Passages from the History of My Creed*. London: J. Chapman, 1850.

Newsome, David. *The Parting of Friends: A Study of the Wilberforces and Henry Manning*. London: Murray, 1966.

Newton, John A, and Mervyn Davies. *A Thankful Heart and a Discerning Mind: Essays in Honour of John Newton*. London: Lonely Scribe, 2010.

Nicholls, David, and Fergus Kerr. *John Henry Newman: Reason, Rhetoric and Romanticism*. Bristol: Mich.: Bristol Classical Press, 1991.

Nichols, Aidan, OP. *From Newman to Congar: The Idea of Doctrinal Development from the Victorians to the Second Vatican Council*. Edinburgh: T & T Clark, 1990.

Nichols, Aidan. "Littlemore from Lucerne: Newman's Essay on Development in Balthasarian Perspective." In *Newman and Conversion*, edited by Ian Turnbull Ker, 100–116. Edinburgh: T & T Clark, 1997.

———. *Catholic Thought since the Enlightenment: A Survey*. Leominster: Gracewing, 1998.

———. "The Theology of Jean Daniélou: Epochs, Correspondences, and the Orders of the Real." *New Blackfriars* 91, no. 1031 (2010): 46.

Nockles, Peter. "The Oxford Movement: Historical Background, 1780–1833." In *Tradition Renewed: The Oxford Movement Conference Papers*, edited by Geoffrey Rockwell, 24–50. London: Darton, Longman and Todd, 1986.

———. "Oxford, Tract 90 and the Bishops." In *John Henry Newman: Reason, Rhetoric and Romanticism*, edited by David Nicholls and Fergus Kerr, 28–87. Bristol: Bristol Press, 1991.

———. "Church Parties in the Pre-Tractarian Church of England 1750–1833: The Orthodox - Some Problems of Definition and Identity." In *The Church of England, c.1689–c.1833: From Toleration to Tractarianism*, edited by Colin

BIBLIOGRAPHY

Haydon, Stephen Taylor, and John Walsh, 334–59. Cambridge: Cambridge University Press, 1993.

———. *The Oxford Movement in Context: Anglican High Churchmanship 1760–1857.* Cambridge: Cambridge University Press, 1994.

———. "Church and King: Tractarian Politics Reappraised." In *Newman: From Oxford to the People. Reconsidering Newman and the Oxford Movement*, edited by P. Vaiss, 93–123. Leominster: Gracewing, 1996.

———. "The Waning of Protestant Unity and Waxing of Anti-Catholicism? Archdeacon Daubeny and the Reconstruction of 'Anglican' Identity in the Late Georgian Church, c.1780–c.1830." In *Religious Identities in Britain, 1660–1832*, edited by Gibson William and Robert G. Ingram, 179–229. Aldershot: Ashgate, 2005.

———. "The Current State of Newman Scholarship." *British Catholic History* 35, no. 1 (2020): 105–27.

Norman, Edward R. *The English Catholic Church in the Nineteenth Century.* Oxford: Clarendon Press, 1984.

Norris, Thomas. *Newman and His Theological Method.* Leiden: Brill, 1977.

———. "The Development of Doctrine: A Remarkable Philosophical Phenomenon." *Communio: International Catholic Review* 22, no. 3 (1995): 470–87.

———. *Only Life Gives Life: Revelation Theology and Christian Living according to Cardinal Newman.* Dublin: Columba Press, 1996.

———. "Newman's Approach to the Act of Faith in the Light of the Catholic Dogmatic Tradition." *Irish Theological Quarterly* 69, no. 3 (2004): 239–61.

Oberman, H. *The Dawn of the Reformation: Essays in Late Medieval and Early Reformation Thought.* Edinburgh: T & T Clark, 1992.

"Obituary - Bishop Lloyd." *Gentleman's Magazine and Historical Chronical* 99 (1829): 560–63.

O'Collins, Gerald. "Newman's Seven Notes: The Case of the Resurrection." In *Focus on Jesus: Essays in Christology and Soteriology*, edited by Gerald O' Collins and Daniel Kendall, 135–48. Leominster: Gracewing, 1996.

O'Donovan, Oliver. *On the Thirty Nine Articles: A Conversation with Tudor Christianity.* London: SCM Press Ltd., 2011.

O'Leary, Joseph. "Impeded Vision: Newman against Luther on Justification." In *John Henry Newman: Reason, Rhetoric and Romanticism*, edited by David Nicholls and Fergus Kerr, 53–193. Bristol, Mich.: Bristol Press, 1991.

O'Malley, John, Joseph Komonchak, Stephen Schloesseer, Neil Ormerod, and David Schultenover. *Vatican II: Did Anything Happen?* London: Continuum, 2007.

Ormerod, Neil. "'The Times They Are a Changin': A Response to O'Malley and Schoessler." *Theological Studies* 67, no. 4 (2006): 834–55.

Palmer, William, and John Henry Newman. "Tract 15: On the Apostolical Succession in the English Church." Messrs. Rivington's, 13 December 1833.

BIBLIOGRAPHY

Palmer, William Patrick. *A Treatise on the Church of Christ: Designed Chiefly for the Use of Students in Theology.* 2 vols. London: J. G. and F. Rivington, 1838.

———. *A Narrative of Events Connected with the Publication of the Tracts for the Times. With Reflections on Existing Tendencies to Romanism, and on the Present Duties and Prospects of Members of the Church.* Oxford and London: J. G. F. and J. Rivington and J. H. Parker, 1843.

Parker, Kenneth L., and C. Michael Shea. "Johann Adam Möhler's Influence on John Henry Newman's Theory of Doctrinal Development." *Ephemerides Theologicae Lovanienses* 89, no. 1 (2013): 73–95.

Patavius, D. *Opus de Doctrina Temporum: Auctius in Hac Nova Editione Notis & Emendationibus Quamplurimus, Quas Manu Sua Codici Adscripserat Dionysius Petavius.* Paris: Lutet, 1627.

Pattison, Mark. "Tendencies of Religious Thought in England 1688–1750." In *Essays and Reviews*, edited by John William Parker, 254–329. London: Longmans, Green and Co., 1860.

Pattison, Robert. *The Great Dissent: John Henry Newman and Liberal Heresy.* Oxford: Oxford University Press, 1991.

Peel, Robert. *An Inaugural Address Delivered by the Right Hon. Sir Robert Peel, Bart., M.P., President of Tamworth Library and Reading Room.* 2nd ed. London: James Bain, 1841.

Pelikan, Jaroslav. *Development of Doctrine: Some Historical Prolegomena.* New Haven, Conn.: Yale University Press, 1969.

Pentin, Edward. "Full Text and Explanatory Notes of Cardinals" Questions on 'Amoris Laetitia.'" *National Catholic Register.* Accessed February 29, 2020. http://www.ncregister.com/blog/edward-pentin/full-text-and-explanatory-notes-of-cardinals-questions-on-amoris-laetitia.

Perceval, Arthur Phillip. *An Apology for the Doctrine of Apostolical Succession: With an Appendix on the English Orders.* London: J. G. F. and J. Rivington, 1839.

———. *Collection of Papers Connected with the Theological Movement of 1833.* London: J. G. and F. Rivington, 1842.

Pereiro, James. "S. F. Wood and an Early Theory of Development in the Oxford Movement." *Recusant History* 20, no. 4 (1991): 524–52.

———. *"Ethos" and the Oxford Movement: At the Heart of Tractarianism.* Oxford: Oxford University Press, 2008.

Peterburs, Michael. "Newman and the Development of Doctrine." In *By Whose Authority? Newman, Manning, and the Magisterium*, edited by Alan V. McClelland, 49–78. Bath: Downside Abbey, 1996.

Peterson, Linda H. "Newman's Apologia pro Vita Sua and the Traditions of the English Spiritual Autobiography." *Proceedings of the Modern Language Association*, no. 100 (1985): 300–314.

Phillips, Peter. "Newman, Vatican II and the Triple Office." *New Blackfriars* 94, no. 1049 (2013): 97–112.

BIBLIOGRAPHY

Pink, Thomas. "What Is the Catholic Doctrine of Religious Liberty." June 15, 2012. https://www.academia.edu/639061/What_is_the_Catholic_doctrine_of_religious_liberty.

———. "The Interpretation of Dignitatis Humanae: A Reply to Martin Rhonheimer." *Nova et Vetera* (English edition) 11, no. 1 (2013): 77–121.

Prothero, Rowland Edmund, and George Granville Bradley. *The Life and Correspondence of Arthur Penrhyn Stanley DD, Late Dean of Westminster*. 2 vols. London: John Murray, 1893.

Pusey, Edward Bouverie. "Notice of "Discourses upon Tradition and Episcopacy" by Christian Benson." *Quarterly Theological Review* 26 (1839): 508.

Quantin, Jean-Louis. *The Church of England and Christian Antiquity: The Construction of a Confessional Identity in the 17th Century*. Oxford: Oxford University Press, 2009.

Rahner, Karl. "The Position of Christology in the Church between Exegesis and Dogmatics." In *Theological Investigations*. Vol. 11. Edited by David Bourke, 185–214. London: Darton, Longman and Todd, 1974.

———. "The Historicity of Theology: The Teaching Office of the Church in the Present-Day Crisis of Authority." In *Theological Investigations*. Vol. 12. Edited by David Bourke, 3–30. London: Darton, Longman and Todd, 1974.

———. "Basic Observations on the Subject of Changeable and Unchangeable Factors in the Church." In *Theological Investigations*. Vol. 14. Edited by David Bourke, 3–23. London: Darton, Longman and Todd, 1976.

———. "On the Situation of Faith." In *Theological Investigations*. Vol. 20. Edited by Edward Quinn, 13–32. London: Darton, Longman and Todd, 1981.

———. "Yesterday's History of Dogma and Theology for Tomorrow." In *Theological Investigations*. Vol. 18. Edited by Edward Quinn, 3–34. London: Darton, Longman and Todd, 1983.

———. "Magisterium and Theology." In *Theological Investigations*. Vol. 18. Edited by Edward Quinn, 54–73. London: Darton, Longman and Todd, 1983.

Ramsey, Michael. *Anglican Spirit*. New York: Church Publishing, 2004.

Ratzinger, Joseph. *Theological Highlights of Vatican II*. Mahwah, N.J.: Paulist Press, 2009.

Reid, Alcuin, ed. *Liturgy in the Twenty-First Century: Contemporary Issues and Perspectives*. London, New York: Bloomsbury T & T Clark, 2016.

Rickaby, Joseph. *An Index to the Works of John Henry Cardinal Newman*. London: Longmans, Green and Co., 1914.

Rogers, Frederic. *A Short Appeal to Members of Convocation upon the Proposed Censure of No. 90*. London: James Burns, 1845.

Ronheimer, Martin. "Benedict XVI's "Hermeneutic of Reform" and Religious Freedom." *Nova et Vetera* (English edition) 9, no. 4 (2011): 1029–54.

Rosman, Doreen. *The Evolution of English Churches, 1500–2000*. Cambridge: Cambridge University Press, 2003.

BIBLIOGRAPHY

Rule, Phillip. *Coleridge and Newman: The Centrality of Conscience*. New York: Fordham University Press, 2004.

Sainte-Marthe, D. de. *Histoire de S.Gregoire Le Grand, Pape et Docteur de l"Eglise*. Rouen, 1697.

Schiefen, Richard J. *Nicholas Wiseman and the Transformation of English Catholicism*. Shepherdstown, W. Va.: Patmos Press, 1984.

Schmaus, M. *Dogma 1: God in Revelation*. London: Sheed and Ward, 1968.

Selby, Robin. *The Principle of Reserve in the Writings of John Henry Cardinal Newman*. Oxford: Oxford University Press, 1975.

Shairp, John Campbell. *Studies in Poetry and Philosophy*. Edinburgh: Edmonston and Douglas, 1868.

Shea, C. Michael. "Newman's Theory of Development and the Definition of Papal Infallibility." In *Authority, Dogma, and History: The Role of the Oxford Movement Converts in the Papal Infallibility Debates*, edited by Kenneth L. Parker and Michael J. G. Pahls, 77–93. Palo Alto, Calif.: Academica Press, 2009.

———. "Newman, Perrone, and Möhler on Dogma and History: A Reappraisal of the Newman-Perrone Paper on Development." *Newman Studies Journal* 7, no. 1 (2010): 45–55.

———. "Father Giovanni Perrone and Doctrinal Development in Rome: An Overlooked Legacy of Newman's Essay on Development." *Journal for the History of Modern Theology / Zeitschrift Für Neuere Theologiegeschichte* 20, no. 1 (2013): 85–116.

———. "The "French Newman": Louis Bautain's Philosophy of Faith, Reason, and Development and the Thought of John Henry Newman." *Newman Studies Journal* 10, no. 1 (2013): 28–40.

———. *Newman's Early Roman Catholic Legacy 1845–1854*. 1st ed. Oxford: Oxford University Press, 2017.

———. "Ressourcement in the Age of Migne: The Jesuit Theologians of the Collegio Romano and the Shape of Modern Catholic Thought." *Nova et Vetera* (English edition) 15, no. 2 (2017): 579–613.

Sheridan, Thomas. *Newman on Justification: A Theological Biography*. New York: Alba House, 1967.

Sidenvall, Erik. "Dealing with Development: The Protestant Reviews of John Henry Newman's An Essay on the Development of Christian Doctrine, 1845–1847." *Studies in Church History* 38 (2004): 357–64.

———. *After Anti-Catholicism: John Henry Newman and Protestant Britain, 1845–c.1890*. New York: T & T Clark, 2005.

Sillem, Edward, ed. *The Philosophical Notebook of John Henry Newman*. 2 vols. Louvain: Nauwelaerts, 1969.

Skinner, Simon. *Tractarians and the "Condition of England": The Social and Political Thought of the Oxford Movement*. Oxford: Clarendon Press, 2004.

BIBLIOGRAPHY

———. "History versus Hagiography: The Reception of Tamer's Newman." *Journal of Ecclesiastical History* 61, no. 4 (2010): 764–81.

———. "A Response to Eamon Duffy." *Journal of Ecclesiastical History* 63, no. 3 (2012): 549–67.

Smith, Christopher. "Liturgical Formation and Catholic Identity." In *Liturgy in the Twenty-First Century: Contemporary Issues and Perspectives*, edited by Alcuin Reid, 260–86. London, New York: Bloomsbury T & T Clark, 2016.

Stanley, Arthur Penrhyn, ed. *Life and Correspondence of Thomas Arnold, D.D., Late Head Master of Rugby School and Regius Professor of Modern History in the University of Oxford*. Vol. 2. London: Fellowes, 1844.

Stern, Jean. *Bible et Tradition Chez Newman: Aux Origines de La Théorie du Développement*. Lyon: Éditions Aubier-Montaigne, 1967.

Strachey, Lytton. *Eminent Victorians: Cardinal Manning, Florence Nightingale, Dr. Arnold, General Gordon*. London: Chatto, 1918.

Sullivan, Francis. "Newman on Infallibility." In *Newman after a Hundred Years*, edited by Ian Turnbull Ker and Alan G. Hill, 419–46. Oxford: Clarendon Press, 1990.

Summer, John Bird. *Apostolical Preaching Considered in an Examination of St. Paul's Epistles*. London: John Hatchard, 1815.

———. *A Charge Delivered to the Clergy of the Diocese of Chester, at the Triennial Visitation in 1838*. London: John Hatchard, 1838.

Sweeney, James. "How Should We Remember Vatican II?" *New Blackfriars* 90, no. 1026 (2009): 251–60.

Sykes, Stephen. *The Identity of Christianity*. London: SPCK, 1984.

Sykes, Stephen, John Booty, and Jonathan Knight, eds. *The Study of Anglicanism*. London: SPCK, 1998.

Sylva, Jo Anne Cammarata. "The Italians and the English Cardinal: Italian Exemplars and the Handing Down of Tradition in the Life of John Henry Newman." D.Litt diss., Drew University, 2006.

Tagle, Luis. "The "Black Week" of Vatican II (November 14–21 1964." In *Church as Communion, Third Period and Intersession, September 1964–September 1965*. Vol. 4 of *History of Vatican II*, edited by Giuseppe Alberigo and Joseph Andrew Komonchak, 387–452. Leuven: Peeters, 2003.

Tait, Archibale Campbell. *A Letter to the Rev. the Vice-Chancellor of the University of Oxford, on the Measures Intended to Be Proposed to Convocation on the 13th of February, in Connexion with the Case of the Rev W. G. Ward*. Edinburgh: William Blackwood, 1845.

Tanner, Norman P., ed. *Decrees of the Ecumenical Councils*. 2 vols. Washington, D.C.: Georgetown University Press, 1990.

Taylor, Jeremy. *Of the Sacred Order and Offices of Episcopacy*. Oxford, 1642.

Tennyson, G. B. *Victorian Devotional Poetry: The Tractarian Mode*. Cambridge, Mass.: Harvard University Press, 1981.

BIBLIOGRAPHY

Thiel, John E. "The Analogy of Tradition: Method and Theological Judgement." *Theological Studies* 66, no. 2 (2005): 358–80.

Thieselton, Anthony C. *The Hermeneutics of Doctrine*. Cambridge: Eerdmans, 2007.

Thirwall, Connop. *A Charge, Delivered to the Clergy of the Diocese of St. David's*. London: J. F. and G. Rivington, 1848.

Thomas, Stephen. *Newman and Heresy: The Anglican Years*. Cambridge: Cambridge University Press, 1991.

Thomas, W., and Allies. *The Church of England Cleared from the Charge of Schism, upon Testimonies of Councils and Fathers of the First Six Centuries*. London: James Burns, 1846.

Tracts for the Times, by Members of the University of Oxford (1833–1834). Vol. 1. London & Oxford: J. G. F. and J. Rivington and J. H. Parker, 1840.

Tracts for the Times, by Members of the University of Oxford (1834–1835). Vol. 2. London & Oxford: J. G. F. and J. Rivington and J. H. Parker, 1840.

Tracts for the Times, by Members of the University of Oxford (1836). Vol. 3. London & Oxford: J. G. F. and J. Rivington and J. H. Parker, 1840.

Tracts for the Times, by Members of the University of Oxford (1836–1837). Vol. 4. London & Oxford: J. G. F. and J. Rivington and J. H. Parker, 1840.

Tracts for the Times, by Members of the University of Oxford (1838–1840). Vol. 5. London & Oxford: J. G. F. and J. Rivington and J. H. Parker, 1840.

Trevor, Meriol. *Newman: The Pillar of the Cloud*. London: Macmillan, 1962.

Tristram, Henry. "In the Lists with the Abbé Jager." In *John Henry Newman: Centenary Essays*, edited by Henry Tristram, 201–22. London: Burns, Oates and Washbourne, 1945.

Turner, Frank Miller. *John Henry Newman: The Challenge to Evangelical Religion*. New Haven, Conn.: Yale University Press, 2002.

Vaiss, Paul. *From Oxford to the People: Reconsidering Newman and the Oxford Movement*. Leominster: Gracewing, 1996.

Vincent of Lerins. "Commonitorium." In *Corpus Christianorum: Series Latina*. Vol. 64. Turnhout: Brepols, 1953.

Walgrave, Jan Hendrick. *Newman: Le Développement Du Dogme*. Tournai: Casterman, 1957.

———. *Newman the Theologian: The Nature of Belief and Doctrine as Exemplified in His Life and Works*. Translated by A.V. Littledale. London: Geoffrey Chapman, 1960.

———. *Unfolding Revelation: The Nature of Doctrinal Development*. London: Hutchinson, 1972.

Ward, Maisie. *Young Mr. Newman*. London: Sheed and Ward, 1948.

Ward, Wilfrid Philip. *The Life and Times of Cardinal Wiseman*. 2 vols. London: Longmans, Green and Co., 1912.

BIBLIOGRAPHY

———. *Life of John Henry Cardinal Newman Based on His Private Journals and Correspondence*. Vol. 2. London: Longmans, Green and Co., 1912.

———. *Last Lectures of Wilfred Ward Being the Lowell Lectures, 1914 and Three Lectures Delivered at the Royal Institution, 1915*. London: Longmans, Green and Co., 1918.

Ward, William George. *The Ideal of a Christian Church Considered in Comparison with Existing Practice: Containing a Defence of Certain Articles in the British Critic in Reply to Remarks on Them in Mr. Palmer's "Narrative."* London: James Toovey, 1844.

———. *An Address to Members of Convocation in Protest Against the Proposed Statute*. London: James Toovey, 1845.

Watkin, Edward Ingram. *Roman Catholicism in England: From the Reformation to 1950*. London: Oxford University Press, 1957.

Whately, Richard. *Letters on the Church by an Episcopalian*. London: Longman, Rees, Orme, Brown and Green, 1826.

Whitaker, William. *Disputatio de Sacra Scriptura, Contra Huius Temporis Papistas, Inprimis Robertum Bellarminum Iesuitam ... Pontificium in Collegio Romano, & Thomam Stapletonum Regium in Schola Duacena Controversiarum Professorem: Sex Quoestionibus Proposita et Tractata*. Cambridge: Ex officina Thomae Thomasii, florentissimae Cantabrigiensis Academiae Typographi, 1588.

Wilberforce, Henry. "F. Newman's Oxford Parochial Sermons." *Dublin Review (New Series)*, 12 (1869): 309–30.

Wilberforce, Samuel. *A Charge, Delivered to the Candidates for Ordination; and a Sermon, Preached at the General Ordination, in the Cathedral Church of Christ, Oxford, December 21, 1845*. London: Francis and John Rivington, 1846.

Williams, Rowan, ed. "Newman's Arians and the Question of Method in Doctrinal History." In *Newman after a Hundred Years*, edited by Alan G. Hill and Ian Turnbull Ker, 263–85. Oxford: Clarendon Press, 1990.

———. Introduction to *The Arians of the Fourth Century, Their Doctrine, Temper, and Conduct, Chiefly as Exhibited in the Councils of the Church, between A.D. 325 and A.D. 381*. Birmingham Oratory Archives. Millenium ed. Leominster: Gracewing, 2001.

Wilson, James Matthew. "Doctrinal Development and the Demons of History: The Historiography of John Henry Newman." *Religion and the Arts* 10, no. 4 (2006): 497–523.

Winstanley, Denys Arthur. *Unreformed Cambridge*. Cambridge: Cambridge University Press, 1935.

Wiseman, Nicholas. *Lectures on the Principal Doctrines and Practices of the Catholic Church*. 2 vols. London, 1836.

———. "Tracts for the Times: Anglican Claim of Apostolical Succession." *Dublin Review* 4 (1838): 307–35.

———. "Tracts for the Times: Anglican Claim of Apostolical Succession." *Dublin Review* 5 (1838): 285–309.

———. "Tracts for the Times: Anglican Claim of Apostolical Succession." *Dublin Review* 7 (1839): 139–80.

Wix, Samuel. *Reflections Concerning the Expediency of a Council of the Church of England and the Church of Rome Being Holden, with a View to Accommodate Religious Differences*. London: F. C. and J. Rivington, 1818.

Woodruff, Douglas, ed. "Newman and the Modern Age." In *John Henry Newman: Centenary Essays*, 55–67. London: Burns, Oates and Washbourne, 1945.

Documents of the Holy See

International Theological Commission. *The Interpretation of Dogma*. 1989. http://www.vatican.va/roman_curia/congregations/cfaith/cti_documents/rc_cti_1989_interpretazione-dogmi_en.html.

Congregation for the Doctrine of the Faith. "Letter to the Bishops Regarding the New Revision of Number 2267 of the Catechism of the Catholic Church on the Death Penalty." August 1, 2018. http://www.vatican.va/roman_curia/congregations/cfaith/ladaria-ferrer/documents/rc_con_cfaith_doc_20180801_lettera-vescovi-penadimorte_en.html.

Pope Benedict XVI. "Ad Romanam Curia Ob Omnia Natalicia." *Acta Apostolicae Sedis* 98 (December 22, 2005): 40–53.

Pope Francis. *Amoris laetitia*. Post-Synodal Apostolic Exhortation on Love in the Family. March 19, 2016. http://w2.vatican.va/content/francesco/en/apost_exhortations/documents/papa-francesco_esortazione-ap_20160319_amoris-laetitia.html.

———. "Epistula Apostolica Ad Excellentissimum Dominum Sergium Alfredum Fenoy, Delegatum Regionis Pastoralis Bonaërensis, Necnon Adiunctum Documentum (de Praecipuis Rationibus Usui Capitis VIII Adhortationis Post-Synodalis "Amoris Laetitia"), 5th September 2016." *Acta Apostolicae Sedis* 108, no. 10 (2016): 1071–72.

———. "Inauguration of the Judicial Year of the Tribunal of the Roman Rota." January 22. 2016. https://w2.vatican.va/content/francesco/en/speeches/2016/january/documents/papa-francesco_20160122_anno-giudiziario-rota-romana.html.

Pope John Paul II. "Letter to Archbishop Vincent Nichols on the Occasion of the 2nd Centenary of the Birth of Cardinal John Henry Newman." February 27, 2001. http://www.vatican.va/holy_father/john_paul_ii/letters/2001/documents/hf_jp-ii_let_20010227_john-henry-newman_en.html.

Pope Paul VI. "Declaratio de Libertate Religiosa." *Acta Apostolicae Sedis* 58 (1966): 929–41.

BIBLIOGRAPHY

Pope Pius XII. *Ai Partecipanti al I Congresso Nazionale Dell"Unione Giuristi Cattolici Italiani*. November 6, 1949. http://w2.vatican.va/content/pius-xii/it/speeches/1949/documents/hf_p-xii_spe_19491106_giuristi-cattolici.html.

———. *Aux Participants Au Ier Congrès International d"histopathologie Du Système Nerveux*. September 15, 1952. http://w2.vatican.va/content/pius-xii/fr/speeches/1952/documents/hf_p-xii_spe_19520914_istopatologia.html.

———. *Discorso Di Sua Santità Pio PP. XII Ai Partecipanti al VI Congresso Internationale de Diritto Penale*. October 3, 1953. http://w2.vatican.va/content/pius-xii/it/speeches/1953/documents/hf_p-xii_spe_19531003_diritto-penale.html.

———. *Mediator Dei*. November 20, 1947. http://w2.vatican.va/content/pius-xii/en/encyclicals/documents/hf_p-xii_enc_20111947_mediator-dei.html.

INDEX

Alexandria, church of, 47, 58–59, 60–61, 63, 142
Algiers, 115
Ambrose, St., 22, 23, 115, 116, 117, 151, 259
Amoris laetitia, 3, 272–74
Anabaptists, 96, 188, 189
analogy, 69, 171, 182, 217, 227, 240, 242–43, 246, 249, 255, 258
Anselm, St., 260
anti-Catholicism, 210, 259
Antichrist, 26, 58, 109, 161
anti-Erastianism, 39
Antioch, church of, 58–59, 60, 61, 138
Apollinarianism, 18, 136, 138, 141, 225, 235
Apollonius of Tyana, 43
Apostles' Creed, 97, 124, 235
apostolicity, 93, 105, 132, 135, 165, 174, 175, 185, 186, 259
Apostolic Succession, 38, 90, 92, 93–94, 99, 106–7, 145, 146–47, 148, 163
Aquinas, Thomas, St., 7, 236
Arianism, 40–41, 138, 142, 144, 225
Aristotelianism, 7, 274
Arius, 59, 103, 173
Arminianism, 187, 190
Arnold, Thomas, 31, 210
Athanasian Creed, 30, 236
Athanasius, St., 60, 115, 141, 142, 177, 196, 224, 228, 236, 249, 259, 260, 261
Athenagoras, 66
Augustine, St., 22, 64, 129, 149, 150–51, 152, 153, 156, 159, 171–72, 177, 255
Aurelian, 151
authority, scriptural, 34, 62, 84n33, 106, 158

Bagot, Richard, Bishop of Oxford, 178n205, 195, 196
Bampton Lectures, 39
baptism, 45, 61, 100, 106, 173, 188, 189, 220, 225, 250, 254
Barberi, Dominic, Bl., ix
Baring-Gould, Sabine, 112
Baronius, Caesar, 52
Barrow, Isaac, 170
Basil, St., 60, 80, 101, 117, 156, 177
Bays, Marguerite, St., ix
Beatific Vision, 221
Becket, Thomas, St., 260n236
Bede, St., 260n236
Bellarmine, Robert, St., 100, 168, 257
Benedict XVI, Pope, 5, 7, 10, 15n47, 269
Benson, Christopher, 171
Bernard of Clairvaux, St., 223, 236, 259, 260n236
Bible Society, 36–37
Birmingham Oratory, 17, 138
Bloxam, J. R., 174, 178
Boleyn, Anne, 149
Bossuet, Jacques-Bénigne, 7, 8
Bowden, John William, 88n60, 90, 91n74, 116n182, 122n222, 145n53, 153, 155, 156n105, 162, 177, 210n23, 223n65, 224
Bramhall, John, Archbishop of Armagh, 188
branch theory, 93, 109, 144, 147, 149, 158, 169, 185
Breisach, Ernst, 8
Brighton, 40, 45, 54
British Critic, The, 78, 125, 154, 157, 161–62, 164, 171, 175, 178, 180–81, 186, 203, 205, 209, 251, 259

309

INDEX

Brownson, Orestes, 267
Buenos Aires, 272
Bull, George, 48, 52, 63, 89, 114, 212
Bunsen, Christian Karl Josias von, 198
Burton, Edward, 87
Butler, Joseph, 25, 27, 28, 29, 34, 36, 38, 99

Calvinism, 109, 158, 176, 187, 190
Cambridge, 12, 54
Canons of the Church of England (1604), 85, 176
Carlyle, Thomas, 210
Carthage, Third Council of, 151
Catechism of the Catholic Church, 3, 270
Catholic Relief Act (1829), 26n37, 56, 75
Cave, William, 52
celibacy, 194, 248, 250
Chalcedon, Council of, 137, 142, 144, 247–48, 275
Charles I, King, 118, 158, 176, 187, 188, 189
Chillingworth, William, 235
Christie, John Frederick, 82, 88, 90n70
Christology, 41, 133, 144, 184, 202, 218, 225, 247, 252
Church, R. W., 181, 192, 229
Church Temporalities (Ireland) Act (1833), 56, 90, 170
Churton, T. T., 190n253
Cicero, 43
Cieszkowski, August von, 274n24
Clarke, Samuel, 49
Clement of Alexandria, St., 69, 78, 79, 80, 82–83, 84n34, 87, 142
Clergy, Civil Constitution of the, 119
Coleridge, Samuel Taylor, 13, 212
conscience, 51, 257–58
Congar, Yves, 9
consent, marital, 272
conversion, 178–79, 199, 205, 223, 235, 266
Convocation, 95, 158, 176
Cranmer, Thomas, Archbishop of Canterbury, 111, 170
Cullen, Paul, Cardinal, Archbishop of Dublin, 268n9

Cyprian, St., 115–16, 144, 170, 171, 173
Cyril of Alexandria, St., 23, 65, 142, 144

Davenport, Christopher (Francis of Santa Clara), 193
death penalty, 3, 270–72, 274
Deutero-Nicene Council, 166–67
Dignitatis humanae, 4
Dionysius of Alexandria, 137, 173
Dionysius the Areopagite (Pseudo-Dionysius), 137
disciplina arcani, 17, 42, 55, 61–65, 67, 69, 70, 74, 76, 77–89, 101, 104, 168, 202, 215, 217, 225, 238–39, 263–64, 275
doctrine, development of. *See* Newman, John Henry
Dodgson, Charles (Lewis Carroll), 117n187
Dodsworth, William, 162n162, 178n205
Dodwell, Henry, 170
dogma, x, 8–9, 17, 19–20, 41, 48, 51, 52, 62, 64, 65, 72–73, 89, 133, 142, 144, 150, 161, 168, 208, 213, 214, 215–22, 223, 249–50, 258, 265, 266, 268, 275
Donatism, 129, 139, 149–51, 153, 163, 174, 178, 203
Drey, Johann Sebastian, 8
Dublin, Ireland, 50
Dublin Review, 135, 144, 146, 153, 163, 196

Eastern churches. *See* Orthodox churches
economy, principle of, 64–65, 83, 87, 145
Edward VI, King, 176
Eichhorn, Johann Gottfried, 31
eisegesis, 104
Elizabeth I, Queen, 176
Emancipation, Catholic. *See* Catholic Relief Act
Ephesus, Council of, 251
Erastianism, 56, 93, 113, 169–70, 190
Eusebius, 116
Eutyches, 137–38, 139, 142, 159
evangelicalism, 12, 15, 20, 22, 24, 30, 36–37, 50n171, 78, 83, 84n33, 97n101, 98, 183, 190, 218–19

INDEX

Faber, George Stanley, 83–84, 87, 253
Falconer, Thomas, 83, 84, 85n39, 86, 104, 105, 207n12
fasting, 178
Fathers of the Church, 7, 14, 18, 19, 21–22, 25, 42–43, 44, 45, 50, 60, 64, 67, 68, 69, 81, 87, 100, 101, 108, 111–17, 122, 127, 131, 132, 136, 149, 150, 151, 157, 158, 165, 169, 170, 173, 197, 222, 225, 227, 230, 235, 237, 247, 248, 261, 264, 275. *See also* patristics
Fisher, Cowley, 233n109
Foot, Sarah, 12
Francis, Pope, 2–4, 269, 271–72, 274. *See also Amoris laetitia*
Frederick Wilhelm IV, Emperor, 198
French Revolution, 75, 119
Froude, Mrs., 16n49, 21n6, 22n13, 29, 85, 208, 224, 225, 226n73, 227n77
Froude, Richard Hurrell, 53n180, 54, 56, 88, 90, 92n82, 94, 116n187, 117, 118n194, 121n214, 122n223, 124, 125n241, 126, 130n267, 179n206, 192n266, 193n266

Gallicanism, 123n230, 172
geologists, 210
Gibbon, Edward, 48, 52
Giberne, Maria, 130, 195, 197, 198, 228n83
Gilley, Sheridan, 12
Gladstone, William, 157, 194
Golightly, Charles Portales, 90n70, 93n84, 190n253
Gramsci, Antonio, 274n24
Gregory Nazianzen, St., 247

Hackney Phalanx, 79
Hadleigh, 56, 90
Hales, William, 79n13
Hall, Joseph, Bishop of Norwich, 34n87, 76
Hampden, Renn, 125, 218
Hampstead, 28
Harding, Stephen, St., 260n236
Harrison, Benjamin, 118, 120–21, 123n232

Hawkins, Edward, 30–38, 40, 56, 61, 62, 68, 87, 99, 124, 164, 192
Hegelianism, 274
Henry VIII, King, 260n236
heresy, 13, 42, 52, 59, 65, 66, 70, 85, 103, 110, 126, 134, 136, 138, 140n30, 141–42, 148, 163, 166, 168, 178, 191, 204, 207, 214, 215, 217, 226n73, 252, 253, 264, 267, 273n21
hermeneutics, 2, 5, 7, 10, 13, 18, 51, 140n30
Hickes, George, 170
Hippolytus, 66
Holmes, Mary, 259, 260
Homilies, Books of, 150
homosexuality, 15
Hooker, Richard, 34, 97–98, 100, 102, 109, 111, 113, 126, 130–31, 157, 167
Horsley, Samuel, 49

Ignatius of Antioch, St., 117
Ignatius Loyola, St., 197, 259
Incarnation, doctrine of, 85, 102, 137, 182, 219, 220, 221, 248
indulgences, 168, 188, 189, 195
infallibility: of the Church, 166, 214, 234, 256–57, 259, 260, 261, 276; papal, 225, 258, 266, 268, 275
Irenaeus of Lyon, St., 62, 248

Jager, Jean-Nicolas, 17, 64, 77, 86, 104, 111, 143, 164, 169, 170, 174, 176, 185, 203, 204, 207, 208n12, 235, 236–37, 264, 266; correspondence with Newman, 118–32
James, St., 117
James VI and I, King, 249
James, William, 38, 94
Jebb, John, Bishop of Limerick, 119
Jenkinson, Robert, 2nd Earl of Liverpool, 79
Jerusalem, bishopric of, 135, 186–200, 203
Jewel, John, 111, 150
John of Constantinople, 151
John Chrysostom, St., 99, 115–16
John Paul II, Pope, St., 269, 270, 271, 173

311

INDEX

Jones, William (Jones of Nayland), 34, 158
Judaism, 25, 28, 59, 244, 248
judgment, prudential, 3, 154, 214, 270
Julius III, Pope, 96n99
Justin Martyr, St., 23

Kaye, John, Bishop of Bristol, 79–83, 84, 88, 89, 238
Keble, John, 58, 70, 83, 94, 97n101, 144, 147n57, 153, 157–58, 179n206, 180, 181, 186, 193, 196n283, 197, 198, 222–25; Assize Sermon, 89–90, 92
Kingsley, Charles, xi, 159, 224n71, 275
Knox, Alexander, 119, 120n203

L'Univers Religieux, 120, 123
Lactantius, 23
Latitudinarianism, 15, 32, 190
Laud, William, Archbishop of Canterbury, 34n87, 130, 158, 187, 189, 193n266
Le Moniteur Religieux, 123
Leeds, 157
Lefebvre, Marcel, Archbishop, 4
Leibniz, Gottfried, 8
Leo, St., 137, 261, 275
liberalism, 15, 22, 44, 51, 70, 141, 210, 234, 253
Liddell, Alice, 117n187
Liddell, Henry, 117n187
Littlemore, 23, 196, 204, 213
liturgy, 6, 85, 86, 91, 101, 269
Lloyd, Charles, Bishop of Oxford, 24–27, 29, 37, 45
Lonergan, Bernard, 9
Lubac, Henri de, 9
Lutheranism, 96n99, 158, 176, 187
Lyall, William Rowe, 46, 47, 54–55, 57, 67–69, 71, 77, 80, 84
"Lyra Apostolica," 115–16, 223

Maclaurin, W. C. A., 180
Magisterium, 5, 121, 273, 275
Maidstone, Lord, 54, 118n194
Maimbourg, Louis, 48
Maistre, Joseph de, 26, 27, 38
Mankidiyan, Mariam Thresia Chiramel, St., ix

Manning, Henry, Cardinal, 14, 146, 156–57, 164, 224
Marin-Sola, Francisco, 9
Marxism, 274
Mary, Blessed Virgin, xiv, 167, 203, 211, 215, 219, 248, 250, 251
mathematics, 241, 243
Methodius, St., 248
Migne, Jacques-Paul, 120
Milman, Henry Hart, 210
Milner, Joseph, 21–22, 52, 118, 164
miracles, 43–44, 162
Möhler, Johann Adam, 8, 22–23, 24, 27, 32
monasticism, 213, 250
Monophysitism, 135–44, 145, 154n100, 155, 159, 178, 179n206, 196, 203, 226n73, 235, 247
Moriarty, David, Bishop of Ardfert, 268n9
Mossheim, Johann Lorenz von, 52
Mozley, James, 155n104
Mozley, Thomas, 183, 193n267, 198n292
Murray, John Courtney, 4, 6, 7

Nestorianism, 85, 137
Newman, Francis, 118n94, 179–86, 202, 203, 205, 207, 230, 245
Newman, Harriett, 22n12, 46n147, 50, 59n224, 85n41, 90n72, 115n176
Newman, Jemima (Mrs. John Mozley), 43n123, 54n187, 85, 154n99, 163n138, 207n12, 208n13, 210n23, 222n58
Newman, John Henry, St.: *Apologia pro vita sua*, xi, 20, 21, 22, 27, 33, 43, 44, 47, 71, 89, 92, 94, 114, 123, 134, 138–39, 140n30, 152, 154, 155, 160–61, 177, 192, 224, 226n73; *Arians of the Fourth Century*, 17, 19–20, 26, 33, 42–74, 76, 78, 80–81, 83, 84, 88, 89, 114, 136, 196, 208, 218, 223, 235, 238; beatification, 15n47; canonisation, ix, 276; childhood, 20; "Churchman, A." (letters), 92; conversion to evangelicalism, 20–21, 24, 30; conversion to Roman Catholicism, x, 11, 12, 22, 32, 60, 105, 122; curacy at St. Clement's, 24, 27, 28,

312

INDEX

30, 40, 158; *Essay on the Development of Christian Doctrine*, ix–x, 1–2, 10, 13–14, 16, 18, 21–22, 26–27, 29, 32, 69, 85, 127, 135, 182, 184, 201–2, 205, 207, 208–22, 222–62, 263, 265, 266–68, 275–77; *Grammar of Assent*, ix; *Idea of a University*, ix; *Lectures on the Prophetical Office of the Church*, 64, 77, 86, 111, 123, 130, 131, 136, 176, 264; *Lectures on Justification*, 148; *Loss and Gain*, 123n228, 206; "Private Judgement," 205–6; sermons, 16–17, 18, 19, 23, 27–30, 36, 40–41, 85–86, 160, 181, 183, 185, 199, 201, 202–8, 209, 210–11, 212–13, 214, 216, 217–18, 219, 220, 221–22, 226, 230, 249; *Tract 1 (Thoughts on the Ministerial Commission)*, 91n75, 94; *Tract 2*, 91n75; *Tract 3*, 91n75; *Tract 6*, 91n75; *Tract 7*, 91n75; *Tract 8*, 91n75, 98; *Tract 10*, 91n75; *Tract 11*, 91n75, 106; *Tract 15*, 91n75, 107; *Tract 19*, 91n75, 99; *Tract 20*, 91n75, 109; *Tract 21*, 91n75; *Tract 31*, 91n75; *Tract 33*, 91n75; *Tract 34*, 91n75, 99–101, 102; *Tract 38*, 91n75, 109; *Tract 41*, 86n48, 103, 105, 109; *Tract 45*, 91n75, 102, 111; *Tract 47*, 91n75; *Tract 71*, 91n75, 102, 109; *Tract 73*, 91n75; *Tract 74*, 91n75, 147n57; *Tract 75*, 91n75; *Tract 76*, 91n75; *Tract 79*, 91n75; *Tract 82*, 91n75; *Tract 83*, 91n75, 161; *Tract 85*, 33, 91n75; *Tract 88*, 91n75; *Tract 90*, 83, 91n75, 96, 135, 179, 186–200, 203, 204, 228, 237
Newton, Isaac, 239
Nicea, Council of, 64, 65, 66, 126, 247
Nicene Creed, 52, 53, 65, 69, 77, 103, 126, 237
Non-jurors, 157, 189
Novatian, 66
novelty, doctrinal, 6, 172, 190, 203–4, 207, 217
nullity, matrimonial, 272

Oakeley, Frederick 223
O'Connell, Daniel, 146
Optatus, 150
orders, Anglican, 17, 107, 108, 163

Orthodox churches, 149n67, 156
Oxford, 15n47, 45, 50, 56, 57, 60, 125, 146, 147, 152, 157, 158, 204, 263; Christ Church, 24; Oriel College, 19, 24, 29, 30n57, 31, 33, 38, 39, 42, 45, 50, 56, 70, 94, 136, 181, 192, 221; St. Alban's Hall, 39, 42, 50; St. Clement's church, 24, 27, 28, 30, 40, 158; St. John's College, 30n57; St. Mary the Virgin (university church), 28, 30, 42, 56, 157, 222; University of, 12, 56, 89, 95n96, 228
Oxford Movement, 14, 33, 56, 57, 73, 75, 76–77, 90, 91n74, 92, 106, 118, 144, 154, 169, 176, 180, 191, 192, 218, 222, 223, 236. *See also* Tractarianism

paganism, 43, 44, 69, 249
Palmer, William Patrick, 75n1, 90, 91n75, 107n39, 158, 193, 194, 218, 219, 226
Pattison, Mark, 268
patristics, 22, 25, 36, 43, 45, 49, 60, 68–69, 79, 80, 87, 111, 112, 114, 116, 131, 151, 159, 170, 171, 173, 200, 204, 264
Paul VI, Pope, St., ix, 4
Pavan, Pietro, 4
Peel, Robert, 56, 75
Pelagianism, 225
penance, 220, 250
Perceval, Arthur, 91, 118, 163
Perrone, Giovanni, 23, 267
Persia, 183
Pétau, Denis (Petavius), 8, 23, 52, 243
Phillipps, Ambrose Lisle, 196
Pink, Thomas, 5n10
Pius V, Pope, St., 236
Pius XII, Pope, 7, 270, 271
Polycarp, St., 117
Pontes, Dulce Lopes, St., ix
Pope, Simeon Lloyd, 50
positivism, theological, 6–7, 104, 221, 266, 268, 275
possession, theory of, 135, 162–79, 186, 196–97, 200, 203, 259, 275
praxis, 273–74
proof-texting, 7, 30, 36, 113–14

313

INDEX

Prosper of Aquitaine, 7
Protestantism, 15, 17, 32, 35, 55, 67, 68, 69, 77, 80, 97, 109, 110, 112, 119, 131, 135, 139, 148, 189, 190, 192, 198, 199, 200, 229, 234, 236, 244, 250, 253, 256, 264
psychoanalysis, 15
Ptolemy, 239
Purgatory, 166, 167, 168, 227, 248, 250
Pusey, Edward Bouverie, 25, 45, 91n75, 123n230, 131, 144, 153, 156–57, 158, 171, 176, 191, 193, 211, 224

Quinn, Michael, 146

Rahner, Karl, 8–9
rationalism, 13, 60, 65, 141, 142, 176, 222
Reimarus, Hermann Samuel, 31
relics, 189, 250
Revolution of 1688, 176
Rickards, Samuel, 37, 52, 118n194
Rivington, Francis, 47n153, 54, 58, 91
Rogers, Frederic, 91n75, 137, 141, 143, 145n53, 152, 153, 154, 155n101, 160, 161, 180, 181n212, 275n27
Rome, Venerable English College at, 146
Rose, Hugh James, 46–49, 50, 51, 53–55, 56, 57, 67, 77n7, 78, 79n11, 80, 82, 84, 87, 90, 91n74, 92n80, 114, 115, 117–18, 120n205, 223n64
Russell, Charles William, 122, 123

Sadducees, 244
Sainthe-Marthe, Denys de, 112
saints, cult of, 166, 167, 188, 223, 250
schism, 4, 60, 103, 106, 107, 108, 148, 149, 151, 156, 163, 165, 166, 169, 174, 197, 199, 228n80, 257
Schleiermacher, Friedrich, 31
Schönborn, Christoph, Cardinal, 274
Scott, Robert, 117n187
Scott, Thomas, 21
Second Vatican Council. *See* Vatican Council, Second
Shrewsbury, earl of, 178
Smedley, Edward, 43
Socialists, 210

Socinianism, 176
Socratic dialogues, 164, 166
sola scriptura, 32, 96n99, 97n102, 98, 99, 110, 167, 219
Sophism, 59, 115
soteriology, 187
Southampton, 28
Stillingfleet, Edward, 130, 170
subordinationism, 40
Sumner, John Bird, Archbishop of Canterbury, 37–38, 164, 197, 199
Synods, Ordinary, 272

Tatian, 66
Tertullian, 23, 79, 101
Theophilus, 66
Thirty-Nine Articles, 31, 95–96, 103, 110, 172, 177, 187–95
Thornton, Charles, 117n187
Thornton, Henry, 117n187
Tillement, Louis-Sébastian Le Nain de, 52
Tisserant, Eugène, Cardinal, 4
Toovey, James, 16
Tracts for the Times. See Tractarianism
Tractarianism, x, 17, 22, 31, 39, 79, 80, 103, 107, 113, 141, 143, 145, 147, 148, 149, 151, 156, 157, 158, 161–62, 163, 164, 169, 178, 223, 250, 265
tradition, Newman's idea of, 17, 19, 30, 34–35, 36, 37, 40, 55, 62, 67–69, 70, 78, 80, 87, 89, 97, 100, 101, 105, 120–21, 124–28, 131, 164, 176, 235, 264, 269
transubstantiation, 188, 189
Trent, Council of, 49, 96n99, 108, 110, 121, 172, 191, 193, 237, 252
Trevern, Jean François Marie Lepappe de, 119
Trinity, doctrine of the, 38, 40, 63, 66, 73, 81, 83, 85, 102, 105, 136, 202, 218, 219, 220, 221, 225, 227, 237, 243, 251
Tübingen, University of, 8
Turrill, John, 54

Ultramontanism, 26, 266, 268–69, 275
Unitarianism, 70, 183

INDEX

Valens, emperor, 117
Vannini, Giuseppina, St., ix
Vatican Council, First, 6, 129, 258, 266, 268, 275
Vatican Council, Second, 4–5, 6, 267, 268–69
via media, x, 17, 18, 77, 95, 97n101, 103, 109, 110, 111, 120, 121, 130, 131, 132, 133–34, 135, 137, 138, 139, 140n30, 142, 145, 147, 152, 154, 159, 162, 167, 169, 176, 177, 200, 226n73, 264, 275
Vincent of Lerins, St., 63–64, 68, 69, 74, 76, 77, 120, 127, 167, 203, 225, 236, 237–38, 264, 275
Vincentian Canon. *See* Vincent of Lerins

Ward, Catherine, 234n115
Ward, William George, 23, 190, 228, 265–66
Waterland, Daniel, 34, 52, 105
Whately, Richard, Archbishop of Dublin, 31n67, 38–40, 43, 49, 50, 164
Whitaker, William, 100
White, Blanco, 70–71, 141
Wilberforce, Henry, 81, 82n24, 88n61, 114, 125n244, 153–54, 157, 160, 161, 162, 196, 198n292, 228n79

Wilberforce, Robert, 122n224, 137, 141
Williams, Isaac, 136, 137, 141, 192n266
Williams, Robert, 145n53, 146, 152, 153–54, 157, 159, 178, 191
Williams, Rowan, Archbishop of Canterbury, 48, 60, 65, 69, 71, 72, 73, 80, 84, 89, 144, 208
Wilson, Robert Francis, 228n80
Wiseman, Nicholas, Cardinal, Archbishop of Westminster, 18, 23, 128, 129, 130, 135, 143, 144–62, 163, 164, 165, 169, 171, 172, 174, 175, 176–78, 179n206, 180, 185–86, 196, 203, 226n73, 235, 260n236, 264
Wix, Samuel, 193
Wood, S. F., 14, 85, 104, 128, 145n53, 153, 154, 160, 161, 178n203, 198, 207n12, 208n12
Woodgate, H. A., 57, 94n88, 106n136
Word, Catholicism of the, 17, 18, 75–132, 133, 137, 145, 162, 164, 169, 219, 236, 264, 275

Zwinglianism, 158

315

John Henry Newman and the Development of Doctrine: Encountering Change, Looking for Continuity was designed in Filosofia by Kachergis Book Design of Pittsboro, North Carolina. It was printed on 55-pound Natural Offset and bound by Maple Press of York, Pennsylvania.

www.ingramcontent.com/pod-product-compliance
Lightning Source LLC
Chambersburg PA
CBHW031233290426
44109CB00012B/274